D1710863

Songs, Dreamings, and Ghosts

ʍusɪc/cuʟᴛuʀᴇ
A series from Wesleyan University Press.
Edited by Robert Walser and Susan Fast.

Originating editors, George Lipsitz, Susan McClary, and Robert Walser.

Songs, Dreamings,

and Ghosts

The Wangga of North Australia

Allan Marett

Wesleyan University Press ◈ Middletown, Connecticut

Published by Wesleyan University Press,
Middletown, CT 06459
www.wesleyan.edu/wespress

Published with the cooperation of Charles Darwin
University Press.

The publisher gratefully acknowledges assistance
from the Dragan Plamenac Publication Endowment
Fund of the American Musicological Society and
the University of Sydney.

Printed in the United States of America
5   4   3   2   1

ISBN 0-8195-6617-9 (cloth)
ISBN 0-8195-6618-7 (paper)

Cover Photo: Ambrose Piarlum dances as a
Walakandha. (Photograph by Mark Crocombe,
Wadeye, 1992.)

Frontispiece: Charlie Brinken's painting of Ma-yawa
performing ceremony. (Photograph published with
permission of the artist's family.)

Design by Chris Crochetière, and set in Minion,
Meta, and Bosin type by BW&A Books, Inc.

Cataloging-in-Publication Data is available
from Library of Congress

For Linda

contents

Illustrations

Figures

Plates

Tables

Musical Examples

The Wongga melodies are particularly haunting and powerful.
. . . This music is hypnotic and unforgettable.

—Trevor Jones, *Arnhem Land Music*

During my first tentative weeks of fieldwork in 1986, I was asked by a young Aboriginal man why the songs of his people—songs of such beauty and deep poetry that they took my breath away—were not more highly valued in the non-Aboriginal community. Why was it that Aboriginal painting had a high profile, and music virtually none? It was an interesting question, and not one that is easy to answer. There is a great deal of ambivalence within Australian society about the contribution that Aboriginal knowledge and modes of expression can and should make to the national consciousness, ranging from those who embrace Aboriginal ways of being in the world as the key to understanding how to be in Australia, to those who reject them totally as primitive, inimical to development, or simply irrelevant to "civilized" values. But this does not tell us why the visual arts have been widely embraced, while music has not. Nor does it account for the fact that not all Aboriginal music is marginalized. In a recent undergraduate survey, I found that the only piece of Australian music (from a sample of about twenty pieces) that everyone in the class recognized was the Arnhem Land band Yothu Yindi's resistant anthem "Treaty."

Part of the answer must surely lie in the fact that both paintings and popular songs are easily commodifed, while traditional songs are not. They do not lend themselves to reframing within a European modernist tradition in the way that paintings do. Moreover, traditional songs work in ways that are unfamiliar to most audiences and are sung in languages that nobody outside their home communities understands. They tend to be intensely local, focused on places that are frequently unknown to any but those who have rights to the country. They rest on cosmologies and ways of being that are radically different from those shared by the majority of the Australian community.

There is, moreover, a palpable nervousness about traditional song. Knowing that some songs are "secret" and potentially harmful, people—frequently people of goodwill, who are merely trying to show proper respect—choose to avoid them completely. This has inhibited the degree to which Australians have been able to engage with Aboriginal music, and this in turn has affected the extent to which Aboriginal song is known and appreciated both within Australia and internationally. And yet my own experience is that, provided restrictions on esoteric knowledge are respected and cultural ownership of public knowledge is properly acknowledged, most Aboriginal communities, at least in the north of Australia, want their music to be more widely disseminated and better understood. There is deep concern over the lack of value accorded Indigenous performance traditions within the national heritage and the rate at which extinctions are occurring. These views were confirmed clearly and unambiguously in a statement that emerged from the recent Garma Symposium on Indigenous Performance, which brought together senior Aboriginal leaders and non-Aboriginal academics in an Arnhem Land community:

> Songs, dances and ceremonial performances form the core of [Aboriginal] cultures in Australia. It is through song, dance and associated ceremony that Indigenous people sustain their cultures and maintain the Law and a sense of self within the world. Performance traditions are the foundation of social and personal wellbeing, and with the ever-increasing loss of these traditions, the toll grows every year. The preservation of performance traditions is therefore one of the highest priorities for Indigenous people.
>
> Indigenous songs should also be a deeply valued part of the Australian cultural heritage. They represent the great classical music of this land. These ancient musical traditions were once everywhere in Australia, and now survive as living traditions only in several regions. Many of these are now in danger of being lost forever. Indigenous performances are one of our most rich and beautiful forms of artistic expression, and yet they remain unheard and invisible.[1]

One of my primary motivations in writing this book is to respond to the challenge implicit in that young man's question issued all those years ago, and in the more recent Garma Statement on Indigenous Music. By focusing on one of the major genres of Aboriginal music, I hope to enhance our ability to understand the significance of performances and the role of the musical gestures that lie at the heart of their cultural work.

In 1978 I arrived at the University of Sydney as a junior lecturer fresh from writing a dissertation in the field of Sino-Japanese music history at Cambridge and was asked by the Professor of Music Peter Platt to prepare a course on Aboriginal music. Some years later, it was my first graduate student, Ray Keogh, who showed me, through his own work on Aboriginal songs from the Western Kimberley, how engagement with Aboriginal knowledge through song can teach us ways of relating to this Australian land. Much more recently, a certain Brazilian ethnomusicologist and former Buddhist monk more or less convinced me in a bar in Hiroshima that I should not talk about Buddhism in a book like this. But I find that I cannot begin without telling you the following.

Last year, when the Sydney Zen Centre opened its Ancient Ground Temple (Kodoji) at Gorrick's Run, west of Sydney, I sang, with the permission of its senior custodian Frank Dumoo, a *wangga* from his country at Yendili in far northwest Australia. The song is an injunction to look after country. I sang it first in Marri-tjevin, "Yendili yendili arrgirritni, yendili yendili arrgirritni, aa ye-ngina," then in English, "Yendili, Yendili, you will look after it, my children." I then drew on the power of Aboriginal song to extinguish geographical distance by bringing the song down to the place where we were all sitting by singing in English, "Ancient ground, ancient ground, you will look after it, my children," before returning it home by singing it in its original form one more time in Marri-tjevin.

To have sung this song before my elders, my old teacher Robert Aitken Rōshi and my present teacher Subhana Bazaghi Rōshi, at a site that lies on one of the old Aboriginal pathways heading to the sacred mountain, Mount Yungu, surrounded by family and friends—this was a moment of true belonging.

I tell you, it is worth engaging with these songs. I only hope that I have done them justice.

June 2004

Acknowledgments

My deepest debt of gratitude is to the *wangga* songmen without whose support this book would not have been written. Foremost among these were Alan Maralung (Barunga), Tommy Barrtjap, Billy Mandji, Bobby Lambudju Lane, Kenny Burrenjuck, Timothy Burrenjuck, Roger Yarrowin, Simon Moreen (Belyuen), Thomas Kungiung, Maurice Ngulkur, Les Kundjil, Philip Mullumbuk, Charles Kungiung (Wadeye), Colin Worumbu Ferguson (Belyuen/Wadeye), Martin Warrigal Kungiung (Peppimenarti), Phillip Pannikin (Kununurra), Jack Dann, and Paul Chapman (Mowanjum/Dodnun). Thanks are also due to the didjeridu players Robert Daly (Peppimenarti), Nicky Jorrock, Ian Bilbil, Peter Chainsaw (Belyuen), Gerald Longmair, Columbanas Wanir (Wadeye), Jack Chadum, and Peter Manaberu (Barunga), and to the doyen of dance, Ambrose Piarlum (Wadeye). I am particularly indebted to the singers, dancers, and ritual specialists who guided my work and acted as my primary teachers: Alan Maralung, Bobby Lambudju Lane, Martin Warrigal Kungiung, and Frank Dumoo.

An extraordinary group of knowledgeable women at Belyuen assisted in the translation and explication of songs, and I offer them all my thanks. These include Esther Burrenjuck, Agnes Lippo, Audrey Lippo, Marjory Bilbil, Ruby Yarrowin, and Alice Jorrock. At Belyuen, thanks are also due to Daniel and Lorraine Lane, Eddie Shields, Henry Moreen, and council president JS (recently deceased).

At Wadeye another group of senior people worked intensively with me on this and related projects. In addition to the songmen acknowledged earlier, these include Marie Long, Jeannie Jongmin, Mary Jongmin, and Ruth Parmbuk. Other elders who have provided valuable assistance include Patrick Nudjulu, John Chula, Laurence Kolumboort, Elizabeth Cumaiyi, Mary Magdalen (Manman) Birrari, Rita Tharwul, Gypsy Jinjair, John Nummar, Pius Luckan, Clement Tchinburur, and Benedict Tchinburur. The Melpi family, including Colin Worumbu's wife Mercy, her brother Leon, and their father Leo, have consistently taken a keen interest in my work. Felix Bunduck, council president for much of the time I have worked at Wadeye, has also been unfailingly supportive.

Among the non-Aboriginal scholars with whom I have worked, I wish first to acknowledge the linguist Lys Ford's invaluable and generous assistance over many years. Linda Barwick, to whom this book is dedicated, has been my companion, adviser, interlocutor, and critic through much of this journey. I have benefited from many illuminating hours of discussion with John von Sturmer and with my friend and colleague Nicholas Routley, who not only gave me encouragement when it was most needed, but also kindly checked my musical transcriptions. JoAnne Page has provided dance transcription and analysis and helped me orient myself in the unfamiliar field of dance. Sally Treloyn kindly made available her recordings of *wangga* from the western Kimberley and drew my attention to a number of important sources on *wangga* for that area.

Nicholas Reid and Francesca Merlan gave invaluable assistance at the early stages of the project. Numerous people, including Ray Keogh, Jim Franklin, Corin Bone, Lisa Bone, Beatrice Marett, and Lucy Rhydwen-Marett, have worked as research assistants or helped in other ways on the project. The setting of the musical examples was carried out by Nicholas Ng with additional help from Matthew Hindson. Maps are by Peter Johnson and Andrew Wilson. Natalie Shea and Amanda Harris assisted in proofreading the text.

Friends and colleagues who have generously read and made comments on my text at various stages in its evolution include Alberto Furlan, Father Hilary Martin, Steven Meucke, Michele Morgan, Deborah Bird Rose, and Alan Rumsey. Over the years I've benefited greatly from conversations with Greg Anderson, Kim Barber, Diane Austin-Broos, Anne Boyd, Aaron Corn, Cath Ellis, Ken Lum, Susan McClary, Michele Morgan, David Nash, Beth Povinelli, Mari Rhydwen, Jane Simpson, Peter Toner, Sally Treloyn, Michael Walsh, and Stephen Wild.

At Wadeye, Mark Crocombe, the director of the Wadeye Aboriginal Language Centre and curator of the Yile Kanamgek Museum, has provided advice and assistance in many areas both intellectual and practical. I am grateful to Evan Costello for his hospitality at Wadeye. Thanks are also due to Cathy Winsley, Theresa Timber, and Lorna Tennant of the Belyuen Community Council. Daniel Suggart and David Newry of the Mirima Language Centre facilitated my work with *wangga* singers in Kununurra, and in Derby, the Ngarinyin Aboriginal Corporation, the late David Mowaljali, Paddy Neowarra, and Tony Redmond were of great assistance. Janet Sincock of the North Australian Research Unit in Darwin has over the years generously provided invaluable and generous logistical help.

I would like to offer particular thanks to my editor, Maura High for her professionalism, patience and grace in guiding this project to fruition; also to Chris Crochetière and Darwin Campa of BW&A Books, Inc. for their stunning design work and for bringing my rather complex text so successfully into production. I am also grateful to Suzanna Tamminen of Wesleyan University Press and to Susan McClary, originating editor of the Music/Culture series, for their faith in and support for the project, and to Bill Henry for his meticulous and remarkably painless copyediting.

The research for this book has been supported by grants from the Australian Institute for Aboriginal and Torres Strait Islander Studies, the Australian Research Council, the Research Grants Council (Hong Kong), the Research Institute for the Humanities and Social Sciences (University of Sydney), and the Australian Academy of the Humanities.

The spelling system for Marri-tjevin and Marri-ammu, which are closely related dialects of the same language, has been developed by Lysbeth Ford in consultation with the staff of the Wadeye Language Centre and the teacher aides at the Wadeye school. The spelling system for Batjamalh was also developed by Lysbeth Ford in consultation with fluent speakers at Belyuen.

How to Read Marri-tjevin/Marri-ammu Words

Vowel	Marri-tjevin/Marri-ammu	English (Standard Australian unless otherwise stated)
middle **i**	n**i**din (country)	b**i**t
end **i**	wud**i** (water)	sk**i**
u	k**u**wa (he/she stands)	p**u**t
a	m**a**-yawa (Marri-ammu ancestor)	b**u**t
e	y**e**ndili (place name)	b**e**t

Consonant		
t	**t**itil (clapstick)	**t**ar
d	ni**d**in (country)	hi**d**
rt	**rt**adi (back, on top)	American English "pa**rt**"
th	**th**anggurralh (Marri-ammu and Marri-tjevin people)	Not in English but as in Italian "**tu**"
dh	walakan**dh**a (Marri-tjevin ancestor)	and **th**is
tj	**tj**iwilirr (Hairy Cheeky Yam)	**ch**at
dj	**dj**in**dj**a (here)	**g**in**g**er
p	**p**urangang (salt water)	**p**ut
b	**b**ugim (white)	**b**ut
k	**k**uwa (he/she stands)	**c**ut
g	**g**apil (big)	**g**ut
rz	**rz**amu (sea turtle)	Dr. **Zh**ivago
sj	gis**j**i (like this)	fu**s**ion

Consonant	Marri-tjevin/Marri-ammu	English (Standard Australian unless otherwise stated)
v	**v**erri (foot)	**v**ery
n	**n**idin (country)	**n**ut
ny	pumini**ny** (spring)	oni**on**
m	**m**ana (brother)	**m**ud
ng	**ng**ata (house)	si**ng**
l	wu**l**umen (old man)	ho**l**y
lh	kavu**lh** (he/she lies down)	stea**lth**
rr	ve**rr**i (foot)	trilled r as in Scottish "spo**rr**an"
r	ye**r**i (child)	ve**r**y
y	**y**eri (child)	**y**es
w	**w**udi (fresh water)	**w**et

How to Read Batjamalh Words

Vowel	Batjamalh	English (Standard Australian unless otherwise stated)
middle **i**	y**i**ne (what?)	b**i**t
end **i**	nga-m**i** (I sit)	sk**i**
u	nya-m**u** (sit)	p**u**t
a	y**a**garra (Oh no!)	b**u**t
e	w**e**rret (quick)	b**e**t
ü	tj**ü**t (foot)	f**ew**

Consonant		
t	tjü**t** (foot)	cu**t**
d	**d**awarra (belly)	**d**ot
tj	ba**tj**amalh (language)	ba**tch**
dj	ba**dj**alarr (place)	ba**dge**
p	nga-**p**-pindja-ng	ha**pp**y
b	**b**angany (song)	**b**ut
k	ma**k**a (for; perfective marker)	la**cq**uer
g	ya**g**arra (Oh no!)	bu**gg**er
v	nga-**v**e (I go)	ha**v**ing
n	**n**üng (him)	**n**ut
ny	**ny**ung (for)	oni**on**
m	**m**aka (for; perfective marker)	**m**ud

Consonant	Batjamalh	English (Standard Australian unless otherwise stated)
ng	**ng**a-mi (I sit)	si**ng**
l	badja**l**arr (place)	ho**l**y
lh	batjama**lh** (language)	stea**lth**
rr	badjala**rr** (place)	trilled r as in Scottish "sporran"
r	**r**ak (patri-country)	ve**r**y
y	**y**agarra (Oh no!)	**y**es
w	**w**erret (quick)	**w**et

What the Walakandha Have Always Done

It is late afternoon in the remote Aboriginal community of Wadeye, or Port Keats, as it is still widely known, and in the shade of an ancient boab tree, a group of men sing, "This is what the Walakandha have always done."[1] Male dancers, led by sinuous old men in red loincloths and hair-string belts, dance with an astounding vigor, kicking up dust and calling out with the voices of their Walakandha ancestors. Their bodies are ochered and imprinted with the image of Walakandha hands. A line of women dancers in brightly colored frocks edges around the dance ground, swaying gracefully and moving their arms from side to side. The deep throb of the didjeridu, mingling with the cries of the dancers and the voices of the singers, grounds everything. The singers, dancers, and the solitary didjeridu player are all enacting ancestral precedent, singing and dancing as the ancestral dead, whom they call Walakandha. This is a circumcision ceremony, a ritual action that also invokes ancestral precedent. This is the proper way for a boy to leave childhood behind and be reborn as a man.

On another day, in the community of Belyuen, several hours to the north, the chattels of a recently deceased person are being ritually burned. The ceremonial ground is decked with multicolored bolts of cloth, and the songmen sing, "Sing the song for me, and dance! Sing the song for me, and dance! Dance a song for us both."[2] They are reproducing the song of a ghost, a Wunymalang, who first sang it to one of the songmen in a dream while he lay sleeping; "us both" in the song refers to the living songman and the song-giving ghost. The ancestral dead call on the living to perform their songs and to dance as Wunymalang. By following this ancestral precedent, the worlds of the living and the dead draw near and interpenetrate. The Wunymalang ghost of the person whose chattels are being burned passes between the two worlds.

The songs and dances performed on both these occasions are *wangga*, a genre of song and dance from the Daly region of northwest Australia, that is, the largely coastal region lying immediately to the north and south of the Daly River (see introduction figure 1). *Wangga* articulates fundamental themes of death and regeneration. The Marri-tjevin people, whose country lies to the north of Wadeye on the Moyle River, address their ancestral dead as "Walakandha." For

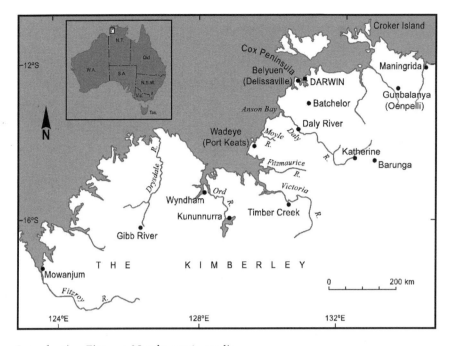

Introduction Figure 1. Northwest Australia

them, this ceremonial action is central to the completion of a cycle of birth, death, and reincarnation that is conceived poetically as the ebb and flow of the tides.

To the Marri-ammu people, who live just north of the Marri-tjevin, the ancestral dead are known as "Ma-yawa." The mingling of the living Marri-ammu and their ancestral dead that is enacted in ceremony is expressed metaphorically in their *wangga* as the mixing of salt and fresh water.

In the *wangga* songs of the Wadjiginy people, a group who over the past hundred years or so migrated from their traditional county near the Daly River to the community of Belyuen near Darwin, the voices of the Wunymalang dead can be heard in ceremony, calling on their living descendants to join with them in song and dance. Wunymalang are a different order of being from Walakandha and Ma-yawa and reflect modifications that people at Belyuen have made to the cosmologies associated with *wangga*. Because they now live at a greater distance from their ancestral country than the Marri-tjevin and the Marri-ammu, the way that these people conceive of conception and death differs from that of people living close to their country in the Daly region. This is reflected in both the genesis and the ceremonial function of songs.

Through its fundamental association with death and regeneration, *wangga* facilitates other types of change: from boyhood to manhood, from student to graduate, from callow youth to hero. The many social changes—settlement, migration, marginalization—that attended European intrusion on Aboriginal domains in the Daly region are reflected in, and mediated by, *wangga*.

The Major Themes and Performance Conventions of *Wangga*

This book is about performances such as those that I have just described, and in particular the ways in which song and dance articulate broad cosmological, ontological, political, and historical themes. When I began this project, my primary aim was to add to our knowledge of Australian Aboriginal music by describing one of its major genres. As the project unfolded over a period of fifteen years, however, I found myself increasingly engaged with the problem of understanding how performers work within the music and dance conventions of *wangga* to articulate social meaning. The integration of musical and social analysis has long been held as an aim of ethnomusicology, but it has rarely been achieved. To grapple with such matters is no easy task, requiring, as it often does, engagement with unfamiliar traditions of performance situated within unfamiliar worlds.

Chapter 1 opens with an exploration of a single song—a *wangga* about the cosmogonic ancestor Tulh—in order to show some of the ways that formal elements of music are linked to broader social concerns. Here, in a thumbnail sketch, we encounter for the first time some of the musical and textual conventions that underlie *wangga*'s capacity to signify, as well as specific—though limited—details of the Daly cosmology. The chapter then goes on to explore the major cosmological and ontological categories of Daly thought through the discussion of fundamental concepts such as Dreaming (*ngirrwat*), conception Dreaming (*meri-men.ngu*), Dreaming sites (*kigatiya*), and orders of being like the Walakandha, Ma-yawa, and Wunymalang ancestors.

The themes associated with *wangga* are intertwined and overlapping, and nowhere is this clearer than in individual songs. In a single poetic couplet, the Walakandha *wangga* song "Truwu," for example, expresses all the following: the essential interconnectedness of the living and the dead through ceremony, the mutual responsibilities of the living to look after each other in everyday affairs, the exigencies of everyday life, and the intimate relationship that the living and the dead maintain with a sentient landscape. "Truwu" is discussed in detail in chapter 5. In the course of this book, I will undertake close-grained studies of a number of songs like "Truwu," since it is only by examining the fine detail of text and music that we can discern the processes by which broader themes, such as those enumerated hereafter, are enacted in particular performative moments.

The Relationship between the Living and the Dead

Wangga provides the primary locus of human engagement with the ancestral dead. This interaction of the living and the dead occurs in two principal contexts: in the process of song composition and in ceremony. The processes by which new songs are learned by songmen from their deceased ancestors in dream provide the focus for chapter 2. Ceremony is discussed in chapter 3.

The principal ceremonial context for *wangga* is the mortuary ceremony, the primary function of which is to facilitate the passage of the recently deceased from the society of the living to that of the dead. The creation of a liminal space in which the worlds of the living and the dead interpenetrate, and in which the deceased can transmigrate, is achieved by living songmen singing the *wangga* songs given to them by the dead, and by living dancers dancing as the dead. The second major ceremonial context is the circumcision ceremony, where a boy, in a process analogous to mortuary rituals, is made to "die" to childhood in order to be reborn as a man.

Ceremonial Reciprocity

The reciprocal obligations of the dead to give songs to the living and for the living to perform these in ceremony on behalf of the dead provide the model for forms of reciprocal obligation that apply among the living in Daly societies. Perhaps the most important of these is the obligation placed on *wangga*-owning groups to perform ceremony for other groups.

In the late 1950s and early 1960s, a tripartite system of ceremonial reciprocity developed at Wadeye whereby the groups associated with three genres of song—*wangga*, *lirrga*, and *dhanba*—perform ceremony for one another. Created in response to specific social pressures at the Port Keats (Wadeye) mission, this system has since played a major role in stabilizing social relationships within the community. (The nature of these pressures is examined more fully in chapter 1.) Chapter 3 contains a detailed description of a mortuary ceremony in which one social group works for another.

Relationships between People and Country

Reciprocal obligations like those that hold between the living and the dead, and among the living in matters of ceremony, also condition the relationships that both the living and the dead have to country. In the Daly region, country is conceived of as living and sentient, and as the source from which the living spring and to which the dead eventually return. The purpose of the joint work performed by the living and the dead in the production and performance of *wangga* is to ensure the continuity of this existential journey to and from country, a process that, in the poetry of the Walakandha *wangga*, is expressed as the ebb and flow of the tide. Performances of *wangga* are thus an enactment of the joint responsibilities of the living and the dead to the life source.

Singers call out to country in their songs, and dancers communicate their presence through their sweat, and by beating the ground with their feet. Invocations and references to country and its associated Dreamings and Dreaming sites permeate the imagery of *wangga*. As we shall see repeatedly throughout this study, it is not only texts but also elements of music such as melody and rhythm that articulate relationships between people and country. Through manipulations of the conventions of music, an accomplished singer like Maurice Ngulkur is, for example, able to express complex and shifting relationships between social groups and country (see chapter 6). Similarly, the fluid relationships that people living at Belyuen have with their primary place of residency, on the one hand, and with their distant ancestral countries, on the other, are reflected in both the text and music of songs such as those in Bobby Lambudju Lane's repertory (see chapter 8).

Liminality

The association of *wangga* with liminal states of being—dream states, and the states of being in the twilight zone between life and death, or between childhood and adulthood—is enacted in ceremony and reflected in its poetics. Animals who can exist in both salt- and freshwater environments, the mixing of fresh and salt water at the Marri-ammu *wudi-pumininy* spring, the ebb and flow of the tide: all these allude to the intermingling of the living and dead within the liminal context of ceremony.

The Mediation of Social Change

The poetics of *wangga* mediate change, not only as it occurs in the course of a person's life—at death or at the point where a boy becomes a man through circumcision—but also in broader social contexts. The enormous effect that the pressures of European settlement and internal colonization have had on the peoples of the Daly region for more than a century is reflected in many aspects of song. Not only have new ritual complexes been brought into the region to replace those seen to have no further efficacy, but also the *wangga* tradition itself has been profoundly affected by the very social and historical factors that it attempts to mediate. New repertories of song, including the Walakandha *wangga*, were created in response to changing social circumstances at the Port Keats mission. The ancestral sources from which some *wangga* repertories spring have altered as cosmologies fracture. Social forces also significantly affect what is sung and what is danced, what is passed down and what is lost. Even the fine details— the way a melodic phrase is turned, or a rhythm articulated—are shaped by the social pressures that exist at the moment of performance.

The association of *wangga* with change is reflected in many of its formal conventions. Musical and textual structures must be fluid enough to signify changing relationships between people, and between people and country, in different ways at different times, as the political and legal landscape shifts. At the same time, the conventions must be sufficiently stable to allow singers and dancers to perform strongly in unison. The most systematic account of the music and dance conventions and their primary semantic associations is given in chapter 4, where in the course of a detailed examination of two *wangga* songs, "Bangany-nyung Ngaya" and "Yendili no. 2," the main formal elements of *wangga* are identified. These include the broad division of songs into melodic sections, instrumental sections, and codas; the role of the didjeridu in articulating rhythm and grounding melody; the characteristics of sung melody and the structuring of melody within melodic sections; the rhythmic and metrical organization of text; the role of clapstick beating in articulating meter and its relationship to dance; the main ground patterns, phrases, and movements of the dance; and the conventions for fitting dance to music.

In this book, the most specific and detailed explanations of modes of signification are given in the chapters on four important *wangga* repertories: the Walakandha *wangga* (chapter 5) and the Ma-yawa *wangga* (chapter 6) from Wadeye; and the *wangga* repertories of the Belyuen singers Tommy Barrtjap (chapter 7) and Bobby Lambudju Lane (chapter 8). These four case studies are followed by a summary of the main formal elements of *wangga* and their significance (chapter 9). In a final chapter (chapter 10), I examine the ways in which musical conventions are extended and modes of signification are modified when *wangga* is performed in a wider diaspora outside the Daly region.

In attempting to show how the music and dance of *wangga* articulate meaning, I rely quite heavily on musical and (to a lesser extent) dance transcription and analysis. Although analysis is not particularly fashionable within ethnomusicology today, I am strongly of the view that it provides our best methodological tool for isolating significant (and signifying) moments of performance. I am not so naive as to assume that Western notation can ever accurately represent the totality of the sound world of *wangga*—or indeed any complex sound world—but I believe that transcription can, if sensitively handled, be used to direct the listener to salient features of the music, much as maps direct travelers to salient features of the landscape. Just as maps are socially constructed documents with their own sets of conventions, and just as they can never represent every aspect of a landscape without simply replicating the landscape in its entirely, so too are transcriptions socially constructed documents that can never totally encode the sound world to which they relate. But insofar as they help us navigate through an unfamiliar music, they can be extremely helpful.

The reason that I use Western notation—despite its obvious shortcomings—is because it is the most widely understood way of graphically representing musical sound. Many of the recordings on which my transcriptions and analyses rest are presented in the accompanying CD, and I invite readers to judge the efficacy of the transcriptions, and their associated analyses, with regard to the extent to which they open up the music and render it intelligible.

We move now from a consideration of themes and conventions to the location of my study of *wangga* within the scholarly traditions of Australian Aboriginal music research and within the broader domains of musicology and ethnomusicology.

Traditions of Scholarship in the Study of Aboriginal Music

Insofar as my work seeks to comprehensively document and explain the musical conventions of a single Aboriginal song genre, it continues and extends a focus on genre that A. P. Elkin and Trevor A. Jones began in the 1950s and Alice Moyle continued in the 1960s and 1970s. Elkin and Jones based their 1958 monograph *Arnhem Land Music* on recordings made by Elkin in northern Australia in 1949 and 1952. In part 1 of *Arnhem Land Music*, Elkin describes many extramusical aspects of his recordings—texts, ceremonial practices, associated mythologies—under a series of headings, some of which are the names of musical genres and some not.[3] One of the strengths of Elkin's work is his reliance on indigenous song categories. This approach strongly influenced later musicological research on Aboriginal song and dance, which now tends to focus either on genre or on specific song series within genres.[4]

Elkin's approach contrasts with that of Alice Moyle in that her work (for example, A. Moyle 1967, 1974) concerns itself primarily with classifying Aboriginal songs with reference to nonindigenous taxonomies—on the basis of their instrumental accompaniment, according to perceived religious categories, or according to aspects of musical style such as melodic range, rhythmic organization, and the nature of the accompanying instruments. Her methods were undoubtedly influenced by the project, then current in ethnomusicology, of identifying unitary methods of analysis that could be applied to all music and by the musical mapping projects then being undertaken under the aegis of the International Folk Music Council.

In part 2 of *Arnhem Land Music*, Trevor Jones undertook transcription and musical analysis of recordings for each of the repertories identified by Elkin, focusing in each case on scale, melody, rhythm, and form. Jones's approach was, in a number of regards, very much of its time. In focusing primarily on musical data, it reflected current musicological attitudes concerning the autonomy of musical systems and the role of musical analysis in defining them. In that the fieldwork data were collected by Elkin and only later analyzed by Jones, there was a separation of the fieldwork and laboratory phases of the ethnomusicological work that limited Jones's ability to investigate the meanings that the music held in its home environment.[5] Jones's interpretation of his data was, moreover, informed by evolutionist and primitivist notions current in the ethnomusicological literature of the time (for example, Sachs 1943 and Nettl 1956).[6] In pointing this out, however, I wish in no way to belittle Jones's work, which has proved invaluable for later generations. There is no doubt that Jones was deeply moved by what he heard, and that by drawing attention to many salient features of the repertories he surveyed, he engendered a wider appreciation of Aboriginal song. Elkin's recordings and Jones's commentaries were what drew me to *wangga* in the first place, and their work has also been invaluable to Aboriginal people for what it preserves today from earlier generations.[7]

A desire to identify the significant elements of Aboriginal music and to increase the appreciation and understanding of it in the wider community also inspired Catherine Ellis, the musicologist who has been the most successful in using musical analysis as a key to understanding both the structures of Aboriginal music and the wider social meanings that they convey in performance. It was Ellis who established some of the key procedures that we now follow in the analysis of Aboriginal music. It was she, for example, who showed that text and its associated rhythm operate as a system independent of melody, and that melody and text/rhythm are combined in the moment of performance, giving rise to different realizations in different contexts. It was she who most successfully related the categories established in musical analysis to dance structures and to wider aspects of ceremonial and social signification. This ranged from pointing out the association of particular melodies with particular Dreamings (and hence the places associated with those Dreamings) to demonstrating how elements of musical form are manipulated to reflect different degrees of sacredness and differing levels of knowledge among performers: "The more powerful the song, the more intricate the overlay of patterning [of formal elements of dance, design, clapstick beating, text, etc.] and their meanings" (Ellis 1980, 725).[8]

The question of how best to combine social and musical analysis has been a central, and indeed unavoidable, issue in research on Aboriginal music. Because of the centrality of song and dance in Aboriginal life, they have formed the focus not only of musicological work but also of research within anthropology (see, for example, Dussart 2000; Keen 1994; Merlan 1987; von Sturmer 1987), linguistics (Donaldson 1984, 1987; Dixon 1984), and literary studies (Strehlow 1971; Clunies Ross 1978). Because anthropological, linguistic, or literary studies that ignore the forms of music and dance are ultimately as impoverished as musicological studies that focus on musical structure alone, scholars from nonmusicological disciplines have been drawn into dialogue with musicologists. A critical event in the creation of dialogue was a multidisciplinary symposium on Aboriginal song and dance held in the context of the 1984 conference of the Australian and New Zealand Association for the Advancement of Science (ANZAAS) and subsequently published as Clunies Ross, Donaldson, and Wild 1987. It was John von Sturmer's paper on the ontology of performance, delivered on this occasion, that convinced me to seriously engage in research in Aboriginal music and dance. Some of the most successful work that has been done on Australian Aboriginal music has occurred when scholars from several disciplines have worked collaboratively (for example, Ellis, Barwick, and Morais 1990; Clunies Ross and Wild 1982, 1984; Dixon and Koch 1996).

One of the most successful integrations of elements of musical and social performance (in this case, the performance of gender roles), through a detailed analytical understanding of the processes that produce a performance, occurs in a paper by Linda Barwick (1995). Barwick focuses "on instances of gross melodic disagreement" in a mixed-sex performance of Central Australian music, in which it is clear that the men (who sing together as a group) sometimes have quite different ideas from the women (who also sing together) about how texts should be fitted onto the flexible melodic contour. Barwick argues "firstly that the *form* of the men's disagreements can be described in terms of different applications by men and women of musical principles that are operating in the intermeshing of text and melody; and secondly, *that the degree to which the men persist* is symbolic of potentially competing claims by men and women to ritual authority in mixed-sex performances of series owned by women" (97).

Barwick's focus on specific details of performance, located through careful analysis and transcription, and her explanation of these as enactments of specific social agendas have had no small influence on the present work. In her research, she maintains a keen sense of the different perspectives derived through analysis and performance, and, like Ellis, insists on the inclusion of performers' perspectives in any interpretation of a performance (see Barwick 1990).

The distinction between the perspectives of the analyst and of the performer is related to a distinction, identified by sociologists such as Howard Becker (1989) and Peter Martin (2002), between "decoding" and "enactment." To view performances as repositories of embedded meaning in need of decoding is to foreground the role of the analyst, whereas to view them as enactments of wider cultural forms is to foreground the perspectives of the performers, which the analyst hopes ultimately to integrate into his or her understanding.

This brief survey has focused on the work that has most directly affected my approach, but even in this regard it is limited. Stephen Wild and Margaret Clunies Ross's work on Arnhem Land clan song, with its emphasis on song text, musical form, and the location of the songs within a broad social matrix illustrated by sound recordings, film, and wider ethnographic writing is something that I use regularly in my teaching and have absorbed almost by osmosis (Clunies Ross and Wild 1982, 1984; Clunies Ross and Mundrugmundrug 1988; Clunies Ross and Hiatt 1978; Wild 1986; McKenzie 1980; Hiatt 1965). Richard Moyle's wide-ranging studies of the music of a number of Central Australian communities (R. Moyle 1979, 1986, 1997), based on detailed transcription and analysis, have challenged me and shaped my thinking in various ways, as has the work of my students Ray Keogh, Greg Anderson, Margaret Gummow, Sally Treloyn, and Alberto Furlan, all of whom take what I have to offer and then return it in forms that both enrich and challenge.

The Integration of Musical and Social Analysis

As stated earlier, ethnomusicology has, since its inception, espoused the integration of musical and social analysis as the sine qua non of its methodology. Writing in 1971, John Blacking stated that the purpose of musical analysis in ethnomusicology was "not simply to describe the cultural background of the music as human behavior, and *then* to analyze peculiarities of style . . . but to describe *both* music *and* its cultural background as dialectically interrelated parts of a total system" (Blacking 1995, 56). Yet, as Richard Widdess recently observed, "While most ethnomusicologists assume that a direct connection exists between the substance of music and its context, this remain largely an article of faith." Widdess adds, with reference to Blacking's dictum, that "ethnomusicological description often goes no further than *either* 'describing the cultural background of the music' *or* analysing its 'peculiarities of style'" (1999, 1).

Stephen Blum, in his thorough review of the role of analysis in ethnomusicology, identifies the universalist baggage that ethnomusicology inherited from its precursor, comparative musicology, as one of the major factors that has inhibited the integration of social and musical analysis. Comparative musicology's preoccupation with the development of an analytical method that could be applied to all musics did not cease when comparative musicology metamorphosed into ethnomusicology. As late as 1971, Blacking wrote: "We need a unitary method of musical analysis which can not only be applied to *all* music, but can explain both the form, the social and emotional content and the effects of the music, as systems of relationships between an infinite number of variables" (Blacking 1995, 93).

Blum is blunt in his assessment of the universalist project: "The development of many regional musicologies has cast doubt on the adequacy of analytical techniques that were designed to be widely or even universally applicable." He adds, "by resisting the various proposals for 'a unitary method of musical analysis' . . . we have learned more than might otherwise have been possible about the multiple meanings of musical activity in many regions" (1992, 208, 209).

The incorporation into analyses of ways of talking about music that are indigenous to those traditions has been a major step forward. Nonetheless, the extent to which different regions and different traditions have language for discussing formal aspects of music can vary greatly, ranging from environments where there is a highly developed indigenous metalanguage for the discussion of music, as in the case discussed by Regula Qureshi where "participants themselves identify the musical features of *qawwali* in terms of their association with its function" (1987, 67), to the case of Australian Aboriginal music, where there is a conspicuous dearth of indigenous musical terminology. Debates over whether particular methods of analysis remain sensitive to (or do violence to) indigenous conceptual frameworks are therefore not uncommon within the community of scholars working on Aboriginal music.[9]

Working within a musical culture where musicians have had no need to develop an elaborate metalanguage around performance, I have, as already stated, found transcription and analysis invaluable in isolating elements of musical form and observing how they are used. As Anthony Seeger noted, transcription (which, after all, is a form of analysis) can "reveal aspects of the performance that native categories do not highlight" (1987, 102). Like Seeger, I have used transcription as "a tool for raising questions" (102). The analytical categories that I have discovered have been confirmed through discussion with specialist musicians and through participation in performance.

At this point I would like to turn my attention away from ethnomusicology and briefly consider some recent developments in other areas of musicology that I have found helpful in clarifying my own ideas about the relationship of musical and social analysis. During the time I have been conducting research for this book, that is, in the period from 1986 to the present, a not-so-quiet revolution has been occurring in the field of Western historical musicology, as scholars such as Susan McClary, Rose Subotnik, Richard Leppert, Gary Tomlinson, and others have argued for an integration of musical discourse with other social, cultural, and historical perspectives. The rejection of the idea that music is an autonomous and arcane art, and that musicology is, by extension, an autonomous domain of music itself, has opened the way for musical scholarship to engage more fully in the debates that have flourished in cognate disciplines of the humanities and social sciences.[10]

One of the areas that has figured most prominently in recent debates is that of musical analysis. Because analysis is so central to positivist musicology's attempts to support "the notion that music shapes itself in accordance with self-contained, abstract principles that are unrelated to the outside world" (Leppert and McClary 1987, xii), any questioning of the view that formalist analysis is a scientific, objective, and value-free approach to music tends to be seen as an attack on musical analysis itself. Within historical musicology, however, a series of close, socially grounded readings of key works both from the Western canon and from popular music (see, for example, McClary 1987, 1993, 2000; Subotnik 1987) has shown that, on the contrary, musical analysis has much to offer to the enterprise of reading meaning into musical works.[11]

One of the important results of debate within musical scholarship over how best to integrate musical and social analysis is that it has encouraged productive dialogue between the different branches of the enterprise: historical musicologists, ethnomusicologists, scholars of popular music, and music sociologists are talking to one another as perhaps never before. The music sociologist Peter Martin, for example, is critical of the fact that in attempting to integrate social and music analysis, the so-called new musicologists such as McClary and Subotnik have been strongly influenced by Adorno's attempts to "decode or decipher the 'sedimented Geist' which is immanent in musical works" (Martin 2002, 132).[12] Another sociologist of the arts, Howard Becker, speaking to the Annual Meeting of the Society for Ethnomusicology in 1988, was convinced that the project of "decoding" had infiltrated ethnomusicological method to such an extent that he felt compelled to offer ethnomusicologists an alternative. "Sociologists . . . aren't much interested in 'decoding' art works, in finding the work's secret meanings as reflections of society. They prefer to see those works as the result of what a lot of people have done jointly" (1989, 282).

In this book I have used transcription and analysis not to uncover "encoded meanings" but to identify the detail of gestures that have significance in performance. Musical performances fly past so quickly that without resort to transcription, it is difficult to identify these moments.

Fieldwork and Working Methods

I was drawn to *wangga* primarily because I found it beautiful and because it moved me. But it also seemed to have potential as a focus for research on a single complete song genre. The apparent concentration of *wangga* within a relatively small area, roughly within a triangle, the corners of which are Wadeye, Belyuen, and Barunga (see introduction figure 1), appeared to make its investigation a manageable project. I began working at Barunga and Belyuen in 1986 and for most of 1988 continued my work in these communities while extending it to others, most particularly Wadeye and Peppimenarti. It soon became apparent, however, that *wangga* is first and foremost a genre belonging to peoples whose traditional country lies to the north and south of the Daly River, and who speak the languages designated linguistically as "Daly languages" (Tryon 1974; Dixon 2002, 674–79), and that when *wangga* is found outside this area, it is as a result of its having been exported from the Daly region along trade routes and via other means. *Wangga*-owning groups are concentrated most heavily at Wadeye and Belyuen, and for this reason I have focused on these communities since the early 1990s, visiting them almost every year for periods ranging from a few weeks to several months. I also did some fieldwork in the Kimberley during this period, where I was able to investigate the changes that occur when *wangga* is adopted in a wider diaspora.

Each of the Daly language groups who nowadays own *wangga* has only a small number of fully competent speakers, many of whom are elderly.[13] At the time I began this study, none of these languages had been described in any detail by linguists. Fortunately I have been able to work closely with Lysbeth Ford, a linguist who during the course of my research wrote dissertations on two of the languages—Batjamalh and Emmi—spoken at Belyuen, and then went on to document the two languages—Marri-tjevin and Marri-ammu—in which *wangga* are sung at Wadeye. Working together, we were able to establish reliable texts as a necessary precursor to musical transcription and analysis, and as a catalyst for broader discussions of local cosmologies, ceremony, and other broader issues. Our methodology involved working not so much with individuals as with groups of senior men and women, some of whom were singers and some not, but all of whom were knowledgeable about song. Both Ford and I, and sometimes Linda Barwick, participated in these sessions, and the process benefited greatly from the combination of musicological and linguistic perspectives as both linguistically and musicologically trained ears were brought to bear on this task. In the final analysis, however, it is Ford who is responsible for the grammatical analyses that underpin the texts.

As the work of transcribing and analyzing the music progressed, the results were integrated into our discussions of performance dynamics and the significance of various elements of music and dance. In recent times, my ability to sing *wangga* songs has advanced to the point where I have been invited to sing alongside songmen such as Kenny Burrenjuck (Barrandjak) and Colin Worumbu (Warambu) Ferguson in minor ceremonies. These opportunities have allowed me to test in live performances what I had learned through transcription, analysis, and discussion.

Much of the dance analysis presented in this book was initially conducted back in Sydney with ethnochoreologist JoAnne Page using videotapes of performances. My recent participation in performances has led to a greater understanding of what in the music is essential for the dancers, and what happens to the dance when you get these things wrong. While this book is primarily a study of music, the identification of the formal elements of dance has proved invaluable on a number of fronts. It has allowed me to understand the role of *wangga* dance in enacting ancestral precedent, and it has clarified aspects of musical form and their significance. Terms used for different types of rhythmic beating and tempo, for example, derive from a description of dance movements: "quick foot" describes the dance but is also applied to the tempo of the clapsticks that accompany the song.

Just as *wangga* songs are owned by groups, so too is knowledge about songs. What was imparted to us in our working sessions with senior Aboriginal men and women was what the group felt it appropriate for us to know and for me to disseminate in the form of a book. This is one of the ways in which a community of knowledgeable elders controls knowledge. Tim Rice, citing James Clifford (1988), warns against the invention of generalized authors—The Nuer, The Balinese (we might add The Marri-tjevin or The Wadjiginy)—in ways that disempower and render anonymous the specific authors and actors (Rice 1994, 11). Apart from exceptional cases, however, it would not be appropriate for me to identify individual viewpoints when discussing group-sanctioned knowledge.

There are nonetheless cases where I identify individuals, particularly in the case of singers or ritual specialists who have the authority to speak as individuals about their own songs, or about the meaning of a ceremony. In these cases I have identified the "authors"—singers like Alan Maralung, Tommy Barrtjap, Bobby Lambudju Lane, and Thomas Kungiung (Kanggiang), or ritual specialists like Frank Dumoo (Dumu)—by name. Like many performers worldwide, *wangga* singers have proud reputations, and they do not want me to conceal their names, but I name such people only with permission.[14]

The presentation of knowledge as group owned rather than individually owned means that the dialogic nature of my research is not always evident from my text. During 2001 and 2002, however, inspired by the example of Steven Feld (1987), I attempted to read sections of my book to the appropriate groups. While some members of the group wished to engage in this process, most were simply not interested. As Feld observed, it is not an easy process to make a text composed for a Western academic audience accessible to a group of people whose knowledge system is so radically different. Those who chose to listen concentrated on correcting fact, rather than engaging with my arguments and interpretations. There was certainly none of the air of contestation noted by Feld with regard to his Kaluli interlocutors over the strategies he adopted in constructing his text.

In a previous article, I pointed out that my Aboriginal informants expect me, as an author, to take responsibility for my text, much as ceremonial performers are expected to take responsibility for their enactment of knowledge.[15] While one is bound to adhere to what was said and witnessed by a group, and while errors or the transgressions of boundaries between esoteric and non-esoteric knowledge will be quickly corrected, in the end you are expected to tell your own story, and to stand by it.

These matters can best be understood from the perspective of the reciprocal responsibilities that lie at the heart of most of the cultural work done by *wangga*. Just as different social groups work for each other to produce ceremony, so too do the living and the dead work reciprocally to ensure the efficacy of ritual and the continuity of human existence (see chapter 3).

In one of Tommy Barrtjap's songs, a song-giving ghost sings:

> What have I come to do?
> I'm going to sing, and then I'm going back.
> Now you sing![16]

Wangga composers are expected to use what they have been given by the dead, but they are also expected to shape it to the needs of the living. It is this act of cultural bestowal and trust that provides, I believe, the best key to understanding my relationship as an author to those who have sung to me and bestowed on me knowledge about songs. Some are back there at Wadeye and Belyuen, but most are already among the dead. Now it is up to me to sing what I have learned.

chapter one

Repertories, Histories, and Orders of Being

Old Man Tulh

At Pumurriyi in far northwestern Australia (see figure 1.1) stands a rock that is the embodiment of Old Man Tulh, an ancestor of the Marri-ammu people in whose country the rock lies. At the beginning of time, in the period referred to in English as the Dreaming, Old Man Tulh returned from hunting and, impatient for food, attempted to eat a hairy cheeky yam (*tjiwilirr*) that had not been properly prepared to remove its toxins. He became angry at his wives for their lack of care and responsibility and in his fury threw pieces of the yam around. Near the Tulh rock are two further rocks—one white and one black—that are the pieces of ancestral Hairy Cheeky Yam that Tulh threw around.

A Story about Old Man Tulh

Edward Nemarluk, a senior Marri-ammu man, told the story of Old Man Tulh as follows:

> I'm going to sit down and tell the story about Hairy Cheeky Yam that the old people used to tell me. They used to come to this place whose real name is Pumurriyi. Old Man Tulh came here to meet them.
>
> In the beginning, when he was human, Old Man Tulh went out hunting. He went and threw sticks at animals. He went after Magpie Geese, Burdekin Duck, Chestnut Teal. It was dark when he got back here. He ran back to the camp. He put down the meat [but he was hungry for something to eat right away, for Hairy Cheeky Yam]. It was that tucker that made him angry. He threw it away. He kept throwing it away at this very place [Pumurriyi]. He got angry at it.
>
> Then he came down. He went down to that place over there now. He sits down now at the place of Tulh. He was sitting down right here. As for the Cheeky Yams, they spread everywhere. He got angry at that Cheeky Yam. Two clumps of Cheeky Yams stand up at Pumurriyi. [They are two rocks, the black one cooked, the white one raw.] And that fellow made his camp at Ngirin, at Tulh.[1]

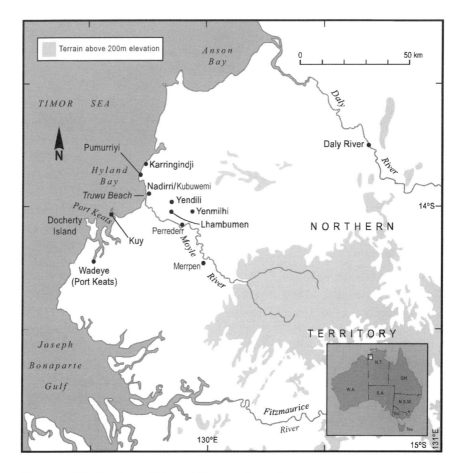

Figure 1.1 The Southern Daly and Fitzmaurice regions

Old Man Tulh is a *ngirrwat,* or as people say in English, a "Dreaming." Like many such figures throughout Aboriginal mythology, he is a world-creating ancestor who was active at the beginning of time, depositing creative essences at certain points in the landscape before metamorphosing into a feature of the landscape itself. The place where Tulh became a rock is a *kigatiya,* one of the eternal life centers to which the Marri-ammu trace their existence.

The Marri-ammu are one of the Daly language groups that compose and perform *wangga.*[2] Old Man Tulh's activities are recorded not only in story but also in painting and in *wangga* songs. He is a Ma-yawa, one of the ancestral dead who give *wangga* songs to the Marri-ammu.[3] Most Ma-yawa congregate near the *wudi-pumininy,* a freshwater spring that flows from the seabed into the saltwater sea at Karri-ngindji.[4] Others—of whom Tulh is an example—reside at other places in Marri-ammu country. Let us consider the painting and the songs in turn.

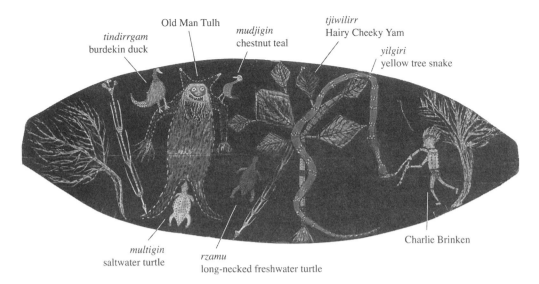

tindirrgam
burdekin duck

Old Man Tulh

mudjigin
chestnut teal

tjiwilirr
Hairy Cheeky Yam

yilgiri
yellow tree snake

multigin
saltwater turtle

rzamu
long-necked freshwater turtle

Charlie Brinken

Plate 1.1 Charlie Brinken's painting of Old Man Tulh. (Photograph published with permission of the artist's family.)

A Painting of Old Man Tulh

A painting by the Marri-ammu painter Charlie Niwilhi Brinken (plate 1.1) depicts the transmission of a song about Tulh and the Hairy Cheeky Yam from the Ma-yawa Tulh to a songman who, according to senior Marri-ammu informants, represents Charlie Brinken himself. Old Man Tulh is the hairy character to the left.[5] To the right of Tulh, touching his left arm, is the Hairy Cheeky Yam, entwined in which is a yellow tree snake (*yilgiri*), a species commonly found in the jungle near Pumurriyi.[6] The snake in turn touches the clapsticks held in the hands of the songman, on the right of the painting. On Tulh's shoulders are two of the ducks that he hunted in Edward Nemarluk's story. The duck on his left shoulder is the chestnut teal (*mudjigin*), and the one on his right is a burdekin duck (*tindirrgam*).[7] Both are freshwater birds who move to the salt water at Pumurriyi and drink at the *wudi-pumini333* at Karri-ngindji. These actions—moving between fresh and salt water, and drinking at the freshwater spring that lies under the saltwater sea—mark the birds as liminal. Both give songs both to Tulh and to human songmen. Like other song-giving beings, they move between the worlds of the living—symbolized as freshwater—and the dead—symbolized as salt water. This symbolism is also evident in the two turtles, who are a long-necked freshwater turtle (*rzamu*) and a saltwater turtle (*multigin*).

As already mentioned in the introduction, the interpenetration of the worlds of the living and the dead is evident in two important contexts: when Ma-yawa appear to living songmen in dreams to give them songs, and when humans perform in ceremony the songs and dances given to them by the Ma-yawa. As we shall see in more detail later, the efficacy of the ceremonies that are performed for the recent dead relies specifically on this mingling of the living and the dead.

Table 1.1 Text of "Wulumen Tulh" performed in the unmeasured vocal section transcribed as musical example 1.1

Sentences	Marri-ammu text	English gloss
1a	*wulumen tulh kidin-mitit-a-gu*	It made Old Man Tulh angry,
1b	*wulumen tulh kidin-mitit-a-gu*	it made Old Man Tulh angry,
1c	*miyi-gu tjiwilirr nal kisji*	that food, Hairy Cheeky Yam, just like this.
2	*kuwa-butj kani-ya*	He kept throwing it away.
3	*kuwa-rrin kisji*	Now it grows everywhere like this.

A Wangga Song about Old Man Tulh

"Wulumen Tulh," Charlie Brinken's song about Old Man Tulh and the Hairy Cheeky Yam, was sung by the late Maurice Tjakurl Ngulkur. The two versions of the song—one unmeasured and one measured—that form the basis of the following analysis may be heard on tracks 1 and 2 of the accompanying CD.[8]

Like Edward Nemarluk's story, the text of the song is in Marri-ammu and narrates how Old Man Tulh got angry over the Hairy Cheeky Yam, how in his anger he threw pieces of the yam around, and how, as a result, it now grows everywhere in the area surrounding Pumurriyi. As can be seen from table 1.1, the song text is made up of three sentences that make perfect sense in everyday spoken language and even reflect the language of the story: the Marri-ammu expression translated as "he kept throwing it away" is exactly the same in the song as in the spoken version. This degree of correspondence between song language and the language of everyday speech, while common in *wangga*, is relatively uncommon in other genres of Aboriginal song.

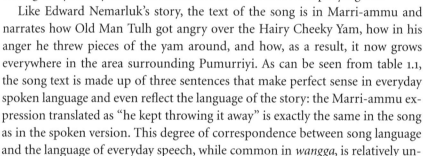

Before going any further, I need to explain some of the basic musical features of *wangga*. *Wangga* songs are performed by one or two (or occasionally more) songmen, who accompany themselves on wooden clapsticks and are accompanied in turn by another performer playing the didjeridu, a long trumpet fashioned from a tree branch that has been hollowed out by termites (plate 1.2). *Wangga* songs typically comprise a number of bursts of singing, which I term "vocal sections," which are accompanied by didjeridu and, in some cases, clapsticks. Vocal sections are separated from one another by a number of "instrumental sections," which are performed using clapsticks and didjeridu, with occasional spoken, sung, or hummed interjections by the songman.[9] In many cases, it is in the instrumental sections that dancing comes to the fore.

The *wangga* repertory may be divided into two broad musical types.[10] In the first, which I call "unmeasured," the singer alternates didjeridu-accompanied

Plate 1.2 Philip Mullumbuk, Les Kundjil, and Colin Worumbu Ferguson (farthest right) perform *wangga*, accompanied on didjeridu by Philip Jinjair (center). (Photograph by Mark Crocombe, Wadeye, 1992.)

vocal sections without clapstick accompaniment with instrumental sections performed by both clapsticks and didjeridu.[11] In the second, "measured" type, the singer accompanies himself with clapsticks throughout the whole song, and the delivery of the text in the vocal sections is constrained by the metrical framework established by the sticks and the rhythmic ostinato of the didjeridu.

The first version of "Wulumen Tulh" (the first vocal and instrumental sections are transcribed as musical example 1.1) is of the unmeasured type.[12] While there is not usually any accompanying clapstick beating in unmeasured *wangga* songs, in this performance Ngulkur—somewhat idiosyncratically—strikes the clapsticks together at the beginning of each of the first two phrases. More substantial and metrically regular clapstick beating occurs during the instrumental section.

Vocal sections that are unmeasured are typically more textually and melodically complex that those that are measured. In this first, unmeasured example, the first sentence, which may be divided into three text phrases, is the most rhetorically complex, with the subject of the sentence (the Hairy Cheeky Yam) being withheld until the third phrase, thus: "(a) It made Old Man Tulh angry, (b) it made Old Man Tulh angry, (c) that food Hairy Cheeky Yam, just like this" (see table 1.1).

The melody supports and reflects the structure of this text (see musical ex-

Example 1.1 "Wulumen Tulh" performed in unmeasured style (Cro00, viii, vocal section 1)

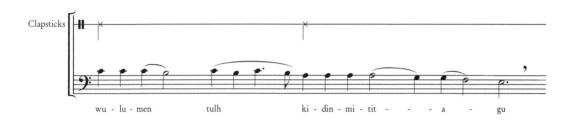

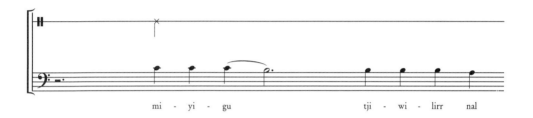

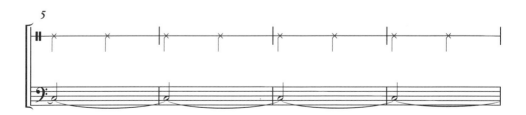

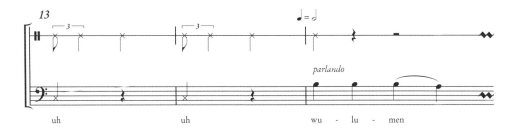

uh   uh   wu - lu - men

ample 1.1). The first two phrases take the first two segments of sentence 1, and like them are virtually identical. The third phrase—which covers the complete range of the song, beginning on the high C and cadencing, somewhat unusually, on the A below the didjeridu-defined tonic, C—takes the remainder of the text.[13] In the vast majority of *wangga* songs, vocal sections conclude on the tonic defined by the didjeridu drone, rather than on another pitch.

Because of its narrative quality, it is important for the meaning of the text to be conveyed to the audience, and so in singing, Ngulkur marks most word divisions rhythmically in order to make the syntax of the sentences clear. Take, for example, the first text phrase. The final syllable of each word, *wulumen, tulh,* and *kidin-mitit-a-gu,* is drawn out, usually over several pitches, and this pattern persists throughout the vocal section. The use of rhythm to support the structure of text in this way is quite typical of public song genres like *wangga.* When songs are associated with restricted knowledge, however, syntactic boundaries are often obscured rather than clarified by the rhythmic setting, so that the meaning of the text becomes unclear to all but the initiated.

In the measured version (CD track 2), the meter of the vocal section is established by the clapsticks, which repeat the pattern ♩♩♩ throughout the item at a tempo in the range of mm 136–46 (see musical example 1.2).[14] A number of different tempos and clapstick-beating patterns are used across the various repertories of *wangga* discussed in this book, but in Ngulkur's repertory, all but one of the measured songs are sung at this tempo and with this beating pattern. In this repertory, the four-beat meter (expressed in the musical example as 4/4) articulated by the ♩♩♩ clapstick-beating pattern is always matched to a compound duple meter (expressed as 6/4) in the vocal part. That is, the metrical relationship of the vocal rhythm to the clapstick beating is six against four. Taken together, these features—the morphology of the clapstick beating, the tempo, and the polymetrical relationship of the vocal part to the clapstick beating—constitute

Example 1.2 A vocal section of "Wulumen Tulh" performed in measured style (Cro00, vii, vocal section 2)

Table 1.2 Text of "Wulumen Tulh" performed in the measured vocal section transcribed as musical example 1.2

Sentences	Marri-ammu text	English gloss
1a	*wulumen tulh kidin-mitit-a kisji*	It made Old Man Tulh angry, like this,
1b	*wulumen tulh kidin-mitit-a kisji*	it made Old Man Tulh angry, like this,
1c	*miyi-gu kisji nal kisji*	that food, like this, just like this.
2	*kidin-mitit-a-gu*	It made him angry.

what is referred to throughout this book as a "rhythmic mode." A fuller explanation of this concept is given in chapter 4.

The text of the measured version is set out in table 1.2. It can be seen immediately that this text is rhetorically more straightforward than that in the unmeasured style. In turn it is supported by melodic structures that are less complex. Irrespective of whether a text is performed in a measured or unmeasured style, however, word boundaries are marked by lengthening in order to maximize the comprehensibility of the text. Musical example 1.2 is more typical of the *wangga* genre as a whole in that its melody cadences unproblematically on the didjeridu tonic, C.

The Principal Repertories of *Wangga* and Their Locations

Today there are two main centers for the composition and performance of *wangga*, namely, the communities of Wadeye (a large community of about 2,500 people, widely known by its old name of Port Keats) and Belyuen (a smaller community of about 300 people) (see introduction figure 1). These are the communities to which, over the past one hundred years or more, people have migrated from their traditional countries in the regions of the Daly and Moyle rivers, leaving their traditional homelands relatively depopulated.[15] Wadeye was first established as a Roman Catholic mission in 1935 by Father F. D. Docherty; Belyuen was established in 1941 as a government ration depot and, until it came under community control in 1979, was known as Delissaville.[16]

It is generally said that *wangga* has always existed at Wadeye. Although only two repertories—the Walakandha and Ma-yawa *wangga* ("Wulumen Tulh" belongs to the latter)—survive in Wadeye today, a number of other repertories were performed there in the past. The full range of *wangga* repertories remembered by people living at Wadeye today, together with known recordings, is set out in table 1.3.

Today it is the Walakandha *wangga* repertory that is dominant at Wadeye. The reasons for this go back to a set of extraordinary decisions made by Wadeye elders almost fifty years ago. During the late 1950s and early 1960s, a conscious

Wangga repertory	Song-giving ancestors	Owning language group	Performed today	Recordings
Wangga ma-walakandha	Walakandha	Marri-tjevin	Yes	See appendix table 1.1
Wangga ma-yawa	Ma-yawa	Marri-ammu	Yes	See appendix table 2.1
Wangga ma-warrgat	unknown	Marri-thiyel	No	AIATSIS: A8197 (Stanner 1954, tape 5A)
Wangga ma-merren	Mani ma-merri	Ngan'gityemerri	No	AIATSIS: A8198A (Stanner 1954, tape 8A)
		Ngan'giwumerri Marri-dan Marri-ngarr		
Wangga ma-yirri	Yirri	Matige (at Yederr)	No	None
Wangga ma-kinwurri	Kinwurri	Matige (at Kuy)	No	None
Wangga kardu-kunhbinhi	Kardu-kunhbinhi	Murrinhpatha	No	AIATSIS: A8196, (Stanner 1954, tape 4B), Rei74:1

decision was made to create three new repertories of song—the Walakandha *wangga*, *lirrga*, and *dhanba*—as the basis of a new tripartite system of ceremonial reciprocity.[17] According to this system, which is described in more detail in chapter 3, the language groups associated with *wangga*—primarily Marri-tjevin, Marri-ammu, and Matige—perform *wangga* songs and dances in ceremony for members of the *dhanba*- and *lirrga*-owning groups. In turn, the Murrinhpatha-speaking groups associated with *dhanba* perform *dhanba* songs and dances in ceremony for members of the *wangga*- and *lirrga*-owning groups, while the Marri-ngarr perform *lirrga* in ceremony for members of the *dhanba*- and *wangga*-owning groups.

The immediate impetus for the establishment of this system was the rapid expansion of the population of the Port Keats mission that had occurred during the late 1940s and 1950s. The expanded community included groups who had long histories of conflict with one another and therefore required a new mechanism to maintain social harmony. The tripartite ceremonial system established at that time continues to function to the present day and is pointed to as a source of ongoing stability within the community.

It is generally agreed that *lirrga* was the first of the new repertories to be established and that this occurred in the late 1950s as a result of a decision by a number of Marri-ngarr men—among whom Tommy Karui Moyle, Brian Nummar, and Bob Wak Jongmin were prominent—to create a localized form of the more easterly tradition of *gunborrg* music and dance. The second repertory, *dhanba*, was established not long afterward by Robert Dungoi Kolumboort and Harry Luke Kolumboort of the Diminin clan of the Murrinhpatha language group. The models for *dhanba* were public Kimberley song genres such as *junba* and *balga*, which had previously been encountered by Murrinhpatha men working on cattle stations in the Kimberley.[18]

The last of the new repertories to be created was the Walakandha *wangga* (*wangga ma-walakandha*), which was first composed by the Marri-tjevin songman Stan Mullumbuk in the early 1960s. Unlike *lirrga* and *dhanba*, which were both localized forms of genres from distant places, *wangga* is, as I have already observed, said to have always existed in the Daly region. But this was a new repertory of songs, composed expressly to accommodate the new ceremonial arrangements. As will be shown in more detail in the following chapter, Walakandha *wangga* songs continue to be composed and performed by songmen (*ngalinangga*) from a number of Marri-tjevin lineages on behalf of the Marri-tjevin and at least two other language groups, the Marri-ammu and the Matige. On the other hand, the Marri-ammu Ma-yawa *wangga* repertory (*wangga ma-yawa*)—the repertory to which "Wulumen Tulh" belongs—represents an older, largely pre-1960s practice, now on the point of extinction. The Ma-yawa *wangga* is taken up in chapter 6.

The earliest concrete glimpses we get of the Walakandha *wangga* are in recordings made by linguist Michael Walsh in 1972 (Wal72) and by lay missionary Lesley Reilly (née Rourke) in 1974 (Rei74). None of Stan Mullumbuk's songs recorded on those occasions were still performed by the time I reached Wadeye in 1988. Instead, an entirely new repertory of Walakandha *wangga* songs, composed largely by Thomas Kungiung and members of the Dumoo family, held sway. It is this latter body of songs that forms the basis for the chapter on Walakandha *wangga* (chapter 5).[19]

The community of Belyuen comprises almost exclusively northern Daly people —the Wadjiginy (speakers of Batjamalh), Emmiyangal (speakers of Emmi), Mendheyangal (speakers of Mendhe), Kiyuk, as well as some Marri-tjevin and Marri-ammu—all of whom identify as *wangga* owners. Significant differences exist between the ritual practices at Belyuen and those at Wadeye and other southern Daly communities. These in turn reflect both the different histories and different relationships to land that have developed as a result of those histories.

Four main lineages are recognized at Belyuen, each associated with a particular songman (*medjakarr* in Batjamalh), namely, Tommy Barrtjap (Wadjiginy), Bobby Lambudju Lane (Wadjiginy), Jimmy Muluk (Mendheyangal), and Billy Mandji (Marri-tjevin). The first two of these form the focus of chapters 7 and 8 respectively. As at Wadeye, a number of earlier repertories existed, some of which have been incorporated into these four. These will be considered in more detail when I discuss lineage and transmission in the next chapter.

Wangga is also performed outside the Daly region. In the past, *wangga* appears to have been regularly performed in the more easterly communities of Barunga, Beswick, and Gunbalanya (Oenpelli), though in recent decades these traditions have waned. *Wangga* has for many decades also been traded into the Kimberley region, where it maintains a great popularity from Timber Creek to Mowanjum, near Derby (Western Australia), though here the deeper significance of *wangga* is usually not completely understood, even by singers (see introduction figure 1). The role of *wangga* in the wider diaspora is considered in chapter 10.

Dreamings, Conception, and Song

Both Wadeye and Belyuen are settlements located in the traditional country of non-*wangga*-owning groups: Belyuen is located in Larrakiya country; Wadeye is located in Murrinhpatha country. While Daly people at Wadeye live relatively close to their traditional estates and have thus been able to maintain regular contact with them, those who live at Belyuen far to the north were, for many decades, unable to maintain regular contact with their estates in the Daly region. This has significantly affected the way in which people at Belyuen relate to country. These differences have in turn affected the subject matter of the *wangga* of the two communities, as well as the ideologies surrounding song creation (see chapter 2) and the role of song in ceremony (see chapter 3). An understanding of the nature of the cosmologies that inform the creation and performance of *wangga* is fundamental to an understanding of differences in the significance and role of *wangga* between the two communities.

Table 1.4 sets out some key terms relating to orders of being in the languages of the groups who today own *wangga*, namely, Marri-tjevin, Marri-ammu, and Batjamalh, as well as in Murrinhpatha (the language used in the two major ethnographies of Wadeye, Stanner 1989 and Falkenberg 1962) and English.

In the past, *wangga* has been characterized as "secular" rather than "sacred." Elkin and Jones, for example, place *wangga* in the category of "secular music" along with other didjeridu-accompanied genres such as *manikay-bunggurl* and

Table 1.4 Terms for orders of being and sites in languages relating to *wangga*

English (Murrinhpatha)	Marri-tjevin	Marri-ammu	Batjamalh
Dreaming (*ngakumarl*)	*ngirrwat*	*ngirrwat*	*durlk*
Dreaming site (*ngugumingki*)	*kigatiya*	*kigatiya*	*durlk-nyini*
Conception Dreaming (*ngepan*)	*meri-men.ngu*	*meri-men.ngu*	*maruy*
Baby spirit (*ngarrith-ngarrith*)	*wudi*	*wudi*	*maruy*
Ghost (*wurl*)	*nguwatj*	*nguwatj*	*wunymalang*
Ancestor [various]	*walakandha*	*ma-yawa*	[none]
Person (*kardu*)	*meri*	*meri*	*nganang*

gunborrg, which are characterized as "purely 'entertainment' music" (1958, 342). The meaning of the term "secular" is a particular one, which in ethnographic writing of the time denoted songs sung at unrestricted (that is, nonsecret) ceremonies. Nevertheless, the idea that *manikay-bunggurl,* the multiple repertories of song and dance that form part of the property of patrilineal clans in East and Central Arnhem Land, is "purely entertainment music," and therefore independent of the spiritual life of those who own and perform the songs, would nowadays hold little credence, as any number of studies show (see, for example, Keen 1994; Morphy 1984; Anderson 1992; Clunies Ross and Wild 1984; Clunies Ross and Mundrugmundrug 1988; Toner 2001).

It is also clear that the celebration in *wangga* of the actions of seminal ancestors such as Old Man Tulh challenges the idea that *wangga* is a form of music associated only with social, nonsacred aspects of life. Evidence to this effect will accumulate throughout this study: later in this chapter, we will examine the poetics of *wangga* and the processes whereby songs are given to songmen by various orders of being; and in the following chapter, we will see how in ceremony *wangga* songs and dances provide the means whereby human singers and dancers metamorphose into those nonhuman forms. Before taking up the matters of song poetics, composition, and ceremony, however, we must examine in more detail some of the broader concepts that lie behind them.

Marri-tjevin and Marri-ammu Orders of Being

NGIRRWAT

The most common word in southern Daly languages for the concept usually translated in English as "Dreaming" or "Dreamtime" is *ngirrwat.* The most common word used at Belyuen today is *durlk,* although there is evidence that in the past *ngirrwat* was also used. *Ngirrwat* refers to totemic ancestors who, like Old Man Tulh, were active in the world-creating period and whose essence resides for all time at certain sites in the landscape. T. G. H. Strehlow maintained that the core meaning of *altjira,* the Arrernte term cognate with *ngirrwat,* is "that which derives from . . . the eternal, uncreated, springing out of itself," or that which has "sprung out of its own eternity" (Strehlow 1971, 614; see also Swain 1993, 21).[20] The way the Murrinhpatha at Wadeye spoke to Stanner about the Rainbow Serpent Dreaming (Kunmanggurr)—to be discussed in more detail in chapter 3—resonates with the definition of *altjira* recorded by Strehlow. Kunmanggurr was said to be a *kardu bangambitj,* a "self-finding" person (that is, "self-creating and self-subsistent") (Stanner 1989, 249).

The self-manifesting and eternally active nature of *ngirrwat* is vividly articulated in some *wangga* songs. For example, table 1.5 shows the text of another of Maurice Ngulkur's songs, his *wangga* about the Sea Breeze Dreaming (Tjerri).

Here the idea of self-manifestation is expressed in the verb *kinyi-ni,* which combines the third-person singular form of the intransitive verb "he moves" or "he is active" (*kinyi*) with the third-person masculine reflexive suffix (*ni*) to mean "he makes himself active." The notion of the Dreaming springing out of

Table 1.5 Text of Maurice Ngulkur's song about the Sea Breeze Dreaming (Tjerri)

karra mana tjerri	Oh, brother Sea Breeze
kagandja kinyi-ni kavulh	He is eternally making himself active right here and now

the eternal is carried by the auxiliary verb *kavulh*, "he has done it forever," and *kagandja*, "right here and now."

Nonverbal performative aspects such as dance may articulate these meanings more directly than words. During some rather tortuous discussions of the meaning of the expression *kinyi-ni*, Ambrose Piarlum, a leading *wangga* dancer, stood up and danced its meaning. By rotating a cloth held in his hand (traditionally a goose wing would be used for this action), he performed in that place and in that moment the self-manifesting nature of the Tjerri's wind activity. What we were witnessing right there and then was an enactment of how Sea Breeze has manifested throughout eternity.

Other Marri-ammu *wangga* express the eternal presence of Dreamings in similar ways and through parallel text construction underline that this aspect is shared by a number of Dreamings and Dreaming sites. In the Ma-yawa *wangga*, the Sea Breeze Dreaming is forever blowing, the Jungle Fowl Dreaming (Malhi-manyirr) is forever calling out as she piles up earth to make her nest, and the Old Men, the Ma-yawa, are forever singing, dancing, playing didjeridu, and performing ceremony:

> This is what the Old Man [Ma-yawa] has always done.
> This is what the Old Man has always done.
> At that country Rtadi-wunbirri-wunbirri, just like this.[21]

KIGATIYA

The animate places, or Dreaming sites, where *ngirrwat* reside and are eternally active are referred to in Marri-tjevin and Marri-ammu as *kigatiya*. *Kigatiya* are permanent sources of life. Both humans and nonhuman phenomena born of these sites are seen as incarnations or manifestations of the *ngirrwat*. Tony Swain has suggested that this belief—that people are incarnated from the sites where a cosmogonic Dreaming ancestor (*ngirrwat*) left his creative power—is perhaps the most fundamental element in Aboriginal ontology (Swain 1993, 39).

People refer to nonhuman phenomena that emanate from the same *kigatiya* as that to which they trace their own existence as their *ngirrwat*, or as *kandjirra-yigin* (my Dreaming) or *kandjirra-ngina* ("Dreaming," marked for emotional intensity with *ngina*), and address them as *mana* (elder brother). In English the most commonly used terms are "my Dreaming" or "my totem."

Johannes Falkenberg, using Murrinhpatha terminology (which I have replaced here with italicized Marri-tjevin and Marri-ammu cognates), describes the process by which phenomena emerge from *kigatiya* as follows:

A *kigatiya* [Dreaming site] is the permanent life-centre for all the *ngirrwat* [Dreamings] which are associated with that *kigatiya*. . . . A single specimen of a *ngirrwat* is a single *meri-men.ngu* [conception Dreaming] which has been temporarily torn loose from the *kigatiya* and assumes substance as an animal, plant, or spear. The animal, plant, or spear is the vessel of a specific *meri-men.ngu* which will return to its *kigatiya* when the vessel disintegrates. (After Falkenberg 1962, 85)

Just as Dreamings are always active, so too are *kigatiya*. Just as the Ma-yawa are forever singing and dancing, and the Sea Breeze is forever blowing, so too is Menggani, the *kigatiya* for the Butterfly Dreaming, eternally producing butter-flies. Maurice Ngulkur sings:

> This is what Menggani has always done.[22]

The land, as in many other Aboriginal cosmologies, is thus conceived of as alive and sentient—not only the source of all life, but also responsive to human events.[23] A Walakandha *wangga* song attributed to John Dumoo refers to the drying up of a billabong at Yendili Hill when his mother died:

> I hear bad news about the family.
> The water at Yendili is drying up on us now.[24]

As we shall see later in more detail, part of the function of ceremonial action is to communicate to country the presence of its human offspring. Between songs, dancers call out to country using a particular ritual cry referred to as *marri* in Marri-tjevin and Marri-ammu (*malh* in Batjamalh), and during the songs, the beating of their feet is felt by the land on which they dance. Wala-kandha *wangga* singers frequently call out "Nidin-ngina!" (Oh, my dear coun-try!) in the course of their songs.

MERI-MEN.NGU

Meri-men.ngu refers to the manifestation of the *ngirrwat* in the everyday world as a phenomenon—that is, as the aspect of being that can be seen, heard, smelled, or touched, which casts shadows and can be photographed or mechan-ically recorded. The term *meri-men.ngu* is frequently translated as "conception Dreaming" or "conception totem" because, in human terms, it is the primary agent in conception. From time to time a *meri-men.ngu* manifests itself as a spirit child, and these spirit children, or baby spirits (known variously as *ngar-rith-ngarrith* or simply as *wudi*, "freshwater"), seek out women from whom to be born (Falkenberg 1962, 238).

As a human ages and passes through various age grades, it is the *meri-men.ngu* aspect of being that is transformed: the babe in arms becomes a tod-dler; the toddler, a young child; the child, an adult; the adult, an old person; and at death the living human becomes a ghost (*nguwatj*). At two key points in this process of transformation, ceremonies to which *wangga* singing and dancing are central are performed: namely, when a male child becomes an adult, and when one of the living becomes one of the dead.

WALAKANDHA AND MA-YAWA

At death, a person does not cease to exist but, following appropriate ceremonial action, becomes one of the ancestral dead. These are the beings known in Marri-tjevin as *ma-walakandha* and in Marri-ammu as *ma-yawa*. Both are marked linguistically as being essentially human: *ma-* is a human class marker that is always applied by native speakers when speaking of Ma-yawa in English, but only irregularly applied to (Ma-)Walakandha. Following this usage, I refer to one (Ma-yawa) with the class marker, and the other (Walakandha) without. It is clear, however, that the term "Walakandha" is not simply a name applied by living Marri-tjevin to the ancestral dead. It is also what the dead call the living. "Walakandha," then, is a reciprocal term, and one that indicates that all Marri-tjevin regard themselves as being fundamentally Walakandha. Unless otherwise specified, however, in this book "Walakandha" will be used to refer to the Marri-tjevin dead and "Ma-yawa" to the Marri-ammu dead.

After appropriate ceremony, the Walakandha dead begin a journey back toward the *kigatiya* from which they emerged. The Walakandha *wangga* emphasizes this existential flux through the pervasive metaphor of tide. In song, the journey of the living from birth to death is referred to metaphorically as the outgoing tide—weak at first as the high tide turns (just as a baby or child, recently sprung from its totemic birth site, is weak), gathering strength as the tidal flow gains its greatest power (the child grows into its adult strength), and weakening as it approaches the turn at low tide (the adult's strength weakens at the approach of old age). The turn of the tide—the moment of stillness—is death itself. The Marri-tjevin songman sings:

> Brother Walakandha, the tide has gone out on him at Nadirri.
> Ah, brother, the tide has gone out on him.[25]

Following death, the incoming tide once again begins to flow and gain strength. Just as the outgoing tide stands metaphorically for the existential journey of the living, the incoming tide stands for the existential journey of the Walakandha dead. Mirroring the progress of the living, the dead progressively gain strength after death, moving backward from old age into adulthood, once again weakening as they move through childhood to babyhood and eventually approach the opposite turn of the tide—the again-still moment when they return to the totemic birth site from which they originally sprang.[26]

Philip Mullumbuk sings of the inevitability of regeneration:

> As a matter of inevitability, it [the tide] is always coming in on us.[27]

My Marri-ammu collaborators are adamant that in contrast to Walakandha, who continue to move through a cycle of reincarnation, the Ma-yawa dead reside in Marri-ammu country for all eternity. I have already noted how the texts of Ma-yawa *wangga* songs—for example, those about the Sea Breeze Dreaming, the Ma-yawa Dreaming, and the Butterfly Dreaming site—tend to stress eternal aspects of being. In my discussion of Old Man Tulh, I also noted how the freshwater dimension of the *wudi-pumininy* is associated with the eternal dimensions of life, and this association is implicit in other songs. Maurice Ngulkur sings of his "brother," the Ma-yawa in human form, sitting on the cliffs and at the *wudi-pumininy*:

> Brother is sitting [where the cliff] stands up, right here like this.
> It's the Dreaming in human form who is right here like this.
> Brother Ma-yawa. *Wudi-pumininy-pumininy*![28]

It could not be put more clearly. Ma-yawa, like Walakandha, are "Dreamings in human form." They are forever manifesting themselves at their *kigatiya* Karringindji, a cliff on top of which is the Ma-yawa's dancing ground at Rtadi-wunbirri and at the foot of which is the *wudi-pumininy* spring. One Ma-yawa, Old Man Tulh, has his *kigatiya* further south at Pumurriyi. The main dreaming site for the Walakandha lies at Wudi-djirridi, a cave at the base of Yenmilhi Hill, from which they emerge to dance at their ceremony ground at Pelhi, although individual Walakandha may reside at other sites—see, for example, the case of Wagon Dumoo, discussed in the following chapter. Both Walakandha and Ma-yawa wander freely in their country. At night you can see their fires and hear them singing.

Song Composition and Ceremony: Two Contexts for the Drawing Together of the Living and the Dead

As previously mentioned, there are two main contexts in which *wangga* draws together the worlds of the living and the dead: in the process of song giving, where Walakandha and Ma-yawa appear to living singers in dream; and in the performance of ceremony that draws together the worlds of the living and of the dead through the performance of the songs and dances of the dead.

When—as referred to in the introduction—Thomas Kungiung sang, "This is what the Walakandha have always done," he was referring both to the role of Walakandha in giving songs to the living and to the replication of their singing and dancing in ceremony. When it was first sung to Kungiung in a dream, the meaning of the Walakandha's declaration was "This [i.e., my singing you a song in a dream] is what the Walakandha have always done." That is, Walakandha have always given songs to living songmen. When Kungiung in turn reproduced the song in ceremony, it took on another meaning: "This [i.e., what I am now singing in ceremony] is what the Walakandha have always done." And for the dancers, the didjeridu player, and the witnessing audience, the text has the meaning "This [i.e., what we are doing now] is what the Walakandha have always done." That is, Walakandha provide the prototypes of ceremonial action.

By joining with their Walakandha ancestors, through singing their songs, playing didjeridu, dancing their dances, painting the marks of Walakandha on

Plate 1.3 The dance ground for a *burnim-rag* ceremony held at Merrpen in 1998. (Photograph by Allan Marett.)

their bodies, and witnessing the production of their ceremonial forms, the living participants draw close to and interpenetrate with the dead. It is within this context that the spirits of the deceased are released from their attachments to the living and are freed to join the ancestral dead (see plates 1.3 and 1.4).

Orders of Being at Belyuen

SOME HISTORICAL REASONS FOR WHY CONCEPTION
DREAMINGS IN THE FORM OF GHOSTS HAVE BECOME
THE FOCUS OF *WANGGA* AT BELYUEN

At Belyuen there are no beings that are equivalent to Walakandha and Ma-yawa. Rather, the source of *wangga* songs and the focus of their associated ceremonies are ghosts (*wunymalang*). While Walakandha and Ma-yawa are, to use Ngulkur's expression, "Dreamings in human form—that is, mirrors of the living—Wunymalang ghosts are conception Dreamings; they are phantasmagorical rather than real manifestations of the dead. To understand why attention is shifted to the conception Dreaming aspect of being in this way, we must reflect on how Daly people came to be at Belyuen, and examine how their migration from the country of their forebears to the country in which they now find themselves has impinged on the cosmologies associated with the composition and performance of song.

Plate 1.4 *Wangga* dancers painting themselves with handprints representing the hands of the Walakandha, Peppimenarti, 1998. (Photograph by Allan Marett.)

Following its settlement in 1867, Port Darwin provided a powerful attraction to Aboriginal people, including many Wadjiginy and Kiyuk people, who were among the first to migrate north from the Daly region (see figure 1.2). They moved to the Cox Peninsula at Charles Point, on the western edge of Darwin Harbour (Basedow 1906, 4), where they were already settled when the lighthouse was built in 1893. H. W. Christie (1906), the first lighthouse keeper, tells how he was initiated into the "Wogait tribe," and there are records of the Wagaitj, that is, the Wadjiginy and Kiyuk, performing joint ceremony with the traditional owners of the Cox Peninsula, the Larrakiya, even earlier than this (Povinelli 1993, 74). According to Elizabeth Povinelli, another wave of migrants, ancestors of the Emmiyangal and Mendheyangal now living at Belyuen, probably arrived in the late 1940s to early 1950s, which is also about the time when Marri-ammu and Marri-tjevin people began to settle there.

It is because Belyuen people are farther removed from the country in which

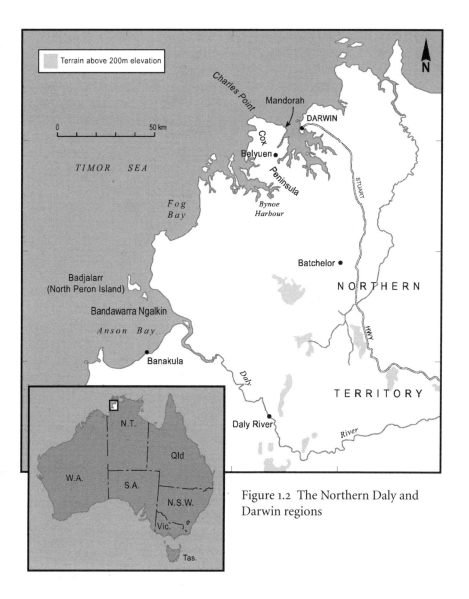

Figure 1.2 The Northern Daly and Darwin regions

their totemic Dreamings reside that there is a greater focus on the *meri-men.ngu* (or, as they call it, *maruy*) aspect of being, both with regard to conception and death and with regard to the subject matter of *wangga* songs and the ideologies associated with their creation and ceremonial performance.[29]

Unlike at Wadeye, where conception spirits are associated with specific Dreaming sites in a person's country, for the older generations at Belyuen there is no regular association of *maruy* with Dreaming sites either in the vicinity of Belyuen or on the Daly to the south. As Povinelli writes:

> Although in some Aboriginal groups conception and birth totems "come out of" an estate totem or Dreaming nearby—one of the permanent marks

that mythical ancestral creatures left in the landscape—Belyuen Aborigines do not always associate a conception totem with a known nearby Dreaming. In fact it seems that [there is] only a generalized conception association with the Belyuen water-hole ("All a kid been come from that Belyuen"). (1993, 140)[30]

Elkin and Povinelli agree that links to *kigatiya* sites on the Daly were already seriously weakened by the 1940s.[31] This view is supported by evidence from song. In the repertory of Tommy Barrtjap, for example, there are no direct references to named sites on the Daly. The texts of his songs are, insofar as they are made up entirely of utterances made by ghosts, heavily focused on *maruy*. Although he never named sites in his songs, he did, in a couple of cases, associate songs with specific places.

Even though "Nyere-nyere Lima Kaldja" has a text made up almost entirely of incomprehensible ghost language, it was said by Barrtjap to refer to Banakula, the cliffs known in English as Red Cliff to the south of the Daly River mouth, which are in his *rak*, or ancestral patri-country.

The first line of the text of "Yagarra Nedja Tjine Rak-pe" is in human speech, while the second is made up of both everyday speech and untranslated ghost talk (shown in italics):

> Yagarra, my son! Where is my country/camp?
> Yagarra *rama rama kama.*[32]

Not long before his death in 1993, Barrtjap told me that this text referred to "my place . . . my country long way back," by which I took him to mean both that the country lay at a great distance from Belyuen and that it had been his since time immemorial. When asked the name of the country, he replied, Djakaldja, Barakbana (South Peron Island), Barrabumalh, and Djedjekana. All these places lie in the general vicinity of the Daly mouth.

While I was in Belyuen in 2002, however, Barrtjap's widow, Esther Burrenjuck, gave a significantly different interpretation of this text, namely, that it had been given to Barrtjap by the ghost of his mother when she returned to the family camp near Milik, on the western coast of the Cox Peninsula, and found it deserted.

As already noted, song texts often contain elements of ambiguity that permit a variety of different exegeses. In this case the word *rak*, which means both "patrilineal inherited estate" and "camp," provides the key.[33] The tension between the two interpretations draws us to matters of more recent history, namely, the way in which songs reflect the experience of Belyuen people engaged in the longest-running land claim in Australian history.

The Kenbi land claim made under the Northern Territory Land Rights Act over much of the Cox Peninsula and the adjacent islands was formally lodged in 1979 and finally resolved only in 2000. During this twenty-year period, there was ongoing and unsettling contestation over the rights of Daly people to remain on the Cox Peninsula.

Povinelli accounts for seemingly contradictory statements, of which the two explanations of "Yagarra Nedja Tjine Rak-pe" are examples, as follows:

> Belyuen families were forced to confront their origins and remember where they came from [namely, the Daly region] because the traditional process by which secondary rights [to residency on the Cox Peninsula]—derived from land use and prompted by colonial disruptions to regional Aboriginal life—are transformed into primary rights [or rights to permanent residence] was interrupted prematurely by the Kenbi Land Claim. (1993, 134)

Barrtjap's statements concerning the connection of his songs to his estates on the Daly derive from the fact that he was "forced to confront [his] origins and remember where [he] came from": he continued to assert his ownership of country that he had inherited through his father both because that was his right and because it represented a fallback position should he and his family lose their rights to live, hunt, and perform ceremony for the country around Belyuen. Following the favorable resolution of the case in 2002, however, his widow was able to give an interpretation that emphasized the family's long-standing residence on the Cox Peninsula.[34]

CONCEPTION, DEATH, AND REINCARNATION

While the two sides of existence—the eternal, unchanging aspect of existence associated with Dreamings (nowadays named *durlk* rather than *ngirrwat* at Belyuen)[35] and the constantly changing aspect associated with conception Dreamings (called *maruy* rather than *meri-men.ngu*)—are both present in the Belyuen cosmology, a person's *durlk* Dreaming is seen more as an inheritance from the father than as an aspect of being that actively emerged from a patrilineally inherited Dreaming site on the Daly at the time of conception. Filiation with country is thus primarily through the *maruy* aspect, and it is to country in the vicinity of Belyuen that existence is traced.[36]

When a person dies, the *maruy* ceases to be a human and becomes a ghost—a Wunymalang.[37] Wunymalang who have been properly conducted away from human society through correct ceremonial performance may either live in the bush around the settlement or return to the person's ancestral country. If they continue to inhabit the country that they frequented when alive, that is, the country around Belyuen, they have the capacity to "come out" from the country when they sense the presence of relatives (whom they look after) or strangers (from whom they will protect relatives). In this sense they behave rather like Ma-yawa and Walakandha ancestors, who love nothing more than to associate with their descendants and repel strangers. Wunymalang who have not been properly conducted away, however, are, like Walakandha and Ma-yawa farther south, regarded as dangerous and potentially harmful to living humans. At death, a similar ceremony to that encountered at Wadeye is carried out at Belyuen to release a person's spirit so that it can return to the country from which it emerged. But here the focus is exclusively on the *maruy* aspect of being in the form of ghosts, rather than on Walakandha or Ma-yawa.

To complicate matters, Wunymalang ghosts may also return to Badjalarr (North Peron Island), which lies off the coast northwest of the Daly mouth and is the ancestral country of the Wadjiginy and Kiyuk peoples. Just as the Belyuen water hole has become a generalized conception site for all the children of the community, so too has Badjalarr become a generalized island of the dead, where the ghosts of Belyuen people congregate, irrespective of language group affiliation. Swain notes a similar "Land of the Dead far from their homes" for the Yolngu people of northeast Arnhem Land and reports that the Yolngu say that the souls of the dead both return to their totem life centers in their clan estates and go to the more generalized land of the dead (Swain 1993, 174–75).[38]

The *wangga* repertory of Bobby Lambudju Lane makes frequent references to Badjalarr and other sites in the immediate vicinity. As will be shown in some detail in chapter 8, the ambivalent associations of songs with country noted earlier with regard to Barrtjap's repertory are also encountered in Lambudju's repertory.

REFERENCES TO DREAMINGS AND DREAMING
SITES ON THE COX PENINSULA

A small number of songs in the present-day repertory of *wangga* mention *durlk* (*ngirrwat*) Dreamings or Dreaming sites in the Belyuen area, for example, Barrtjap's song about the Cheeky Yam Dreaming (Wilha) and Lambudju's song about the Channel-Billed Cuckoo Dreaming (Kurratjkurratj).[39] At first sight, these songs appear not to be specifically about Dreamings and their activities in the way the Marri-ammu or Marri-tjevin *wangga* are, but rather about everyday events associated with them. Deeper levels of exegesis, underscored by certain musical aspects, reveal a greater strength of association with the Dreamings than is first apparent.

At a surface level, the text of Barrtjap's song about the Cheeky Yam Dreaming, "Yagarra Delhi Nye-bindja-ng Barra Ngarrka," seems relatively mundane, referring as it does to an incident where a specific person was frightened by *what he thought* was this highly dangerous Dreaming. The Cheeky Yam Dreaming is not, however, directly named in the song, and one explanation that I was given went so far as to suggest that it was a buffalo rather than the Hairy Cheeky Yam Dreaming that was the cause of the panic. However, this song uses a ritual call associated with the Cheeky Yam Dreaming, and atypical melodic and rhythmic modal usages mark them as having a deeper association with the Dreaming (see chapter 7).

Likewise Lambudju's song "Benmele," which appears at first sight to be a simple song about a kookaburra singing to a man, is revealed to be, at a deeper level, a song that refers to death and sorcery, and their association with the Channel-billed Cuckoo Dreaming and its Dreaming site, a banyan tree near Milik on the Cox Peninsula (see chapter 8).

Despite these two references to local Dreamings, there is in the repertory of *wangga* recorded at Belyuen over the past sixty years a complete absence of any reference to song-giving ancestral Dreamings of the same order as Walakandha and Ma-yawa. If the dominant groups such as the Wadjiginy, Emmiyangal, and Mendheyangal now resident at Belyuen ever received songs from beings of the Walakandha or Ma-yawa type, they do not now. Wunymalang are nowadays the only song-giving beings mentioned in relation to Belyuen repertories.

I have previously observed that at both Wadeye and Belyuen, song composition and ceremony provide the two main contexts associated with *wangga* where the worlds of the living and the dead are drawn together. These two contexts will now be examined in greater detail, beginning in chapter 2 with song composition and proceeding in chapter 3 to a consideration of ceremony.

Chapter 2 begins with a detailed account given by the Barunga singer Alan Maralung of how he received a *wangga* song in dream from a spirit agent called Balanydjirri. Even through it comes from a singer from outside the Daly region, this is a good place to begin, since it is the most detailed story I ever recorded about the receipt of a *wangga* song. We then move to accounts of song creation from Wadeye and Belyuen, all of which resonate with Maralung's story and contribute new perspectives on the process of composition.

I then question in detail what exactly the ancestors give to songmen. Do they give fully fashioned songs, or rather the elements of song—text, melody, rhythm —which the songman is expected to fashion into a more fully fledged song composition?

Having completed this exploration of the processes by which *wangga* songs come into being, I will then examine how tradition is sustained. At both Wadeye and Belyuen, there are clearly established song lineages, which play an important role in the maintenance of tradition. How are these lineages formed? How well do they maintain tradition? What factors determine which songs are lost and which survive? An understanding of lineage also provides a foundation for the more detailed studies of specific repertories that will be undertaken in chapters 5–8.

chapter Two

Dreaming Songs:
Sustaining Tradition

Dreaming Songs

Maralung's Story about the Song "Minmin Light"

During the late 1980s, Alan Maralung, a *wangga* singer resident at Barunga (see introduction figure 1), told me a number of stories about how he had been given songs in dream. These were the most detailed accounts I recorded of the role that spirit agents play in the composition of songs, and although Maralung's *wangga* does not form a major focus in this study, these stories provide a good starting point for my discussion of song creation.

On one occasion, he described in detail how, on the previous evening, he had received a *wangga* song about a spirit light, which he referred to as a "minmin light," from his two song-giving agents, the ghost of a deceased songman called Balanydjirri and a small bird called Bunggridj Bunggridj.[1] Maralung's story narrates how the bird and the ghost came to him and woke him (within his dream) and taught him the song.

> I call the song "Minmin Light" because Balanydjirri got up and went to it. I was watching him. When that light appeared, he followed it. It was dangerous. He got the song from there. Then he came to me. Bunggridj Bunggridj was there too. . . .
>
> Next minute, Balanydjirri showed me the corroboree. He gave me this "Minmin Light" song and I learnt to sing it.
>
> "Boy," he said, "are you asleep? I'm coming up. Bunggridj Bunggridj and I are coming." Both of them came up and Balanydjirri said, "Get up! Come here! We're going to sing for you." Then he said to me, "Boy, you listen. Don't be frightened. Come here."
>
> I said, "I can see you."
>
> "Well," he said, "we've got to show you this song, 'Minmin Light.' "
>
> I said, "You come out here and sing to me." I got that song, yeah. And that Bunggridj Bunggridj, he sang it too. They were together then. . . .
>
> This is how he got those corroboree sticks, you know. They came out, where he got them, all of a sudden. He got them all of a sudden. He split

that cloud. Oh ho. Fuck me dead. They were really big, those corroboree sticks.

That didjeridu player, he sat down beside him. Balanydjirri called the didjeridu player "son." It wasn't a short one, that didjeridu. Really big! Really long! And he blew that didjeridu right there for me. When he blew that didjeridu—oooh—it was really big! . . .

Then he went back. "Don't lose this song." That's what he said. "Well, I'll take you back now, son." That's what he said to the didjeridu player. "Bye-bye," he said. "Don't you lose it. You keep this one. I sang this *wangga* for you." He spoke kindly like that.

Well I said, "*Wuhra* [all right]." Yeah, that's what I said.

"OK, don't lose it," he said. "You've got to remember it properly, this good song. This 'Minmin Light' of yours."[2]

The principal song-giving agent in this story is the ghost Balanydjirri, whom Maralung first encountered when, as a healer and ritual specialist, he attended a young man who was possessed by an evil spirit. Balanydjirri is the benign ghost (what Maralung called a *wahrdu*) of a songman who lived long ago—so long ago, in fact, that Maralung did not know any details of the man's life. Balanydjirri and Maralung called each other *lambarra*, a reciprocal term used between men of opposite moieties who bestow wives on each other and between whom there are other reciprocal obligations. While reciprocity is an essential element of the relationship between the living and the dead both in the Daly region and at Barunga, the structural relationships are significantly different.[3]

Balanydjirri is accompanied by a somewhat mysterious bird called Bunggridj Bunggridj, who is also involved in singing "Minmin Light" to Maralung. Maralung told me that he used to "follow up" the bird Bunggridj Bunggridj when he was "a young boy," but he never clearly spelled out its relationship to Balanydjirri beyond indicating that the ghost and the bird were two manifestations of the same entity.[4]

It may be significant, however, that as a young man, Maralung had been active as a songman in the eastern Kimberley region. In public genres of songs from the Kimberleys such as *nurlu*, *junba*, and *balga*, both birds and ghosts are involved in the creation of songs and are regarded as manifestations of conception Dreamings. As an agent of conception, a conception Dreaming takes the form of a bird and after death becomes a ghost. The model that Maralung used to describe the process of song creation was therefore probably adopted from this area.[5]

Peter Manaberu, a well-known painter who often accompanied Maralung on the didjeridu, painted the two beings on the pair of clapsticks shown in plate 2.1. Bunggridj Bunggridj, here depicted as a pair of birds, is on the larger of the two clapsticks; Balanydjirri is on the smaller. Here too the relationship between the two song-giving agents is mysterious and dynamic, the two coming together to create music whenever the sticks are struck against each other.

In Maralung's account, Balanydjirri obtained the song from the Minmin

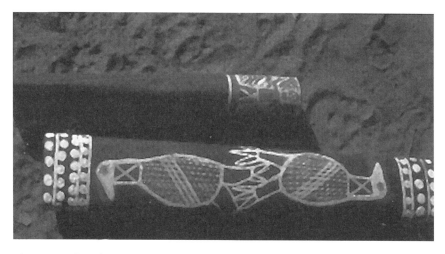

Plate 2.1 Balanydjirri and Bunggridj Bunggridj painted on a pair of clapsticks by Peter Manaberu. (Photograph by Allan Marett, 1988.)

Light, which in the Barunga region is regarded as a Dreaming.[6] Balanydjirri thus appears to act as an agent between the songman Maralung and the dangerous Minmin Light Dreaming. Had I known, while Maralung was still alive, what I now know about the cosmologies associated with the creation of *wangga* in the Daly region and of *nurlu*, *junba*, and *balga* in the Kimberley, I may have been able to better refine my understanding of the relationships between the Dreaming, the ghost, and the bird.

Before leaving the topic of birds, I should note that song-giving birds are also encountered in the Daly region, although I have never heard any suggestion that they are manifestations of conception Dreamings. In Charlie Brinken's painting of Old Man Tulh (plate 1.1), for example, the two ducks sitting on Tulh's shoulder are said to give songs both to Ma-yawa and to living songmen. In a Murrinhpatha myth about the murder of the Rainbow Serpent at a *wangga* corroboree (considered in detail in the following chapter), a darter acts as songman, and a troop of birds (brolga, Australian bustard, jabiru, chestnut teal, burdekin duck, and the black kalawipi) forms the company of dancers.

The words of the song "Minmin Light" were, as is usual for Maralung's repertory, entirely in ghost language (Maralung 1993).

> *Ga djero ganaga andibarranana*
> *Djero ganaga andiba*
> *Ga djero ganaga andibarrana ga ya ya*
> *A ga na ya ya ga ga*

While at Wadeye and Belyuen, songmen normally translate the texts of songs from spirit language to human language, in Maralung's song, Balanydjirri's words remain untranslated and hence unintelligible to humans. The texts of all Maralung's songs are, moreover, unstable and vary from performance to performance. What Maralung received from Balanydjirri was clearly not fixed, a point that will be taken up later in the chapter when I investigate the question of what exactly ancestors give to songmen.

How Walakandha and Ma-yawa Wangga Are Received

At Wadeye, it is Walakandha and Ma-yawa, rather than ghosts, that give *wangga* to songmen. Even though Walakandha and Ma-yawa are viewed as embodying both *ngirrwat* and *meri-men.ngu* aspects of being, accounts of song giving give little or no emphasis to the ghostly side of existence. Song composition does not involve the intervention of an intermediary such as Maralung's ghost, Balanydjirri. This is clearly shown in Frank Dumoo's account of how his brother John received a *wangga* song from a group of Walakandha while sleeping near their *kigatiya* Dreaming site at Wudi-djirridi. According to Frank, the Walakandha appeared to his brother in dream and sang the following song as an invitation for him to come with them to a corroboree.

> Brother! Let's all go now, let's all go now!
> Pelhi, the ceremonial ground, is there, there behind Yenmilhi Hill.
> Brother! There are clapsticks for us all.
> Come with us.[7]

While in this case it was a group of unnamed Walakandha who bestowed the song on John Dumoo, in some cases songmen remember the identity of the ancestor who gave them a song. Philip Mullumbuk, for example, told me that his song "Karra Yeri-ngina" was given to him by another of the Dumoo brothers, Wagon, after Wagon had gone to join the Walakandha dead. Wagon sings of his sadness at having to leave his living descendants and return to his *kigatiya* at Na-pumut, the Headache Dreaming place from which he originally emerged.

> My children!
> I can just see them faintly, behind me at the creek.
> My descendants! Come here!
> I've got to stay here at the point at Yenmungirini, at Na-pumut.
> The Headache Dreaming [Pumut] resides here.[8]

Similarly, Wagon's wife, Maudie, received a song from one of her ancestors, Bob Wak, which she gave to her husband to sing. This case is discussed in more detail in the next chapter.

Walakandha *wangga* texts may also contain the names of specific Walakandha ancestors such as Munggum, Wutjeli, Berida (Berrida), and Munggumurri. These now-deceased figures stand two or three generations back from living songmen; the precise relationships will be discussed later in the chapter, when I consider the Marri-tjevin song lineages. The songs about Munggum, Berida, and Munggumurri are discussed in chapter 5, and the song about Wutjeli in chapter 10.

Although both in Maralung's "Minmin Light" and in the Walakandha and Ma-yawa *wangga* repertories the song text comprises the words of the song-giving spirit agent, there is a significant difference. In "Minmin Light" the words of the ghost are retained in their original spirit language, whereas in the Walakandha and Ma-yawa *wangga* the words of the ancestors are translated into human speech in their entirety: into Marri-tjevin in the case of songs given by Walakandha, and into Marri-ammu in the case of songs given by Ma-yawa. There are only two exceptions to this rule. The first is the untranslatable vocable *karra*, which occurs frequently in both repertories, often appearing at the beginning of many text phrases and marking them as the utterances of the ancestral dead.[9] The second occurs in songs such as the following—one of the early, now-defunct Walakandha *wangga* songs by Stan Mullumbuk—where the text retains the untranslated words of the Walakandha, *yene yene yene yene*, in the form of a quotation.

> "*Yene yene yene yene*"
> Walakandha always sing like this.[10]

Although as a whole this song might appear to be more a description of what Walakandha *do* than a reproduction of what a Walakandha *said*, the whole song is nonetheless ultimately regarded as a Walakandha utterance.

In the southern Daly region, songmen translate the words of their deceased ancestors into human speech only when the ancestors belong to their own language group. This is thrown into relief by the counterexample of the Murrinhpatha songman Joe Malakunda Birrarri, who in addition to singing and composing the *dhanba* typical of his language group also sang and composed *wangga*.[11] Although the Murrinhpatha do not usually sing *wangga*, Malakunda was given a repertory of *wangga* songs by a Ma-yawa whom he encountered while living in Marri-ammu country with the Marri-ammu composer and painter Charlie Brinken. The Ma-yawa appeared to Malakunda while he slept, and took him on a dream journey to a cave on Docherty Island, where he taught him *wangga* songs. Because Malakunda was not Marri-ammu, however, he was unable to translate the songs into human language, so the texts remain in Ma-yawa language and, like those of Maralung, make no sense to living humans.

Song Dreaming at Belyuen

As noted in the previous chapter, at Belyuen it is not Walakandha or Ma-yawa but Wunymalang ghosts that give songmen *wangga*. Bobby Lambudju Lane told me that he received songs in dream from two Wunymalang: the ghost of his father's brother, Aguk Malvak, and the ghost of his adoptive father, Nym Mun.gi.[12] While they were alive, both these men taught songs to Lambudju, passing on to him their own songs and the inherited songs of their tradition. After their deaths, they continued to teach him by appearing as Wunymalang in his dreams and giving him new songs. These two elements, the receipt of the existing repertory from living singers and the composition of new songs through interaction with Wunymalang ancestors, are the sine qua non of a person's being accepted as a songman (*medjakkarr*). Lambudju likened the experience of receiving songs from a ghost in a dream to that of watching a movie of Frank Sinatra or Bing Crosby. This image is particularly apt, since images preserved on film are also regarded as *maruy* conception Dreamings.

The other singer with whom I principally worked in Belyuen, Tommy Barrtjap, received songs from his father's brother, Jimmy Bandak, who when alive taught many songs to young Barrtjap, and then, after death, appeared to him in dream as a Wunymalang to give him new songs. Bandak's relationship to Barrtjap, namely, father's brother, precisely parallels the relationship between Aguk Malvak and Lambudju. In both cases the songmen would have called their father's brothers "father." These two Wunymalang stand, moreover, in the same patrilineal relationship to the songmen as the Walakandha and Ma-yawa do to songmen in the southern Daly region.

As is the case for the Walakandha and Ma-yawa *wangga* repertories, the songs of both Barrtjap and Lambudju comprise the utterances of ancestors, many of which have been translated into normal human language: here, Batjamalh. At Belyuen, however, some untranslated ghost language is frequently retained in the form of unintelligible text.

One of Barrtjap's songs is particularly revealing with regard to his interaction with his song-giving Wunymalang:

> Yagarra! I'm singing!
> Yagarra! What have I come to do?
> I'm going to sing and then go back.
> Yagarra! You sing!
>
> Yagarra! I was sitting on the edge of the open beach and singing *ni*.
> Yagarra! You sing! [13]

This text is effectively a record of Barrtjap's interaction with the Wunymalang in the process of receiving a song. Notice how closely the words of the song approximate the events in Maralung's story. Barrtjap's ghost sings: "I'm singing. What have I come to do? I'm going to sing and then go back. You sing." Maralung's ghost says: "We're going to sing for you. . . . We've got to show you this song, 'Minmin Light.' I sang this *wangga* for you. It's yours. . . . Bye-bye. Don't you lose it." The announcement of the ghost's intention to sing, the handing over of the song to the songman, and the announcement of the ghost's intention to return to the spirit world in Maralung's account appear in a more pithy form in the text of Barrtjap's song.

The fact that at Belyuen *wangga* songs can record this sort of instruction was confirmed by Lambudju, who in explaining his song "Bangany Nye-bindja-ng" commented: "This spirit tells me to repeat that song, what I been singing now. I got to repeat that song every now and then when I sing it. . . . It says 'sing me a song' and that's what it is. . . . I just keep on repeating, that same word: 'bangany nye-bindja-ng nya-mu.' " [14]

We observed in chapter 1 that at Belyuen the song-giving agents are not *ngirrwat* Dreamings such as Walakandha or Ma-yawa but *maruy* conception Dreamings in the form of Wunymalang ghosts. Irrespective of whether they are Walakandha, Ma-yawa, or Wunymalang, however, the beings that are the agents in song giving are also the focus of ceremony. This alignment is central to ceremonial efficacy.

What Exactly Do the Ancestors Give to Songmen?

The discussion of song creation up to this point begs the question, In the process of creating songs, what exactly do the ancestral dead give to songmen? Is it a complete song already fully formed, or is it something more unformed and malleable—something that the songman must then work up into a fully realized song?

Philip Mullumbuk from Wadeye suggests that it is the latter. He told me that after he receives a song from a Walakandha, it takes him about a month to get the song straight. As soon as he wakes from a dream in which a Walakandha has sung him a song, he begins working with what he has been given. He talks about this process as "getting the words in the right order" and "making the song go straight" and compares this to the compositional work of rock or country-and-western musicians.

Mullumbuk's account resonates with less-explicit statements by singers from other communities. Lambudju, for example, acknowledged a degree of human agency in the creation of his songs. He told me that after he had received a song, he would walk around singing it to himself until he was happy with it, before "setting" it by singing it in ceremony.

I once witnessed Maralung rehearsing a new song that he had just received. He sang fragments of melody and text sotto voce and quietly beat out short rhythmic patterns, adjusting the various elements until he was happy with them. Later that day he was able to perform the song for a recording; this perhaps suggests that he required less composition time than Mullumbuk.[15] One should bear in mind, however, that Maralung's songs involve a much greater degree of improvisation than Mullumbuk's. They continually evolve and never attain the degree of stability sought by Mullumbuk, or indeed by Lambudju. When songs are not regularly performed in ceremony, as is the case with Maralung's repertory, they never become "set," and their form invariably remains unstable from performance to performance. Nevertheless, both forms—those set by performance in ceremony, and those that continue to evolve from performance to performance—equally represent the collaborative work of humans and ancestors.

Sustaining Tradition

Transmission of Wangga at Wadeye

Since 1988, when I first visited Wadeye, the *wangga* songmen (*ngalinangga*) resident there have all been either Marri-tjevin or Marri-ammu. *Wangga* have been described as "individually-owned songs" (Moyle 1974, 75–76, 161–62), but although at Wadeye songs are individually *composed*, they are owned by larger groups and performed by a number of specialist songmen from within those groups.

Of the two *wangga* traditions at Wadeye, the Walakandha *wangga*—the repertory composed to represent the *wangga* "mob" in the tripartite ceremonial arrangements established in late 1950s—is overwhelmingly the more dominant. During the period in which I undertook research there (1988–2000), the Mayawa *wangga* tradition, which began with Charlie Brinken, was rarely performed, and with the death of Maurice Ngulkur in November 2001, it is unlikely to continue. For this reason, the following discussion will focus on the Marri-tjevin families responsible for the transmission of the Walakandha *wangga*.

The Walakandha *wangaa* repertory is closely associated with Nadirri, an important Marri-tjevin coastal site near the mouth of the Moyle River, which is now the location of the principal Marri-tjevin outstation community. Nadirri has, since time immemorial, been the country of three families, the Mullumbuk, the Kungiung, and the Berida. The first Walakandha *wangga* songs were composed by Stan Mullumbuk around the early 1960s. Other Marri-tjevin families such as the Dumoo and the Ngurndul (Kundjil), whose country lay inland, also played an important role in the composition and development of the Walakandha *wangga* at that stage.[16] A number of Marri-ammu families have joined with the Marri-tjevin to form a "company" called Thangguralh, and these families—in particular the Ngulkur and the Nemarluk families—have been prominent as dancers in the Walakandha *wangga* tradition, which is sometimes also referred to (particularly in the Kimberley region) as the "Thangguralh *wangga*." Matige men have also been prominent as dancers in the Thangguralh company.

An understanding of lineage is fundamental to an understanding of the cultural work that is done when *wangga* songs are performed. In later chapters we will see how themes of cooperation and tension between different lineages, and between the different language groups associated with *wangga*, can influence important aspects of performance such as the shape of melody, the adoption of one rhythmic pattern instead of another, and the maintenance of modal consistency.

MARRI-TJEVIN LINEAGES

Four Marri-tjevin lineages, focused on the Mullumbuk, Kungiung, Dumoo, and Ngurndul families, now carry the Walakandha *wangga* tradition. The involvement of several Marri-tjevin families with their Marri-ammu and Matige countrymen in the performance and transmission of the Walakandha *wangga* is what challenges the characterization of *wangga* as being individually owned (Moyle 1974).

Lineage 1 (figure 2.1) is carried by the descendants of Mullumbuk, the second oldest of three brothers associated with the coastal country near Nadirri. The names of two of Mullumbuk's sons, Munggumurri and Wutjeli, appear in Wala-

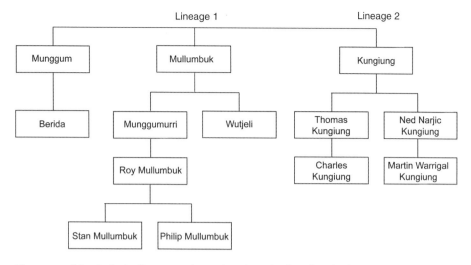

Figure 2.1 Marri-tjevin lineages 1 (Kungiung) and 2 (Mullumbuk)

kandha *wangga* songs together with the names of Mullumbuk and Kungiung's brother, Munggum, and his son Berida.[17] As already noted, it was Mullumbuk's great-grandson, Stan (born 1937), who composed the first Walakandha *wangga* songs around early 1960s. At that time two other traditions of *wangga* flourished at Wadeye: the now almost extinct Ma-yawa *wangga* and the now defunct *wangga kardu kunhbinhi* sung by Joe Malakunda Birrarri. According to Frank Dumoo, before the establishment of the Walakandha *wangga*, these two traditions were supplemented by *wangga* performed by visitors from Belyuen such as Jimmy Bandak, Tommy Barrtjap, Billy Mandji, and Jimmy Muluk, and it was these Belyuen repertories that provided Stan Mullumbuk with his model. Stan Mullumbuk had already passed away by the time I arrived at Wadeye in 1988, but recordings of his singing survive from 1972 and 1974. By the mid-1990s, Stan's younger brother Philip Mullumbuk (born 1947) had emerged as a senior singer for the Walakandha *wangga* tradition, a position that he maintains to the present.

Lineage 2 comprises the group of singers who have descended from Kungiung, the youngest of the three brothers. Kungiung's son Thomas sang the first Walakandha *wangga* songs with Stan Mullumbuk and then took over as the senior singer after his death. From the late 1970s until the early 1990s, Thomas Kungiung (1934–1992) was the most active singer and composer in Wadeye, and his singing is legendary. His son Charles (born 1968) is becoming increasingly active as a singer and didjeridu player. Being only in his thirties, however, Charles is junior to Les Kundjil (lineage 4) and Philip Mullumbuk (lineage 1), the two older singers who lead the Walakandha *wangga* tradition today. Martin Warrigal Kungiung (now also deceased), the son of Thomas's half brother, Ned Narjic Kungiung, was another very active lineage 2 singer in the 1980s and 1990s. It was Warrigal who took me under his wing when I first arrived in the Daly region. He introduced me to other songmen in the Walakandha *wangga* tradition, and I acknowledge him as one of my main teachers.

Plate 2.2 Les Kundjil, Philip Mullumbuk (obscured), Thomas Kungiung, John Dumoo, Maurice Ngulkur, Frank Dumoo (didjeridu), and Ambrose Piarlum (seated right to left) performing at a circumcision ceremony at Wadeye in 1992. (Photograph by Mark Crocombe.)

Lineages 3 and 4 are relatively straightforward and do not require genealogical charts. Lineage 3 descends from Dumoo, whose country lay not on the coast but inland at Yenmungirini, near the site of the present-day outstation of Perrederr (see figure 1.1). The sons of Dumoo were also major players in the development of the Walakandha *wangga* tradition. Two of his sons (now both deceased), John (born about 1922) and Wagon (born about 1926), composed songs. Wagon was also a prominent singer, while John was renowned primarily as a didjeridu player. Two other sons, Frank (born about 1936) and Terence (born about 1943), are prominent dancers, and Frank is also an important ritual specialist. Frank is also one of my main teachers.

Lineage 4 descends from Ngurndul. Ngundurl was one of three brothers. As a result of ongoing intertribal conflict, he moved from his inland estates to Anggeleni, just north of Nadirri, while his brothers, Billy Mandji and Harry Worumbu Ferguson, moved north to Belyuen, where Billy Mandji founded one of the four Belyuen lineages, and Harry Worumbu Ferguson became a leading didjeridu player. Harry Worumbu Ferguson's son, Colin Worumbu Ferguson, is active as a singer at both Belyuen and Wadeye. In addition to singing the songs of the Walakandha *wangga* tradition, he sings the songs of his father's brother, Billy Mandji, as well as those of other singers from Belyuen such as Bobby Lambudju Lane.

Plate 2.2, a photograph taken in 1992, shows a performance group in which the Thangguralh company is represented by all four lineages and the Marri-ammu singer Maurice Ngulkur: from right to left these are Les Kundjil (lineage 4), Philip Mullumbuk (obscured; lineage 1), Thomas Kungiung (lineage 2), John Dumoo (lineage 3), Maurice Ngulkur (Ma-yawa *wangga* singer), Frank Dumoo (playing didjeridu; lineage 3), and Ambrose Piarlum (a splendid dancer associated with lineage 3). In chapter 1, plate 1.2 shows a more recent performance in which Les Kundjil and Colin Worumbu Ferguson (lineage 4) sing with Philip Mullumbuk (lineage 1).

The four lineages that now carry the Walakandha *wangga* tradition are also connected by the fact that most of the key players married children of a Marri-ammu man, Ngenawurda, and his wife Nimineddi. The mother of the Dumoo brothers John, Wagon, Frank, and Terence (lineage 3) was a Ngenawurda, as was the mother of Stan and Philip Mullumbuk (lineage 1), and the mother of Les Kundjil and Colin Worumbu Ferguson (lineage 4). Moreover, Thomas Kungi-ung's half sister (lineage 2) married one of the Ngenawurda brothers, Detpil Ngenawurda, and their children, Alan Nama and David Nyilco, became important musicians at Belyuen. These marriages clearly had political implications, closely binding together as they did the Marri-tjevin and Marri-ammu, two of the principal groups in the Thangguralh company, and they underscore just how closely politics, marriage, and transmission are intertwined.

Transmission of Wangga at Belyuen

Each of the four *wangga* repertories at Belyuen is "individually composed" and in the past would have been "individually owned." With the death of the principal composers, however, several people have now gained rights to each of the repertories. For generations, the various Daly language groups and the Larrakiya have intermarried and performed ceremony for one another at Belyuen. So successful have been the strategies adopted to ensure continuity of tradition that the community has had over the past few generations an incredible richness of talented singers. In this relatively small community, it is possible to distinguish four lineages, two of which—those associated with Barrtjap and Lambudju—are examined in detail in this book.

Lineage 1 is associated with Tommy Barrtjap (now deceased) and is the least linguistically diverse, comprising as it does only Wadjiginy songmen. It can be traced to Barrtjap's father's brother, Jimmy Bandak. Barrtjap, who added many new songs to the repertory, has in turn been succeeded by his son Kenny Bur-renjuck, who has also composed songs as well as inheriting rights to the songs of his maternal grandfather, Jimmy Muluk (lineage 3). With the passing of time, and the increasing intermeshing of families through marriage, the distinction between the Belyuen lineages is becoming increasingly blurred as younger singers inherit rights to two or more lineages. Barrtjap himself inherited songs from two other traditions: the last of the Larrakiya songmen, Tommy Imabulk Lyons, publicly handed his songs to Barrtjap together with the right to sing and

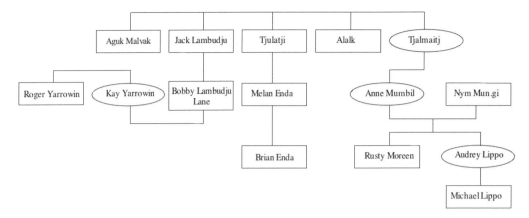

Figure 2.2 Belyuen lineage 2 (Bobby Lambudju Lane)

compose new songs for the Cox Peninsula, while the last Kiyuk songman, Mosek Manpurr, also handed down his songs to Barrtjap. However, none of those living today at Belyuen remember Barrtjap ever publicly singing any of these songs, and they have certainly not been passed on to his sons. Barrtjap's actions in this regard seem to reflect a strong desire on his part to preserve the patrilineality of his tradition while at the same time sweeping up the rights to any defunct traditions. As we will see in chapter 7, the desire to keep the tradition "in the family" is reflected in the strong homogeneity of the corpus: all but one of his songs belong to the same mode; texts are constructed according to principles distinctive to this tradition; and the way in which texts are rhythmicized and matched to melodies follows a strict set of conventions.

The second Belyuen lineage is associated with Bobby Lambudju Lane (also now deceased), and here the pattern of transmission is much more complex, involving initially both Wadjiginy and Emmiyangal singers, and nowadays crossing several language groups (see figure 2.2). Three of Lambudju's father's brothers (whom he called "father"), Aguk Malvak, Alalk, and Tjulatji, were leading Wadjiginy songmen at Belyuen in the first half of the twentieth century.[18] Lambudju, however, was too young to learn their songs before they died, so Lambudju's father (Jack Lambudju) arranged for the songs to be kept in trust by his sister's daughter's husband, the Emmiyangal songman Nym Mun.gi, until Lambudju was old enough to learn them. Mun.gi also shared repertory with his mother-in-law's brother's son, Melan Enda, and nowadays it is, with a few notable exceptions, difficult to distinguish which songs were originally Wadjiginy and which Emmiyangal.[19]

Lambudju's songs were also passed on to Emmiyangal singers such as Mun.-gi's grandson, Michael Lippo (now deceased), and Lambudju's brother-in-law, Roger (Rossie) Yarrowin, as well as to his own Wadjiginy patriline in Melan Enda's son Brian (also now deceased). Moreover, just as Mun.gi had looked after the Wadjiginy repertory for Lambudju, Lambudju in turn looked after Mun.gi's Emmiyangal repertory for Mun.gi's son, Rusty Benmele Moreen, one of the foremost singers of this repertory, who passed away at a tragically young age. Today Lambudju's repertory is sung by the Marri-tjevin singer Colin Worumbu Ferguson (Marri-tjevin lineage 4), who was brought up by Lambudju's mother, as if he were Lambudju's brother. In general, there is considerable freedom with regard to the rights of lineage 2 songs. In 2002 I also heard Kenny Burrenjuck (Wadjiginy) and Simon Moreen (Kiyuk) sing these songs.

Belyuen lineage 3 descends from the Mendheyangal songman Jimmy Muluk (born 1925), one of the most important singers of his generation, who had already passed away by the time I arrived in Belyuen in 1986. He was the maternal grandfather of Kenny Burrenjuck, who—as I have just mentioned—in addition to the repertory of his father Barrtjap, has inherited that of Muluk. Kenny has told me, moreover, that although he is Wadjiginy, it is Muluk's Mendheyangal songs that are his real favorites. Colin Worumbu Ferguson also sings a number of Muluk's songs, which he has rights to through his father, Harry Worumbu Ferguson, who was Muluk's principal didjeridu player.

Belyuen lineage 4 descends from Billy Mandji, one of two Marri-tjevin brothers—the other was Harry Worumbu Ferguson—who migrated to Belyuen about sixty years ago. This lineage is intertwined with lineage 4 of the Walakandha *wangga* tradition. Harry Worumbu Ferguson's son, Colin Worumbu Ferguson, has inherited Mandji's repertory as well as rights to the Walakandha *wangga*. As already discussed, the third brother, Ngurndul, remained in the southern Daly region, and his son, Les Kundjil, in addition to being one of the two leading singers in the Walakandha *wangga* tradition presently active at Wadeye, also sings Billy Mandji's songs.

Perhaps because of the quite complex patterns of tradition at Belyuen, transmission of songs is formalized by a small ceremony. The passing of the sticks under the arms to put underarm sweat on them is necessary for a singer to be considered a songman. Lambudju described the process of Mun.gi's making him a songman as follows: "He gave me his *nangga*, his little clapping sticks. He rubbed this through his arms [applied underarm sweat] and gave me these knocking sticks and here I am."

The right to play didjeridu also appears to be transmitted, by preference, patrilineally. Nicky Jorrock, the principal didjeridu player at Belyuen, learned from his father and is now training his son Luke to take over. Harry Worumbu Ferguson's grandson, Ian Bilbil, also frequently plays didjeridu in ceremony, but in this case the inheritance has passed via his mother.

The right to play didjeridu, like the right to sing, may also be passed on by means of a ceremony that involves the novice's drinking water that has been spat through the didjeridu by a formally recognized didjeridu player. Nicky Jorrock (Mendheyangal) received that ceremony from two didjeridu players other than his father, namely, Roy Burrburr and Roy Bigfoot, both of whom were Emmiyangal. In the following chapter, we will see that water spat through the didjeridu is conceived of as being the spit of the Rainbow Serpent, swarming with baby spirits. The symbolism of the ceremony, with its emphasis on seminal potency, is clear.

Repertory Loss

Wangga repertories change significantly over time. Many songs fall quickly from the repertory with the death of their composers, while some survive for several generations. New songs quickly emerge as new songmen take over. At Wadeye, for example, none of the original Walakandha *wangga* songs by Stan Mullumbuk that were recorded in 1972 by Walsh and in 1974 by Reilly were performed between 1988 and 1992. The loss of Stan Mullumbuk's songs occurred despite the fact that Walsh recorded both Thomas Kungiung and Les Kundjil singing with Stan Mullumbuk in 1972. It is not as if Thomas Kunglung did not know the songs; it is just that in taking over as the main singer, he chose to develop a new repertory based on his own compositions and those of the Dumoo family. Neither Kungiung nor Kundjil maintained any of Stan Mullumbuk's songs in their repertories. Nor, more importantly, does Stan's brother, Philip.

Although they do not form the core of the present study, Walsh's and Reilly's recordings (Wal72; Rei74) reveal that in the 1970s the musical practices associated with the Walakandha *wangga* were significantly more complex than they were in the late 1980s. Whereas today individual songs are only ever sung in one rhythmic mode, that is, at one tempo and with only one form of clapstick beating, in Stan Mullumbuk's time several different rhythmic modes were used. The simplification of rhythmical and metrical practices by the late 1980s is almost certainly related to the reduction in the number of styles of dance that were performed to the Walakandha *wangga*, which in turn is related to the social pressures inherent in making one repertory serve the interests of several language groups. As will be shown in chapter 5, several other aspects of form in the Walakandha *wangga* are related to these pressures.

In 1988, when I spent a lot of time with the Walakandha *wangga* group, the Dumoo and Kungiung families provided the bulk of the singers and didjeridu players (Thomas Kungiung, Martin Warrigal Kungiung, Wagon Dumoo, John Dumoo), and their songs were most prominent on ceremonial occasions. Of the fourteen songs recorded from 1988 to 1992, twelve have named composers. Of these, half are attributed to members of the Dumoo family, three to Thomas Kungiung, and three to Philip Mullumbuk. Of these, only five have survived to the present.

The situation at Belyuen is typified by Kenny Burrenjuck, who has inherited rights to the repertories of both his father and his maternal grandfather, Jimmy Muluk. Burrenjuck sings only half of the repertory that was recorded by his father, and an even smaller proportion of Jimmy Muluk's songs. He has, however, added to the repertory a small number of songs that he has composed himself.

Colin Worumbu Ferguson, by dint of his close family associations with both the Walakandha *wangga* and Billy Mandji, sings songs from both these repertories, as well as at least three others to which he has rights by other forms of association. His practice reflects an approach to lineage that is evident both in the Marri-tjevin lineages and in Belyuen lineage 2 (Bobby Lambudju Lane), which emphasizes the interpenetration of family interests, rather than the dominance of one family's repertory.

At a performance at Peppimenarti in late 2002, Ferguson sang a bracket of fourteen items that included songs from all four Belyuen lineages, as well as one, "Truwu," from the Walakandha *wangga* repertory, although shortly after Ferguson began singing "Truwu," Philip Mullumbuk, who by then was the most senior songman in the Walakandha *wangga* tradition, took over the performance of this song. The contexts of performances always influence what repertory is sung, and how it is sung. Perhaps it was the fact that he was performing in the southern Daly region, away from Belyuen, that emboldened Ferguson to draw so widely on the Belyuen traditions. At the same time, the presence of Mullumbuk probably inhibited Ferguson from singing the Walakandha *wangga*, though I have heard him sing several songs from this repertory on other occasions.

Nonetheless, it is also clearly the case that the four main traditions that I have identified at Belyuen are becoming increasingly entwined, and that, by and large, the songs of all lineages are increasingly regarded as common property. This fact was further underlined in 2002 when, during the negotiation of access to recordings for a local sound archive at Belyuen, the community elders decided that all Belyuen songs should be accessible to the whole community, irrespective of their family affiliation.

We turn now to an examination of the role of *wangga* in ceremony. Chapter 3 begins with an examination of a Murrinhpatha myth that, I will argue, establishes ancestral precedents for the ceremonial role of *wangga* today. Foremost among these are themes that associate *wangga* with death, and with profound social and religious change. We can also detect within this myth themes of ceremonial reciprocity, such as those that govern the tripartite system that has held sway at Wadeye for around half a century.

We then move to a consideration of the main ceremonial contexts in which *wangga* is performed. It will be argued that the texts of *wangga* songs suggest that *burnim-rag* ceremonies—which are performed to conduct the recently dead away from the living and into the society of the ancestral dead—provide the main context for the performance of *wangga*. The performance of *wangga* songs, whose texts are saturated with metaphors of death and rebirth, for the circumcision ceremony draws attention to the fact that the transition of an initiand from boyhood to manhood is also seen as a form of death and rebirth. By focusing on a *burnim-rag* ceremony that was performed at the Marri-tjevin outstation in 1988, I will draw out some of the main themes associated with the ceremony —themes of purification, transmigration, and reciprocity—and consider how these are facilitated by, and expressed in, song and dance. Then, by focusing on a *burnim-rag* ceremony performed at Belyuen in 1995, I will explore some of the ways in which the themes encountered in the southern Daly region have been modified as a result of the Belyuen people's migration from their ancestral country.

The discussion of circumcision first explores ways in which the themes articulated in *burnim-rag* ceremonies are rearticulated in the process of initiating boys into manhood. Through comparison of a circumcision ceremony undertaken in 1988 with W. E. H. Stanner's detailed accounts of circumcision ceremonies between 1935 and 1945, I will argue that the form that the circumcision ceremony takes today represents a significant modification of earlier ceremonial practice.

Following a brief account of the role of *wangga* in circumcision ceremonies at Belyuen, I will consider some of the other contexts—funeral, civil ceremonies, cultural festival—in which *wangga* is performed.

chapter Three

Ceremony

Myth

The Death of the Rainbow Serpent and Wangga: *Themes of Death and Regeneration*

In 1954 the anthropologist W. E. H. Stanner recorded a myth about the ancestral Bat (Tjinimin) and his father, the Rainbow Serpent (Kunmanggurr or Kanamgek). The narrative culminates in Tjinimin's spearing of his father at a *wangga* ceremony, following which the dying Rainbow Serpent moves around the country, creating many features of the landscape. Stanner interpreted this story as being primarily about ritual palimpsest, that is, the replacement of the cult of the Rainbow Serpent by a new secret male rite.[1] This new rite forms the central focus of *On Aboriginal Religion*, Stanner's monumental study of Murrinhpatha religious life, and is performed in Wadeye to this day.

Given the close association of *wangga* with death, the myth's placement of Tjinimin's act of patricide within a *wangga* ceremony cannot be insignificant. The primary ritual context for the performance of *wangga* today is, after all, the *burnim-rag* mortuary ceremony, and the ancestral dead form the primary focus of *wangga* songs and dances. But *burnim-rag* ceremonies and *wangga* songs are not just about death. They also vouchsafe important continuities of existence. The purpose of the ceremony is not only to assist the living to come to terms with death, and to restore social harmony, but also to free the deceased from their attachment to the living so that they can join the society of the dead and in this way continue their existential journey toward reabsorption into country and the possibility of rebirth. The poetic imagery of *wangga* songs expresses themes of continuity in a number of ways. In the Walakandha *wangga*, the journey of the Walakandha back to the Dreaming site from which it emerged before birth is expressed in the image of the incoming tide. Singers of the Ma-yawa *wangga* celebrate their dead who are forever dancing at the ancestral ground at Rtadi-wunbirri. References to the journey of the deceased back to its place of origin are also to be found in the repertory of Bobby Lambudju Lane from Belyuen (see chapter 8).

Continuity is also a central theme in this Murrinhpatha myth about the death of the Rainbow Serpent: following his spearing, the dying Rainbow Serpent leaves seminal marks on the landscape, many of which are the Dreaming sites from which new life, both human and nonhuman, eternally springs. Although this myth was recorded a half century ago, it continues to be retold today in a variety of forms, not just among the Murrinhpatha but also among the Daly peoples, whose *wangga* songs and dances figure so centrally in the myth and whose ritual lives are enmeshed with those of the Murrinhpatha. Visual reminders of the myth abound at Wadeye.[2]

The following version of the myth of Tjinimin's patricide is an extract the version published in *On Aboriginal Religion* (Stanner 1989, 91–93).[3]

> Tjinimin returned to Kimul [a site on the Fitzmaurice River to the south of Wadeye], where Kunmanggurr, the Rainbow Serpent, was. Kunmanggurr said: "My son is returning."
>
> Tjinimin stayed for one day. Then he said to his father: "I am going that way." "Where?" Tjinimin pointed to the north. "I am going for a bamboo."
>
> He visited all the people. He said to them: "Hear! We shall dance at the open place at Kimul. Kanamgek, The Old One, The Leader-Friend, is there."
>
> He gathered all the people, and they went to Kimul. He said to Maminmangga the Diving Duck,[4] "I cannot leave you here; you are the singing-man; you must come with me." Maminmangga brought a big bamboo [dijeridu] for Kunmanggurr. Tjinimin called to come Kularkur the Brolga,[5] the skillful dancer; Mundoigoi the Turkey,[6] Tjimeri the Jabiru,[7] the Ducks Laidpar[8] and Ngulpi,[9] and the Black Kalawipi (unidentifiable) for the women's dance (*mamburki*). They all went, and came out at Kimul.
>
> Tjinimin went first to Kunmanggurr, who asked him: "What news?" Tjinimin replied: "Many people are coming to dance. We shall have a big *wangga.*"
>
> Maminmangga gave the drone-pipe to Kunmanggurr and said: "I will sing." Kunmanggurr began to play *kidnork, kidnork, kidnork!* and Maminmangga to sing:
>
> > Kawandi, kawandi, kawandi, kawandi.
> > Mutjingga[10] tjalala, purima marata,
> > Krrk, krrk, krrk, krrk.
>
> Tjinimin danced. All danced. Tjinimin came close. Kunmanggurr said to his son: "You have brought something?" "Nothing." He had brought only his fire-stick and womerah. He had hidden his spear.
>
> There were many people, and much noise. Tjinimin danced so as to make the women desire him. He and Kularkur, the Brolga, were the leaders. With many tricks and artifices, they danced close to the singing-man. . . . As he danced he drew the hidden spear towards him by his toes. To himself, he said, without words: "Not long now. From this place I will throw the spear." . . .

Now all were tiring. Kunmanggurr blew; Maminmangga sang . . . and then he stopped. Now the other people danced, but Tjinimin ran to the spear, grasped it, and came close. While they danced, and Kunmanggurr blew his pipe, Tjinimin did that thing. *Prrp!* (the sound of the womerah). *Trrr!* (the sound of the spear). It hit there in the back!

"Yeeeeee!" cried Kunmanggurr. He threw the drone-pipe in the water there. *Pub!* (the sound of falling). The Old One, The Friend-Leader, is finished.

Like Old Man Tulh, both Kunmanggurr the Rainbow Serpent and Tjinimin the Bat are Dreamings: *ngakumarl* in Murrinhpatha; *ngirrwat* in Marri-tjevin and Marri-ammu. According to Stanner, "Kunmanggurr, the main proper name, carries the sense of The Oldest One, He Who Perennially Is-Acts, Is-Acts Now." Stanner also observes that Kanamgek, one of the alternative names used for the Rainbow Serpent in the version of the myth just quoted, contains the compound verb form *kanam*, meaning "a repeated, habitual or continuous state of being" (1989, 82).

Just as Old Man Tulh left signs of his activities at the beginning of time, so too did Kunmanggurr. "Any manifestation of a rainbow is 'his spit,' 'his tongue,' or 'water spat through his drone-pipe' (*maluk*)." Water spat through the didjeridu is said to contain flying foxes and spirit children (*ngarrith-ngarrith*) (Stanner 1989, 96). But undoubtedly the most important marks left by Kunmanggurr are the Dreaming sites (*ngugumingki* in Murrinhpatha, *kigatiya* in Marri-tjevin and Marri-ammu) at which, in the process of dying, he deposited his creative power for all eternity. The myth continues:

The Old One rolled about (in agony). He plunged into the waters at Maiyiwa. *Bu!* (the sound of plunging into water). He cried out to his son, Nindji, The Black Flying Fox, "Pull out the spear." Nindji did as his father bid. "Throw it." Nindji threw it afar. That spear is now at Toinying. (Stanner 1989, 93)

The Rainbow Serpent then went on to the rock shelter, Purmi, where his image appears on the rock, and then to a large number of other places, of which Stanner recorded thirty, where he performed miraculous feats and left many marks: parts of his body, the shape of his body and footprint, his blood (Stanner 1989, 93–94).[11]

Song Genres and Ceremonial Reciprocity at Wadeye

In the Tjinimin myth, the ceremonial reciprocity that is so central to ritual practice at Wadeye today is established as ancestral precedent. Indeed, this telling of the myth in the period immediately before the establishment of the new system of ceremonial reciprocity is highly significant. It shows the extent to which such matters were on people's minds. At the beginning of the story, Tjinimin goes north from Kimul to ask his *wangga*-owning neighbors to perform ceremony for him. The singers and dancers that Tjinimin brings to his murderous corroboree include several birds that are specifically associated with *wangga*-owning groups. The singer, Maminmangga the darter, is strongly associated with the Marringarr, who, before the development of their localized *lirrga*, were *wangga* singers.[12] The dancers, Laidpar the Chestnut Teal and Ngulpi the Burdekin Duck, are the same two ducks that appeared on Old Man Tulh's shoulders in Charlie Brinken's painting and drink at the *wudi-pumininy* that is referred to in a number of the Marri-ammu Ma-yawa *wangga* songs (see chapter 1). By performing *wangga* for non-*wangga*-owning groups today, Marri-tjevin and Marri-ammu singers and dancers enact the ancestral precedents laid down when Maminmangga, Laidpar, Ngulpi, and the others performed at the behest of Tjinimin.

For as long as we have records, *wangga* has been associated with the maintenance of social harmony. According to Stanner, the disruptive forces felt in the Daly-Fitzmaurice region following European intrusions into the area from the 1870s onward led not only to the introduction of new cults but also to a new importance being given to circumcision ceremonies—the ceremonies then most strongly associated with *wangga*—which provided opportunities for exchange and trade with other more distant groups (1989, 110). During the 1930 and 1940s, as now, more than one musical tradition was associated with circumcision. At that time, however, two of the three musical genres belonged to groups who lived at a significant distance from Port Keats. According to Stanner, *lirrga* was brought in from the east by the Maielli or some other Gunwingguan group, and *dinggirri* was a desert complex performed by the Djamindjung to the south.[13] Of the twenty-three instances of circumcision about which Stanner was able to obtain information between 1935 and 1945, four had been performed using *wangga*, seven using *lirrga*, and ten with *dinggirri*.

The question of the extent to which the *wangga* repertories performed at that time were local or imported is difficult to answer. The evidence of Stanner's 1954 field tapes (see table 1.3) shows that by 1954, at least one repertory (Joe Malakunda Birrarri's *wangga kardu-kunhbinhi*) was local, and two repertories (the Marri-thiyel *wangga ma-warrgat* and the Ngan'gityemerri *wangga ma-merren*) were from nearby. We have also noted that in the 1950s, immediately before and during the period when the first Walakandha *wangga* songs were composed, there was a heavy reliance on singers from Belyuen to provide *wangga*. This view is supported by Stanner's recordings. Those from 1957 contain Belyuen *wangga* sung by an as yet unidentified Emmiyangal singer, as well as by Barrtjap's "father" and teacher, Jimmy Bandak, and a Larrakiya singer, who was possibly George King. The Ma-yawa *wangga* tradition also dates back to this period, though it was not recorded by Stanner.

As already discussed, around the end of the 1950s, three new repertories were created as the basis of a tripartite system of ceremonial reciprocity. The primary impulse for the creation of these new repertories of song was the need to create social stability in a community whose population had grown rapidly during the 1950s and now contained groups that had traditionally been enemies. All three repertories were composed by local songmen with the assistance of local song-giving Dreamings, and all refer to local places and articulate cosmological principles held in common by all three groups.

The first of the new traditions, *lirrga*, was established, at least in part, to give the Marri-ngarr—who came into the mission relatively late—a clear identity, and to legitimize the Marri-ngarr's occupation of the country that they now inhabit, following their migration from country farther north (Ford 2005). The Marri-ngarr had previously been ejected from the *wangga*-owning company as a result of the intertribal conflict associated with their incursions south.

Lirrga songs, which like *wangga* are sung by male singers accompanied by didjeridu, are received from the mermaid (*kanybubi*) Dreamings who live in billabongs near Wudipuli in the Marri-ngarr's present country. Their texts celebrate the Muyil (floodplain) country around Wudipuli and its associated Dreamings. The principal singers and composers—Pius Luckan and Clement Tchinburur and members of the Narjic family—developed the repertory into an extraordinary corpus of well over one hundred songs (Barwick 2005).[14]

The second of the new repertories, *dhanba*, is a localized version of public song series such as *junba* and *balga* from the Kimberley. Like *wangga* and *lirrga*, *dhanba* songs are given to individual composers in dream—in this case by the "little people" known as *kardu dhanba* (*kardu* marks *dhanba* as human)—and refer to local country and Dreamings, in this case the Murrinhpatha Diminin clan who own them. Like the Kimberley genres to which they are related, *dhanba* are sung by men and women who accompanied themselves with clapsticks—didjeridu is not used for this genre—and isorhythm plays a significant part in the organization of text.[15]

The origin of the name *dhanba* is somewhat difficult to determine. Dhanba is the name of a major cult figure in the secret *kuranggara* rites of the Kimberley (Lommel 1952, 97; Meggitt 1955). However, while there are some elements in common between *dhanba*, which at Wadeye is a public rite, and *kuranggara*, the secrecy associated with *kuranggara* makes this a difficult topic to pursue.

The Walakandha *wangga* repertory, the establishment of which was discussed in chapter 1, also refers to local country and Dreamings, in this case of the Marri-tjevin. All three repertories, however, celebrate the country and Dreamings of only one of the owning clans or language groups in a company. In the case of the Walakandha *wangga*, Marri-ammu and Matige people must identify with a corpus of *wangga* songs that celebrate not their own country and Dreamings but those of the Marri-tjevin. In the case of the Marri-ngarr, clans other than those associated with Wudipuli must identify with a corpus of songs that primarily celebrate the country of the Rak Wudipuli clan. In the case of the

Murrinhpatha, it is songs about the Dreamings that live in Diminin clan country that are identified with by other Murrinhpatha-speaking clans.

Ceremonies

It is clear that in present-day practice, mortuary rites rather than circumcision ceremonies provide the primary ritual context for the performance of *wangga*. This is not, however, the impression that one gets from reading Stanner's account of ritual life at Wadeye, in which *wangga* is strongly associated with circumcision and not at all with mortuary rituals. Are we to conclude, therefore, that ceremonial practice has changed in this regard since Stanner undertook his field research in the period from the 1930s to the 1950s, or might there be another explanation for the discrepancy?

One explanation for Stanner's not having made a connection between *wangga* and death in his interpretation of the myth of Tjinimin and the Rainbow Serpent is simply that he did not witness any mortuary rituals. Stanner's account of "the mortuary rite" (1989, 118–25) is based entirely on what was reported to him about a then-defunct ceremony. There is no mention of *burnim-rag* ceremonies of the type performed at Wadeye today nor of the performance of *wangga* in such contexts. We know, however, from Simpson (1951) and Elkin (Elkin and Jones 1958) that *wangga*-accompanied *burnim-rag* ceremonies were being performed at Belyuen in the 1940s and 1950s.

Secondly, it is clear that Stanner did not investigate the texts of the *wangga* songs in the depth that would be required to reveal their association with death. Indeed, Hiatt has criticized Stanner for a lack of attention to the "liturgical arts" that articulated the worldview he describes: "Stanner's ontological formulations are superstructures ingeniously, but gratuitously, raised on the more prosaic foundations of rites of passage. . . . A sounder procedure is to work within a problematic anchored to exegeses offered in good faith by local authorities" (1989, xxvi).

Unfortunately there are no recordings of the performances heard by Stanner in the 1930s and 1940s, and although Stanner's recordings made in 1954 contain examples of the now-extinct *wangga* repertories *wangga ma-merren* and *wangga ma-warrgat* (see table 1.3), the quality of the recordings makes it impossible to obtain translations of them. Nonetheless the evidence of the older Ma-yawa *wangga* tradition and of the Belyuen repertories that were regularly performed at Wadeye before the establishment of the Walakandha *wangga* is that the association of *wangga* with death is a long-standing one.

Burnim-rag *Ceremonies*

Marri-tjevin, the language spoken by the most active *wangga*-owning group at Wadeye, has no proper noun for the ceremonies that are performed to conduct the recently dead away from the company of the living and into the society of the dead. People will simply announce the ceremony by saying something like

"Thawurr ngumbun bin-djeni" (We all have to burn those things now), thus emphasizing the ritual burning of the belongings of the deceased that lies at the center of the ritual and is the major coercive act practiced by the living to compel the dead to leave. The Batjamalh noun used for this ceremony at Belyuen, *kapuk*—also a verb meaning "wash" or "bathe" (Ford 1997, 54–55)—emphasizes the purifying function of the ceremony and refers to the ritual bathing that occurs at the end of the ceremony. In naming this ceremony, I have adopted the widely used Aboriginal English expression *burnim-rag* (-*im* marks the verb "burn" as transitive; *rag* refers to the deceased's belongings).

"NOW THIS PLACE IS CLEAR, AND I AM HAPPY"

The *burnim-rag* ceremony is most frequently spoken of as being a ceremony for the removal of the pollution associated with death. The essence of a deceased person, commonly referred to in Aboriginal English as "sweat," remains in the belongings that he or she habitually used in life.[16] Typically this includes items such as clothes, bedding, cooking and hunting utensils, and particularly cherished objects such as a woven basket or a favorite rifle. While they prepare for the ceremony that will see the eventual destruction of the "rags," relatives of the deceased look after these chattels. For the objects to remain in human society for any length of time, however, risks sickness and anxiety, and ideally they should be burned within a year or so of the death.

Once a ceremony has been completed, those who have held the chattels will declare relief that the place where they live has been made "clear."[17] The quotation that heads this section—"Now this place is clear, and I am happy"—was said to me by a senior Matige man, Patrick Nudjulu, following a *burnim-rag* ceremony conducted at his outstation Kuy in 2001. Following the ceremony, restrictions on the use of a deceased person's name were also lifted.

At Belyuen, where the theme of purification is more strongly articulated, the *burnim-rag* ceremony concludes with the ritual bathing of all participants. First the oldest men, then the oldest women, pour water over themselves, and then one by one all other participants advance to the drum of water placed on the dance ground and do the same. While ritual bathing may also occur in the southern Daly region, it is usually done in a more casual manner that is not integral to the ceremony itself.

"WE WANTED TO MAKE HER FREE TO WALK AROUND IN HER COUNTRY ALL THE TIME, AND WE WANTED THE PEOPLE LEFT BEHIND TO FEEL GOOD"

Although less frequently articulated than the theme of purification, it is clear that the major theme of the *burnim-rag* ceremony is the release of the "sweat" of the deceased into their country, so that they may join the company of their ancestral dead. Referring to a *burnim-rag* ceremony for a young female relative at the Marri-tjevin outstation of Nadirri in 1988, Frank Dumoo, a senior Marri-tjevin ritual specialist, said, "We, the countrymen of the dead girl, wanted to dance for her. We wanted her to feel us dancing and to hear the songs for that country. We wanted to make her free to walk around in her country all the time, and we wanted the people left behind to feel good."

In the southern Daly region, the return of the "sweat" of a deceased person to his or her country is the central element of the ceremony; *burnim-rag* ceremonies are therefore almost always carried out in the country of the deceased, and according to Frank Dumoo, this is what has always been done. Stanner's account of the discontinued mortuary ceremony that he describes but did not witness confirms that this is a long-standing practice (Stanner 1989, 119). According to what Stanner was told, the final stage of the ceremony involved the cremation of the deceased, the burning of his or her chattels and the burying of the ashes of the deceased in his or her country. Cremation is, under mission influence, no longer practiced in the southern Daly region, but burning and burying the ashes of the deceased's chattels in his or her country remains central to *burnim-rag* ceremonies today. The reason why the 1988 ceremony referred to was conducted at Nadirri was because this was the patri-country of the young girl.

As to the nature of the "sweat," Frank Dumoo told me that when the "rags" are burned, both *meri-men.gu* (conception Dreaming) and *ngirrwat* (Dreaming) aspects of being are released from them. The *meri-men.gu* aspect stays around the place where the ceremony took place, where it may, from time to time, manifest to people in the form of a ghost (*nguwatj*). This aspect of being will, however, fade over time as people's memories of the deceased fade. The *ngirrwat* aspect, on the other hand, is eternal, and in time it returns to the Dreaming site from which it originally emerged. Wagon Dumoo's song about returning to his *kigatiya* at Na-pumut, the Headache Dreaming place (quoted in chapter 2), refers to this process, as does the metaphor of the incoming tide. Walakandha also manifest as the archetypal Dreamings that reside at Wudi-djirridi and whose actions provide the ancestral precedent for all ceremonial action.

I have already observed that ceremony is one of the two contexts where the living and the dead are drawn together around song—the other being song creation—and that song texts both embody the words of the dead and describe their actions. Thus, when Thomas Kungiung sings, "This is what the Walakandha have always done," or Maurice Ngulkur sings, "This is what the Old Man [Ma-yawa] has always done," they are not only describing the song-giving actions of the ancestors but also affirming that the ceremonial action they are presently performing rests on ancestral precedent. When Maurice Ngulkur sings, "Fresh water and salt water [mix] like this,"[18] or when Charlie Brinken paints saltwater turtles beside freshwater turtles, or saltwater- and freshwater-inhabiting chestnut teal and the burdekin duck sitting on Old Man Tulh's shoulder, they are pointing to the interpenetration of the world of the living and dead in ceremony. By singing the songs of the ancestors, and by dancing following ancestral precedent, ceremonial performers draw together the worlds of the living and the dead, and in the liminal environment thus created—a space that is both of the living and of the dead—the deceased person who is the focus of the ceremony is able to cross over and join with the ancestral dead.

This is the principle, but actual ceremonial practice is complicated by the third of the themes evident in *burnim-rag* ceremonies, namely, ceremonial reciprocity.

"I AM PAINTING MYSELF WITH THE DESIGNS OF KUNHBINHI"

In the southern Daly region, the central ritual acts of burning and burying the ashes of the deceased's belongings are accompanied not by the songs of the deceased's own language group but by those of a language group that stands in an exogamous relationship to that of the deceased. Ideally this should be the language group of the mother, though another exogamous groups can be called on to fulfill this role. Thus it is not the songs given by the patri-ancestors of the deceased that are performed at key points of the ritual, but those of another group. The places named in these songs are not those of the deceased's patri-country, into which he or she is being released, but rather those of the exogamous group who perform ceremony. Nor are the beings invoked in the songs the patri-ancestors of the deceased. The ceremonial efficacy of each genre of public songs rests not on the particular places and beings that they celebrate but rather on the set of cosmological principles that underpins them all. Indeed, one senior *dhanba* singer told me that ceremonial reciprocity would not work unless participants in ceremony were able to interpret the imagery of other genres as equivalent to their own. This system, whereby elements from one genre can be mapped onto another, is unlikely to have come about by chance. It must have been a deliberate strategy at the time the new traditions were being developed.

The accommodation of ceremonial reciprocity into the central ritual act leads to an enactment of ancestral precedent not at the level of the specific cosmologies associated with the deceased but rather in terms of the underlying cosmological principles held in common by all language groups.[19] This is not to say, however, that the songs of the deceased's patriline, with their references to the country of the deceased and its associated cosmology, need be excluded from the ceremony. If they are performed, however, it will only be after the main ceremonial action of burning the "rags" and burying their ashes has been completed.

The ceremony performed at Nadirri in 1988 provides an example of how this works in practice. The songs and dances performed to accompany the burning of the young girl's belongings were carried out not to the Marri-tjevin *wangga* repertory of her father but to the *dhanba* songs and dances of her Murrinhpatha mother's patri-group. The principal mourners were her maternal grandmother and her grandmother's sister, both senior Murrinhpatha women of high ritual status. As flames and smoke leaped from the hole in which the rags were burning, these two women cried out, wept, and cut their heads with sharp rocks so that the blood flowed. Affinal relations of the women struggled with them on the edge of the fire pit to prevent them from inflicting serious damage on themselves. It was during this phase of the ceremony that the singing and dancing were at their strongest.

The *dhanba* songs were performed by a Murrinhpatha songman and the widow of a deceased Murrinhpatha ritual specialist. In the case of *dhanba*, which is the only one of the three principal genres that has both male and female singers, a wife often learns to perform the songs of her husband's language group. She will also be expected to dance in the style inherited from her father. The dancers in this case included a range of people with senior Murrinhpatha men and their wives, as well as younger Murrinhpatha women.

The *dhanba* songs performed referred not to the local Marri-tjevin cosmology but to sites in the deceased's mother's country and to the associated song-giving ancestral beings for that country. One *dhanba* song, for example, has the text "dhanba kunhbinhi dirrmu mempatha watha dim," which means "I am painting myself with the designs of Kunhbinhi." The *kardu dhanba* (also known as *kardu kunhbinhi* or *kardu wakal* [little people]), who are the Dreaming beings that—like Walakandha and Ma-yawa—give people ceremony, live in the vicinity of Kunhbinhi, a hill in the country of the Murrinhpatha Diminin clan. This site is the equivalent of Wudi-djirridi for the Marri-tjevin or Rtadi-wunbirri for the Marriammu. The designs painted on the body during the performance of this song refer to Diminin country, to the *dhanba* ancestors whose actions are reproduced in ceremony, as well as to other important Dreamings of the Diminin clan.

Another *dhanba* song has the text "la-ngadhe-ngadhe la-ngarra-ngarra." This is the song that begins a *burnim-rag* ceremony. The text is about remembering the appearance of the deceased after the body has been destroyed and asking where the deceased has gone. Such sentiments are felt at all *burnim-rag* ceremonies, irrespective of the genre being performed.

"YENDILI YENDILI! LOOK AFTER IT, MY DESCENDANTS!"

On the occasion of the Nadirri ceremony, *wangga* was also performed by the relatives of the deceased as soon as the Murrinhpatha *dhanba* group had completed their section of the ceremony. The young girl's father and father's brother formed the core of the men's dancing group, another of her father's brothers formed part of the singing group, and yet another played the didjeridu. Close female relatives on the father's side—for example, her father's brother's wife, and her aunt (father's mother's brother's daughter)—led the women's dancing. This section of the ritual also had a role in releasing the girl so that she could be "free to walk around in her country all the time." By dancing and singing the songs of the country, her surviving relatives wanted her to feel their presence through the footsteps of the dance and, by hearing the voices of the living, to understand the proper relationship between the living and the dead.

Seventeen *wangga* song items were performed on this occasion, most of them to accompany dance. The seventeen items were, however, made up of only three individual songs: "Walakandha no. 1" (one item), "Truwu" (five items), and "Yendili no. 2" (eleven items). During the performance of all three songs, dancers performed the role of Walakandha, reproducing both their everyday actions, such as walking with a limp, brandishing spears and woomeras, following tracks, and the vigorous and elaborate dance movements that the Walakandha themselves perform in the ceremony. An analysis of the dancing at this ceremony is given in the following chapter.

When sung in ceremony, the song "Walakandha no. 1" is primarily a formalized call from the living to the dead (although since "Walakandha" is a reciprocal term, it also reproduces the call made to the songman from the song-giving Walakandha when the song was first given). Its text consists simply of the vocable *karra* followed by the single word "Walakandha!"[20] the last syllable of which is set to an elaborate vocal melisma, the melody tracing an elaborate downward track to settle on the bedrock of the didjeridu drone. As is often the case in Aboriginal song—we will see this in more detail in chapters 5 and 6—not only the texts but also the melodies of song carry meaning, and melodic identity can be the basis for an association between songs with different texts. The melody of "Walakandha no. 1" is shared with a song that was not, in fact, sung on this occasion, which has the following text:

> Brother Walakandha, the tide has gone out on him at Nadirri.[21]

This song text refers to a death at Nadirri, the Marri-tjevin outstation community that provided the location of the young girl's *burnim-rag* ceremony, but by referring to the death as an ebb tide, it implicitly holds the promise of a return journey toward reabsorption and eventual reincarnation, a journey on which the young woman had already embarked. Even when used in singing a text as simple as *karra walakandha*, the melody has the power to evoke the ebb and flow of existence itself.

The theme of the tide is also evident in the second of the songs, "Truwu." This song, which has already been referred to briefly in chapter 2 and will form the focus of extensive discussion in chapter 5, describes a Walakandha called Munggum looking out at his living descendants as they struggle against the exigencies of life, poetically conceived of as waves crashing on the beach.[22] Here the Walakandha expresses sympathy for the grieving living, just as the living, by singing this song in ceremony, enact their obligations to the dead.

The third song, "Yendili no. 2," also refers to the obligations that the living have to the dead, in this case the obligation to look after country. The text of "Yendili no. 2," which provided the heading for this section, is simply

> Yendili Yendili! Look after it!
> Yendili Yendili! Look after it!
> My descendants.[23]

Yendili Hill is one of the most prominent landmarks in Marri-tjevin country and the location of one of the major Marri-tjevin Dreaming sites. As such, it is emblematic of all Marri-tjevin country, and indeed Marri-tjevin identity itself. All Marri-tjevin lineages sing songs about this site.

The text of "Yendili no. 2" refers simultaneously to mutual obligations between the living and the dead, and to those between different language groups among the living. The most commonly given explanation of this song is that the words were spoken by the song's composer, Maudie Dumoo, to her children when she and her husband were leaving Nadirri to go back to Wadeye for supplies. At a deeper level, however, this is a call from the ancestral dead to the living to look after the country from which they, both the living and the dead, were born, and to which they will all eventually return. The Marri-ngarr word translated as "look after" is *arr-girrit-ni. Girrit* means "hold," *arr* indicates the use of hands, and *ni* marks the verb as expressing intentionality. "Looking after the country" means hunting and foraging on it, conducting ceremony for it, protecting it from strangers, and looking after the environment—the annual burning of the long spear grass toward the end of the dry season is often cited as one form of this environmental work.

"Yendili no. 2" is almost unique among the various *wangga* repertories in that it was composed by a woman, Maudie Dumoo, the wife of one of the Marri-tjevin "fathers" of the deceased girl. It is also unusual because it was given to her not by a Walakandha but by the "spirit" of one of her deceased Marri-ngarr ancestors.[24] The exhortation to look after perhaps the most potent and emblematic of Marri-tjevin sites comes therefore from a "spirit" who is simultaneously of the dead and of an affinal language group. Performance of this song in ceremony reinforces the fact that those who will in the future look after Marri-tjevin country are descended not only from Marri-tjevin men but also from the wives that Marri-tjevin men have received from groups such as the Marri-ngarr and Murrinhpatha. It reminds us of the somewhat obvious fact that continuity of existence is no less dependent on reciprocity in matters of marriage than it is in matters of ceremony.

"THE WIND IS AT MY BACK, AND I AM GOING TO BADJALARR FOREVER"

The types of adaptation—evident in matters such as conception beliefs, song creation, and broader aspects of cosmology—that result from Belyuen's being located so far from the traditional countries of its residents also affect the *burnim-rag* ceremony. Rather than being held in the traditional country of the deceased, as is the case in the southern Daly region, the ceremony is usually held at Belyuen, adjacent to the house where the deceased person lived. Colin Simpson, writing of a *kapuk* held at Belyuen (then known as Delissaville) in 1948 for the first wife of "Barrajuk" (Barrtjap in this text), records that the ceremony ground was constructed "close to the ripple-iron hut of Burrajuk, the widower, where Mabalang [the deceased] lived" (Simpson 1951, 173). Some forty-five years later, I witnessed a *kapuk* for the sister of Barrtjap's last wife, the ceremony ground for which was constructed next to the house in which the deceased had lived. In recent times, as people from Belyuen have established outstations on their traditional country, ceremonies are again being held in the Daly region, albeit rarely.

The central purpose of the *kapuk* ceremony at Belyuen is essentially the same as that of the *burnim-rag* ceremony in the southern Daly region, namely, to free the "sweat" of the deceased by burning his or her belongings. There are, however, a number of significant differences (in addition to the location of the ceremony), and these too represent adaptations that Belyuen people have made to accommodate their particular patterns of residence.

First, when people at Belyuen refer to "sweat," they mean *maruy*, that is, the aspect of being denoted by the Marri-tjevin word *meri-men.gu*. While I would not wish to deny that at Belyuen eternal aspects of being are present in the concept of "sweat," there can be no doubt that it is *maruy* in the form of Wunymalang ghosts that form the primary focus of the ceremony. The singer sings songs given to him by Wunymalang, and the dancers perform as Wunymalang, just as dancers perform as Walakandha or Ma-yawa in the southern Daly region. Among the actions that mark the dancers as the ancestral dead are tracking, looking backward over the shoulder, standing in number four leg (with one leg crossed over the other at the knee), and performing the formal stamping movements that replicate the ceremonial activities of ghosts. Many of these actions are, as noted earlier, also associated with Walakandha and Ma-yawa ancestors.

Second, as already noted in chapter 1, Wunymalang, like the Walakandha dead, inhabit multiple places. These sites are, however, at a far greater distance from one another than the places that Walakandha inhabit. Wunymalang may remain in the area of the Cox Peninsula near Belyuen but may also be present at the island of the dead, Badjalarr (North Peron Island), which is located in the Daly region, far to the south. The quotation at the head of this section, which is from a song in Bobby Lambudju Lane's repertory, is a Wunymalang's account of his journey to Badjalarr.[25] In chapter 8 we will see that Lambudju's songs, and the exegeses that surround them, are replete with references that resonate simultaneously with sites both on the Cox Peninsula and at Badjalarr.

Third, while ceremonial reciprocity is also evident at Belyuen, the fact that almost all the residents belong to *wangga*-owning groups means it is much less conspicuous—there is no song-genre-centered system as there is at Wadeye. In the past, when many of the language groups at Belyuen had their own repertory—Barrtjap and Lambudju for the Wadjiginy and Kiyuk, Mun.gi for the Emmiyangal, Jimmy Muluk for the Mendheyangal, Billy Mandji for the Marri-tjevin—these patterns would have been more noticeable, but by the mid-1980s, when I first visited Belyuen, Barrtjap's repertory had become dominant. Like the Walakandha *wangga* at Wadeye, Barrtjap's corpus was pressed into service on behalf of a number of family groups and has become a *wangga* for the whole Belyuen community. This dominant position was one that Barrtjap himself actively promoted and maintained. Following his death, which was followed soon afterward by that of Lambudju, the distinctions between different song traditions, noted in chapter 2, have tended to break down even further.

I observed in the previous chapter that *wangga* songs received by Barrtjap and Lambudju at Belyuen encapsulate the words of their ghostly ancestors, just as those sung by Marri-tjevin or Marri-ammu singers articulate the words of Walakandha or Ma-yawa. Similarly, just as the reproduction of the songs of the

Walakandha and Ma-yawa ancestors in ceremony leads to an interpenetration of the world of the living and the dead, so the reproduction of songs given by the Wunymalang ghosts at Belyuen lead to a similar interpenetration of worlds. But at Belyuen there is yet another twist.

Here it is not just the words, melodies, and rhythms of the song-giving ghost that are reproduced in ceremony, but the very voice of the ghost itself. One of the most important things that an apprentice songman learns at Belyuen is to imitate his teacher's voice. So closely did Barrtjap's voice resemble that of his "father," Jimmy Bandak, that when listening to a recording made in 1952 by Elkin, Belyuen elders, including some who were present when the recording was made, were unable to distinguish which of the two was singing. They said that this was because the two singers "had the same voice." For further discussion of this case, see chapter 7. After he died, Bandak, now in the form of a Wunymalang, continued to give songs to Barrtjap, so that when people heard Barrtjap singing in ceremony, it was unclear whether they were hearing his voice or that of the ghost of Jimmy Bandak. The fact that not only the texts, melodies, and rhythms of the songs are sourced to Wunymalang, but also that the voice itself is that of a ghost, adds to the power of the song to create the liminal space wherein the deceased can leave the society of the living and join that of the dead.

When I discussed the matter of voice quality with singers at Wadeye, some of whom, like Les Kundjil, have spent large amounts of time at Belyuen, they confirmed that the reproduction of the voice of the ancestor was central to Belyuen singing, but asserted that it was not part of the practice at Wadeye. Perhaps this maintenance of a distinction between the voices of the living and those of the dead reflects a greater emphasis on maintaining social distinctions in the patterns of ceremonial reciprocity found at Wadeye.

A *kapuk* ceremony that was held at Belyuen in 1995 for Agnes Lippo, a senior woman who had died about eighteen months previously, can provide a concrete example of the way songs and dances work in the Belyuen context. The overall shape of the *burnim-rag* is very similar whether it is performed at Wadeye or Belyuen, and irrespective of which musical and dance tradition—*wangga*, *lirrga*, or *dhanba*—is performed. In this case, certain aspects of the ceremony were shaped by the life and character of the deceased, who had not only been the women's ritual leader but had also brought up a number of adopted children. Her role as women's ritual leader was reflected in the unusually prominent role played by women dancers, and in particular by the first two women that she had put through ceremony. Second, one of the young males she had raised was allowed to lead certain key phases of the dancing, despite his youth. He was the first to dance on the filled-in pit in which the ashes had been buried. This is often regarded as a dangerous phase of the ceremony because of potential danger from the angry spirit of the deceased. At the Nadirri ceremony, this phase was accomplished first by senior men, and only later were young dancers allowed to approach the filled-in pit. The fact that at the Belyuen ceremony there was no sense of danger very much reflected the benign nature of the deceased woman and the affection in which she was held.

This ceremony occurred after the death of Tommy Barrtjap. His son, Kenny Burrenjuck, who lives far away at Snake Bay on Melville Island but visits Belyuen regularly, was unable to attend, and another of Tommy's sons, Timothy, was forced into the relatively unaccustomed role of songman. In all, six songs were sung in the ceremony. On average, each was performed six times, and the total number of song items was thirty-eight. As is typical of Barrtjap's repertory, all the songs performed contained a mixture of Wunymalang language (in the form of untranslatable vocables) and instructions from the ghost that had been turned over into human language. These included "Bangany-nyung Ngaya," the most popular of Barrtjap's songs, which will be discussed in detail in the following chapter, and a number of songs that contained a very high proportion of untranslatable Wunymalang language. "Yagarra Ye-yenenaye" (Barrtjap's *wangga* song 12) is an example of this sort of song.

> Yagarra! *Ye-yenenaye,*
> *Ye-yeneyene kavemaye,*
> *Ye-yeneyene abemaye.*
>
> Yagarra! Say to him,
> "Sing for the two of us, right now."[26]
>
> *Yeneyene yenenaye,*
> *Ye-yeneyene kavemaye,*
> *Ye-yeneyene.*

By singing the words of the dead, in the voice of the dead, the songman brought into the ritual space not only his own voice but the voices of his ancestors. The dancers, dancing as ghosts, assisted in closing the gap between the worlds of the living and the dead and allowed the dead woman's spirit to depart in peace.

Circumcision

I have argued that mortuary rituals constitute the primary ceremonial context for *wangga*. Circumcision ceremonies, however, also draw on the death-related imagery of *wangga* songs to enact the moment where a boy "dies" to his childhood and becomes a man.[27] I have encountered only one *wangga* song, at either Wadeye or Belyuen, that appears to refer to circumcision, namely, the song "Watjen Danggi," (Dingo or Wild Dog), from the Ma-yawa *wangga* complex. Stanner notes that a boy who has been removed from his kin to be circumcised is referred to as a "wild dog" (*kuwere* in Murrinhpatha) (1989, 85). Hiatt has suggested that this is done to highlight the boy's liminality (1989, xxxii–xxxiii).

In the Ma-yawa *wangga*, the wild dog is marked in several ways as liminal. For example, the shoreline along which he walks is used in a number of Ma-yawa *wangga* songs as a symbol of liminality.

> He looks right back all along, wild dog!
> Brother, he was making his prints, wild dog!
> He is walking toward Yilhiyilhiyen Beach.[28]

Ngulkur told me that, unlike most of the subjects of the Ma-yawa *wangga*, the "wild dog" is not a Dreaming. He is walking up the beach from the cliffs at Karri-ngindji (the home of the Ma-yawa) to the beach at Yilhiyilhiyen. Like a novice, the dingo keeps looking back, though it should be borne in mind that looking back is also one of the actions associated with the dead—an action that is frequently reproduced in dance.

The primary association of all other *wangga* texts used for circumcision is, however, with death. Indeed, as I will show shortly, almost exactly the same songs were performed at the 1988 circumcision ceremony at Wadeye as at the Nadirri *burnim-rag* ceremony described in the previous section.

CIRCUMCISION AT WADEYE

As performed today, the circumcision ceremonies at Wadeye represent a revival of the rites discontinued in the mid-1940s under influence from the Catholic mission at Wadeye, then Port Keats.[29] The exact date of the revival is difficult to ascertain, though it seems reasonable to assume that it coincides with the creation of the new repertoires of *wangga*, *lirrga*, and *dhanba* in the late 1950s or early 1960s. Frank Dumoo says simply that they resumed "after the war." Throughout the period of the ban, however, circumcisions did continue elsewhere. Elkin encountered them in the settlements of Delissaville and Old Beswick (nowadays known respectively as Belyuen and Barunga) in 1952 (Elkin and Jones 1958, 149–52), and it is said that during the time they were banned at Port Keats, the circumcision ceremonies continued to be performed secretly in the bush nearby.

It is clear, from a comparison of Stanner's detailed account of the circumcision ceremonies he observed in the 1930s with those performed today, that the ceremony has been adapted to the current circumstances of people living at Wadeye. One major difference is that it is performed today less frequently than in Stanner's time. Whereas Stanner ascertained that at least twenty-three circumcisions were held between 1935 and 1945, for a similar ten-year period from 1988 to 1998, only five ceremonies were performed at Wadeye: in 1988, 1990, 1992, 1996, and 1997.[30] A second difference concerns the scale of the ceremonies. From Stanner's descriptions, it is clear that in earlier times the ceremonies were more family-based affairs than those conducted today, and that each ceremony normally involved the circumcision of only one boy. By contrast, the ceremonies performed between 1988 and 1998 involved the whole community or large sections of the community, in some cases lasted several days, and involved the circumcision of a number of boys on each occasion. The patterns of ceremonial reciprocity were the same as those already described for the *burnim-rag* ceremonies.

Another increase in scale concerns the range of styles of music and dance performed in a single ceremony. According to Stanner, between 1935 and 1945 a father would have chosen only one of three available ceremonial styles, and hence only one genre of song and dance, for the circumcision of his son, and the whole ceremony would have been in that style. Today a single ceremony might involve three or more genres of song and dance, and a higher proportion of these are likely to be local than was the case in Stanner's time.

One of the main criteria that a father uses in choosing which ritual complex is to be performed remains, however, the establishment of social networks outside the community. A man maintains throughout his life a special relationship with the men who sing and dance for his circumcision, and if this group is from a relatively distant community, this acts to the young man's (and his father's) advantage in that it significantly expands his social horizons—particularly with regard to access to potential wives. For this reason, nonlocal genres, sung by visitors from afar, continue to appear in circumcision ceremonies, whereas in *burnim-rag* ceremonies only local genres seem to be used.

The Ritual Journey   In the past, the circumcision rite began when the boy was led away from his family to be taken into distant country where he would meet new people and encounter songs, dances, and languages he had never witnessed before. This was undertaken in the company of a guardian (*malakunbara*), usually a person who stood in the relationship of mother's brother, and a number of other close kin. The period of removal, which in the old days would have lasted from six weeks to two months, not only enlarged the range of the boy's social world but also subjected him to a number of disciplines appropriate to his new status. Older men at Wadeye tell of their own precircumcision seclusions at remote places like Banakula, south of the Daly River, or near Tjindi (the place where the dingo referred to in the song "Watjen Danggi" walked). The separation of the boy from his family before the ritual tour was an important element of the ceremonial complex, which included feasting, singing, and dancing, as well as formal grieving.[31]

When the party returned, it was expected that they would bring with them a large number of people—in much the same way that Tjinimin brought back people for his ceremony. Before the boy's return, relatives would sing each evening. Elkin recorded an Emmiyangal singer performing in such a context at Belyuen in 1952.[32] The boy's return, immediately before circumcision, was announced dramatically during the ongoing singing and dancing that attended his expected arrival.

Nowadays, boys continue to be taken into seclusion, but usually for significantly shorter periods of time, and to closer locations. For example, boys who are to be circumcised to *wangga* may be taken to nearby outstations in the country of *wangga*-owning language groups, such as the Matige outstations at Yederr or Kuy, each of which is little more than an hour's drive from Wadeye, and kept there for "a couple of weeks." On the other hand, in certain cases, modern transportation allows boys to travel to even more distant communities such as Ngukurr or Barunga. In the past it was rare for boys to be circumcised without their having undertaken the preinitiation journey, but this is more common today. Nowadays the departure and return of the boy is not usually marked by singing or dancing.

The Act of Circumcision   In the past, the actual circumcision traditionally took place on the day after the boy's return. Stanner characterized the ceremony as "one of high spectacle and sustained emotion." His descriptions of this phase in *On Aboriginal Religion* are vivid, but too extensive to reproduce in full here. This section of the rite developed in three phases, the first of which involved the painting of the initiand, after which the boy's guardians danced toward his relatives seated on the ceremonial ground, who broke into expressions of grief. The second phase involved leading the boy in a procession onto the ceremony ground toward his kin. Stanner notes:

> All semblance of order then disappeared. Female kin, who had been
> sitting or standing behind the men of Mununuk [the father's camp], rose
> to their feet and sought to break through the line; male kin tried to wrest
> the boy from the throng of *wunggumangi* [those who had returned with
> the boy]; child-siblings threw stones and dirt at "those with the flesh."
> All the boy's kin wept uninhibitedly. The hotheads ran to take spears and
> boomerangs; the cool heads tried to restrain them; heavy struggles went
> on in the midst of the broil where father and mother were clasping and
> weeping over their son. (Stanner 1989, 115)

The third phase was the circumcision itself, during which the boy was concealed from the women and children by a dense screen of male bodies. He was placed on a platform of interlaced legs, formed by the boy's mother's brothers, and the act of circumcision was performed by a ritual specialist (Stanner 1989, 114–16). This was, for the most part, the end of the ritual sequence involving song and dance. A feast followed immediately, and then, some time later, one final purification rite.

Although not as elaborate as Stanner's, an account by Elkin of a *wangga*-based circumcision at Old Beswick settlement (Barunga) in 1952 contains many of the same elements: the painting of the boy, the ritual procession, the move to the camp of the boy's social group for the operation (though not the provocation of the relatives and resultant turmoil), and the way the operation was conducted (Elkin 1958, 151–52). How does this compare with how the ceremony is performed today?

Nowadays the conduct of the ceremony at Wadeye, while retaining many of the same elements, lacks the clearly defined structure present in Stanner's account. On the only occasion when I was able to attend a circumcision ceremony at Wadeye, it lasted for three days (rather than a few hours), and there was talk of extending it to a fourth, because of the number of boys to be circumcised. Boys were circumcised on each of the three days in batches of one to three boys.

I did not witness the painting-up phase, which was carried out at some distance from the main ceremony ground, which had been constructed in front of the clinic by the local council, who had truckloads of sand brought in. I first saw the initiands when they arrived in a procession containing their guardians and the musicians, not to their family camp but to the door of the clinic (see plate 3.1). Compared to Stanner's account, this was a relatively subdued affair.

Plate 3.1 The *wangga* group (Les Kundjil, Thomas Kungiung, Martin Warrigal Kungiung, Maurice Ngulkur, and Ambrose Piarlum) leads up a candidate for circumcision. (Photograph by Mark Crocombe, 1988.)

There was no provocation of the boy's relatives by the guardians, and while close relatives still grieved, the grieving was relatively subdued.

The form of this second phase (according to Stanner's sectionalization) varied according to a number of circumstances. In the *wangga* procession I witnessed, the initiand-enclosing group moved in a slow and orderly fashion to the door of the clinic over a distance of about one hundred meters. This is similar to the procession that begins the *burnim-rag* ceremonies, in that a number of *wangga* songs were sung but there was no dancing.

The circumcision itself was done inside the community clinic under anesthetic, the operation being carried out not by clinic staff (as was the case in the early days of the Port Keats mission, and indeed is the case today at Belyuen) but by a traditional "cutter," a ritual specialist who traveled specially from the relatively distant community of Maningrida. While at Wadeye the practice of circumcising in sterile conditions under anesthetic is maintained, I am told that particularly troublesome boys are still taken out into the bush and circumcised in the old way. Certainly these old methods, which do not include the benefit of anesthetic, continue to be practiced at Peppimenarti, the community about an hour's drive from Port Keats, where a generally tougher regime prevails.

One effect of the present practice, however, is that the act of circumcision itself, once concealed from all but the central participants by a wall of bodies, is now made invisible by the walls of the clinic. Obscured though the act may have been under the old regime, it was still witnessed by the relatives of the initiand and the visitors in a way that present practices render impossible.

During the circumcision, the singers and dancers outside the clinic continued to perform songs and dances in the appropriate tradition. However, this was part of a much more generalized structure, according to which each of the main traditions—*wangga*, *lirrga*, *dhanba*, and sometimes *wurlthirri*—was performed in sequence with little apparent relationship to whether circumcision was taking place or not. Singing and dancing typically began at about nine or ten in the morning and continued to about 5 p.m. with little or no break. The *wangga*, *lirrga*, and *dhanba* singers and dancers sat in separate groups, the location of each "camp" lying in the general direction of their traditional country: the *wangga* group toward the northwest, the *lirrga* group toward the northeast, and the *dhanba* group toward the south. On a typical day, the sequence might be an alternation of three or four brackets of *lirrga* and *dhanba* singing and dancing, each lasting up to an hour or more, followed by an hour of *wangga* dancing, or alternation of brackets of *lirrga* and *wangga* followed by *dhanba*.

To show exactly which *wangga* songs were sung, and to reflect on their significance, I will focus now on the final bracket sung late in the afternoon of the ceremony's final day. On this occasion, a total of five songs were sung, with a total of twenty-three items. These include the same three songs, "Walakandha no. 1" (six items), "Truwu" (two items), and "Yendili no. 2" (eight items), that were performed at the 1988 *burnim-rag* ceremony at Nadirri examined earlier. The circumcision ceremony preceded the Nadirri *burnim-rag* ceremony by about two months. The other two songs that were performed were "Yendili no. 1" (three items) and "Nadirri" (three items). This conforms fairly closely to what was performed on other days.

"Nadirri" was discussed earlier as the song that shares a melody with "Walakandha no. 1," and refers to the tide going out at Nadirri as a metaphor of death. The text of "Yendili no. 1" refers to a Walakandha giving a song about Yendili Hill and is related to "Yendili no. 2." In short, precisely the same sites and Dreamings, and the same references to the tide as a metaphor for death and rebirth, are present here as were present in the *burnim-rag* ceremony. There should be few remaining doubts that the primary images produced through the singing and dancing of *wangga* at circumcision ceremonies are essentially the same as those projected at *burnim-rag* ceremonies, and that the same themes of ritual transformations, broadly conceived of as death and rebirth, inhabit both contexts.

CIRCUMCISION AT BELYUEN

Although I have never had the opportunity to witness a circumcision at Belyuen, its general form and themes have been described to me in detail by a number of ritually knowledgeable people at Belyuen. In general, the structure follows that of Wadeye. As at Wadeye, the act of circumcision normally takes place under medical supervision in the clinic.

Just as ritual bathing was more central to the Belyuen form of the *burnim-rag* ceremony than it is in the southern Daly region, so too does ritual bathing play a more prominent role in the circumcision practices at Belyuen.[33] After being circumcised, boys are taken to the Ngura-nyini (Penis Dreaming site) on the north coast of the Cox Peninsula to be bathed in salt water, and then to Belyuen water hole to be bathed in freshwater. The bathing at the Ngura-nyini site ensures that their "sweat" is introduced to important Dreamings to the east and south, including the dangerous Wilha Dreaming, and to Dreamings as far south as the Peron Islands. After this the boy is safe to enter or sail upon these waters. The bathing at Belyuen water hole, on the other hand, takes their sweat to certain freshwater sites via the Kenbi (Didjeridu Dreaming) underground "tunnels" that connect Belyuen to a number of freshwater sites, especially on the islands to the west.[34]

Other Performance Contexts

Funerals, which occur within days of a death, are normally conducted, at both Wadeye and Belyuen, as Christian rituals, into which traditional elements are incorporated in varying degrees. In some cases a funeral may have no traditional elements at all, particularly if the deceased is a child or a person with low status in the community. At Wadeye, the same groups who work for each other in the context of the *burnim-rag* ceremony provide singing and dancing for a funeral. In appropriate cases, *wangga* singing and dancing (or, indeed, that of any of the other public genres) may occur at a number of points in the ceremony, such as during the procession of the coffin to the church or within the church in the course of a requiem mass. Singing, but not dancing, may also occur during the procession of the coffin from the church to the cemetery. As the procession moves forward, songs are interspersed with items of the Christian liturgy such as the Lord's Prayer or the rosary.

Wangga are also sung in a number of other ceremonies that might be termed "quasi-ceremonial." Some quasi-ceremonial contexts have obvious relationships to the two main ceremonial contexts of *burnim-rag* and circumcision, both of which involve significant transformation in the status of the person who is the focus of the ceremony. Graduation ceremonies at the Batchelor Institute of Indigenous Tertiary Education are usually accompanied by the traditional songs and dances of the graduands, including, when appropriate, *wangga*.

The analogies between this new rite of passage and other more traditional ones are not difficult to discern. Like the funeral services described earlier, the new rite represents an essentially European ritual form into which *wangga* or related genres have been incorporated. Other ceremonial occasions that include *wangga* but are not strictly traditional include book or record launches, for example, the launches of Lysbeth Ford's Batjamalh dictionary and the CD *Rak Badjalarr* at Belyuen, or civic ceremonies such as the conferring of a bravery award on a young man from Peppimenarti by the administrator of the Northern Territory.

On other occasions, such as the winning of a major land rights case, or the visit of the newly crowned Queen Elizabeth II to Toowoomba in 1953, or the protests that were held in Sydney on Australia Day 1988 (to protest against bicentennial celebrations that took little account of the negative impact of European settlement and colonization on Aboriginal people), the performance of *wangga* mediates moments of important social change in ways that are not dissimilar to the role of *wangga* in mediating ritual change in the Tjinimin myth.

Wangga are also frequently performed at occasions of cultural exchange ranging from tourist corroborees, such as those which performers from Belyuen have presented at the Mandorah Hotel and other venues in Darwin over a number of decades, to festivals, such as the 1988 Barunga Festival, where a large contingent of dancers from Peppimenarti danced the Walakandha *wangga* over a period of several days.

Wangga is, as it was in the past, also frequently associated with economic exchange. For this reason *wangga* songs have sometimes been referred to in the literature as "trade songs." Accounts of ceremonial practice from the 1940s to the 1960s suggest that at that time there was a strong relationship between *wangga* and trade. This took two main forms, the first of which involved ceremony that was conducted primarily for the purposes of trade, and the second, the trading of goods "in the shadow," as Stanner puts it, of ceremonies held for other purposes, such as circumcision.

The first of these forms, "trade ceremonies," is discussed by the Berndts (Berndt and Berndt 1964, 131). It is clear that in 1949 Elkin witnessed a ceremony of this type, using *walaka* singing and dancing—*walaka* is the Jawoyn word for *wangga*—at Tandandjal (near Beswick Creek),[35] which led him to characterize *walaka* as a "trade dance":

> The Walaka is a "trade dance" of the Wadaman and other tribes on the southwest of Arnhem Land. It had spread to the Yangman and Djauan [Jawoyn] who made the recording. It is performed when groups from different tribes meet with goods to exchange. At such gatherings marriages are arranged and friendships made. The exchange of articles is often preceded by temporary exchanges of women during the singing, a sign of the good relations existing between all present. (Elkin and Jones 1958, 62)

So far as I know, the performance of *wangga* for ceremonies solely focused on trade no longer occurs.

The second type of economic exchange, namely, the kind that takes place after a ceremony when guests are invited "for a smoke," undoubtedly occurs, but it was hardly a conspicuous part of any of the ceremonies I have witnessed—indeed, the speed with which visitors tend to pack up and leave at the end of a ceremony is nowadays quite striking. This does not mean, however, that there is an absence of exchange *as part of* the ceremony (the presentation of cloth by visitors to a *burnim-rag* ceremony, the provision of food and goods for the performers) but rather suggests that *wangga*-based ceremonies such as *burnim-rag* or circumcision do not seem to provide a primary context for trade exchange as they did in the past, unlike the restricted men's ceremonies, where trade is still a central element of the proceedings. Perhaps changing economic circumstances and vastly improved transportation opportunities mean that *wangga*-based ceremonies no longer need to fulfill this function.

Wangga has, however, always been a highly flexible genre, associated in formal ways with ceremonies associated with death and renewal, by metaphorical extension with other formal ceremonies that mark other major life changes, and by further extension with occasions that celebrate social change and interchange.

chapter four

Conventions of
Song and Dance

To set the stage for the examination of how singers of different *wangga* repertories enact broader social themes within specific performances, this chapter will provide an introduction to the musical conventions—the "nuts and bolts" of performance—that performers manipulate to achieve these ends. Through an analysis of a performance of Tommy Barrtjap's song "Bangany-nyung Ngaya" given at Belyuen in 1968, I will identify the major elements of form and develop a set of analytical terms that can be used in subsequent discussions. I will then examine a performance of the Walakandha *wangga* song "Yendili no. 2," from the 1988 *burnim-rag* ceremony at Nadirri discussed in the previous chapter, and extend the analysis to include elements of dance. The focus here will be on identifying the main formal elements of dance and explaining how they are matched to those of the music. Finally, I will return to the myth of Tjinimin's murder of the Rainbow Serpent discussed in the previous chapter, in order to more closely examine the song sung by the Darter, Maminmangga, for what it tells us about the meanings that adhere to various formal elements of song and dance.

Susan McClary has suggested that "[musical] conventions always operate as part of the signifying apparatus," and has observed that this is so "even when they occupy the ground over which explicit references and encodings occur: in other words, it is not the deviations alone that signify, but the norms as well" (2000, 6). The need to focus not only on how performers play against conventions to generate meaning, but also on the meanings embedded in the conventions themselves, is as important for the study of *wangga* as it is for McClary's study of the blues or Beethoven's A Minor Quartet.

To discuss how a songman manipulates the melody of a *wangga* song so as to articulate his relationship to his country and to that of neighboring language groups, for example, we need to clearly understand what melody signifies in Aboriginal musical systems. Here I will draw on research on melody and signification from other areas in Australia. In Central Australia, for example, melody is thought of as being the "taste" or "scent" of a totemic ancestor.

> R. Moyle [1979, 71] gives as the Pintupi terms used for melody, *mayu* "scent," *yatjila, yakuntjirra* "taste," and *ngurra* "taste." These concepts, as

also among the Pitjantjatjara [see Ellis et al. 1978, 74] refer to the melodic characteristics which enable a song to be recognized by terms related to other senses than hearing. It is possible to surmise, then, that not only are creators of the song "naming" the ancestral characters of the Dreaming, but the melody represents their most characteristic qualities of taste and smell. (Ellis 1984, 171)

Because songs about the activities of a single ancestor or group of ancestors have the same melody, and because Dreamings are associated both with people and with sites, melody has enormous power to signify relationships between people, their Dreamings, and their country.[1] This observation holds true not only for Central Australia but also more generally in Aboriginal culture. In North East Arnhem Land, for example, melodies are identified with specific groups of people and are regarded as a form of clan property (Anderson 1992; Keen 1994; Toner 2001), and in the Daly region, *wangga* melodies and modes are associated with specific language groups and with hereditary lineages within these language groups.

When melodic disagreements occur during performances, they may, as Linda Barwick has observed, reflect a struggle for dominance between different groups (Barwick 1995). In the chapters to come, I will examine numerous instances where the treatment of melody may be seen as the enactment of relationships between different social groups. Different forms of a melody may, for example, be performed to underscore the fact that one hereditary lineage of singers is independent of another. Or a text about a site in the country of one language group may be set to a melody belonging to another language group to express solidarity between the two groups. In many cases, the identity of group interests is expressed at the level of mode, while the existence of independent interests within a group is expressed at the level of melody. To broach these matters, we need a developed language to talk about melody—about how it is structured and segmented, about how pitch is used in this context rather than that, about the use of melisma, about the omission of certain scale degrees in certain contexts, and so on. Part of the work that we must do here is to apply the language already developed to describe formal aspects of Aboriginal music to *wangga*, and where necessary develop new terminology.

Melody is not, however, the only element of form that can carry significance. To take but one example, because of the close relationship between clapstick beating and dancing, clapstick beating often signifies the footsteps or the gait of an ancestor. In Jimmy Muluk's *wangga* song about a Wunymalang in the form of a buffalo, *slow* clapstick beating is used to accompany the section of the dance where the buffalo swims from Mandorah to Mica Beach on the Cox Peninsula, and is replaced by *fast* beating when the buffalo arrives and dances on the beach. Similarly, performers of the Walakandha *wangga* use an unmeasured rhythmic mode to accompany enactments of the everyday, unstructured activities of Walakandha ancestors, and fast beating to accompany the enactment of the Walakandhas' ceremonial dancing. The terms used here and elsewhere to describe elements of rhythm—"slow" and "fast" clapstick beating, "rhythmic mode," and others—will all be defined in the course of this chapter.

Of course, in thinking about the specific ways that performers manipulate form in order to enact meaning in specific local contexts, we should not forget that the relationship between the performative and the social is not a one-way street. As Clifford Geertz has observed with regard to painting, the formal elements of a work of art both inform, and are informed by, the wider social realm: "One could as well argue that the rituals, or the myths, or the organization of family life, or the division of labor enact conceptions evolved in painting as that painting reflects the conceptions underlying social life" (Geertz 1983, 101).

Nor should we forget that in the moment of singing or dancing, the articulation of social themes, whether they are overt and on the surface of the performance or so deeply embedded that they do not even rise to the level of consciousness, is not the primary focus of attention for performers. Inevitably they focus most on the performance itself: on putting it all together in a way that works in terms of conventions and aesthetics, and on the delight given by the various elements of music and dance—the sinewy voice quality of an experienced singer, the old, familiar melodies and the startling new twists imparted to them, the rhythmic impulses that drive the dance, the extravagant dance movements that punctuate key moments. To develop an appreciation of how singers and dancers put their performances together is to approach the core of the poetics and aesthetics of their tradition. It is these matters, as much as any other, that they would have us understand. For this reason, I have structured the following sections as a series of activities: establishing meter and tempo in the instrumental introduction, structuring the vocal and melodic sections, structuring text and realizing it rhythmically in song, breaking up the singing with instrumental sections, wrapping up the performance in the coda, and stabilizing form.

"Bangany-nyung Ngaya": A Measured *Wangga* Song from Belyuen

Barrtjap's "Bangany-nyung Ngaya" is one of the most widely performed *wangga* at Belyuen and was one of those performed in the 1995 *burnim-rag* ceremony described in the previous chapter. Thirty performances of the song, spanning more than twenty years and involving six different leading songmen, have been recorded (see appendix table 3.2). While all these performances have been taken into account in the following analysis, my primary focus will be on one: a particularly accomplished performance by Barrtjap recorded at Belyuen (then Delissaville) by Alice Moyle in 1968.[2] A recording of this performance is reproduced on track 3 of the accompanying CD and is transcribed as musical example 4.1.

Example 4.1. "Bangany-nyung Ngaya" (Moy68:5, v)

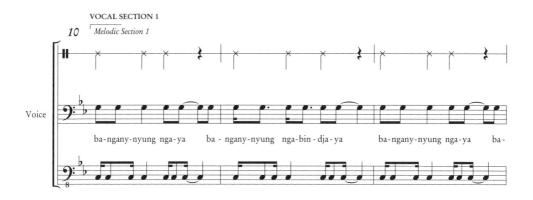

ba - ngany-nyung nga - ya   ba - ngany-nyung nga-bin - dja - ya   ba - ngany-nyung nga - ya   ba-

ngany-nyung nga-bin-dja - ya   ya-ga - rra nga-bin-djang nga-mi ya-ke - rre   ye   mm

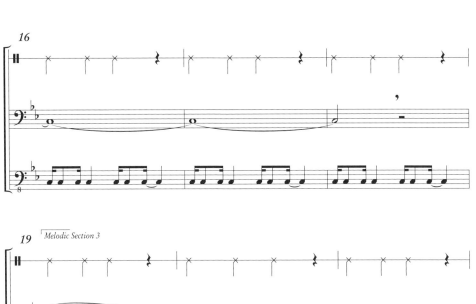

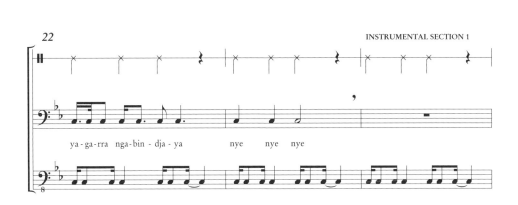

ba-ngany-nyung nga-ya   ba-ngany-nyung nga-bin-dja-ya   ya-ga-rra   nga-bin-djang nga-mi

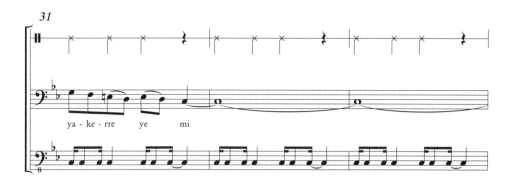

ya-ke-rre   ye   mi

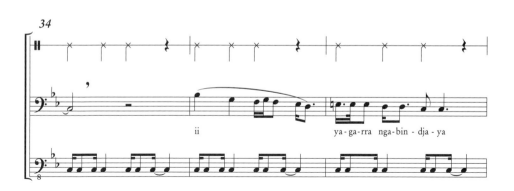

ii   ya-ga-rra nga-bin-dja-ya

INSTRUMENTAL SECTION 2

nye   nye   nye   ya-ga-rra nga-bin-dja-ya

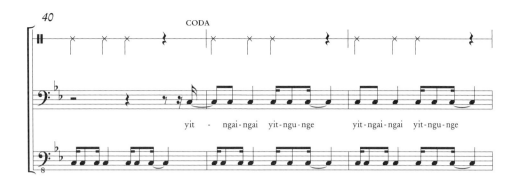

yit - ngai-ngai yit-ngu-nge   yit-ngai-ngai yit-ngu-nge

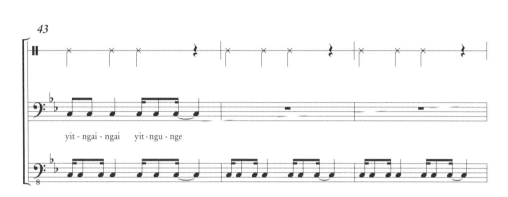

yit - ngai - ngai   yit-ngu - nge

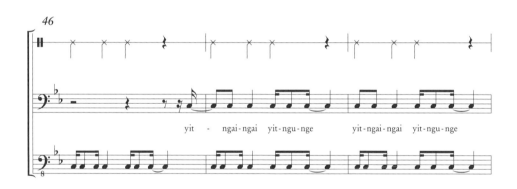

yit - ngai-ngai yit-ngu-nge   yit-ngai-ngai yit-ngu-nge

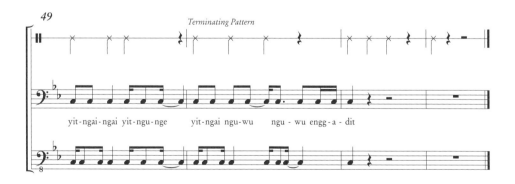

Terminating Pattern

yit-ngai-ngai yit-ngu-nge   yit-ngai ngu-wu   ngu - wu engg-a - dit

85

Establishing Meter and Tempo in the Instrumental Introduction

All *wangga* songs begin with an "instrumental introduction," in which the didjeridu commences. The didjeridu player plays a rhythmically patterned drone, which establishes both the pitch that will function as the singer's tonic (henceforth the "didjeridu tonic") and the meter and tempo of the song. When a singer is taking up a new song, he will usually indicate the rhythmic pattern and tempo that he requires of the didjeridu player by singing a vocalization of the didjeridu rhythm before commencement. Sung versions of didjeridu patterns will, following A. Moyle 1974, be referred to as "didjeridu mouth-sounds." Because this particular performance is the second item in a pair, however, it is not preceded by any vocalization of the pattern.

The four-beat pattern performed by the didjeridu at the beginning of "Bangany-nyung Ngaya" consists of two almost-identical elements, each two beats in length (see musical example 4.1, where the pattern is first given in its complete form in measure 2). The slight rhythmic differentiation between the two halves of the pattern gives the meter a quadruple, rather than a duple, feel. In measured *wangga* items such as this, the patterned drone normally continues virtually unchanged from the beginning to the end of the song item, significant deviation occurring only in the special "terminating patterns" that conclude the performance.

Three measures before he begins singing, that is, at measure 7, Barrtjap commences a cyclical clapstick-beating pattern, ♩♩♩𝄾, which continues unchanged until the end of the song. Songmen usually begin beating one or more full cycles before they begin singing, though in some cases they delay the clapstick beating until the point where they begin to sing. The asymmetrical shape of the clapstick pattern reinforces the quadruple meter established by the didjeridu. This is one of five different beating patterns used by Barrtjap; his full range of clapstick-beating patterns and the meters they imply are described in chapter 7 under the heading "Barrtjap's Use of Rhythmic Mode."

In addition to establishing meter, the clapsticks and didjeridu set and maintain the tempo of songs. If the singer is not entirely satisfied with the tempo that the didjeridu player has established, he can adjust it at the point where he begins beating the clapsticks, as Barrtjap does, in fact, in this instrumental introduction. If you listen carefully to the CD, you will notice that at the point where the clapsticks enter (measure 7), the didjeridu player has to adjust the tempo to bring his pattern completely into phase with that of the songman's clapstick-beating pattern. The tempo of the clapstick beating in the performance, once it is established, is mm 136. Within the recorded performances of Barrtjap singing this song, the tempo does not deviate from within a range of mm 134–36.

Measured songs in Barrtjap's repertory occur in four "tempo bands": the tempo of songs with clapstick beating in a similar range to that of "Bangany-nyung Ngaya" is termed "fast"; clapstick beating at about half that tempo is termed "slow"; and beating at a tempo double that of fast is termed "fast doubled." Beating also occurs in the range of mm 117–20, and this tempo is termed "moderate." I have established all these terms for the purpose of analysis, but indigenous terminology does support the concept of tempo bands, as will be shown later in this chapter.

Throughout this book, I use another term, "rhythmic mode," to refer to repeatedly encountered configurations of clapstick-beating patterns and tempo bands. For vocal sections (that is, the sung sections of a song), rhythmic mode is defined in the first instance by the presence or absence of clapstick beating, and then, within vocal sections that have beating, by the combination of clapstick-beating pattern and tempo. In some cases—as, for example, in the performance of "Wulumen Tulh" discussed in chapter 1—the relationship between vocal rhythms and clapstick-beating rhythms may also be a factor in defining rhythmic mode. Rhythmic modes also have associations with mood: the rhythmic mode without clapstick beating is associated with a mood of seriousness, while fast rhythmic modes are regarded as "happy." A summary of all the rhythmic modes used to accompany singing in the repertories under consideration in this study is given in table 9.1. A more detailed exploration of Barrtjap's deployment of these modes, and their significance, is given in chapter 7.

While the didjeridu player also plays a part in articulating rhythmic mode, the degree of variation between the patterns that different players from different traditions adopt for different modes has made it difficult to codify this aspect of performance. For this reason, the didjeridu rhythm has not generally been included as a defining aspect of rhythmic mode. Barrtjap's repertory is unique, however, in that a vocalized form of the didjeridu pattern always appears in the final section (what I have termed the "coda") of each song (see musical example 4.1). This makes it possible—in this repertory at least—to make meaningful observations about the role of the didjeridu in articulating rhythmic mode. In the case of "Bangany-nyung Ngaya," the vocalization used is *yit-ngai-ngai yit-ngunge*. As can be seen from the end of measure 40 on, the rhythmic asymmetry of the vocalization (which is reflected in the morphology of the text) matches the asymmetry of the rhythm performed by the didjeridu.

Structuring the Vocal and Melodic Sections

The voice enters at the beginning of vocal section 1, that is, at measure 10. Vocal sections are one of the two main structural elements of a song, since it is here that the text and melody are enunciated. The other main element is the instrumental sections, where dancing comes to the fore. In most cases, and certainly in the case of Barrtjap's repertory, both text and melody are unique to a song. When they are not, something significant is usually happening (see chapters 5 and 6).

As can be seen from musical example 4.1, this performance comprises two virtually identical vocal sections. Although the number of vocal sections sung in a performance is not fixed—singers are free to lengthen a performance by adding extra vocal sections if circumstances require—most comprise two or three. In all but two of the eight performances of "Bangany-nyung Ngaya" recorded by Barrtjap himself, there are two vocal sections: in only one performance is the length extended to three. The greatest number of vocal sections that I have encountered in any performance by Barrtjap—that is, over his whole repertory—is five, and this unusually long performance occurred in the rather atypical context of a tourist corroboree when the dancers became so engaged in bantering with the audience that the singer was obliged to continue far beyond the normal length.

Each vocal section is in turn made up of a number of "melodic sections," which are normally sung in one breath and usually describe a wide-ranging descending melodic contour that cadences on the didjeridu tonic. In the present song, two of these sections, melodic sections 2 and 3 (commencing respectively at measures 14 and 19), conform to this pattern, with each having a range of a minor seventh. In the other, melodic section 1 (commencing at measure 10), the range is confined, somewhat unusually, to a single pitch. In Barrtjap's repertory, and in *wangga* generally, vocal sections are made up of either two or three melodic sections.

As he ends one melodic section, Barrtjap begins the next either directly (as is the case between melodic sections 1 and 2) or after a short rest (as between melodic sections 2 and 3). The duration of this rest is, within small limits, variable. The length of instrumental sections that separate vocal sections is similarly variable (see Marett 1992, 198).

Before leaving the subject of melody entirely, I will briefly address the question of mode. As will be shown in more detail in chapter 7, all of Barrtjap's songs except one (the song about the Cheeky Yam Dreaming Wilha, "Yagarra Delhi Nye-bindja-ng Barra Narrka") use melodies that are in the same mode, by which I do not mean simply that they use the same pitch series, but also that they habitually emphasize the same pitches in the series, employ pitches in specific ways in particular contexts, and adopt certain melodic moves in important structural positions. All but one of Barrtjap's songs use the note set C–D–E/E-flat–F–G–A–B-flat, with C and G being particularly strong degrees and with the third degree being unstable. The fact that in "Bangany-nyung Ngaya," melodic section 1 is entirely sung on G reflects the strength that the fifth degree typically has in Barrtjap's modal usage. Melodic section 3, in both occurrences (that is, those beginning at measure 19 and measure 35), shows the unstable nature of the third degree as the song approaches the tonic. Closely allied to this is another feature of Barrtjap's modal usage, namely, the use of a descending figure over the pitches E–D–C, usually approached from below (and often from E-flat), which terminates most vocal sections.

Structuring Text and Realizing It Rhythmically in Song

Like most songs in Barrtjap's repertory, the text of "Bangany-nyung Ngaya" embodies the words of a song-giving ghost singing in the songman's dreams.[3]

> I'm singing in order to give you a song,
> I'm singing in order to give you a song.

Yagarra, I'm singing, yagarra *ye mm*!
Ii. Yagarra, I'm singing *nye nye nye*.

For now, I want to focus on the structure rather than the meaning of the text, postponing a fuller explication of meaning until chapter 7. Table 4.1 divides the text into text phrases and gives a morpheme-by-morpheme gloss. Free morphemes are marked with a plus sign (+); bound morphemes are marked with an equal sign (=).[4] In table 4.1, text in Batjamalh, together with untranslatable vocables (conceived of emically as ghost language), is written in the upper line, the former in roman type and the latter in italics. A gloss is added below the text.

Text phrases comprise a single unit of meaning, normally a complete sentence. A distinctive feature of *wangga* is, however, that it uses text phrases in a number of different ways. "Bangany-nyung Ngaya" displays the three most commonly encountered arrangements: text phrases that are immediately repeated or comprise repeated texts (these are termed "cyclical"); text phrases that are not repeated (these are termed "through-composed"); and text phrases that are a mixture of the two.

Table 4.1 Text of "Bangany-nyung Ngaya"

Text phrase 1

bangany=	nyung	*ngaya*	bangany=	nyung	nga+	bindja=	*ya*	
song	PURP	voc	song	PURP	1 MIN S/A	sing	voc	
bangany=	nyung	*ngaya*	bangany=	nyung	nga+	bindja=	*ya*	
song	PURP	voc	song	PURP	1 MIN S/A	sing	voc	

Text phrase 2

yagarra	nga+	bindja=	ng	nga+	mi	yakerre	*ye*	*mm*
EXCL	1 MIN S/A	sing	SIM	1 MIN S/A	sit	EXCL	voc	voc

Text phrase 3

ii	yagarra	nga+	bindja=	*ya*	*nye*	*nye*	*nye*	
voc	EXCL	1 MIN S/A	sing	voc	voc	voc	voc	

Key

1	Speaker
A	Agent of transitive sentence
EXCL	Exclamation
S	Subject of intransitive sentence
MIN	Minimal (thought of as one person)
PURP	Purposive (specifying action as deliberate)
SIM	Simultaneous
voc	Untranslatable vocable (ghost language)

Text phrase 1 is an example of a cyclical text phrase. Here the text segment *bangany=nyung ngaya bangany=nyung nga+bindja=ya* is sung twice in its entirety. Cyclical text phrases whose repetitions are limited to a fixed number are termed "discontinuous." In discontinuous text phrases, the repetitions comprise complete utterances of the whole text phrase. In this text phrase there is a strong internal rhyme between the two halves of the text phrase: *bangany=nyung ngaya* and *nga+bindja=ya*. As we will see in chapter 7, Barrtjap uses rhyme in other songs to similarly subdivide his text.

Text phrase 2, *yagarra nga+bindja=ng nga+mi yagarra ye mm*, is "noncyclical," or "through-composed," while text phrase 3 combines both cyclical and noncyclical text: the initial vocable *ii* (which is not repeated and hence technically through-composed) is followed by *yagarra nga+bindja=ya nye nye nye*, which may be repeated indefinitely (or at least until the singer's breath runs out) and can break off at any point in the cycle. Cyclical text phrases of this type are termed "continuous."

Text phrases may in turn be divided into words. The basis for this division is described in Lysbeth Ford's grammar of Batjamalh (Ford 1990) and is informed by discussions of word boundaries that Ford and I undertook with fluent Batjamalh speakers.[5] Batjamalh, like all Daly languages, is agglutinative and highly inflected; that is, its words have a complex morphology, whose elements are ordered in respect to one another. It has distinct word classes consisting of nominals, verbs, adverbs, and particles: the class of nominals generally denotes entities or attributes; verbs denote actions, processes, or states; adverbs modify the verb; particles modify the clause.

In many cases, words are made up of several morphemes. In Batjamalh, core arguments (subject, agent, and object) are all marked on the verb.[6] The subject (S) of an intransitive verb (a verb with only one argument), or the agent (A) and the object (O) of a transitive verb (a verb with more than one argument), are shown in a single, verb-initial portmanteau prefix. The term "portmanteau" means that these prefixes cannot be unpacked into separate segments.

We can see in table 4.1, for example, that the verb-initial morpheme *nga* of the transitive verb *bindja* (sing) shows who is singing, while the verb-initial morpheme *nga* of the intransitive verb *mi* (sit) shows who is sitting. Both modality (the attitude of the speaker toward a particular verbal notion expressed by his or her utterance) and tense (the time of the action or state expressed by a verb in relation to the time of utterance) are expressed by affixes. In the case of *nga+bindja=ng*, the suffix *ng* indicates the action of the verb: singing is occurring at the same time as the word "sing" is being uttered. When the singer sings, "I am singing," he is actually, at that moment, singing. The inseparability of these elements, that is, their coexistence as elements of what I am here calling a single "word," is indicated in table 4.1 by the use of plus and equal signs, thus: *nga+bindja=ng*.

Texts may also contain ordered clitic particles specifying the nature of an action or state as either purposive (PURP) or completed at the time of speaking (PERF). These clitic particles are bound morphemes that may attach to any host word, especially a semantically compatible clause-initial constituent. An example of this can be seen at the beginning of text phrase 1. Here the noun *bangany* (song) is cliticized by *nyung*, which expresses the idea of "for the sake of a song" or, to more fully expound this somewhat elliptical expression, "for the sake [of giving you] a song." The two bound morphemes, joined by an equal sign (since *nyung* never stands alone), make up a single word.

In table 4.1, untranslatable vocables are in italics and are marked "voc." In most cases these are treated as free morphemes. Only where the vocable is a clear extension of the previous phoneme is the vocable regarded as being bound to the previous morpheme. For example, at the end of text phrase 1, the final syllable *bindja* is prolonged by the addition of a vocable extension: *bindja=ya*.

It is not my intention here to give a full account of the grammar of Batjamalh, nor even to fully explicate this text in terms of its linguistic structure. My point here is to demonstrate that text phrases and word boundaries can be identified by purely linguistic criteria, and that the morphology of texts exists independently of any treatment to which they might be subjected in song. To explain how the two systems, language and music, are brought together in performances of songs, it is essential to have identified the formal elements of texts of the two systems according to independent criteria. Not to do so would be to risk circularity, for if text phrases were identified only in terms of melodic sections, and melodic sections only in terms of text phrases, or if words were identified by the way they are treated rhythmically in song, and rhythmic units defined in relation to words, it would impossible to talk sensibly about the structural relationship of music and text.

I turn now to the question of how text is treated rhythmically in *wangga*. Cyclical texts are always treated isorhythmically; that is, the relationship between text and rhythm is fixed for all repetitions of the text, whether this involves the repetition of whole text phrases or of text segments within a text phrase. Thus, in the case of text phrase 1, both occurrences of the text segment *bangany=nyung ngaya bangany=nyung nga+bindja=ya* have the same rhythmic setting. This can be seen at measures 10–13 and measures 26–29.

While text phrase 3 is not entirely cyclical, much of it is, and the cyclical section of text phrase 3 is also treated isorhythmically. In the performance of "Bangany-nyung Ngaya" that I am examining here, the text phrase ends at the end of the second cycle of *bangany=nyung nga+bindja=ya nye nye nye* in vocal section 1 (at measure 23) but gets only halfway through the second cycle in vocal section 2 (measure 38). In other performances, however, the cyclical text continues significantly longer; we may conclude that the isorhythmic repetition here is "continuous."

Isorhythm is the governing principle of song in Central Australia, the Western Desert, and the Kimberley, as well as of a number of northern Australian genres, particularly those associated with restricted male cults. In all these contexts, however, isorhythm constitutes the main unifying principle of musical organization. Rather than being applied willy-nilly to some text phrases and not to others (as it is in *wangga*), isorhythm is always sustained throughout a whole song item. In *wangga*, isorhythm is never used as the central organizing principle in this way and is invariably confined to individual melodic sections (as in the case of melodic section 1), or even parts of a melodic section (as in melodic section 3). Thus, while isorhythm is an overarching principle of rhythmic organization in Central Australian song, it is but one of several principles of rhythmic organization that *wangga* composers draw on to construct a repertory of richly varied songs.

This brings us to text phrase 2, which is not cyclical but through-composed, and is therefore not treated isorhythmically, as can be seen at measures 14–18 and measures 30–34. It also brings us to the question of how text-phrase boundaries and word boundaries are treated rhythmically.

In Barrtjap's repertory, the ends of text phrases are always marked by rhythmic extension, and this is normally the case in other *wangga* repertories. There is, however, a significant difference in the way that extension is achieved in noncyclical, as opposed to cyclical, texts. In noncyclical texts the final *syllable* is prolonged for several measures. This is shown clearly in text phrase 2 of "Bangany-nyung Ngaya" (see measures 15–18), where the final note is prolonged for eleven beats. By contrast, in cyclical text phrases, the extension of the melodic section's final note is sustained by the *repetition* of the text, and there is no final syllable prolongation (see measures 20–23).

In *wangga* there is a general tendency to maximize the comprehensibility of the song texts by marking word boundaries by prolongation. This is not the case here, however, nor indeed is it the case in most of Barrtjap's repertory, which in this regard may be considered somewhat atypical of *wangga*. Barrtjap tended to mark internal word boundaries only in cases where the text diverges in some way from his text formulary (that is, when there is a danger of his audience not understanding the text), but this occurs only rarely. This matter is taken up in more detail in chapter 7. "Yendili no. 2," which I will examine later in the chapter, is more typical of *wangga* in the way that it marks word boundaries with prolongation.

Breaking Up the Singing with Instrumental Sections

Instrumental sections provide an interlude between vocal sections, and (in some cases) between the final vocal section and the coda. As already noted, in measured *wangga* songs such as "Bangany-nyung Ngaya," the instrumental sections that occur between the vocal sections continue in the same rhythmic mode as the vocal section that precedes them (see, for example, measures 24–25). Both the vocal sections and the instrumental sections of "Bangany-nyung Ngaya" are in rhythmic mode 5c, which designates the use of the pattern ♩♩♩𝄾 in the fast tempo band.

In some instances, however, an instrumental section may be in a different rhythmic mode from the vocal section that precedes it. This is always the case for unmeasured *wangga* where vocal sections in the unmeasured rhythmic mode are inevitably followed by an instrumental section in one of the measured rhythmic modes. In measured *wangga*, changes of rhythmic mode rarely occur between a vocal section and an instrumental section.

In the case of Barrtjap's repertory of measured songs, it is unusual for any vocal material to be performed during the instrumental section, but this is not the case for all *wangga* singers. As we will see later in this chapter, in the Walakandha *wangga* repertory, singers often reproduce the calls of Walakandha during instrumental sections, and other singers such as Maurice Ngulkur and Bobby Lambudju Lane also frequently add didjeridu mouth-sounds and other vocable material in this position.

Dancing may also occur during the instrumental sections, in which case they may become more extended than they are in this performance. The dance performed to rhythmic mode 5c is briefly described in the following section, and a more extensive and technically focused treatment of dance is given in the analysis of "Yendili no. 2."

Wrapping Up the Performance in the Coda

No *wangga* singers apart from Barrtjap and his sons perform codas of the type encountered in this performance of "Bangany-nyung Ngaya" (musical example 4.1, from the end of measure 41), and the use of codas throughout Barrtjap's repertory is one of its most distinctive stylistic traits. In most cases, measured *wangga* simply extend the final instrumental section to bring an item to its end. As I have already noted, Barrtjap's codas are distinctive for his use of didjeridu mouth-sounds, which he sings on the didjeridu tonic. Although he does not do so in "Bangany-nyung Ngaya," Barrtjap may even adopt for the coda a different rhythmic mode from that used in the instrumental section (see table 7.3).

Where dance is present, it is in the coda that it comes particularly to the fore. Rhythmic mode to a large extent determines the form of the dance. The dance style used by men for rhythmic mode 5c, the mode of "Bangany-nyung Ngaya," is quite distinctive. The normal pattern is for dancers to enter the dance ground toward the end of a vocal section and to dance vigorously during the instrumental sections and the coda. It is during the coda that the most extensive dancing occurs, and the singer may shorten or lengthen the coda to accommodate dance sequences of different lengths, just as he may with the instrumental section. The main feature of the dance is that it comprises two alternating patterns of dance steps—the right foot stamps, the left foot stamps, the right foot stamps, and the pose is held with the left leg raised off the ground in front of the dancer. This is followed by the reverse sequence: left–right–left–hold. Each of the stamps coincides with one of the three clapstick beats of the rhythmic mode 5c pattern. Women's dancing is similar to that described later for "Yendili no. 2."

Because codas are variable in length, it is necessary to have clear procedures for coordinating the point at which the singer(s), didjeridu player, and (where present) dancers finish. The key point in this regard is where the singer signals the approaching end of the coda by moving out of the repeated didjeridu mouth-sound patterns into a short terminating pattern. Each rhythmic mode has its own concluding formula, which differs according to the meter. In "Bangany-nyung Ngaya" this concluding formula comprises the vocables *yit-ngai nguwu nguwu enggadit* (this is marked "terminating pattern" in musical example 4.1 and occurs at measure 50), and the singer concludes the song on the final syllable *dit*. The rhythm of the singer's vocalization is exactly matched by the didjeridu player, who concludes at the same point as the singer. The clapsticks continue for another full cycle, with the dancers executing their last step on the final clapstick beat.

Stabilizing Form

Because *wangga* are created and performed in an oral culture, songs do not have fixed forms. In a society without writing, it is not a score or an original version that constrains a performance, but a set of musical conventions understood and conformed to by singers, didjeridu players, and dancers alike. The relatively high degree of stability from performance to performance of the same song that is revealed in Barrtjap's praxis derives from the performances' conformity to the conventions just outlined. In no way do I mean to imply, however, that the selected performance is a template for other performances of the song. The metaphor of a template, taken from print technology, could not be more in-appropriate in a culture to which the idea of a fixed written text holds little sway.[7] If stability in oral performances is, as Leo Treitler has suggested, the result of a performer repeatedly following "paths . . . worn smoother the more he sang the melody" rather than a template (1975, 12), the stability of Barrtjap's performance may be seen as being due to his having followed the same musical track, with very little straying, over many years.

One factor that produces stability in *wangga* songs is regular performance in ceremony. In ceremony the ideal for the singers is to produce a strong unison, or at least a limited heterophony, and to do so, there must be a stable text form and clear musical conventions that are understood by all singers. The dancers too need clear musical structures to work within. The easiest way to produce these is to maintain a degree of stability from performance to performance. The need for stability was well understood by Barrtjap in his role both as composer and as performer, as it is today by other ritually active singers. By contrast, the performances of *wangga* singers such as Maurice Ngulkur (chapter 6) and Alan Maralung (chapter 10), who almost never performed for ceremony (and therefore not for dance) and tended to sing without the support of a second singer, vary much more from performance to performance. Unconstrained by the need to coordinate with another singer or a group of dancers, Ngulkur was able to realize a song text using a variety of melodies and rhythmic modes. Maralung too was free to explore different paths, putting text, rhythm, and melody together in different ways from performance to performance.

"Yendili no. 2": An Unmeasured *Wangga* from Wadeye

The performance of "Yendili no. 2" that I consider here was recorded in 1988 at the *burnim-rag* mortuary ceremony at Nadirri discussed in the previous chapter. It is included primarily for what it tells us about dance, although it also stands in contrast to "Bangany-nyung Ngaya" as an example of an unmeasured, as opposed to a measured, *wangga.*

In broad terms, the form of the dance follows that of the song. During the unmeasured vocal sections, male dancers perform unstructured gestural actions—looking for footprints, brandishing spears—that represent everyday activities of the Walakandha. During the instrumental sections, which are in general more extensive than those encountered in the performance of "Bangany-nyung Ngaya," the dancers change to a style characterized by more overtly structured dance phrases that involve vigorous and rhythmical stamping and spectacular extensions of the body. It is these movements that are seen as enacting ceremonial precedents established by the Walakandha. Women's dancing also occurs in two phases, each corresponding either to an unmeasured vocal section or to a measured instrumental section. In the former, women dancers travel toward or around the dancing ground, whereas in the latter they remain stationary on the edge of the dance ground while performing a rhythmical arm action whose movement extends through the body. This is seen as replicating the ceremonial action of female Walakandha.

Plate 4.1 shows women performing the second phase of the dance at the circumcision ceremony performed at Wadeye in 1988 and described in the previous chapter.

Plate 4.1 Women performing the second phase of the dance at a circumcision ceremony at Wadeye in 1988. (Photograph by Mark Crocombe.)

Musical Structure

THE INSTRUMENTAL INTRODUCTION AND VOCAL SECTIONS

The style of delivery used by the singers in the vocal sections of "Yendili no. 2" could best be described as *parlando*. Apart from the prolongation of word-final syllables and the melismatic delivery of the vocable *aa* that begins melodic section 3, the text is delivered in a rhythm close to that of everyday speech. When the meter is unconstrained by regular clapstick beating—this occurs only in vocal sections—it is termed rhythmic mode 1. The Marri-tjevin refer to this rhythmic mode as *ambi tittil* (without clapsticks), and singers may announce that they are about to take up this mode by saying something like "Thawurr-mandhi ngu-munit kurzi ambi tittil" (The song that I am going to take up is without clapsticks).

In the instrumental introduction that precedes the entry of the voice, the didjeridu articulates a fairly regular pulse that anticipates the duple meter used in the measured instrumental sections, rather than the more unstructured meter of the vocal section. As soon as the voice enters at the beginning of the vocal section, however, the didjeridu player—who in this case was the highly skilled John Dumoo—follows the irregular rhythms of the vocal line quite closely. As can be seen from musical example 4.2 (and heard on the CD on track 4), while not perfectly matched, the didjeridu follows the rhythms of the singer at significant points: providing articulations at the beginning of key words, such as *karra* and *arr+girrit=ni*, for example, or matching the vocal rhythm exactly as at the second occurrence of *yendili*. In performances of this song by less-skilled didjeridu players, the didjeridu rhythm tends not to match that of the voice to quite this degree and proceeds independently of the vocal rhythms.[8] We might regard what happens in this performance as particularly accomplished. Once the clapsticks enter at the beginning of the instrumental section, the didjeridu part becomes metrically regular and locks into the rhythm of the clapsticks.

In this performance of "Yendili no. 2" there are four vocal sections, only the first of which is transcribed in musical example 4.2. As was the case with "Bangany-nyung Ngaya," the number of vocal sections is, within limits, variable: other performances of "Yendili no. 2" have between two and four vocal sections (and hence between two and four instrumental sections).

In chapter 3, I explored ways in which the text of "Yendili no. 2" ("Yendili Yendili! Look after it! Yendili Yendili! Look after it! My descendants") articulates themes of reciprocity both among the living and between the living and the dead. As was the case when I examined the text of "Bangany-nyung Ngaya," however, the focus in the present chapter is more on the structure, rather than the meaning, of the text. Each text phrase of "Yendili no. 2" is shown in table 4.2, placed within a structural framework that represents the most common form taken by texts in the Walakandha *wangga*. In this repertory, text phrases often comprise some or all of the following: an initial vocable, an initial vocative formula (that is, a call to an aspect of country, a spirit being, or a relation), a core sentence that articulates the main activity portrayed in the text, and a conclud-

Example 4.2. "Yendili no. 2," vocal section 1 and instrumental section 1 (Mar88:38, v)

ka-rra yen-di - li

ing vocative formula. In "Yendili no. 2," the first two text phrases lack the concluding vocative formula, but this is supplied in text phrase 3, which in turn
lacks the initial vocative formula and the core sentence. The way in which these
broader aspects of structure are manifested more broadly in the Walakandha
wangga repertory will be discussed more fully in the following chapter.

Apart from the initial vocable *karra*, the final syllables of each of the words of
the text, *yendili yendili* (the reduplicated form counts as one word), *arr+gir-
rit=ni*, and *ye–ngina*, are lengthened, and in a manner typical of unmeasured
vocal sections, each prolongation carries a vocal melisma. In the matter of word-
final prolongation, "Yendili no. 2" is, as already observed, more typical of the
wangga genre as a whole than "Bangany-nyung Ngaya."[9]

Each vocal section comprises three melodic sections. Melodic sections 1 and 2
share the same melody and articulate the same text, that is, text phrases 1 and 2
respectively. Melodic section 3 comprises a different, though closely related,
melodic contour and is sung to different text. Each melodic section ranges over
an octave.

Although it is not particularly clear from vocal section 1 of the present performance, where the first two melodic sections are sung solo and the third is

Table 4.2 Text of "Yendili no. 2"

Initial vocable	Initial vocative formula	Core sentence	Concluding vocative formulas
Text phrase 1			
karra	yendili yend**ili**	arr+girrit=**ni**	
karra	*Yendili! Yendili!*	*Look after it.*	
Text phrase 2			
karra	yendili yend**ili**	arr+girrit=**ni**	
karra	*Yendili! Yendili!*	*Look after it.*	
Text phrase 3			
aa			ye=ngi**na**
aa			*My descendants*

sung with a strong unison, later vocal sections tolerate a small degree of dis-agreement between the singers, particularly in the first two melodic sections (as can be heard on the CD). This degree of heterophony arises from the fact that in *parlando* style, singers deliver the text at slightly different speeds, and with a de-gree of individual melodic decoration. A more straightforward example of unisonal singing can be heard on the following track (track 5) of the CD.

Plate 4.2 shows an example of the sort of unstructured dancing that occurs during the vocal sections. Walakandha are highly suspicious of strangers. As one

Plate 4.2 Edward Nemarluk, Tommy Moyle, and JC as Walakandha behaving suspiciously toward strangers. (Photograph by Mark Crocombe.)

song text says: "Who are they? They look different! One of them is coming toward me!"[10] Here Edward Nemarluk, Tommy Moyle, and JC (recently deceased) enact Walakandha on the lookout for strangers.

INSTRUMENTAL SECTIONS

In all but one of the songs in the Walakandha *wangga* repertory (as defined in chapter 5; see table 5.1), the instrumental sections take the same basic form: one set of clapstick-beating patterns is used for the last instrumental section, and another for all nonfinal sections.[11] We might therefore regard these as being the standard Walakandha *wangga* clapstick-beating patterns.

Because it is in the instrumental sections that formal male dancing comes to the fore, we will now focus on the clapstick-beating patterns that function as primary points of reference for the male dancers.

Figure 4.1 sets out clapstick-beating patterns of both final and nonfinal instrumental sections in the performance of "Yendili no. 2" under discussion.

In the first instrumental section, a sequence of twenty-four even clapstick beats (labeled A) is performed and then followed by a cueing pattern (labeled B). This is in turn followed by twelve even clapstick beats (A), which are again followed by the cueing pattern (B). In the second and third instrumental sections (the other nonfinal instrumental sections) of this performance, the length of A is variable. In the second there are twenty-six beats in the first sequence and twelve in the second. In the third there are twenty-two beats in the first section and ten in the second. In all cases, the second A section is shorter than the first.

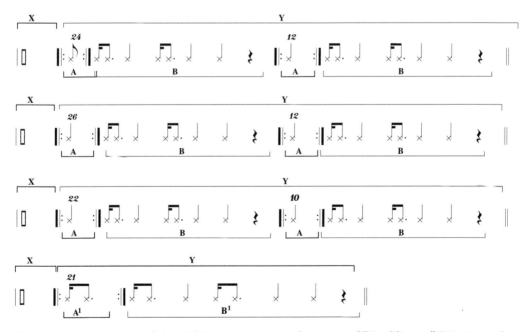

Figure 4.1. Arrangements of clapstick beating in one performance of "Yendili no. 2" (Mar88:38, v)

Before the commencement of the final instrumental section, the main singer signals its approach with a number of even but metrically free taps played quietly on the clapsticks (these can be heard on the CD). The main singer then begins performing an uneven short-long pattern with his clapsticks, while a second singer may insert a clapstick beat immediately after the main player's short beat (not notated in figure 4.1).[12] This sequence (labeled A^1 in figure 4.1), which in the current performance comprises twenty-one occurrences of the pattern, is followed by another version of the cueing pattern (B^1). In all the unmeasured songs of the Walakandha *wangga* repertory (that is, in all but one song), instrumental sections in nonfinal positions have the same basic ABAB structure, while all instrumental sections in final position have an A^1B^1 structure.

Irrespective of whether they are final or nonfinal, instrumental sections are made up of both fixed and variable elements. While the cueing pattern, B, always has exactly the same form and the same length in nonfinal instrumental sections, the length of A can vary considerably. In the 1988 *burnim-rag* ceremony, the length of A ranged between eight and thirty clapstick beats. In final instrumental sections, the number of clapstick-beating patterns in A^1 varied between fourteen and thirty. The variability of A and A^1 arises from the need to accommodate dance sequences of different lengths (as is the case in codas with Barrtjap's performances), while the more fixed morphology of B and B^1 (like the concluding vocal and didjeridu formulas in Barrtjap's songs) provides a point of fixed reference for the interlocking of key elements of music and dance as each phase of the dance draws to a close. The didjeridu usually terminates in the final instrumental section, three to four beats before the beginning of B^1.

The Walakandha *wangga* also tends to include a degree of vocalization during the instrumental sections. In this performance of "Yendili no. 2," one of the singers sings an extended *wuu* on the upper tonic, in imitation of a Walakandha's call, and this will be answered, in the second half of the phrase, by a low hum on the lower tonic performed by the other singers. This represents the living and the dead calling to one another. During these sections, the dancers, and occasionally the singers, can also be heard calling out instructions such as *pui*, "come on now!" and other forms of encouragement to the dancers.

Dance Structure

The following observations are based mainly on the dancing that occurred at the *burnim-rag* ceremony conducted at Nadirri in 1988. Like the clapstick beating in the instrumental section, the male dancing that corresponds to it may be divided into phrases of variable and more stable lengths. The structure of men's dancing has five phrases: preparatory movements, generally a walk (W); a run onto the dance ground (R); an action termed a "halt" (H), which serves as a terminating formula to the run; a sequence of stamping actions (S); and an ending sequence of extended movements (E).

These phrases, which are presented in the form of labanotation in figures 4.2–4.6, can be described verbally as follows.

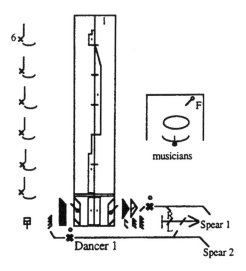

Figure 4.2 Labanotation of the preparatory walk phrase

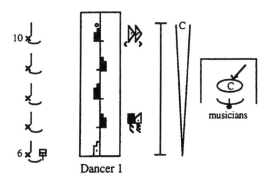

Figure 4.3 Labanotation of the run phrase

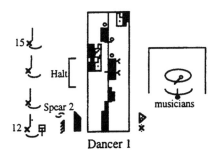

Figure 4.4 Labanotation of the halt phrase

PREPARATORY MOVEMENTS

The preparatory walk serves as a way for the dancer to prepare himself for the dancing, either spatially, by moving toward the dance ground, or physically, by taking up the rhythm and tempo of the beats while walking on the spot (see figure 4.2). As mentioned in the previous section, dancers may begin this movement as soon as the clapsticks enter. It is not uncommon for the songman to create an overlap between the vocal and instrumental sections by beginning to beat his clapsticks even before he has arrived at the tonic. This has the effect of heightening the tension and is reflected in the dancers moving, seemingly impatiently, from foot to foot on the spot.

RUNNING ONTO THE DANCE GROUND

During the run phrase, the dancer moves onto the dance ground. In the context where the present recording was made, the focal point of the dance ground was the filled-in pit in which the ashes of the "rags" of the young Marri-tjevin girl had been buried. It is this dangerous place—the place where the angry spirit of the deceased is most likely to be encountered—that the dancers, led by the most senior dancers, progressively approach throughout the ritual. Although some dancers perform purposeful walks rather than running actions in this phrase, they are distinct from the preparatory walking movements in being directed toward the central dancing area (see figure 4.3).

THE HALT

Before a dancer begins the stamping section, a halt (see figure 4.4) marks the end of the traveling phase of the dance, allowing the dancer to establish his placement in the space and to prepare his body for the nontraveling

Plate 4.3 Ambrose Piarlum at the end of the halt phrase, and just beginning the stamp phrase. (Photograph by Mark Crocombe.)

movements that will follow. Plate 4.3 shows Ambrose Piarlum at the end of the halt phrase, and just beginning the stamp phrase.

THE STAMP PHRASE

The stamp phrase is the phrase most characteristic of male *wangga* dances. Even if a dancer joins in late, toward the end of the dance section, he will always perform a stamp or two before the ending formula. Here the dancers stamp with alternate feet and raise the nonstamping leg high in preparation for its stamp (see figure 4.5). The dancers, performing vigorously in unison, raise clouds of dust, as can be seen in plate 4.4.

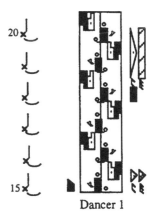

Figure 4.5 Labanotation of the stamp phrase

Plate 4.4 Frank Dumoo executing the stamp phrase. (Photograph by Mark Crocombe.)

THE ENDING PHRASE

The ending phrase marks the end of the dance sequence, which corresponds with the end of the instrumental section. It features an increase in the dynamics of the movements and the use of extended limbs, or the inclusion of additional body parts (see figure 4.6). The ending phrase will be discussed in more detail shortly. See also plate 4.5.

THE SEQUENCE OF DANCE PHRASES

On the evidence of the dancing at the Nadirri *burnim-rag* ceremony, and on the basis of my wider experience of dancing in a good many other contexts, it seems that the order of phrases in a dance sequence is fixed, as set out in table 4.3.[13]

As noted earlier, just as the instrumental section comprises

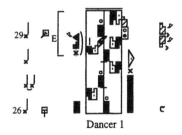

Figure 4.6 Labanotation of the ending phrase

Plate 4.5 Frank
Dumoo executing
the ending
phrase. (Photo-
graph by Mark
Crocombe.)

sections (A and A¹) that are variable in length and cueing patterns (B and B¹) that are fixed, so too does the sequence of dance phrases contain variable elements. The complete dance sequence WRHSE contains two subsequences of this type: the first of these is WRH, where W and R are highly variable in terms of the amount of time a dancer will spend on each, while H (the formula that terminates the first sequence) is more constrained in that it lasts from only one to three beats; the second sequence is SE, where the length of time spent on S is variable, while E, like H, occupies only one to three beats. In table 4.3, the more variable elements of the sequence appear in roman type, while those of a more constrained length are in boldface.

Table 4.3 Patterns of dance phrases

Nonfinal instrumental sections	W R **H** S **E**	R **H** S **E**
Final instrumental sections	W R **H** S **E**	

Table 4.4 Interrelationships between dance phrases and musical phrases

Nonfinal instrumental sections

Dance	W R **H** S	**E**	R **H** S	**E**
Clapsticks	A	**B**	A	**B**

Final instrumental sections

Dance	W R **H** S	**E**
Clapsticks	A¹	**B¹**

Table 4.5 Beginnings of dance phrase E for each beat of B (nonfinal)

Stick beat	♪♩.	♩	♪♩.	♩	♩	₇
Number of occurrences	3	2	36	19	19	1

How Are Dance Phrases Mapped onto the Clapstick Beating?

In table 4.4, the only point of exact coincidence between music and dance structures is where the cueing patterns in the music (B or B¹) coincide with the terminating formulas of the dance sequence (E), which they in fact cue. The elements of more fixed length are once again marked in boldface.

At the Nadirri *burnim-rag* ceremony, the preparatory walk (W) coincided with the beginning of the clapstick beats in only about half the dances performed. Dancers can, in fact, begin their movements onto the dance ground at any time during the clapstick beats, though the various options—ranging from treading impatiently on the spot before launching forward immediately the vocal section ends, to delaying entering the ground until the very last minute—are calculated to have maximum effect.

Neither the point at which the dancers change from a walk to a run (R) nor the point at which they perform the first terminating formula in the dance, the halt (H), interlocks in a precise way with the musical structure of A. Indeed, different dancers perform their halts at quite different times from one another. The halt appears to act more as a point of constraint among other unconstrained features rather than as a point around which specific vertical alignment with the music, and between dancers, occurs.

The point of most fixed coincidence occurs at the intersection of the musical cueing patterns (B and B¹) and the ending sequence of the dance (E). In a very high proportion of the dances performed for the *burnim-rag* ceremony at Nadirri (45 percent), the dancer began his final E pattern on the third beat of B (see table 4.5), and in a further 47.5 percent, the pattern began on either beat 4 or beat 5. The probable reason is that it takes two or more beats for the dancer to respond to the musician's cue. The few cases in which E begins before beat 3 may be accounted for by the fact that singers sometimes give visual cues to the dancers, such as lifting their clapsticks just before they play the cueing pattern.

Intriguingly, while the morphology of the musical terminating patterns B and B^1 is fixed, the morphology of the dance terminating pattern E is highly variable. Indeed, the variety of forms that E takes from dancer to dancer and from occasion to occasion points to an important feature of *wangga* dancing, namely, the high tolerance of individual idiosyncratic variation. There are clear individual variations in the type of actions included as endings and, to a certain extent, in the duration of endings. In the Nadirri performance, the first of the two main dancers, Frank Dumoo, typically used elaborate and sharp actions with extended limbs occurring over one or two beats, while the second dancer, Ambrose Piarlum, more often included a series of head movements with still limbs over three beats. Plate 4.5 shows Dumoo's typically flamboyant perform-ance of the terminating pattern.

Although I have not as yet spoken in terms of rhythmic modes when dis-cussing the instrumental sections, all nonfinal instrumental sections are, in fact, in rhythmic mode 5a, which consists of fast even clapstick beating in the range of around 128–40 beats per minute,[14] while all final instrumental sections are in rhythmic mode 5b, in which the rate of beating maintained by the main singer is, on average, twice that of fast even beating, namely, in the range of 250–85 clapstick beats per minute.[15] Irrespective of whether they are dancing to a final or a nonfinal instrumental section, however, the speed of the dancers' steps is the same, and for this reason they term both rhythmic mode 5a and rhythmic mode 5b "fast foot" (*tarzi verri*). In practice, two styles of *tarzi verri* dancing are performed: a more flamboyant style with a high degree of individual movement, such as the one analyzed earlier, and a more unisonal style adopted when a large group performs. Both styles conform to the same basic structure.

Unisonal dancing is the equivalent of unisonal singing. Since the 1960s, when the Walakandha *wangga* became the public form of song and dance associated with the Marri-tjevin, Marri-ammu, and Matige language groups at Wadeye, unisonal dancing has become an expression of group solidarity among the *wangga* mob. Observing a videotape of a performance of *wangga* at the 1988 Barunga Festival, in which dozens of men from Port Keats and Peppimenarti danced together, Frank Dumoo said, "Ma-ngalvu kuniny kununggu-purr ka-wurr" (a large mob of people stands up and dances). Here the unisonal dance, which was performed by a wider-than-usual range of language groups, was par-ticularly strong and powerful, representing a group solidarity that extended be-yond that normally expressed in performances of the Walakandha *wangga*. This was a public display of the strength of Daly culture presented to the many Ab-original groups assembled from Arnhem Land and central Australia, as well as to an audience of non-Aboriginal Australians that included the prime minis-ter.[16] Even on this occasion, however, there was some dancing in the solo style, as some older dancers emerged from the mob to enact their individual status as senior ceremonial performers in the Walakandha *wangga* tradition.

Observing a videotape of the more flamboyant performance analyzed here, Frank Dumoo said, "Ma-wangga-ngina [our dear *wangga* people] ma-tjitjuk kuniny [two men stand up] kununggu-purr-vini-djen [use two feet now]." That is, there were two dancers, and hence, by implication, a more soloistic style. This style is danced only by older men who have sufficiently high status and personal authority within the tradition.

Maminmangga's Song

In the spoken version of the death of the Rainbow Serpent that Stanner used as the basis for his transcription of the myth (see chapter 3), the narrator gives a little "performance" of Maminmangga's song in which the rhythm and pitch of the didjeridu, the rhythm and pitch of the text, and the clapstick beating are all articulated. Given its location within the narration of a myth that has already furnished us with important insights into the significance of *wangga*, we might expect the performance to offer some clues about the inherent meaning of these musical gestures. After all, this little enactment of a *wangga* is there not just to add color but also to support important themes. A realization of this performance is included as musical example 4.3.

The narrator indicates the pitch and rhythm of the didjeridu pattern used by Kunmanggurr by singing "Kidnork kidnork kidnork!" before his "performance" of the song.[17] That it is Kunmanggurr who plays the didjeridu articulates a fundamental association of the didjeridu with the Rainbow Serpent, which in turn extends to another set of associations related to the tone produced by the didjeridu and to conception beliefs. As already noted, rainbows are seen as manifestations of the water that Kunmanggurr spat through his didjeridu. The practice of spitting water through the didjeridu is employed almost universally in northern Australia, and the usual explanation is that it improves the tone of the instrument and makes it easier to play. Kunmanggurr's spit, moreover, not only improves the sound but is full of baby spirits (*ngarrith-ngarrith*). Thus the didjeridu is linked to fertility and new human life as it springs forth from Dreaming sites.

There is also a close association of the didjeridu and the Rainbow Serpent at Belyuen where the Belyuen water hole is the site of both the Rainbow Serpent and the Didjeridu (Kenbi) Dreaming. Stanner's accounts of a postcircumcision ritual washing of boys at Wadeye also associates the didjeridu with the Rainbow Serpent. According to Stanner, one or two weeks after circumcision, the initiated boy was immersed in a deep pool of water to the accompaniment of singing accompanied by didjeridu (1989, 117). Stanner was told that the playing of the didjeridu protected the boy by calming the Rainbow Serpent, and that the washing gave the boy a new skin that prevented the Rainbow Serpent from smelling him.

Like the actual performances examined in this chapter, the text of Maminmangga's song incorporates the two principles of text construction commonly found in *wangga*, namely, cyclic and through-composed text. The cyclic text (*kawandi kawandi*) is performed isorhythmically, as is normally the case with cyclical text. Stanner has suggested that Tjinimin's murder of the Rainbow Serpent represents the replacement of the cult of the Rainbow Serpent by the restricted men's cult that is now performed at Wadeye, and in view of this, it

Example 4.3 Maminmangga's *wangga*, transcribed from a tape recorded by Stanner in 1954, now cataloged at AIATSIS at 8195B

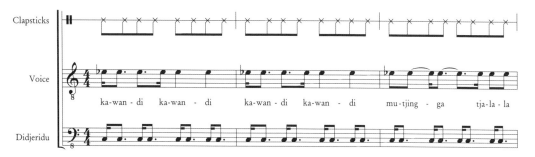

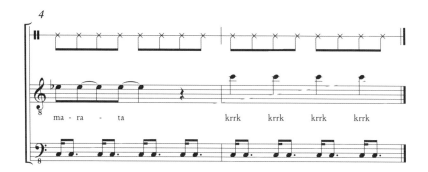

would not be unreasonable to assume that the use of isorhythm here evokes the isorhythm used in male cult singing. This view is supported by the fact that the Old Woman (*mutjingga*) who is the central figure of the men's cult is explicitly named in the second (through-composed) text phrase of the song (*mutjingga tjalala marata*).[18] The device normally adopted in *wangga* to enhance the articulation of text, namely, the lengthening of word-final syllables, is applied here to make "Old Woman" stand out clearly.

While the narrator produces this text rhythmically, it is not given full melodic definition, being sung on a single pitch a minor third above the pitch used to intone the didjeridu drone. The beating pattern is extremely rapid beating and seems to symbolize the frenetic dancing of Tjinimin as he gathers the enormous spiritual power required to execute his dangerous, world-shattering, and ultimately world-creating act of murder. In everyday ritual, the most highly energized dancing accompanies the most spiritually powerful and most dangerous phases of rituals, as, for example, at the point in *burnim-rag* ceremonies where senior dancers gather the power to engage most closely with the deceased by dancing on the filled-in fire pit.

Finally, the cries *krrk, krrk, krrk, krrk* on the upper tonic represent both the call of Maminmangga the Diving Duck and Tjinimin's dance calls. For an audience familiar with *wangga*, these cries resemble those made by singers and dancers in imitation of the Walakandha ancestors and represent themes of reciprocity and the interpenetration of worlds.

Even in this short, not fully realized song, then, certain musical elements emerge as having clear intrinsic associations—the didjeridu with the Rainbow Serpent, isorhythm with dangerous and powerful ceremonies, clapstick beating with dancing, dance calls with the ancestors—and these conventional associations are not only deployed in the context of myth but carried into ceremonial performance, where they form part of the semiotic bedrock on which signification rests.

chapter five

The Walakandha *Wangga*

This is the first of four chapters that will explore important repertories of *wangga*. The Walakandha *wangga*, which forms the focus of this chapter, is not only the strongest of the four traditions but also the youngest, having been established in the early 1960s as part of the reorganization of ritual life at Wadeyc. Here I will examine a number of songs in detail, beginning with "Truwu," the song from this repertory that was most frequently performed during the period of this study.[1] We will see that a number of conventions concerning the structure of song text, meter, rhythm, melody, and modality play an important role in establishing the Walakandha *wangga* as an identifiable corpus, a corpus with which not only the Marri-tjevin but also other members of the *wangga* mob— the Marri-ammu and Matige in particular—identify. The majority of songs in the Walakandha *wangga* repertory conform to one of two models: in the first, songs have through-composed texts made up of a core sentence surrounded by vocable and vocative formulas (group 1); in the second, two identical text phrases precede a third made up largely or entirely of vocables (group 2). A significant proportion of group 1 songs—for example, "Truwu"—have couplet texts (group 1A), while the remainder, like Phillip Mullumbuk's "Walakandha no. 4," have more than two text phrases (group 1B). There is a small number of songs (group 3) whose texts do not conform to either the group 1 or the group 2 model (see table 5.5). All but one song in the repertory use the highly distinctive pair of clapstick-beating patterns already encountered in the discussion of "Yendili no. 2" in the previous chapter. The facts that most songs—like "Yendili no. 2"—have unmeasured vocal sections that are reproduced almost identically from performance to performance, and that a single dance style is regularly used for all songs in the repertory, also create a sense of a unified corpus.

In the course of this chapter, we will see how some of the major themes identified with *wangga*—reciprocity, relationship to country, the articulation of identity—are played out not only in the text of songs but also within the musical fabric of individual performances. For example, the fact that "Truwu" can be sung to two related melodies, each of which is associated with a particular tract of country, allows the shifting relationships between different families of the Marri-tjevin group to be played out in performance. The relatively standard na-

Table 5.1 The Walakandha *wangga* repertory (1988–2000)

Song number	Title
1	Kubuwemi
2	Yendili no. 1
3	Yendili no. 2
4	Yendili no. 3
5	Yendili no. 4
6	Walakandha no. 1
7	Truwu
8	Nadirri
9	Yenmilhi
10	Mirrwana
11	Wutjeli
12	Walakandha no. 2
13	Walakandha no. 3
14	Karra Yeri Ngina
15	Walakandha no. 4
16	Walakandha no. 5
17	Kinyirr
18	Lhambumen
19	Yendili no. 5

ture of the musical and textual structures facilitates unisonal singing as an enactment of group solidarity, but when—as in the songs of Philip Mullumbuk—the musical features become so elaborate that strong unisonal singing is no longer possible, concerns arise about the ability of the repertory to act as the focus of concerted social action within a system of ceremonial reciprocity.

A full list of the nineteen songs on which the analysis in this chapter rests, that is, the corpus recorded between 1988 and 2000, is shown in table 5.1.[2] Recordings of these songs are listed in appendix table 1.1.[3]

"Truwu," the Most Popular of the Walakandha *Wangga*

In "Truwu," we hear the words of one of the Walakandha ancestors as he sings of his living descendants (whom—following reciprocal patterns of address—he calls "Walakandha") swimming in the surf at Truwu Beach near the settlement of Nadirri (see figure 1.1), while another Walakandha, a named ancestor called Munggum, stands watching them.[4]

> Walakandha! The sea stands up and crashes on them.
> Truwu! My country! Walakandha!

Munggum! He stands behind a beach hibiscus and peeps out.
Truwu! My country! Walakandha![5]

Several themes central to the Walakandha *wangga* repertory are evident here. One is the concern that Walakandha ancestors feel for their descendants. The sea, rearing up in the form of waves and crashing on the living Walakandha descendants, signifies the exigencies of life. "Truwu" was sung repeatedly at the 1988 *burnim-rag* ceremony, where it articulated a deep sense of ancestral sympathy for the living as they struggled to come to terms with the death of a close relative.

Country—the source of all life—and people's relationship to it are evoked in the calls "My country!" "Truwu!" Such calls, made by the song-giving Walakandha when he gave the song to its composer, are reproduced by living songmen such as Thomas Kungiung when they perform "Truwu" in ceremony. The sentient landscape hears and responds to the cries of both the living and the dead. Utterances of this type—calls to country, calls to the Walakandha dead, and calls to the living—are so frequent in the Walakandha *wangga* that they can be said to function as vocative text formulas.

"Truwu," then, expresses the essential connectedness of the Walakandha living and dead through song and ceremony, their mutual responsibilities to look after one another, their existential journey, the sentient nature of the land, and the intimate relationship that both the living and the dead have to country.

The Text Structure of "Truwu"

The form of the text—a couplet, with a strong degree of parallelism between the text-phrase pairs—is one commonly encountered in the Walakandha *wangga* repertory. The internal structure of each of the text phrases that make up the couplet in songs from group 1A follows a similar pattern (see table 5.2).

Table 5.2 **The text structure of "Truwu"**

Text phrase	Initial vocable	Initial vocative text formula	Core sentence	Concluding vocative text formulas
1	karra	walakan**dha**	pura**ngang** kuwa-vapa-vinya**nga**	tru**wu** nidin-ng**ina** walakan**dha**
	karra	*Walakandha!*	*The sea stands up and crashes on them.*	*Truwu ! My country! Walakandha!*
2	karra	mung**gum**	kimelha-guwa karrivirri**lhyi**	tru**wu** nidin-ng**ina** walakan**dha**
	karra	*Munggum!*	*He stands behind a beach hibiscus and peeps out.*	*Truwu! My country! Walakandha!*

Table 5.3 Vocative text formulas used in the Walakandha wangga (1988–2000)

Terms addressed to country (all place names except *nidin-ngina* and *purangang*)	*kubuwemi, kilili, ngumali, nidin-ngina* (my country), *rtidim, truwu, yendili, karila-yendili, yenmilhi, purangang* (the sea)
Terms addressed to Walakandha	*mana* (brother), *munggum, walakandha, wutjeli*
Terms addressed to the living	*ye-ngina/yeri-ngina* (my child/ren, my descendants)

They often begin with the untranslatable (and untranslated) vocable *karra*, which marks it as belonging to the ancestral dead. At the heart of each text phrase is a "core sentence," an utterance of a type that could stand alone in normal Marri-tjevin speech: "purangang kuwa-vapa-vinyanga" (The sea stands up and crashes on them) in text phrase 1, and "kimelha-guwa karrivirrilhyi" (He stands behind a beach hibiscus and peeps out) in text phrase 2. This core sentence is framed by vocative text formulas. In text phrase 1 the initial vocative text formula is *walakandha*, and in text phrase 2 it is *munggum* (the name of a Walakandha), while in both text phrase 1 and text phrase 2 the concluding vocative text formulas are *truwu* (Truwu Beach), *nidin-ngina* ("My country!"), and *walakandha*. A full list of these highly charged and oft-repeated calls to country, to named and unnamed Walakandha, and to living humans is shown in table 5.3.

Within the 1988–2000 sample, singers produce the text of all songs (including "Truwu") in a more or less identical form from performance to performance. Apart from occasional alteration of the final string of vocative text formulas—elements may be added, changed, or left out according to the judgment of the singer—there is little variation.

Meter and Rhythm in the Vocal Section of "Truwu"

As in the previously analyzed "Yendili no. 2" (see chapter 4), the vocal sections of "Truwu" are sung in rhythmic mode 1—the rhythmic mode characterized by an absence of clapstick beating—and are followed in the instrumental section by the standard Walakandha *wangga* clapstick-beating patterns already encountered in "Yendili no. 2."

Musical example 5.1 is a transcription of the voice and clapstick parts only of the first vocal section and instrumental section of a performance of "Truwu" recorded at the 1988 circumcision ceremony at Wadeye. The singers are Thomas Kungiung, Wagon Dumoo, and Martin Warrigal Kungiung. A performance of the whole song can be heard on the CD at track 5.

The text of "Truwu" is articulated using a delivery close to normal speech rhythm, and as is so often the case in *wangga*, there is strategic lengthening of final syllables to enhance the clarity of the text. In table 5.2, lengthened syllables are shown in boldface; syllables are regarded as long if—in transcription—they

Example 5.1 Vocal section 1 and instrumental section 1 of "Truwu," performed by Thomas Kungiung, Wagon Dumoo, and Martin Warrigal Kungiung (Mar88:39, ii)

are a crotchet or more in length. In "Truwu," the lengthening that is applied to the final syllables of all vocative text formulas and the final syllable of the core sentence is not applied to all internal word boundaries of the core sentence. While the word boundary between *purangang* and *kuwa-vapa-vinyanga* in text phrase 1 is marked, the boundary between *kimelha-guwa* and *karrivirrilhyi* in text phrase 2 is not. We will see shortly, with regard to a more-complex group 1 text, that the degree of lengthening that occurs in core sentences depends to a large degree on the complexity of the sentence.

In this performance the didjeridu (not transcribed) plays in a metrically free style with little or no coordination between the articulation of the text and that of the didjeridu.

The Melodic Structure of the Vocal Section of "Truwu"

The melody of "Truwu" transcribed in musical example 5.1 is little more than a straight pentatonic descent using the pitches C–B-flat–G–F–E-flat–C. As we will see in more detail shortly, this pentatonic form is extracted from one of two heptatonic modal series used in the Walakandha *wangga* repertory.

In "Truwu," the melodic contours of text phrases 1 and 2 are virtually identical. Indeed, singers say that they have the same tune. Because the two text phrases of "Truwu" have an identical structure, they can be mapped onto this "tune" in the same basic way. In each case, the initial vocable, initial vocative text formula, and core sentence are sung to the upper tetrachord (C–B-flat–G), while the concluding vocative text formulas are sung to the lower tetrachord (F–E-flat–C). This relatively straightforward type of relationship between text and melody is to be found in other songs of the Walakandha *wangga* repertory.[6]

In the transcribed performance, a fragment of the opening of the first text phrase (labeled "Lower-Octave Fragment") is repeated at the lower octave immediately before the instrumental section. This practice of adding lower-octave fragments at the end of a vocal section occurs in only two of the repertories examined in this study: the Walakandha *wangga* repertory and that of Bobby Lambudju Lane. Whereas Lambudju regularly adds a lower-octave fragment at the end of vocal sections, in the Walakandha *wangga* the practice is optional and is encountered relatively rarely. In the present performance, it occurs only in vocal section 1 and not in the two vocal sections that follow it (CD track 5).

Instrumental Sections

As already mentioned, the instrumental sections of "Truwu" use the same two clapstick-beating patterns as "Yendili no. 2." Indeed, these patterns are used for the instrumental sections of all but one of the Walakandha *wangga* songs and for this reason may be regarded as the "standard" Walakandha *wangga* clapstick-beating patterns. They are strongly emblematic of the repertory as a whole and stand as a musical identity marker not just for the Marri-tjevin but for all the Wadeye language groups that identify as members of the *wangga* mob. Approaching an as-yet-unseen ceremony through the bush, one can quickly and easily recognize a Walakandha *wangga* performance, even from a distance. The distinctive clapstick-beating patterns ring out loudly and clearly. The only song in the Walakandha *wangga* repertory that does not use these patterns is "Yenmilhi," the vocal sections and the instrumental sections of which are both in rhythmic mode 5a. I will discuss "Yenmilhi" shortly.

Modality, Melody, and Their Relationship to Song Lineage

Two modal series are used for the Walakandha *wangga* repertory: a "dorian" series (C–B-flat–A–G–F–E-flat–D–C) is used in eight of the nineteen pieces, and a "major" series (C–B–A–G–F–E–D–C) is used in the remaining eleven (see table 5.4).[7] The dorian series is strongly associated with lineages 2, 3, and 4, that is, the traditions carried by the Kungiung, Dumoo, and Kundjil families respectively (see chapter 2). All songs using the dorian modal series were composed by people belonging to these lineages.

The major modal series, on the other hand, is strongly associated with lineage 1. All six songs composed by Philip Mullumbuk use the major modal series, though not all songs using the major modal series are by Philip Mullumbuk: "Walakandha no. 2" is said to have been composed simultaneously by Thomas Kungiung and Terence Dumoo; "Yendili no. 2" was composed by Maudie Dumoo, the Marri-ngarr wife of Wagon Dumoo. It was her song that provided the model for "Yendili no. 3" and "Yendili no. 4," composed by Kundjil and Mullumbuk respectively. I do not know why "Walakandha no. 2" is not in the modal series normally associated with the Kungiung and Dumoo traditions, but I would suggest that the reason why "Yendili no. 2" uses the major modal series is in order to mark it as having emanated from outside the Dumoo patriline, that is, from an affine.

Some aspects of the relationship between the Mullumbuk lineage and the major mode are somewhat puzzling. An early recording (Rei74; see appendix table 1.1) reveals that songs composed by Philip's (now deceased) elder brother Stan—none of which are now sung by Philip, and none of which survive in the repertory under consideration—all use the dorian rather than the major series. By adopting the major modal series for his songs, Philip Mullumbuk seems to have set himself off not only from the Kungiung, Dumoo, and Kundjil lineages but also from the songs of his elder brother. The reasons why Philip has chosen to do so are not easy to determine, but this is clearly a matter of some sensitivity.

More conclusive observations can, however, be made with regard to the relationship between mode and lineage by examining a number of performances of "Truwu" in detail. Although songs share modal characteristics, which in turn link them to family traditions, many have an individual melody. Table 5.4, which sets out all the songs and their associated melodies for the Walakandha *wangga* repertory sung between 1988 and 2000, shows that four groups of songs share the same melody.[8] "Kubuwemi," "Yendili no. 1," and "Lhambumen" all use the Kubuwemi melody; "Nadirri" and "Walakandha no. 1" share the Nadirri melody (the significance of this was discussed in chapter 3); "Yendili no. 2," "Yendili no. 3," and "Yendili no. 4" all use the Yendili no. 2 melody; and four of Philip Mullumbuk's songs ("Karra Yeri Ngina," "Walakandha no. 3," "Walakandha no. 5," and "Kinyirr") share the Karra Yeri Ngina melody. Conversely, two songs are sung to two or more melodies. "Truwu," which is sung to the melodies Truwu A, Truwu B, and Truwu A/B, is one of these.[9]

When singing "Truwu" alone, or when leading a performance such as the one

Table 5.4 Melodies and modal series used in the vocal sections of Walakandha
wangga (1988–2000)

Melodies (dorian)	Songs	Lineage (Composer)
	Songs with a unique melody	
Wutjeli	Wutjeli	2 (Thomas Kungiung)
Yenmilhi	Yenmilhi	3 (John Dumoo)
Yendili no. 5	Yendili no. 5	3 (Wagon Dumoo)
	Songs that share a melody	
Kubuwemi	Kubuwemi	3 (Wagon Dumoo)
	Yendili no. 1	3 (Wagon Dumoo)
	Lhambumen	4 (Les Kundjil)
	Songs with two melodies	
Mirrwana A	Mirrwana	2 (Thomas Kungiung)
Mirrwana B		2 (Martin Warrigal Kungiung)
Truwu A	Truwu	2 (Thomas Kungiung)
Truwu B		4 (Les Kundjil)
Truwu A/B	Truwu	1/2/4 (Philip Mullumbuk, Thomas Kungiung, Les Kundjil)

Melodies (major)	Songs	
	Songs with a unique melody	
Walakandha no. 2	Walakandha no. 2	2/3 (Thomas Kungiung/Terence Dumoo)
Walakandha no. 4	Walakandha no. 4 (Berida and Munggumurri)	1 (Philip Mullumbuk)
	Songs that share a melody	
Nadirri	Nadirri	Unknown
	Walakandha no. 1	Unknown
Yendili no. 2	Yendili no. 2	3 (Maudie Dumoo)
	Yendili no. 3	4 (Les Kundjil)
	Yendili no. 4	1 (Philip Mullumbuk)
Karra Yeri Ngina	Karra Yeri Ngina	1 (Philip Mullumbuk)
	Walakandha no. 3	1 (Philip Mullumbuk)
	Walakandha no. 5	1 (Philip Mullumbuk)
	Kinyirr	1 (Philip Mullumbuk)

transcribed in musical example 5.1, Thomas Kungiung always used the pentatonic form of the melody shown in musical example 5.1, namely, the descending pitch series C–B-flat–G–F–E-flat–C. I call this version of the melody "Truwu A."

Les Kundjil of lineage 4, on the other hand, consistently used a different pentatonic form of the melody, which comprises the pitches C–A–G–F–D–C. This melody, which I call "Truwu B," is shown in musical example 5.2 and can be heard on track 6 of the CD.

Both forms of the melody may be derived from the heptatonic dorian modal series, but each in a different way. As musical example 5.3 shows, the dorian modal series can be analyzed as falling into two parallel tetrachords based on G and C respectively; these are indicated by brackets in musical example 5.3. Truwu A omits the second degree of each tetrachord (A and D), thus preserving the parallelism between the tetrachords. Truwu B also maintains balanced tetrachords, but by omitting the third degree of each (B-flat and E-flat).

What, then, is the significance of these two melodies? The Truwu A melody is associated with Marri-tjevin country on the coast, in the vicinity of Truwu

Example 5.2 "Truwu B" as sung by Les Kundjil of lineage 4 (Mar98:15, xii, vocal section 1)

Example 5.3. The derivation of two contrasting pentatonic series from the same heptatonic dorian series

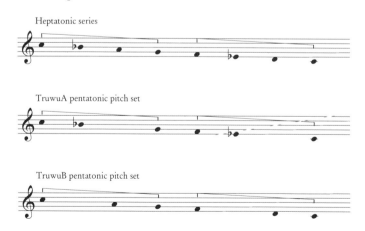

Beach, the area traditionally associated with the Kungiung, Berida, and Mullumbuk families and nowadays also with the Dumoo family (see chapter 2). Truwu B, on the other hand, is regarded as the inland melody, the form associated with the area of Kundjil's principal Dreaming sites. In the very small repertory of five songs that he was singing in the period 1998–2000, three were specifically related to inland sites, namely, "Yendili no. 3," "Yenmilhi," and "Lhambumen" (see figure 1.1). We might interpret this as follows: the common dorian basis of the two melodies is emblematic of commonalities of interest between the two Marri-tjevin men, Kungiung and Kundjil, while the contrasting pentatonic forms represent separate affiliations to different areas of Marri-tjevin country. In the past these might have been associated with different Marri-tjevin clans (see Falkenberg 1962, chap. 11).

In performance, this conventional association of melody with place provides the basis for considerable expressive potential. When the two singers sing the melodies together, a struggle for one melody to dominate the other may erupt, leading either to melodic disagreement or to the silencing of one of the singers. In such a case, volume and persistence are essential for one singer to dominate the other. Similar scenarios emerged in the conflict between men's and women's versions of a Central Australian song series discussed by Linda Barwick (1995) (see introduction). In that case, different ways of fitting texts to melodies also led to melodic disagreements. In my experience, melodic tensions are quickly resolved in *wangga*, either by both singers adopting one or other forms of the melody or by a melodic compromise being reached.

The strength of feeling that can be generated with regard to these melodies was demonstrated to me in 2003, however, when Kungiung's adult daughter exploded angrily when I sang the Truwu B melody to her. She told me that this tune was simply wrong—*mandhi wundjeni* (literally "a bad melody")—and not an alternative at all. I was instructed never again to sing "Truwu" to that melody.

In 1992 Thomas Kungiung and Les Kundjil were singing together at a circumcision ceremony at Wadeye (CD track 7). On this occasion, each singer held to his own form of the melody, Truwu A or Truwu B, when singing alone, but when singing together, they acted to minimize the differences between the two melodies. This was done by reintroducing the notes that are normally omitted in each of their pentatonic forms, thus re-creating the heptatonic form of the melody, which I call Truwu A/B and have transcribed as musical example 5.4.

Here the distinction between the two forms of the upper tetrachord, one of which omits the A, and the other the B-flat, is blurred by the inclusion of both these notes. Kundjil, moreover, omits the conspicuous A–C–A oscillation on the word *purangang* from the A/B form of the melody, since this would emphasize the contrast between his and Kungiung's versions. When the melody gets to the lower tetrachord, both singers again use all four notes, so that the contrast between the two pentatonic versions is again minimized.

But these matters extend beyond lineage 2 (Kungiung's lineage) and lineage 4 (Kundjil's lineage) to the Mullumbuk lineage (lineage 1). "Truwu" is the only Kungiung/Dumoo song included in Philip Mullumbuk's repertory. Given the

Example 5.4 Truwu A/B as performed by Thomas Kungiung and Les Kundjil together (Eni92, viii, vocal section 1)

Example 5.5. Philip Mullumbuk's version of "Truwu" (Mar99:4, iv, vocal section 1)

close association of Truwu Beach with the Mullumbuk family, and the fact that the named Walakandha Munggum was one of Mullumbuk's patrilineal ancestors, his "grandfather" (father's father's brother), it is not altogether surprising that he performs this song. In the late 1990s, I recorded Mullumbuk singing "Truwu" both with Les Kundjil and alone. In both circumstances he used only the Truwu A/B form of the melody, thus keeping alive—as it were—the primary association with the composer, Kungiung (who by that time had passed away), while at the same time acknowledging Kundjil's authority over the song as a more senior Marri-tjevin singer. This was an important strategy in minimizing any conflict that might have arisen between the more senior but less accomplished singer, Kundjil, and the highly talented but junior Mullumbuk. This is the only song that Mullumbuk sings that does not use the major modal series.

In this performance (CD track 8), Mullumbuk nonetheless articulates his right to song by marking it with features of his own flamboyant style, like the flourish at the end of the melody (see musical example 5.5). He also sometimes adds a small textual modification (this does not occur in musical example 5.5)—the introduction of the word *devin* (alone)—into the first text phrase, thus "karra walakandha purangang devin kuwa-vapa-vinyanga." This seems to reflect his preference for longer and more complex texts.

Table 5.5 The Walakandha *wangga* repertory subdivided on the basis of text structure

Group	Songs
1A	"Truwu," "Wutjeli," "Walakandha no. 2," "Walakandha no. 3," "Walakandha no. 5," "Kinyirr"
1B	"Karra Yeri Ngina," "Walakandha no. 4"
2A	"Yendili no. 2," "Yendili no. 3," "Yendili no. 4"
2B	"Kubuwemi," "Yendili no. 1," "Lhambumen"
3	"Mirrwana," "Yendili no. 5," "Walakandha no. 1," "Nadirri, "Yenmilhi"

Text Structure and Melody

In all there are eight songs that—like "Truwu"—are made up entirely of through-composed texts whose text phrases comprise a core sentence framed by vocable text formulas. As noted at the beginning of this chapter, I have designated songs of this type "group 1." The texts of six of the eight songs in this group are in couplet form (group 1A), while two comprise a larger number of text phrases (group 1B). These are set out in table 5.5.

A second major principle of text construction is found in a further six songs in the repertory, designated "group 2," an example of which—"Yendili no. 2"—I examined in the previous chapter. In group 2 songs, two identical text phrases are followed by a third, which largely or entirely comprises vocable text. The first two text phrases are always set to the same melodic contour. Like group 1, group 2 can also be subdivided into two subsets: the three songs in each subset are closely modeled on each other, as we will see in more detail shortly.

A number of other text structures, none of which conform to groups 1 or 2, occur in five songs, and these are designated "group 3." Apart from "Yenmilhi"—which is of interest because of its use of a rhythmic mode that is unique among songs in the Walakandha *wangga* repertory—songs from this group will not be discussed in detail.

Having already examined an example of group 1A in "Truwu," I will now move on to examine each of the other groups, beginning with an example from group 1B.

Philip Mullumbuk's Song about the Walakandha Ancestors Berida and Munggumurri: A Group 1B Song

Philip Mullumbuk's beautiful song about the Walakandha ancestors Berida and Munggumurri ("Walakandha no. 4") has a five-text-phrase structure rather than the couplet form found in group 1A. Moreover, most of the text phrases are longer and more complex than the sentences encountered in "Truwu."

Here a Walakandha stands beside a beach hibiscus and sings while two other

Walakandha, Berida and Munggumurri (Mullumbuk's grandfather), look backward over their shoulders at the flat top of Yendili Hill, where the trees and grasses are standing up like hairs on the back of the neck in response to a death. In the final text phrase, the Walakandha sings of the nonfinality of death: "as a matter of inevitability, it [the tide] is always coming in on us."

Because of the greater complexity of the core sentences in each text phrase, none has all the elements of the "*karra* + initial vocative text formula + core sentence + concluding vocative text formulas" structure found in group 1A songs like "Truwu." Four of the five text phrases contain an initial vocative text formula, but only one has a concluding vocative text formula. Only three of the five begin with *karra*. Nonetheless, as table 5.6 shows, the formal structure of Mullumbuk's text can be read as an elaboration of the text structure found in "Truwu": some structural elements have been omitted, while others—in particular the core sentence—have been expanded. In creating such a structure, Mullumbuk both draws on and extends the model encountered in group 1A.

The greater complexity of the core sentence, and, in one case, of the initial

Table 5.6 The text of Philip Mullumbuk's song "Walakandha no. 4" (Berida and Munggumurri)

Text Phrase	Initial vocable	Initial vocative text formula	Core sentence	Concluding vocative text formula
1	karra	walakandha	ngindji kimi-ninanga-wu**rri** kavulh na karrivirri**lhyi**	
	karra	*Walakandha!*	*One is singing to me as he stands at the beach hibiscus.*	
2	ka**rra**	berri**da** munggumu**rri**	kunya-nin-viyi-ninanga-vini-wu**rri**	
	karra	*Berida! Munggumurri!*	*They stand and look toward the top.*	
3	ka**rra**		wandhi wandhi kiminy-gimi-vi**ni** ku**nya**	
	karra		*They stand and look back.*	
4		karrila-yendili	kuwa-thet-viyi-ngangga -wu**rri**	mana
		Yendili Hill!	*The top is standing upright toward me*	*Brother!*
5		pura**ngang**	kavulh nyinanga-wu**rri**	
		The tide!	*As a matter of inevitability, it is always coming in on us.*	

vocative text formula, requires that the word boundaries be more clearly articulated in order to maintain comprehensibility. For this reason there is a slightly increased tendency for sentence-medial word-final syllables to be lengthened (these are marked in boldface in table 5.6). The sheer complexity of this, and other texts in his repertory, however, makes Mullumbuk's songs difficult for other singers to grasp. This may be one of the reasons why, even as late as 2000, Mullumbuk's songs were not as frequently performed as those of the other lineages. The simple fact of the matter is that none of the other *wangga* singers now living at Wadeye are able to master these songs, leaving Mullumbuk with no backup singer.

As can be heard on CD track 9, these difficulties extend to other aspects of performance. As is typical of Mullumbuk's songs, the melody uses a major, rather than a dorian, pitch series. Mullumbuk's melodies tend, moreover, to be more highly decorated and more flexible than those of other singers in the tradition. They are delivered with a sinuous and flexible voice that is capable of executing elaborate flourishes. As was the case with text structure, melodic structure, while conforming to well-established models, takes them to new levels of complexity. As was the case with text structure, the melody broadly follows the pattern established for "Truwu" but expands it and makes it more elaborate. Instead of each of the first two melodic sections taking one text phrase—as was the case in "Truwu"—in "Walakandha no. 4" each melodic section takes two text phrases. Because of the large amount of text to be sung, each of these melodic sections must be divided into two melodic subsections by a breath, so that each text phrase is in fact set to one melodic subsection. An even greater degree of structural complexity is produced by the addition of a third melodic section.

By using the major mode, singing in a highly individualistic vocal style, and composing texts and melodic structures that are far more elaborate than those found elsewhere in the Walakandha *wangga* repertory, Mullumbuk sets himself apart from other members of the tradition. The fact that the song is about one of Mullumbuk's own ancestors only reinforces this. The *wangga* tradition as a whole is not averse to complexity in performance or to individual singers rising to high levels of virtuosity—as is evidenced by singers such as Barrtjap, or by any number of historical recordings—but the particular history of the Walakandha *wangga* has inhibited such developments. Because this repertory was formed explicitly to unify a number of different language groups into one of the three companies or "mobs" that provide the basis of the tripartite system of ceremonial reciprocity at Wadeye, degrees of virtuosity that place songs beyond the range of average singers are problematic. There is little doubt that Mullumbuk is the heir to the Walakandha *wangga* tradition, but at the same time, his departure from the established models that allow strong unisonal singing weakens the potential for his songs to act as the focus of concerted ceremonial action. At the time of this writing, his position was still somewhat marginal, and the future of his repertory was difficult to predict.

Group 2A Songs: "Yendili no. 2" and Two Songs That Are Based on It

Group 2A songs, the texts of which are set out in table 5.7, are all about one important site, Yendili Hill. The original model for these songs was "Yendili no. 2," the song composed by Wagon Dumoo's Marri-ngarr wife, Maudie Dumoo, the ceremonial usage of which was discussed in chapter 3 and the structure of which was discussed in detail in chapter 4. As can be seen from table 5.7, the text structures of Philip Mullumbuk's "Yendili no. 4" and Les Kundjil's "Yendili no. 3" fol-

Table 5.7 Group 2A: An original song by Maudie Dumoo ("Yendili no. 2") and two other songs based on it ("Yendili no. 3," "Yendili no. 4")

Song title	Text phrase	Initial vocable	Initial vocative text formula	Core sentence	Concluding vocative text formulas
Yendili no. 2 (Maudie Dumoo)	1	karra *karra*	yendili yend**ili** *Yendili! Yendili!*	arr-girrit-**ni** *Look after it!*	
	2	karra *karra*	ycndili yend**ili** *Yendili! Yendili!*	arr-girrit-**ni** *Look after it!*	
	3	**aa** *aa*			ye-ng**ina** *My descendants!*
Yendili no. 4 (Philip Mullumbuk)	1	karra *karra*	yendili yend**ili** *Yendili! Yendili!*	ngirrin-**ni** *We all have to go there.*	
	2	karra *karra*	yendili yend**ili** *Yendili! Yendili!*	ngirrin-**ni** *We all have to go there.*	
	3	**aa** *aa*			nidin-ng**ina** *My country!*
Yendili no. 3 (Les Kundjil)	1	karra *karra*	yendili yend**ili** *Yendili! Yendili!*		karra ma**na** nidin-ng**ina** *karra Brother! My country!*
	2	karra *karra*	yendili yend**ili** *Yendili! Yendili!*		karra ma**na** nidin-ng**ina** *karra Brother! My country!*
	3	**aa** *aa*			karra ma**na** nidin-ng**ina** *karra Brother! My country!*

low that of Maudie Dumoo's original, Mullumbuk's version more closely than Kundjil's.

In both "Yendili no. 2" and "Yendili no. 4," text phrases 1 and 2 comprise an initial vocable *karra*, an initial vocative text formula *yendili yendili*, and a core sentence: *arr-girrit-ni* (Look after it!) in "Yendili no. 2," and *ngirrin-ni* (We all have to go there) in "Yendili no. 4." There is no concluding vocative text formula for text phrases 1 and 2 in either song.

"Yendili no. 3" starts out in the same way but omits the core sentence and moves directly to a pair of concluding vocative text formulas, *mana* (brother) and *nidin-ngina* (my country), which is preceded by *karra*, almost as if it were a new text phrase (which it clearly is not). This is a unique structure within the Walakandha *wangga* and may in fact reflect a weakness in Kundjil's understanding of Marri-tjevin compositional principles. As we will see in the following chapter, Maurice Ngulkur appears to make reference to this odd serial construction in the performance of his composition "Walakandha Ngindji." In all three songs, text phrase 3 consists of the initial vocable *aa*, sung to a melisma, followed by one or more vocative text formulas.

All songs in this group have unmeasured vocal sections, and the pattern of rhythmic prolongation follows that described for "Yendili no. 2": the final syllables of the initial vocable, core sentence, and concluding vocative text formula are all lengthened. In all cases, the instrumental sections follow the same pattern as was described for "Yendili no. 2" in the previous chapter.

The three songs also have very similar melodies. Although clearly related, the melodies of "Yendili no. 2" and "Yendili no. 4" are sufficiently distinctive for them to have become sites of contestation. In attempting to deny any relationship between "Yendili no. 2" and Mullumbuk's lineage, a senior member of the Dumoo family told me categorically that "Yendili no. 2" does not have the same melody as "Yendili no. 4," even though most people, including the composer, would say that it does. The association, through melody, of items from these two lineages clearly causes a degree of discomfort, as does the fact that Mullumbuk took as his model one of the two songs from the Dumoo lineage that uses the major mode that he himself uses for most of his songs.

Group 2B Songs: Three Further Group 2 Songs with Related Texts

Group 2B songs, the texts of which are set out in table 5.8, follow a similar form to those in group 2A. In the first two text phrases of each song, the initial vocable *karra* is followed by a vocative text formula, which in each case is a place name: Kubuwemi, Yendili, or Lhambumen (see figure 1.1). This is followed by the core sentence *kimi-wurri kavulh* (he always sings to me) or *kimi-wurri* (he sings to me). Both forms of the sentence are in fact a truncation of the full form of the sentence *kimi-wurri kavulh-a* (he *has* always sung to me), which is the form always given when a spoken form of the text is elicited. The meanings of these texts are "He sings/he always sings/he has always sung 'Kubuwemi'/'Yendili'/'Lhambumen' to me." "He" in this case is understood to be a song-giving Walakandha.

Table 5.8 Group 2B: Three further group 2 songs with related texts

Song title	Text phrase	Initial vocable	Vocative text formula	Core sentence
Kubuwemi	1	**karra**	kubuwe**mi**	kimi-wurri kavulh
		karra	*"Kubuwemi!"*	*He always sings to me.*
	2	**karra**	kubuwe**mi**	kimi-wurri kavulh
		karra	*"Kubuwemi!"*	*He always sings to me.*
	3	**aa**		
		aa		
Yendili no. 1	1	**karra**	yendi**li**	kimi-wurri kavulh
		karra	*"Yendili!"*	*He always sings to me.*
	2	**karra**	yendi**li**	kimi-wurri kavulh
		karra	*"Yendili!"*	*He always sings to me.*
	3	**aa**		
		aa		
Lhambumen	1	ka**rra**	lhambumen lhambu**men**	kimi-wurri
		karra	*"Lhambumen! Lhambumen!"*	*He sings to me.*
	2	ka**rra**	lhambumen lhambu**men**	kimi-wurri
		karra	*"Lhambumen! Lhambumen!"*	*He sings to me.*
	3	**aa**		
		aa		

Whereas the vocal sections of all three songs in group 2A are sung in rhythmic mode 1, the vocal sections of group 2B songs are sung in a mixture of rhythmic mode 2 (text phrases 1 and 2) and rhythmic mode 1 (text phrase 3). Rhythmic mode 2, which we have not previously encountered, is characterized by slow even beating in the range of 55–65 clapstick beats per minute. A full list of all the rhythmic modes used in the *wangga* repertories is set out in chapter 9 (see table 9.1).

As can be seen from musical example 5.6, the rhythmic setting of the "Kubuwemi" text in rhythmic mode 2 is complex. The first two beats of this short text articulate duple subdivisions of the beat, the third beat is divided into sextuplets, and the fourth beat is left empty. But the most striking feature of text phrases 1 and 2 is the way that the truncation of the full text just referred to is highlighted by an abrupt halt in the rhythm.[10] So striking is this gesture that Maurice Ngulkur was able to use it in his own Ma-yawa *wangga* composition to evoke Marri-tjevin musical practice and identity. The sense of incompleteness that pervades the text and the rhythmic setting is in turn supported by the melody. Melodic sections 1 and 2 do not descend to the tonic but remain suspended on the secondary tonic, G. A recording of "Kubuwemi" can be heard on track 10 of the CD.

Example 5.6 "Kubuwemi" (Mar88:42, viii, vocal section 1)

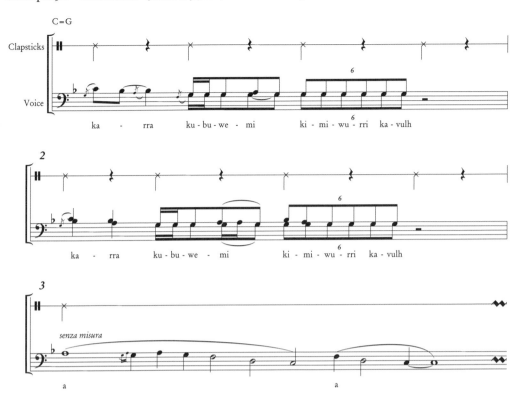

"Yenmilhi": A Song from Group 3

The textual, rhythmic, and melodic structures that have emerged in the study of
groups 1 and 2 are clearly the most representative, but they are not the only
ones. "Yenmilhi," a song from the miscellaneous group, is an important song,
not only by virtue of its association with John Dumoo, who was an important
figure in the creation of the Walakandha *wangga*, but also because it contains
one of our most vivid accounts of the interaction between the living and the
dead. The text of "Yenmilhi" articulates the words of a group of Walakandha
calling the singer away to ceremony: "Brother! Let's all go now, let's all go now.
Pelhi [a ceremony ground] is there, there behind Yenmilhi Hill. Brother! There
are clapsticks for us all. Come with us!"

While the text of "Yenmilhi," which is set out in table 5.9, is basically
through-composed, it does not follow the "vocative text phrase + core sentence
+ vocative text phrase" structure typical of group 1 songs. Rather, its text simply
strings together a series of short text phrases. Although this serial construction
of text occurs in no other Walakandha *wangga* song, it is found in other *wangga*
repertories, albeit rarely. We find it once in the Ma-yawa *wangga*—in the song

Table 5.9 The text of "Yenmilhi"

Text phrase	Text
1	karra ma**na**
	karra Brother!
2	ngumbun-nim djeni ngumbun-nim dje**ni**
	Let's all go now, let's all go now.
3	pelhi yi-dha wandhi yi-dha yi-dha yenmi**lhi**
	Pelhi is there, there behind Yenmilhi Hill.
4	mana tittil kuwa ngangga-**nim**
	Brother, there are clapsticks for us all.
5	djindja-wu**rri**
	Come with us!
6	**e**
	e

"Watjen Danggi" (Dingo) (see chapter 6)—and once in Barrtjap's repertory—in "Be Bangany-nyaya" (see chapter 7).

It is not only the text structure of "Yenmilhi" that is unusual, but also the rhythmic mode in which it is performed. While rhythmic mode 5a (fast even beating) is regularly used for the nonfinal forms of the standard clapstick-beating pattern used in instrumental sections, "Yenmilhi" is the only song in the Walakandha *wangga* repertory that uses even clapstick beating to accompany singing. It is not insignificant that even clapstick beating occurs in only two other songs in my sample, and that these are the same two songs just identified as having serially constructed texts, namely, "Watjen Danggi" from the Ma-yawa *wangga* repertory, and "Be Bangany-nyaya" from Barrtjap's repertory. In "Be Bangany-nyaya," as in "Yenmilhi," the even beating occurs in the fast tempo band, while in the case of "Watjen Danggi" it occurs in the moderate tempo band.[11] Might these three songs be considered to constitute a group—but a group distributed across three different repertories?

Because even clapstick beating is unable in itself to imply meter, all three songs rely on the rhythmic setting of the text to create a sense of meter. In the case of "Yenmilhi," this meter is not entirely regular. While there is a predominance of compound triple meter, it is regularly disrupted by the long prolongations that mark the end of the melodic sections. As a result, the meter of this song feels somewhat irregular, with both compound triple and quadruple groupings emerging at different points. Compound quadruple meter is particularly strong at the beginning and end of vocal sections, and this is reinforced by

Example 5.7 "Yenmilhi" (Mar88:54, iii, vocal section 1 and instrumental section 1)

the quadruple feel of the cueing pattern played by the clapsticks (marked in musical example 5.7) at the end of the instrumental section immediately before the commencement of the new vocal section. It is noteworthy that in "Be Banganynyaya," vocal sections are similarly polymetric (see chapter 7). A recording of "Yenmilhi" can be heard on track 11 of the CD.

Before leaving this song, let me comment briefly on melodic structure and its relationship to the text. As musical example 5.7 shows, the first melodic section takes the first two text phrases, and the third takes the sixth (a vocable sung to a melisma). Overall, this melodic structure reflects that of the text: the text sung to the first melodic section sets up the proposition "Let's all go now," and the second gives the detail of where and why we are going.

Rhythmic Mode and Dance

Only four rhythmic modes are used in the Walakandha *wangga* repertory recorded between 1988 and 2000, of which three are measured and one unmeasured: rhythmic modes 1, 2, and 5a are used in vocal sections (see table 5.10); rhythmic modes 5a and 5b are used in instrumental sections.

As table 5.10 shows, the vast majority of Walakandha *wangga* (fifteen of the nineteen songs) have unmeasured vocal sections, while in only four songs are the vocal sections measured. The unmeasured vocal sections are all performed in rhythmic mode 1. The two modes used for measured vocal sections are rhythmic mode 2 (slow even, which the Marri-tjevin refer to as *darabu*, "slow") and rhythmic mode 5a (fast even, which the Marri-tjevin call *tarzi verri*, "fast foot"). Compared with other *wangga* repertories, this is an unusually high proportion of unmeasured songs and an unusually limited number of rhythmic modes.

I have already observed that the Walakandha *wangga* is characterized by the use of one form of dance to fit all songs. There is no problem with this so long as songs conform to the model of an unmeasured vocal section followed by the standard beating patterns. But what happens when, as in the group 2B songs, rhythmic mode 2 is used, or when, as in "Yenmilhi," rhythmic mode 5a is used?

Table 5.10 Rhythmic modes used in vocal sections of the Walakandha *wangga* (1988–2000)

Clapstick beating	Mode number	Number of songs
Unmeasured		
Without clapsticks (*ambi tittil*)	1	15
Measured		
Slow even (*darabu*) (mm 55–65)	2 (even)	3 (group 2B songs)
Fast even (*tarzi verri*) mm 133–42	5a (even)	1 ("Yenmilhi")
Total		19

When dance is performed to songs in group 2B, most dancers treat the vocal section as if it were in rhythmic mode 1; that is, they perform unstructured mimetic movements. The beating is, after all, rather slow, and the vocal section becomes unmeasured when it moves to its final melodic section. During the slow beating, however, older dancers may sometimes be observed performing slow stamping motions, a style of dance that has, for all intents and purposes, become obsolete.

Because the final melodic section is unmeasured in group 2B songs, the transition between vocal section and instrumental section is identical to that in the majority of Walakandha *wangga* songs. Group 2 songs therefore present no problem to the dancers. Dancers perform as described for "Yendili no. 2" in chapter 2.

The clapstick beating used in the instrumental sections of "Yenmilhi," while in the same tempo band as the standard Walakandha *wangga* clapstick-beating pattern, has some significant differences. The fact that it remains unchanged from vocal section to instrumental sections, and the fact that it does not move to fast doubled clapstick beating in the final section, must surely affect the dance. Unfortunately I have never seen "Yenmilhi" danced, but senior dancers tell me that the young men find anything other than the standard clapstick-beating pattern very difficult to deal with.

During the period 1988–2000, every song in the Walakandha *wangga* repertory was performed in one, and only one, rhythmic-modal setting. "Truwu" was always sung in rhythmic mode 1, as was "Yendili no. 2." "Yenmilhi" was always sung to rhythmic mode 5a, and "Kubuwemi" was always sung to a mixture of rhythmic modes 1 and 2. That this was not always the case is shown by two historical recordings.

It is clear from a recording of Stan Mullumbuk performing at a circumcision ceremony in 1974 (listed as Rei74 in appendix table 1.1) that Mullumbuk frequently performed the same song in two different rhythmic modes. Senior performers today confirm that this was the case and characterize Mullumbuk's practice in this regard as "old-fashioned." In a further recording of unknown date or recordist (listed as Anon. n.d. in appendix table 1.1), Thomas Kungiung demonstrates how a song may be set to a number of different rhythmic modes. On hearing this recording, Frank Dumoo told me that in the early days of the Walakandha *wangga* repertory, it was a common practice for singers to vary songs in this way, even during ceremonies. The reason why songs are no longer sung in multiple rhythmic modes is clearly related to the reason why only one style of dance is used; namely, because this repertory of *wangga* was established expressly to unite the language groups associated with it, issues of performability overrode all other considerations. There was little incentive to maintain a complex rhythmic modal practice if dancers could not maintain the associated dance styles (see chapter 9).

Another indication of a profound shift in dance practice comes from an examination of the clapstick-beating patterns used in the earlier recordings. Here the clapstick-beating patterns (A + B; A¹ + B¹) that today function as key markers of a group identity centered on the Walakandha *wangga* were nowhere to be heard. A quite different pattern was used by Stan Mullumbuk for nonfinal instrumental sections. This involved a series of fast doubled beats (sometimes with interlocking), followed by five fast beats, followed by the same concluding formula (underlined) as used now: . According to senior performers alive today, this "old-fashioned" pattern required a markedly different style of dancing.

In the recording of unknown date or recordist previously mentioned, Thomas Kungiung also introduces a number of patterns that are no longer used (including a version of the one just described for Stan Mullumbuk). Some older men and women still remember how to dance to nonstandard clapstick-beating patterns such as these, but their knowledge is essentially passive, since no one performs songs in those modes today, and younger dancers have no knowledge of them at all.

◈

In the next chapter, we encounter a tradition that tolerates a far higher degree of variability than does the Walakandha *wangga*, namely, the Ma-yawa *wangga*. The Ma-yawa *wangga* stands in a quite different relationship to the ceremonial practice of Wadeye from the Walakandha *wangga*. We will see how the Marriammu singer Maurice Ngulkur uses performance to explore his own relationship to the Walakandha *wangga*, and how, through his manipulation of musical and textual structures, he enacts complex patterns of competing interests.

chapter six

The Ma-yawa *Wangga*

Compared with the Walakandha *wangga*, the Ma-yawa *wangga* is only rarely heard and is already on the verge of extinction. Between 1988 and 2000, only one singer, Maurice Ngulkur, performed this repertory, and he passed away in November 2001. In the months before Ngulkur's death, Colin Worumbu Ferguson attempted to learn some of Ngulkur's songs, but I have yet to hear him perform them. Whether they will emerge as part of Ferguson's repertory (which already contains Walakandha *wangga* songs, as well as songs from a number of Belyuen traditions), and if so, in what form, remains to be seen.

Ngulkur's repertory comprised only twelve songs. Together with the song "Malhimanyirr no. 2," sung nowadays at Kununurra but not at Wadeye, this makes up the total surviving repertory for the Ma-yawa *wangga*.[1] "Malhimanyirr no. 2" is not included in the following analyses but will be discussed in chapter 10. All but the first song, "Walakandha Ngindji," in table 6.1 were composed by Charlie Niwilhi Brinken, a senior Marri-ammu ceremonial leader who died in the early 1990s—the same Charlie Brinken who made the painting of Old Man Tulh that I explored in chapter 1. "Walakandha Ngindji" is the only Ma-yawa *wangga* song composed by Ngulkur, and it will provide the main focus of this chapter.

Although Ngulkur performed this relatively small repertory only rarely, it nonetheless provides important insights into a number of issues central to this book, in particular the ways in which individual *wangga* performances may reflect the relationship a singer has with his Dreamings (*ngirrwat*) and Dreaming sites (*kigatiya*). In its emphasis on Dreamings and Dreaming sites, and in certain other dimensions of its musical practice, the Ma-yawa *wangga* repertory represents a praxis that is older than that of the Walakandha *wangga*. Having been supplanted by the Walakandha *wangga* as the main *wangga* repertory at Wadeye, the Ma-yawa *wangga* is no longer constrained by the social forces that apply to the Walakandha *wangga*. For this reason, a number of the features that have disappeared from Walakandha *wangga* practice in recent times—in particular, the ability to perform individual songs in a variety of rhythmic modes—have been

Table 6.1 The Ma-yawa *wangga* repertory

Song number	Title	Number of recorded items
1	"Walakandha Ngindji" (One Walakandha)	3
2	"Wulumen Kimigimi" (Old Man [Ma-yawa] Dreaming)	2
3	"Rtadi-wunbirri" (Place name: Ma-yawa Dreaming site)	4
4	"Menggani" (Place name: Butterfly Dreaming site)	2
5	"Tjerri" (Sea Breeze Dreaming)	2
6	"Watjen Danggi" (Dingo)	2
7	"Malhimanyirr no. 1" (Jungle Fowl Dreaming)	2
8	"Ma-vindivindi" (Old Man [Ma-yawa] Dreaming)	2
9	"Karri-ngindji" (Place name: Ma-yawa Dreaming site)	2
10	"Thalhi-ngatjpirr" (Place name: Fish Dreaming site)	2
11	"Na-pebel" (Place name)	3
12	"Wulumen Tulh" (Old Man Tulh Dreaming)	4
13	"Malhimanyirr no. 2 (Jungle Fowl)	4

maintained in the Ma-yawa *wangga*. In short, while it is rather old-fashioned, the Ma-yawa *wangga* provides a tantalizing glimpses of older practices.

In the previous chapter, I examined the way in which melodic aspects of "Truwu" were modified to accommodate shifting relationships within the Marri-tjevin group. In this chapter, I turn my attention to how the musical and textual practices of Maurice Ngulkur's composition "Walakandha Ngindji" balance themes of both solidarity and independence. In this case, however, the interaction is not between different lineages of the same language group but rather between two of the language groups who identify as *wangga* owners at Wadeye. In this song, Ngulkur takes the text of the Walakandha *wangga* song "Walakandha no. 2" and sets it to a Ma-yawa *wangga* melody.[2] The very fact that Ngulkur was permitted to set a Marri-tjevin text—a text making reference to speci-fic places and events in Marri-tjevin country—to a Ma-yawa *wangga* melody that is associated with Dreamings and Dreaming places within Marri-ammu country is in itself expressive of a profound degree of solidarity between the groups. Other aspects of the relationship are played out in other dimensions of the performance.

"Walakandha Ngindji": A Ma-yawa *Wangga*
Adapted from a Walakandha *Wangga* Original

In all, I recorded three performances of "Walakandha Ngindji," two in 1998 and one in 1999. The first of the two recordings made in 1998 was an elicited performance recorded on October 6 at Wadeye in the presence of all the singers then active in the Walakandha *wangga* tradition—Les Kundjil, Philip Mullumbuk, and Charles Kungiung—as well as Ambrose Piarlum, one of the doyens of Walakandha *wangga* dance, whose performance I examined in chapter 4. As we will see in the following analysis, the presence of these senior Walakandha *wangga* owners had a significant effect on the performance. The second 1998 recording was made on the next day at Peppimenarti, in the context of a ceremony at which the administrator of the Northern Territory conferred a bravery award on a boy from that community. In the following analysis, I will focus primarily on the Wadeye performance, though additional perspectives will, from time to time, be gleaned by reference to the Peppimenarti performance.

At the 1998 Wadeye performance, Ngulkur sang systematically through his repertory, omitting only three songs: "Rtadi-wunbirri" (which he sang the next day), "Na-pebcl" (which he sang for me the following year), and "Wulumen Tulh" (which he had forgotten in 1998 but had Mark Crocombe record in 2000). Soon after the 1998 recording, Ngulkur became too ill to perform at any length. This is therefore the only recording that I ever made of a sustained performance of the Ma-yawa *wangga*.

Ngulkur began the 1998 Wadeye performance by announcing, "I'm going to begin by singing about Walakandha,"[3] and followed this immediately with a performance of "Walakandha Ngindji." This begs the question, Why did Ngulkur choose to begin his performance by singing a song about a Marri-tjevin Walakandha, rather than one about his own Marri-ammu Ma-yawa or some other Marri-ammu Dreaming? That this was his only composition must surely have been a consideration. A more significant reason, however, was the strong presence of the Marri-tjevin songmen. By beginning in this way, he acknowledged the high status of these singers within the *wangga* tradition and his close association with them. "Walakandha Ngindji" is, above all else, an enactment of Ngulkur's relationship to these men, and to the Walakandha *wangga* tradition in which both they and he shared.

I begin my analysis of "Walakandha Ngindji" with a discussion of its text in order to identify the ways in which "Walakandha no. 2," the song on which it is based, conforms to established models for the Walakandha *wangga*. I then show how Ngulkur transforms this text—a text that is both stable and typical of the Walakandha *wangga*—into one in which key elements of the original are omitted, new elements added, and the order of text phrases altered.

I then examine Ngulkur's treatment of rhythmic mode. In the first vocal section of "Walakandha Ngindji," he presents the text in a rhythmic mode that is typical of the Ma-yawa *wangga*, while in the second vocal section he returns the text to the unmeasured rhythmic mode that it has in Walakandha *wangga* practice. I suggest that he does this to reflect a juxtaposition of Marri-ammu and Marri-tjevin interests.

A balance between Marri-ammu and Marri-tjevin conventions is also achieved in the way that he rhythmicizes the text within the first, measured vocal section. For the first text phrase, he chooses a model drawn from the Walakandha *wangga*, while in the second, he reverts to normal Ma-yawa *wangga* conventions.

The melody that Ngulkur uses for "Walakandha Ngindji" is one used in the majority of songs in the Ma-yawa *wangga* and is thus saturated with associations with Marri-ammu Dreamings and Dreaming sites. By setting it to this melody, he firmly draws the Marri-tjevin text into a Marri-ammu sphere of interest. This is in turn subverted by the way he maps the text onto the melody. To preserve the rhythmical conventions of the Walakandha *wangga* in the first text phrase, Ngulkur makes a dramatic alteration to the form of the melody. Thus we can see that at all levels of the compositional process, different conventions—Marri-ammu ways of doing things as opposed to Marri-tjevin ways of doing things—are being balanced. I would argue that these musical gestures are an enactment of the complex sets of mutual obligations that characterize the relationship between the Marri-ammu and Marri-tjevin in other dimensions of social life—not least in the ritual sphere.

The Text of "Walakandha no. 2" and Its Relationship to "Walakandha Ngindji"

"Walakandha no. 2" is a song about the building of the first house at Kubuwemi, the site of the present-day community of Nadirri, and the return of the Marri-tjevin to their ancestral lands following a period of "sitting down" at the mission. The surprise and delight felt by the ancestral dead at the return of their living descendants—whom they refer to as "Walakandha"—is almost palpable.

> A Walakandha! One is staying for a whole year.
>> Kubuwemi! My country!
> A solitary house with a white roof is there for him.
>> Kubuwemi! My country!

As can be seen from table 6.2, the text of "Walakandha no. 2" conforms in structure to the group 1A pattern advanced in the previous chapter with reference to "Truwu." It is a through-composed text in couplet form, and by and large it conforms to the pattern found in other songs of this form, namely, initial vocable + initial vocative text formula + core sentence + concluding vocative text formulas.[4] When performed as a Walakandha *wangga*, the structure of the text remains identical from performance to performance. A performance of the Walakandha *wangga* version of "Walakandha no. 2" can be heard at CD track 12.

At first Ngulkur maintained the couplet form of the original but truncated each of the text phrases, omitting both the initial *karra* and the concluding vocative formulas *kubuwemi* and *nidin-ngina* from both text phrases (see table

Table 6.2 Text structure of "Walakandha no. 2" compared to that of "Truwu"

Song	Initial vocable	Initial vocative text formula	Core sentence	Concluding vocative text formulas
"Truwu"				
Text phrase 1	karra	walakandha	purangang kuwa-vapa-vinyanga	truwu nidin-ngina walakandha
	karra	*Walakandha!*	*The sea stands up and crashes on them.*	*Truwu ! My country! Walakandha!*
Text phrase 2	karra	munggum	kimelha-kuwa karrivirrilhyi	truwu nidin-ngina walakandha
	karra	*Munggum!*	*He stands behind a beach hibiscus and peeps out.*	*Truwu ! My country! Walakandha!*
"Walakandha no. 2"				
Text phrase 1	karra	walakandha	ngindji kiny warri kurzi	kubuwemi nidin-ngina
	karra	*Walakandha!*	*One is staying for a whole year.*	*Kubuwemi! My country!*
Text phrase 2	karra		ngata devin bugim rtadi-nanga kuwa	kubuwemi nidin-ngina
	karra		*A solitary house with a white roof is there for him.*	*Kubuwemi! My country!*

6.3).[5] The omission of the vocative formulas *kubuwemi* (a reference to the eponymous Marri-tjevin site) and *nidin-ngina* (an expression of deep emotional attachment to [Marri-tjevin] country) might be seen as significant (given that this is not Ngulkur's site or country) were it not for the fact that both of these expressions reappear the second time he performs the song.[6] Addressing Wala-kandha ancestors as "brother," as Ngukurr does in vocal section 2, implies a very strong association between Ngulkur and the Marri-tjevin dead, a relationship that had been built up over decades of dancing as a Walakandha in ceremonial performances. That Ngulkur's use of these expressions in his song drew forth no objections from the Marri-tjevin audience is evidence of a deep bond between them.

In his second item, Ngulkur took text phrase 2 of item i (*ngata devin bugim rtadi-nanga kuwa*, "a solitary house with a white roof is there for him") and used it as text phrase 1 (table 6.4). He then added a completely new text phrase as the second line of the couplet. This is made up entirely of a series of vocable formulas that are all calls to Marri-tjevin Dreamings and country: *mana nidin-ngina kubuwemi mana* (Brother! My country! Kubuwemi! Brother!).

Table 6.3 Text structure of Ma-yawa *wangga* "Walakandha Ngindji" (item i) compared to "Walakandha no. 2"

Version	Initial vocable	Initial vocative text formula	Core sentence	Concluding vocative text formulas
Walakandha wangga "Walakandha no. 2"				
Text phrase 1	ka**rra**	walakan**dha**	ngin**dji** kiny warri ku**rzi**	kubuwe**mi** nidin-ng**ina**
	karra	*Walakandha!*	*One is staying for a whole year.*	*Kubuwemi! My country!*
Text phrase 2	ka**rra**		ngata de**vin** bugim rtadi-nanga ku**wa**	kubuwe**mi** nidin-ng**ina**
	karra		*A solitary house with a white roof is there for him.*	*Kubuwemi! My country!*
Ma-yawa wangga "Walakandha Ngindji," item i				
Text phrase 1		walakan**dha**	ngin**dji** kiny warri ku**rzi**	
		Walakandha!	*One is staying for a whole year.*	
Text phrase 2			ngata de**vin** bugim rtadi (-nanga) ku**wa**	[ma**na** walakan**dha**]
			A solitary house with a white roof is there (for him).	[*Brother! Walakandha!*]

The only text phrase structured as a stand-alone string of vocative formulas that we have previously encountered is the one in Les Kundjil's "Yendili no. 3" (see table 5.7). We might see Ngulkur's use of this text-phrase structure as a nod in the direction of Kundjil, the most senior of Walakandha *wangga* owners present at this performance.

Ngulkur's manipulation of the textual form in item ii shows the extent to which he was unafraid to play around with the Walakandha *wangga* text and create new versions of it. In the rendition of "Walakandha Ngindji" given on the next day in Peppimenarti—when the senior Walakandha *wangga* owners were absent—Ngulkur took this process even further by adding a third text phrase and thus destroying the original couplet structure completely.

Changing the Rhythmic Setting of the Text

As mentioned earlier, Ngulkur's modifications of the form of the original Walakandha *wangga* song extend beyond text to key elements of the musical form

Table 6.4 Text structure of Ma-yawa *wangga* "Walakandha Ngindji" (item ii)

Text phrase	Initial vocative text formula	Core sentence	Concluding vocative text formulas
1		ngata de**vin** bugim rtadi-nanga ku**wa** *A solitary house with a white roof is there for him.*	
2			ma**na** nidin-ngi**na** kubuwe**mi** ma**na** *Brother! My country! Kubuwemi! Brother!*

such as the rhythmic mode and the melody used to set the text. In this section, I will focus on the rhythmic mode of item i.

As can be seen from musical example 6.1, and heard on the CD (track 13), in the first of the items performed at Wadeye, vocal section 1 was measured, while vocal section 2 was unmeasured. The same pattern was replicated in item ii.

In the following discussion, my primary focus will be vocal section 1, since it is here that Ngulkur replaces the rhythmic mode—rhythmic mode 1—that is used for this song in the Walakandha *wangga* with the rhythmic mode—rhythmic mode 5c—most commonly used in the Ma-yawa *wangga*. In the Ma-yawa *wangga*, rhythmic mode 5c is performed in the fast tempo band (mm 134–46), with a polyrhythmic (six against four) relationship between voice and sticks, and an uneven stick-beating pattern. I noted this in chapter 1 with reference to "Wulumen Tulh." The full set of rhythmic modes used in the Ma-yawa *wangga* is set out in table 6.5. From this we can see that rhythmic mode 5c is used in more than half the Ma-yawa *wangga* songs.

In assessing the significance of Ngulkur's use of this rhythmic mode in vocal section 1, we must bear in mind that in both items he followed it immediately, in vocal section 2, with a return to the rhythmic mode of "Walakandha no. 2." It is as if he was saying to the Marri-tjevin singers present at the performance, "I may have appropriated the text of one of your songs to a rhythmic mode typical of my repertory, but I am now returning it to its original rhythmic mode." Just as, during this performance, the Marri-ammu and Marri-tjevin sat side by side as countrymen, so too did these two rhythmic settings sit next to each other in the performance.[7]

There was, moreover, another agenda at work here. By singing each of the two vocal sections in a different rhythmic mode, Ngulkur demonstrated to me a musical practice that is no longer maintained in the Walakandha wangga, namely, the setting of a single text to multiple modes of performance.[8] Like other elements of his performance, such as his constant variation of text, Ngulkur's use of two rhythmic modes within a single song was made possible by the fact that he was not constrained by ceremonial imperatives to produce a strong vocal unison or facilitate strong unisonal dancing.

Example 6.1 "Walakandha Ngindji," item i of the elicited performance recorded at Wadeye (Mar98:14)

ngin - dji   kiny wa - rri ku - rzi

Melodic Section 2

nga - ta de - vin   bu - gim rta - di

ku - wa   ma - na   wa - la - kan - - -

INSTRUMENTAL SECTION 2

dha hm hm hm hm hm hm hm hm hm hm

hm hm hm hm

143

Table 6.5 Rhythmic modes used in vocal sections of the Ma-yawa *wangga*

Clapstick beating	Mode number	Songs	Number of songs
Unmeasured			
Without clapsticks	1	"Rtadi-wunbirri," "Tjerri," "Karri-ngindji"	3 entirely in this mode
		"Walakandha Ngindji," "Wulumen Tulh"	2 partly in this mode
Measured			
Moderate even (mm 117)	4a	"Watjen Danggi"	1 entirely in this mode
Fast uneven quadruple (mm 134–46)	5c	"Wulumen Kimigimi," "Menggani," "Malhimanyirr," "Ma-vindivindi," "Thalhi-ngatjpirr," "Na-pebel"	6 entirely in this mode
		"Walakandha Ngindji," "Wulumen Tulh"	2 partly in this mode

There is, however, more to the changing of the rhythmic mode than simply altering the clapstick-beating pattern and the tempo. The text must also be structured in a way that will allow it to be mapped onto the melody according to the conventions of the Ma-yawa *wangga*.

To explain these conventions, I need to invoke two concepts that I have not previously used, namely, "text cell" and "rhythmic cell." A text cell, in the present context, is a subdivision of the text produced by word-final lengthenings, and a rhythmic cell is a metric unit, which in rhythmic mode 5c has a length of six crotchet beats or a multiple thereof. In most cases, text cells and rhythmic cells are coterminous.

In all measured Ma-yawa *wangga* songs but one, text cells and rhythmic cells are fitted together according to the following conventions:

1. Each syllable of a text phrase except the last is set to one crotchet beat.
2. The final syllable of each text cell is prolonged for as long as is necessary for the text cell to fill out the six-crotchet-beat structure of the rhythmic cell. Thus two-syllable text cells are always set to a two-note rhythmic cell whose elements are 1 + 5 crotchet beats in length, whereas a three-syllable cell is set to 1 + 1 + 4 crotchet beats, a four-syllable cell to 1 + 1 + 1 + 3 crotchet beats, and so on.
3. If a text cell has more than six syllables, the rhythmic cell to which it is matched must be extended by six beats or a multiple thereof.
4. All text phrases are 24 (4 x 6) crotchet beats in length. The normal

Marri-ammu convention is for the final syllable of a text phrase to be prolonged for as long as is necessary to fill out this structure. This often results in the final syllable being prolonged for more than six crotchet beats (see, for example, the final rhythmic cell in table 6.6 and the final rhythmic cell of text phrase 2 in table 6.7).

This division of text phrases into text cells, and their allocation to rhythmic cells, is an organizing principle that underpins the entire Ma-yawa *wangga* repertory, even in other rhythmic modes, where the length of the rhythmic cells may be different (as is the case in rhythmic mode 4a, where rhythmic cells are four beats in length) or even variable (as in rhythmic mode 1). [9]

Table 6.6 shows the normal convention for the fitting together of text cells and rhythmic cells in Ma-yawa *wangga* songs in rhythmic mode 5c as it is applied in an individual song (syllables in boldface indicate lengthened syllables). In "Wulumen Kimigimi," the song that Ngulkur sang immediately after "Walakandha Ngindji," the text is divided into three text cells, the first two of which are fitted to rhythmic cells that are six crotchet beats in length, and the third of which is fitted to a rhythmic cell that is twelve beats in length. As is usually the case at the end of a text phrase, the final syllable is prolonged for quite a long duration in order that it fill out the full twenty-four-beat structure. A performance of "Wulumen Kimigimi" may be heard on track 14 of the CD.

Let us now compare this with the text-rhythmic structure of "Walakandha Ngindji." As can be seen in table 6.3 (where lengthened syllables are again marked in boldface), the pattern of final-syllable lengthening found in the Marri-tjevin version of the text is retained in "Walakandha Ngindji." It is these essentially Marri-tjevin patterns that form the basis for the creation of text cells in Ngulkur's new version of the song. In this way a vital element of the original is retained as the basis for his remolding the text in accordance with Marri-ammu conventions. Ngulkur once again marries Marri-ammu and Marri-tjevin principles of musical and textual organization.

As table 6.7 shows, text phrase 2 of "Walakandha Ngindji" follows the Ma-yawa *wangga* conventions exactly. It is divided into two text cells on the basis of final-syllable lengthening, and each of these is fitted to a rhythmic cell. The first of these is six crotchet beats in length, and the second is eighteen, including the extension of the final syllable.

Table 6.6 The relationship between text cells and rhythmic cells for measured text phrases in "Wulumen Kimigimi"

	Rhythmic cells										
	1 (6 beats)			2 (6 beats)				3 (12 beats)			
Text cells	wu	-lu	**-men**	ki	-mi	-gi	**-mi**	ka	-vulh	-a	**-gu**
Beats	1	+1	+4	1	+1	+1	+3	1	+1	+1	+9
Text rhythm	♩	♩	♩𝅗𝅥	♩	♩	♩	𝅗𝅥	♩	♩	♩	𝅗𝅥𝅗𝅥

Table 6.7 The relationship between text cells and rhythmic cells for measured text phrase settings in "Walakandha Ngindji" (item i, vocal section 1)

Rhythmic cell			1		2		3				(4)

Text phrase 1

Text cells	wa	-la	-kan	**-dha**	ngin	**-dji**	kiny	wa	-rri	ku	**-rzi**	
Beats	1	+1	+1	+3	1	+5	1	+1	+1	+1	+2	(6)
Text rhythm	♩	♩	♩	♩	♩	♫	♩	♩	♩	♩	♩	⁊⁊⁊⁊⁊

Rhythmic cell		1			2						

Text phrase 2

Text cells	nga	-ta	de	**-vin**	bu	-gim	rta	-di	-na	-nga	ku	**-wa**
Beats	1	+1	+1	+3	1	+1	+1	+1	+1	+1	+1	+11
Text rhythm	♩	♩	♩	♩	♩	♩	♩	♩	♩	♩	♩	♩♩♩.

Text phrase 1, however, does not follow this pattern. Although the three text cells are formed on the basis of final-syllable lengthening, and each is assigned to a rhythmic cell of six crotchet beats' duration, the final syllable of the last text cell is not extended to the end of the text phrase in the normal way. Instead the articulation of the text comes to a sudden halt, so that the final six beats of the text-phrase setting—what might have been a fourth rhythmic cell—have no text. The beginning of this potential fourth six-beat cell (marked in parentheses in table 6.7) is, moreover, marked by a grunt on the first beat, as if to emphasize the sudden truncation of the normal structure. Where have we previously seen a sudden truncation like this?

The answer lies, of course, in the analysis of the group 2B songs in the previous chapter. In seeking a model within the Walakandha *wangga* that he could draw on for his measured setting of the "Walakandha Ngindji" text in vocal section 1, Ngulkur had a limited choice. There are only four measured songs in the Walakandha *wangga*, and the group 2B songs—"Kubuwemi," "Yendili no. 1," and "Lhambumen"—account for three of them.

Table 6.8 shows the text-rhythmic structure of "Kubuwemi"—a structure shared by all three songs in group 2B of the Walakandha *wangga*. Here the text is divided into three text cells on the basis of final-syllable lengthening, and each is set to a rhythmic cell. In this case, however, the rhythmic cell is four quaver beats in length, rather than six crotchet beats.[10] The most significant rhythmic feature of "Kubuwemi" (and the other two group B songs), however, is the sudden truncation that occurs at the beginning of what would have been the last rhythmic cell. While in "Walakandha Ngindji," truncation was emphasized by a grunt on the first beat of the final rhythmic cell, in the Walakandha *wangga* group 2B songs, the sense of coming to an abrupt and unexpected halt is underscored by

Table 6.8 The relationship between text cells and rhythmic cells for measured text phrase settings in the Walakandha *wangga* "Kubuwemi"

	Rhythmic cell 1		Rhythmic cell 2			Rhythmic cell 3						Rhythmic cell (4)
Text cells	**ka**	**-rra**	kubu	-we	**-mi**	ki	-mi	-wu	-rri	ka	**-vulh**	
Beats	2	+ 2	1	+ 1	+ 2	2				+ 2		(4)
Text rhythm	♩	♩	♪♪	♪	♩	♪	♪	♪	♪	♪	♪	𝄾𝄾
							3			3		

the withholding of the final syllable of the text (see p. 126) and the lack of prolongation of the last syllable of the cell.

While text phrase 2 conforms to Marri-ammu conventions, text phrase 1 seems to invoke a specific and conspicuous aspect of Marri-tjevin music practice. Just as there was juxtaposition of typically Marri-ammu and Marri-tjevin rhythmic modes in each of the vocal sections, here the contrast between Marri-ammu and Marri-tjevin practice is made at the level of text phrase.

The Setting of "Walakandha Ngindji" to Ma-yawa Wangga *Melody 1*

As Linda Barwick (1995) showed in her study of a combined men's and women's performance, in Central Australia, the process of bringing together text and melody may often provide an important locus for enacting social difference and identity. This is particularly the case where, as is the case in Central Australian song, a single melody is used to set a variety of texts.

The Ma-yawa *wangga* is unusual among *wangga* repertories for the fact that the majority of its songs are sung to a single melody. As can be seen from table 6.9, eight of the twelve songs are sung to the melody that I have called melody 1.[11]

Except when it is used in "Walakandha Ngindji"—which is emphatically not about a Marri-ammu Dreaming—melody 1 is used exclusively for songs celebrating Marri-ammu Dreamings or Dreaming sites. These include the following Dreamings and Dreaming sites: Ma-yawa (referred to both as Wulumen and as Ma-vindivindi– both mean "old man"), Tjerri (Sea Breeze) and Malhimanyirr (Jungle Fowl), Menggani (a Butterfly Dreaming site), Thali ngatjpirr (a Fish Dreaming site), and Karri-ngindji (a Ma-yawa Dreaming site). Melody 1, together with melody 4—which is associated with the Old Man Tulh Dreaming and the Ma-yawa Dreaming place Rtadi-wunbirri—is strongly reflective of the most profound aspects of Marri-ammu being, namely, their association with the places and associated Dreamings to which they trace their existence.[12]

Because the setting of text phrase 1 of "Walakandha Ngindji" is atypical of Ma-yawa *wangga* practice, the way in which "Walakandha Ngindji" is mapped onto melody 1 is also somewhat atypical. To understand what normally hap-

Table 6.9 The melodies of the Ma-yawa *wangga*

	Song title	Number of items
Melodies using the dorian series		
Melody 1	"Walakandha Ngindji," "Wulumen Kimigimi," "Menggani," "Thalhi-ngatjpirr," "Tjerri," "Malhimanyirr no. 1," "Ma-vindivindi," "Karri-ngindji"	8
Melody 2	"Watjen Danggi"	1
Melodies using the major series		
Melody 3	"Rtadi-wunbirri," "Wulumen Tulh"	2
Melody 4	"Na-pebel"	1

pens, let us return to "Wulumen Kimigimi," which, like "Walakandha Ngindji," is set to melody 1.

Musical example 6.2 shows how melody 1 is manifested in vocal section 2 of the second item of "Wulumen Kimigimi." Because Ngulkur varies the form of the melody slightly from performance to performance, it is easiest to consider melody 1 in its outline form, which in the musical example appears above the transcription of "Wulumen Kimigimi."

Melody 1 comprises two melodic sections, each of which is four measures in length. The melodic sections are distinguished on the basis of phrasing (a breath occurs at the end of the first melodic section), and on the basis of their melodic shape.

As we have already seen (table 6.6), the text of "Wulumen Kimigimi" comprises three text cells, each of which is set to a rhythmic cell. These are in turn mapped onto the melody as follows:

1. Each of the two melodic sections takes a full statement of the text.
2. The first two text/rhythmic cells map onto the first two melodic cells (marked off by bar lines in musical example 6.2) of each melodic section, while the third, longer, text/rhythmic cell maps onto the last two melodic cells. We can see this clearly in musical example 6.2, where text/rhythmic cells are boxed.

This model is found not only in "Wulumen Kimigimi" but also in a number of other songs in the Ma-yawa *wangga* repertory.

Because of the atypical text-rhythmic structure of the first text phrase of "Walakandha Ngindji," Ngulkur was faced with a difficult dilemma. He could adopt the normal Marri-ammu conventions for setting text to melody, which

Example 6.2 Melody 1 in outline form, and as realized in "Wulumen Kimigimi" (Mar98:14, iv, vocal section 2)

would preserve the melody intact but render its relationship to the Walakandha *wangga* unrecognizable, or he could maintain text phrase 1 in its Marri-tjevin form but modify the melody. Somewhat surprisingly, he chose the latter.

The way in which he adapted the melody to fit the shorter text was to omit the second melodic cell of melody 1, thereby shortening it from four to three measures and leaving the fourth measure empty (see musical example 6.3).

The implications of this are quite startling and reveal just how sophisticated Ngulkur was in the way he balanced Marri-ammu and Marri-tjevin conventions in this song. Ngulkur takes a Walakandha *wangga* text that was originally sung in rhythmic mode 1 and sets it first in the most typical of the Marri-ammu rhythmic modes—rhythmic mode 5c—and then in the most typical of the Walakandha *wangga* rhythmic modes: rhythmic mode 1. The juxtaposition of a "Marri-ammu" vocal section 1 and a "Marri-tjevin" vocal section 2 mirrors that of the Marri-ammu and Marri-tjevin men who in this performance were sitting side by side, as well as the balancing of Marri-ammu and Marri-tjevin interests that occurs in wider social spheres.

Ngulkur then articulates this balancing of interests in the rhythmic setting of his text. In the setting of text phrase 1 of vocal section 1 (that is, in the measured vocal section), he adopts the model most commonly applied to measured songs in the Walakandha *wangga*, a model that involves the sudden truncation of the text at the beginning of the final rhythmic cell. In text phrase 2, however, he returns to normal Marri-ammu conventions for the setting of the text.

The choice of the most typical of the Ma-yawa *wangga* melodies—a melody suffused with Marri-ammu-ness by dint of its having been used in many songs that celebrate Marri-ammu Dreamings and Dreaming places—for "Walakandha

Example 6.3 Adaptation of melody 1 in the setting of "Walakandha Ngindji"

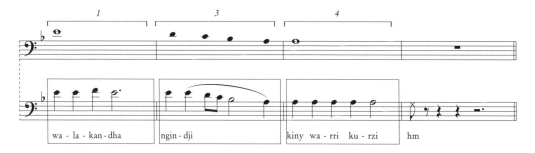

Ngindji" was risky, because it could easily have been interpreted as an unwelcome appropriation. However, any potential offense is mitigated by the fact that,
under pressure from Marri-tjevin principles of text setting, Ngulkur chose to alter his melody. This readiness to modify the very musical element that most co-
gently encodes Marri-ammu identity is a not insignificant compromise and
would have been recognized as such by the Marri-tjevin musicians present.

Looking at social relationships, we find a similar balancing of interests. As
mentioned in chapter 2, not only did all the Marri-tjevin songmen—Thomas
Kungiung, Philip Mullumbuk, Les Kundjil, Colin Worumbu Ferguson—have
Marri-tjevin fathers and Marri-ammu mothers, but their actual mothers were
all sisters. There are also significant enactments of social intimacy and independence in the linguistic sphere. Marri-ammu and Marri-tjvein share a similar
grammar and a high proportion of the lexicon, but as in so many other spheres,
there are sufficient distinctive features for the two languages to remain distinct.
And we must not forget that within the Wadeye community, the camps (and
now the houses) of the Marri-tjevin and Marri-ammu have always occupied the
same quarter of the town.

The most significant interaction for the present context, however, must be
that which occurs around song and dance in ceremonial contexts. There can be little doubt of the dominance of the Marri-tjevin in this realm. It is their repertory—
the Walakandha *wanggu*—replete with all its references to Marri-tjevin country
and Marri-tjevin ancestors, that forms the basis of joint ceremonial action with
the Marri-ammu. It is this repertory, not their own, that the Marri-ammu now
perform ceremonially. Within the *wangga* company, the interests of the two
groups are by no means as finely balanced as they are in Ngulkur's extraordinary
song, but there is nonetheless a significant degree of interdependence.

"Watjen Danggi," an Atypical Song in the Ma-yawa *Wangga* Repertory

In the previous chapter, I noted that the song "Yenmilhi" had much in common
with the Ma-yawa *wangga* song "Watjen Danggi." Neither, however, conforms to
the principles of construction typical of their repertory. In addition to having

a unique melody, "Watjen Danggi" is the only song in the Ma-yawa *wangga* repertory—indeed, the only song performed at Wadeye during the period of my study—that uses even clapstick beating in the moderate tempo band (rhythmic mode 4a). Like "Yenmilhi," but like no other song in the Ma-yawa *wangga* repertory, "Watjen Danggi" has a serial text, where short statements are strung together in a sequence. As in other songs with even clapstick beating, it is the rhythmic cells—which in this case are four beats in length—to which these statements are sung, rather than the clapstick beating, that articulate the meter. The relationship between the rhythm of the clapsticks and that of the vocal line is nonetheless straightforward and in marked contrast to the polyrhythmic relationship that characterizes other measured songs of the Ma-yawa *wangga*.

Although "Watjen Danggi" and "Yenmilhi" are the only two songs performed at Wadeye that maintain even clapstick beating throughout a whole song, the tempo of the former is moderate and the latter fast. Another significant difference

Table 6.10 Text of "Watjen Danggi"

	Initial vocable	Initial vocative text formula	Sentence
Vocal section 1			
Text phrase 1		mana	watjen kani-tjippi-ya kayirra
		Brother!	*Dingo was making tracks all along [the beach].*
Text phrase 2			wandhi-wandhi kimi kayirra watjen-danggi
			He looks right back all along [the beach], that dingo.
Vocal section 2			
Text phrase 1		mana	kani-tjippi-ya kayirra watjen-danggi
		Brother!	*He was making tracks all along [the beach], that dingo.*
Text prase 2			yilhiyilhiyen-gu
			This was at Yilhiyilhiyen Beach.
Vocal section 3			
Text phrase 1	karra	mana	kani-tjippi-ya kani-tjippi-ya wandhi
		Brother!	*He was making tracks, he was making tracks behind.*
Text phrase 2			yilhiyilhiyen-gu
			This was at Yilhiyilhiyen Beach.

lies in the relative stability of the text. Like most Walakandha *wangga*, "Yenmilhi" is performed in more or less the same way from performance to performance. The instability of the text of "Watjen Danggi" is, on the other hand, typical of the generally higher degree of textual instability that occurs in the Ma-yawa *wangga* repertory, which is probably simply a function of its infrequent use in ceremony. An example of "Watjen Danggi" appears on the CD (track 15), and the text is shown in table 6.10.

❖

A feature of Aboriginal music that continues to astound me is the amount of information that can be packed into a performance that lasts less than one minute. This is as true of a *bunggurl* from eastern Arnhem Land, or an *inma* from Central Australia, as it is of *wangga*. Commentators on Aboriginal visual arts such as Nancy Munn and Howard Morphy have revealed the often dense and multivalent layers of semiosis that exist within individual paintings (see, for example, Munn 1973; Morphy 1998), but it is rare for the significance of a single song to be unpacked by a musicologist to the extent that I have attempted here.

The following chapter moves from an intense examination of a small and marginalized repertory to a much broader examination of the largest and most enduring bodies of *wangga* song—Tommy Barrtjap's *wangga*.

chapter seven

Barrtjap's *Wangga*

In contrast to the Ma-yawa *wangga* repertory—a tradition that is on the point of extinction—that of Tommy Barrtjap remains extremely vigorous, even following his death in 1992.[1] Barrtjap was the men's ritual leader at Belyuen, and today, some ten years after his death, his memory is still held in the highest regard throughout the Daly region. The body of recordings made of his repertory is not only large, but it also covers five decades. The historical depth of the recorded sample is thus significantly greater than for any other repertory, including the Walakandha *wangga*. Tommy Barrtjap and his father's brother Jimmy Bandak were recorded by A. P. Elkin in 1952. Alice Moyle made a wonderful recording in 1968, and in 1986 and 1988, I was able to record the old man in the final years of his life. In 1995 and 1997 I recorded his sons Kenny and Timothy Burrenjuck performing their father's songs, and in 2002 I was invited to sing alongside Kenny on a number of occasions.

The repertory that Barrtjap recorded comprises eighteen songs, which are listed in table 7.1 as songs 1–18.[2] By the time I met him in 1986, Barrtjap appeared to no longer sing three of the songs recorded by Alice Moyle, songs 5, 6, and 7. On the other hand, in her 1968 recording, Moyle recorded only songs 1–7. That this was by no means his full repertory is confirmed by the fact that two songs—songs 12 and 13—both of which Elkin recorded in 1952, were still in Barrtjap's repertory in the late eighties and continue as part of the repertory of Kenny and Timothy Burrenjuck.

Both the size and the historical depth of the recorded samples provide the opportunity to address a number of important issues. That we have recordings of eight performances by Barrtjap of song 3, "Bangany-nyung Ngaya," spanning a period of some twenty years, for example, allows us to speak with some confidence about the degree to which he maintained textual, rhythmic, and melodic stability over time. A further eighteen recordings of this song by his sons Kenny and Timothy Burrenjuck (and a further four by other singers) allow us to draw conclusions that hold to the present day, and to confidently assess the degree to which songs change in the course of being passed from generation to generation. Another song, "Dadja Kadja Bangany Nye-ve" (song 13), which was recorded over a period of almost fifty years and has maintained a high degree of stability over the period, will be examined toward the end of this chapter.

Table 7.1 Barrtjap's repertory

Song number	Song title	Number of performances by Barrtjap (and others)
1	"Ya Bangany-nyung Nga-bindja Yagarra"	4
2	"Yagarra Nga-bindja-ng Nga-mi-ngaye"	4 (6)
3*	"Bangany-nyung Ngaya"	8 (22)
4*	"Kanga Rinyala Nga-ve Bangany-nyung"	7 (12)
5	"Yagarra Nga-bindja-ng Nga-mi"	2 (5)
6	"Yagarra Bangany Nye-ngwe"	1
7	"Be Bangany-nyaya"	1
8*	"Nyere-nyere Lima Kaldja"	4 (3)
9*	"Nyere-nye Bangany-nyaye"	4 (7)
10*	"Karra Ngadja-maka Nga-bindja-ng Nga-mi" (text phrase 2)	4 (2)
11*	"Yerrerre Ka-bindja-maka Ka-mi"	5 (1)
12	"Yagarra Ye-yenenaye"	1 (8)
13*	"Dadja Kadja Bangany Nye-ve"	1 (13)
14	"Yagarra Nedja Tjine Rak-pe"	1
15*	"Ya Rembe-ngaya Lima-ngaya"	2 (3)
16	"Yagarra Tjüt Balk-nga-me Nga-mi" (text phrase 2)	1 (5)
17	"Karra Tjine Rak-pe"	1
18*	"Yagarra Delhi Nye-bindja-ng Barra Ngarrka"	1 (1)
19*	"Nga'ngatbat-ba Mangalimpa"	(4)
20*	"Ngaya Lima Bangany-nyaya"	(3)
21*	"Nyala Nga-ve Bangany"	(5)
22*	"Anadada Bangany-nyaya"	(14)
23	"Karra Bangany-nyaya Nga-p-pindja"	(8)

* Songs sung by Kenny Burrenjuck

"Dadja Kadja Bangany Nye-ve" was also recorded at the community of Barunga (Beswick Creek) by Maddock in 1964. In chapter 10, I will focus on this performance in order to show how the formal elements of songs are changed when they are disseminated to a wider diaspora.

On the evidence currently available, Kenny Burrenjuck appears to sing about eleven of the songs that his father sang (songs sung by Kenny are marked with an asterisk in table 7.1), as well as at least two others that he himself has composed. Timothy Burrenjuck sings one further song (song 23) that he inherited from his father, which neither Barrtjap nor Kenny has recorded. On the basis of this evidence, we might reckon that Barrtjap's repertory numbered at least twenty-one songs, only eighteen of which he recorded. This is the largest known repertory for a single *wangga* singer.

This chapter will first examine the way in which performances by Barrtjap enact historical, cosmological, and ontological themes both in the texts and in the musical fabric of the songs. In the course of this discussion, I will also uncover some of the conventions that inform Barrtjap's composition.

Barrtjap's *Wangga* and Its Significance at Belyuen

Song Texts and Their Meanings

Just as texts of the Walakandha *wangga* and the Ma-yawa *wangga* are the utterances of song-giving Dreaming ancestors, the songs of Barrtjap (and other singers at Belyuen) are the utterances of Wunymalang ghosts. Similarly, while the focus of Walakandha and Ma-yawa *wangga* songs is the activities of the song-giving Walakandha and Ma-yawa Dreamings, the focus of Barrtjap's songs is the activities of Wunymalang.

My examination of Barrtjap's performance of "Bangany-nyung Ngaya" in chapter 4 was undertaken primarily to establish the musical and textual conventions of *wangga* as a genre. I will now assess its significance as an item of Barrtjap's repertory. The following is a slightly more literal translation of this song than was given in chapter 4, where, in order to avoid unnecessary complexity, the first line was read unequivocally as the utterance of a ghost.

> I'm singing for the sake of a song.
> Yagarra, I'm singing, yagarra *ye mm*!
> *Ii.* Yagarra, I'm singing *nye nye nye.*

As is so often the case in *wangga*, the first text phrase is elliptical, the effect of the ellipsis being to open the song to multiple interpretations. The first of these, "I'm singing for the sake [of giving you] a song," or (as in chapter 4) "I'm singing in order to give you a song," interprets the words as those of a song-giving ghost. In ceremonial performances of Barrtjap's songs, however, the efficacy of the ceremony relies on the simultaneous presence of two voices: that of the ghost and that of the living singer. When the voice of the living singer is also taken into account, the following interpretation also emerges: "I'm singing for the sake of [performing] a song [in ceremony]," or more expansively, "I'm singing in order to perform this song in ceremony for you all—living and dead." In chapter 1, I noted that references to Dreamings or Dreaming sites in Barrtjap's traditional country on the Daly are conspicuously absent from his texts and that the focus on Wunymalang ghosts in his song texts reflects the Wadjiginy's filiation to the country around Belyuen via conception.

The Song Text Lexicon and Its Rhythmic Realization in Song

One of the most conspicuous formal differences between Barrtjap's repertory and that of the Walakandha and Ma-yawa *wangga* is Barrtjap's tendency not to mark word boundaries and other semantic boundaries by the lengthening of word-final syllables. It was postulated earlier that boundaries tend to be marked in this way to increase the comprehensibility of the texts. Barrtjap's texts, however, contain a far higher proportion of untranslatable vocables (that is, untranslated spirit language) than either the Walakandha or the Ma-yawa *wangga*. Even when text is "turned over" from ghost language into Batjamalh, the text formulary is so restricted and so familiar to Barrtjap's audience that there is usually no need to rhythmically mark internal word boundaries to ensure comprehensibility. The only places in which Barrtjap practices rhythmic marking of word boundaries in a way that is comparable to the conventions of the Walakandha and Ma-yawa *wangga* repertories are where the text either departs from his normal formulary or is unusually complex, or both, as we will see later in the song "Yagarra Nga-bindja-ng Nga-mi."

Compared to other *wangga* singers, Barrtjap employs a relatively small repertory of words and phrases in his texts. Certain phrases, in particular those that contain the words *bangany* (song) or the verb *bindja* (sing), form the core of his lexicon. *Bindja* appears most frequently in the form *nga-bindja* (I sing), but also in the forms *nye-bindja* (you sing), *ka-bindja* (he sings), and *nga-p-pindja-ng* (I will sing), as well as in compound forms such as *nga-bindja-ng nga-mi* (I sing [while seated]).

The text of "Bangany-nyung Ngaya" (see table 4.1) is made up entirely of either vocables (*ngaya, -ya, ye, mm, ii, nye*), exclamations (*yagarra*), or references to singing (*bangany-nyung . . . nga-bindja*, "I'm singing for the sake of a song"; *nga-bindja-ng nga-mi*, "I'm singing [while seated]"; *nga-bindja*, "I'm singing"). A similar observation can be made with regard to "Yagarra Nga-bindja-ng Nga-mi," the text of which is reproduced later in this chapter as table 7.4. The text of another of the songs to be examined in detail in this chapter, "Dadja Kadja Bangany Nye-ve," comprises almost entirely vocables or exclamations, apart from the repeated expression *bangany nye-ve* (you go for a song) (see table 7.9).

Table 7.2 summarizes Barrtjap's text formulary for the entire repertory. Core words and phrases based on the text items *bangany* and *bindja* are boxed together. Additional words and phrases, a high proportion of which refer to the coming and going of the song-giving ghost, are combined with these core words and phrases to make longer utterances. These additional words and phrases are placed outside the boxes. They include expressions such as *nye-ve* (you go), *nga-ve* (I go), *yine* (where?), *dawarra wagatj-maka* (at the edge of the beach), *ngadja-maka* (as for me), *tjitja* (this), and *nga-p-puring djü* (I will go now).

Insofar as economy of text lessens the demand on memory, one might be tempted to regard this reliance on a small formulary as a strategy to assist the reproduction and transmission of songs in an oral context. But Barrtjap was the men's ritual leader at Belyuen, a "memory man" who within the context of men's ceremony would have been required to remember many songs, each with its own distinctive text. A more likely motive is that by repeatedly focusing on songs and the act of singing, Barrtjap focused his audience's attention on the fact that the songs he was singing were received from, and addressed to, Wunymalang.

Table 7.2 Core phrases in Barrtjap's song-text lexicon

nga-ve	bangany	nye-ve	
	bangany		
	bangany-nyung		
	bangany-nyung		
	bangany-nyung bangany	nga-bindja	
	bangany-nyung	nga-bindja	
		nga-bindja	
	yine	nga-bindja	
		nga-bindja-ng nga-mi	
	dawarra wagatj-maka	nga-bindja-ng nga-mi	
	ngadja-maka	nga-bindja-ng nga-mi	
		nye-bindja-ng nya-mu	
	nye-menüng	nye-bindja-ng nya-mu	nganggung djü
		ga-bindja-ng ka-mi	
	tjitja	ga-bindja-ng ka-mi	
		ga-bindja-maka ka-mi	
		nga-p-pindja-ng	nga-p-puring djü
		nga-p-pindja-ng	nga-p-puring djü nüng

The Significance of Melody and Mode

In the previous chapters, we have seen how the widely encountered association in Australian Aboriginal music between melodies, people, and country plays out in other repertories. In the case of the Walakandha *wangga*, related but different pentatonic forms of a single melody refer to inland and coastal country respectively, while in the Ma-yawa *wangga*, the use of two melodies for all the songs about ancestral Dreamings and Dreaming sites in Marri-ammu country imbues these melodies with considerable semiotic power.

By contrast, no two songs in Barrtjap's repertory share the same melody. Nor is any song sung to more than one melody. For this reason, many of the strategies adopted by singers in the Walakandha and Ma-yawa *wangga* traditions were simply not available to him. Moreover, because only one of Barrtjap's texts, "Ya-garra Delhi Nye-bindja-ng Barra Ngarrka," refers to a Dreaming, the sorts of associations that exist between Dreamings, place, and melody in the Wadeye repertories have not developed here.

Nonetheless, Barrtjap has his own strategies. His repertory exhibits a high degree of modal consistency, which marks his songs as belonging to an identifiable corpus. The regular performance, over several decades, of this corpus in ceremony, for a landscape that can hear the voice of the singer and feel the stamping of the dancers, has made it "of that country." Indeed, Barrtjap's adoption of a general modal consistency—as opposed to the more specific relationships between melody and place found in the Ma-yawa *wangga*—could be interpreted as reflecting the more generalized relationship that people from the Belyuen community have with their adopted country (see chapter 1).

Moreover, Barrtjap's modal consistency reflects not only the relationship between his people and their country of residence but also—as was also the case with the Walakandha *wangga*—relationships between the singers within the Barrtjap lineage. The fact that, with only one exception, the melodies associated with Barrtjap share the same melodic mode reflects the fact that the repertory has been passed down within a single family.

The heptatonic pitch series used in Barrtjap's songs is a dorian set with an unstable third degree (C–D–E-flat/E–F–G–A–B-flat–C) that sometimes gives it a mixolydian feel. Modal practice in Barrtjap's usage extends beyond the simple sharing of a pitch series to the structuring of his melodies by the systematic use of a set of finals and subfinals.

In his melodies, the heptatonic dorian series is frequently divided into two disjunct parallel tetrachords based on C and G respectively, just as it was in the Walakandha *wangga* (see musical example 5.3). Barrtjap reinforces the inherent symmetries of the series by frequent cadencing on these degrees. E-flat/E, the pitch of a prominent harmonic in the didjeridu spectrum, forms another cadencing pitch. In addition to these modal characteristics there are also frequently recurring melodic phrases with structural implications, such as the cadential figure (figure z) E/E-flat–D–C, approached from above or below, which regularly precedes the arrival onto the tonic. See, for example, musical example 7.1, "Yagarra Nga-bindja-ng Nga-mi," where it occurs at the end of melodic sections and subsections. A transposed form of this (B-flat–A–G, marked z^1 in the same musical example) is also used for parallel approaches to the secondary tonic, G.

The only exception to this pattern is "Yagarra Delhi Nye-bindja-ng Barra Ngarrka," which uses a major pitch series. It cannot be insignificant that the one modally distinct song in Barrtjap's repertory should also be the only one that refers to a local Dreaming. Melodically it stands out from the rest, not just because of its modality, but because of a strange, high-pitched call made by the singer in the middle of the vocal section. In fact, when I first heard this song, I doubted whether it was a *wangga* song at all: its modal and melodic structure seemed quite different from other *wangga* songs and was certainly different from other songs in Barrtjap's repertory.

Barrtjap's Use of Rhythmic Mode

In general, singers from Belyuen employ a greater range of rhythmic modes in their songs than do the singers of the Walakandha *wangga* and the Ma-yawa *wangga*. While each of the two repertories associated with Wadeye uses only three rhythmic modes, Barrtjap uses seven. Lambudju, as we will see in more detail in the following chapter, used a total of nine.

Table 9.1 shows a complete list of all rhythmic modes used in the four repertories discussed in this book, beginning with unmeasured songs and proceeding
to measured songs. Apart from rhythmic mode 1, rhythmic modes are formed
by combining the parameters of tempo and clapstick beating. Hence a limited
number of clapstick-beating patterns, of which the most common are even
beating and uneven quadruple beating (♩♩♩♪), may be performed in four tempo
bands: slow, slow moderate, moderate, and fast (including fast doubled).[3] Songs
whose vocal sections are performed without beating are designated rhythmic
mode 1; those performed at a slow tempo are grouped under rhythmic mode 2;
those performed at a slow moderate tempo are grouped under rhythmic mode
3; those performed in a moderate tempo are grouped under rhythmic mode 4;
and those performed in a fast tempo are grouped under rhythmic mode 5. The
different stick-beating patterns used to produce different rhythmic modes
within these tempo bands are distinguished by lowercase letters: 5a, 5b, et cetera.

Table 7.3 Rhythmic modes used by Tommy Barrtjap

Tempo band of vocal section	Song number	Vocal sections	Instrumental sections	Coda
Unmeasured				
Without clapsticks	5	1	5b/d	5d
	10	1	5a	5d
Measured				
Slow (mm 58–65)	4	2	2	5d
	17	2	2	5d
	18	2	2	5a
Moderate (mm 117–20)	2	4d	4d	4d
	16	4d	4d	4d
Fast (mm 126–44)	15	5a	5a	5a
	1	5a/b	5a/b	5a/b
	6	5a	5a	5a
	7	5a	5a	5a
Fast (mm 268–88/126–44)	8	5b/c	5b/c	5c
	9	5b/c	5b/c	5c
	12	5b/c	5b/c	5c
	13	5b/c	5b/c	5c
	14	5b/c	5b/c	5c
Fast (mm 126–44)	3	5c	5c	5c
	11	5c	5c	5c

Although Barrtjap used only a subset of the rhythmic modes laid out in table 9.1, I have adopted here, as elsewhere in the book, the nomenclature established there. A survey of the use of all rhythmic mode across all four repertories will be undertaken in chapter 9.

Of the seven rhythmic modes that Barrtjap used, one is unmeasured and six measured. The six measured modes are distributed across three of the four tempo bands: slow, moderate, and fast. These are set out in table 7.3.

SONGS WITHOUT CLAPSTICK BEATING IN
THE VOCAL SECTION (RHYTHMIC MODE 1)

All songs with no clapstick beating in the vocal sections belong to rhythmic mode 1. As can be seen from table 7.3, Barrtjap sang only two songs in this rhythmic mode. One of these, "Yagarra Nga-bindja-ng Nga-mi" (song 5), is examined in detail in the following section.

Barrtjap's rhythmic practice in the instrumental parts of these songs was more varied than that of other singers. As can be seen from the table, he used a number of different forms of rhythmic mode 5 in his instrumental sections, while the coda was always in the fast triple meter rhythmic mode 5d. The move from instrumental section to coda thus frequently involves a shift from quadruple to triple meter.

SONGS IN THE SLOW TEMPO BAND

There is only one rhythmic mode in the slow tempo band: rhythmic mode 2, which comprises even stick beating in the slow tempo band. The rate of clapstick beating used by Barrtjap in this tempo band was normally in the range of 58–65 beats per minute, although in the 1968 recording made by Alice Moyle, the range was significantly higher (mm 69–74), perhaps because—as can be heard on the recording—the general level of excitement was high on this occasion. Kenny Burrenjuck performs this tempo band at mm 57–60, that is, in a range similar to that used by his father.

Barrtjap sang three songs in rhythmic mode 2. Two of these—"Kanga Rinyala Nga-ve Bangany-nyung" (song 4) and "Yagarra Delhi Nye-bindja-ng Barra Ngarrka" (song 18)—will be examined in more detail later.

As can be seen from table 7.3, Barrtjap's practice was to maintain rhythmic mode 2 through both the vocal and the instrumental sections, but to adopt a different rhythmic mode—the fast triple rhythmic mode 5d—for the coda. He did not use this rhythmic mode anywhere other than in the codas of songs whose vocal sections are in rhythmic mode 1 or 2.

SONGS IN THE MODERATE TEMPO BAND

Although Barrtjap did not sing any songs in the slow moderate tempo band, he sang two songs—"Yagarra Nga-bindja-ng Nga-mi-ngaye" (song 2) and "Yagarra Tjüt Balk-nga-me Nga-mi" (song 16)—in the moderate tempo band. A detailed examination of "Yagarra Tjüt Balk-nga-me Nga-mi" is undertaken later in this chapter. Although several rhythmic modes may be performed in the moderate tempo band, Barrtjap used only one: rhythmic mode 4d, which is characterized by quintuple clapstick beating (♩♩♪♩♪). Another of the rhythmic modes in the moderate tempo band was encountered in chapter 6 when I examined the Ma-yawa *wangga* "Watjen Danggi." In that case the clapstick beating was even (rhythmic mode 4a) rather than quintuple. This tempo band is also used by Bobby Lambudju Lane, who employed uneven quadruple clapstick beating to establish rhythmic mode 4b, and a triple form of beating to establish rhythmic mode 4c (see chapter 8).

Barrtjap is the only singer to use quintuple meter in his songs. As we will see shortly, he also adopted it for song 7, "Be Bangany-nyaya," which is in the fast tempo band.

SONGS IN THE FAST TEMPO BAND

In Barrtjap's practice there are four different forms of rhythmic mode 5: rhythmic mode 5a, fast even; rhythmic mode 5b, fast doubled; rhythmic mode 5c, fast uneven (quadruple), in which the meter is articulated primarily by the clapstick-beating pattern ♩♩♪; and rhythmic mode 5d, fast uneven (triple), in which the meter is articulated primarily by the clapstick-beating pattern ♩♩♪ (see table 7.3). The fast tempo band comprises beating in the range of 126–44 beats per minute or, in the doubled form, in the range of 268–88 beats per minute.

Examples of Barrtjap's use of rhythmic mode 5a in "Be Bangany-nyaya" (song 7) and of rhythmic modes 5b and 5c in "Dadja Kadja Bangany Nye-ve" (song 13) will be discussed hereafter. We have also encountered rhythmic mode 5c in the discussion of "Bangany-nyung Ngaya" (song 3) in chapter 4. As noted earlier, rhythmic mode 5d is used only in the codas of songs whose vocal sections are in rhythmic modes 1 and 2.

THE PERFORMANCE OF SUCCESSIVE VOCAL
SECTIONS IN DIFFERENT RHYTHMIC MODES

As we have already noted, a distinctive feature of Barrtjap's practice is the performance of successive vocal sections in different rhythmic modes. In contrast to the current practice for the Walakandha *wangga*, where each song (and hence each vocal section of any one song) is only ever sung in one rhythmic mode, Barrtjap regularly subjected successive vocal sections of certain songs to different rhythmic modes. Whereas Maurice Ngulkur was able, for a dying repertory, to vary successive vocal sections in this way, and while there is evidence that this practice was adopted in the early years of the Walakandha *wangga*, Barrtjap's ability to manipulate rhythmic mode was a conspicuous and vital element of musical practice right up until the time he died, and this survives to the present day in the practice of his son Kenny. This has significant implications for dance, as we shall see in chapter 9.

Six Songs in Six Rhythmic Modes

In the following sections, I examine six songs, each of which is sung in one or more of the six rhythmic modes in which Barrtjap sang his vocal sections. I take up these songs partly for what they tell us about how Barrtjap uses rhythm and meter, but also to examine wider aspects of his musical style, the significance of the songs, and the nature of their transmission.

"Yagarra Nga-bindja-ng Nga-mi" (Rhythmic Mode 1)

In Barrtjap's repertory there are only two unmeasured songs, both of which are notable for their sense of gravitas.[4] In Barrtjap's practice, rhythmic modality seems also to include an element of affect. Not only do these two songs have a deeply serious feel to them, but also, by contrast, the dances used to accompany fast songs in rhythmic mode 5 are sometimes described as *lerri*, or "happy" dances.

The text of "Yagarra Nga-bindja-ng Nga-mi," which was also discussed in chapter 2, contains perhaps the most explicit account that we have in song of the exchange between a song-giving ghost and a living singer.

> Yagarra! I'm singing!
> Yagarra! What have I come to do?
> I'm going to sing and then go back.
> Yagarra! You sing!
>
> Yagarra! I was sitting on the open beach and singing *ni*.
> Yagarra! You sing!

Like most unmeasured *wangga*, "Yagarra Nga-bindja-ng Nga-mi" comprises only through-composed text, but the sheer length of the song—six text phrases—makes it one of the most complex songs encountered in this study (see table 7.4).

The rhetorical form of "Yagarra Nga-bindja-ng Nga-mi" is that the ghost first describes what he is doing and then, in the final text phrase of each melodic section, switches the attention to the songman, commanding him to sing: "You sing!" (*nye-bindja-ng nya-mu*). This rhetorical structure is reinforced by the melodic structure of each of the vocal sections.

As can be seen from musical example 7.1, a transcription of the second of three vocal sections in a performance recorded by Alice Moyle in 1968, the vocal section of "Yagarra Nga-bindja-ng Nga-mi" comprises two melodic sections. Each of these is in turn subdivided on the basis of breath, melodic structure, and rhythm into two subsections. A recording of "Yagarra Nga-bindja-ng Ngami" can be heard on the CD at track 16.

Each subsection is marked by a cadence. The first subsection occupies the full range of the song and cadences strongly on the didjeridu tonic, C, the cadence being approached by the cadential figure z. The second melodic subsection,

Table 7.4 Text structure of "Yagarra Nga-bindja-ng Nga-mi"

Text phrase	Exclamation	Sentence
Melodic Section 1		
1	yaga**rra**	nga-bindja-ng nga-**mi**
	Yagarra!	*I'm singing!*
2	yagarra	yine nga-ve me-**nung**
	Yagarra!	*What have I come to do?*
3		nga-p-pin**dja-ng** nga-p-pu**ring-djü** <u>nüng</u>
		I'm going to sing and then go back.
4	yaga**rra**	nye-bindja-ng nya-<u>**mu**</u>
	Yagarra!	*You sing!*
Melodic Section 2		
1	**yaga<u>rra</u>**	dawa**rra** wa**gatj**-ma**ka** nga-bin**dja-ng** nga-**mi** <u>*ni*</u>
	Yagarra!	*I was sitting on the edge of the beach singing ni.*
2	yaga**rra**	nye-bindja-ng nya-<u>**mu**</u>
	Yagarra!	*You sing!*

Example 7.1 "Yagarra Nga-bindja-ng Nga-mi" (Moy68:5, ix, vocal section 2)

which also cadences on the didjeridu tonic, is simply a slightly elaborated form of the cadential figure z itself. While in most *wangga* songs melodic sections are sung in one breath, here the sheer length of the melody forces Barrtjap to quickly snatch a breath (marked by a comma in musical example 7.1) in the course of the melodic section. The point at which he does so is the junction between the two melodic subsections. This is also the point at which the text switches its focus from the ghost's account of what he has come to do, to his instruction to the songman to sing.

Both breathing and melodic structure thus reinforce the rhetorical structure of the text. Further support is provided by the rhythmic setting. Barrtjap's delivery of the text in rhythmic mode 1 is close to speech rhythm. In this case, however, the delivery is quicker than usual, perhaps because of the large amount of text and melisma to be uttered in one breath. In the text transcription shown in table 7.4, syllables prolonged from one to four beats appear in boldface, and prolongations in excess of four beats are both in boldface and underlined.

Let us focus first on the longest prolongations. Durations in excess of four beats occur in only three positions within each melodic section: at the end of the final text phrase, at the end of the penultimate line, and on the final syllable of the first *yagarra*. In the second of these contexts, the prolongations take the form of a melisma. On the basis of what we already know about the setting of through-composed *wangga* texts, the prolongation of the final syllable of the melodic section is to be expected. Long durations, accompanied by florid vocalizations at the end of the penultimate line, are, however, unusual and are employed here to mark the end of the first phase of the Wunymalang's account, just before the rhetorical shift mentioned earlier.

Earlier in this chapter, I noted that in general Barrtjap does not mark internal word or other semantic boundaries by final-syllable prolongation, and I suggested that this was because of their highly formulaic nature. In this song we have an opportunity to test this hypothesis, since it contains both formulaic text (which we would expect not to exhibit a great deal of final-syllable lengthening) and text that is unique, or almost unique, to this song (which might require such lengthening to make it intelligible). This is in fact what happens. While the shorter sentences such as *nga-bindja-ng nga-mi* and *yine nga-ve me-nung* do not display any lengthening at internal word or morpheme boundaries, the longer sentences like *nga-p-pindja-ng nga-p-puring djü nüng* (melodic section 1, text phrase 3) and *dawarra wagatj-maka nga-bindja-ng nga-mi ni* (melodic section 2, text phrase 1) do. In these cases, all word boundaries and most morpheme boundaries are marked.

"Kanga Rinyala Nga-ve Bangany-nyung" (Rhythmic Mode 2)

Let us turn now to rhythmic mode 2. In Barrtjap's repertory, three songs (songs 4, 17, and 18) are sung in this rhythmic mode. Musical example 7.2 is a transcription of the final melodic section and instrumental section of a performance of song 4, "Kanga Rinyala Nga-ve Bangany-nyung."

Example 7.2 "Kanga Rinyala Nga-ve Bangany-nyung," final vocal section and instrumental section (Moy68:5, vii)

*Bracketed beat = beats that are normally present but not in this case

In all but one of Barrtjap's seven recorded performances of "Kanga Rinyala," he maintains slow even beating throughout all vocal and instrumental sections. In one of the performances recorded by Alice Moyle, however, he suspends the clapstick beating for the first melodic section of the final vocal section. (This performance is included on the CD at track 17.) In musical example 7.2, the beats that were performed in vocal section 1 but omitted in the final vocal section are shown in brackets. The suspension of beating in this way raises a number of questions.

First, in the only other instances of rhythmic mode 2 so far encountered, that is, in the group 2B songs of the Walakandha *wangga* repertory, clapstick beating is similarly suspended for part of a vocal section. In all three songs in that group, the first two text phrases are always sung in rhythmic mode 2 (with slow even beating), but in text phrase 3 the beating is suspended (see chapter 5). Was I right to assume that text phrase 3 is in rhythmic mode 1, or should we regard the whole vocal section as being in rhythmic mode 2, but with the beating suspended in the third text phrase?

Second, to what extent can we regard Barrtjap's suspension of clapstick beating in one performance of "Kanga Rinyala" as representative of normal practice? In this regard, performances by his son Kenny are instructive. When Kenny performs "Kanga Rinyala," he frequently suspends the clapstick beating for a single melodic section, just as his father did. Indeed, as table 7.5, shows, he is more likely than not to suspend the beating in one or another of his melodic sections. Moreover, as was the case in his father's performance, when the clapstick beating is withheld, the metrical structure continues to be maintained by the didjeridu through the strict repetition of a simple duple pattern.

Table 7.5 Inconsistent clapstick beating in performances of "Kanga Rinyala Nga-ve Bangany-nyung"

Singer	Vocal section	Melodic section 1	Melodic section 2
Barrtjap (Moy68:5, vii)	1	slow even beating	slow even beating
	2	no beating	slow even beating
Kenny Burrenjuck (Mar97:9, iv)	1	slow even beating	slow even beating
	2	no beating	slow even beating
	3	no beating	slow even beating
Kenny Burrenjuck (Mar97:8, v)	1	slow even beating	slow even beating
	2	slow even beating	no beating
	3	no beating	slow even beating

This way of proceeding is quite different from what happened when clapstick beating is suspended for the third text phrase of group 2B Walakandha *wangga* songs. There, the text phrase in which the beating is suspended is clearly unmeasured, and there is no clear relationship between the voice and the didjeridu.

I have therefore concluded that when slow even beating is suspended, but the metrical pulse is continued by the didjeridu—as in the case of "Kanga Rinyala"—the piece remains in rhythmic mode 2. When, on the other hand, there is no metrical alignment between the voice and didjeridu—as is the case with the third text phrase of the group 2B Walakandha *wangga* songs—the mode shifts to rhythmic mode 1. This view is confirmed by another of the songs in rhythmic mode 2, "Yagarra Delhi Nye-bindja-ng Barra Ngarrka."

"Yagarra Delhi Nye-bindja-ng Barra Ngarrka" (Rhythmic Mode 2)

In this song, Barrtjap performs the slow even beating typical of rhythmic mode 2 in the instrumental sections that precede and succeed each vocal section, but he suspends the clapstick beating for the *entirety* of each vocal section. As in "Kanga Rinyala," however, the metrical pulse is maintained throughout the vocal section by the didjeridu. Moreover, before the entry of the didjeridu that begins the song, Barrtjap clearly sings the duple didjeridu pattern to be played (this can be heard on the CD at track 18), which is then taken up by didjeridu player, Eric Martin. After three measures, the clapsticks enter and match the tempo of the didjeridu, playing slowly at around 69 beats per minute. At the first word of the text, however, the beating ceases and does not resume until the final text phrase *yagarra di* of the vocal section (see musical example 7.3).

"Yagarra Delhi Nye-bindja-ng Barra Ngarrka" is, of course, Barrtjap's song about the Wilha (Cheeky Yam) Dreaming and as such demands further attention. The text of the song is set out in table 7.6. Following his performance of this song in 1986, Barrtjap told me that it was about an event that occurred when he and a group of other people went hunting on Indian Island, west of Belyuen. There was a strong tide running, and because the dangerous Wilha Dreaming is known to travel on the tide, Barrtjap and the rest of the party chose to climb a small hill and wait out the danger. The husband of one of the women—a man who was not a local but from the Tiwi Islands—went, however, to the southern tip of the island, from where he thought he saw the Wilha Dreaming coming after him. As he turned to run, Barrtjap called him up to the safety of the hill.

Wilha is one of the four traveling Dreamings associated with the traditional owners of the region, the Danggalaba clan of the Larrakiya people. She is described as being ovoid and hairy, like a Hairy Cheeky Yam, with red eyes and arms like seaweed that can ensnare and entrap strangers. Like the Walakandha, she is not particularly dangerous to her own people, or to those who have been properly introduced to her by being bathed on the incoming tide (as in fact all young people at Belyuen are as part of the local puberty ceremonies). But to outsiders Wilha is extremely dangerous, and stories abound of the many tragedies that have taken place in these waters and are attributed to her. Various

Example 7.3 "Yagarra Delhi Nye-bindja-ng Barra Ngarrka" up to the end of vocal section 1
(Mar86:3, v)

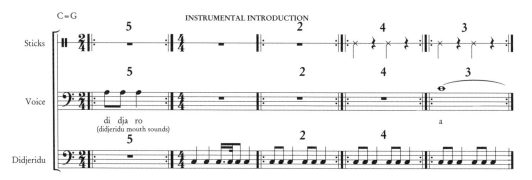

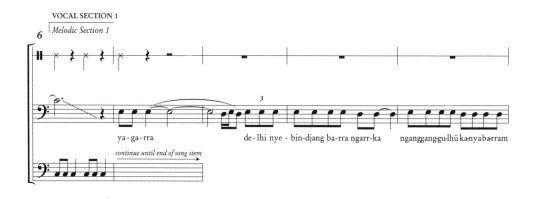

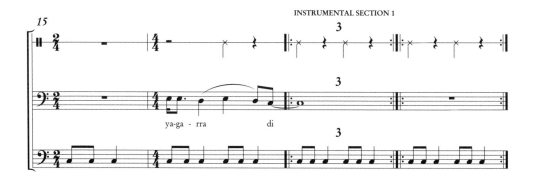

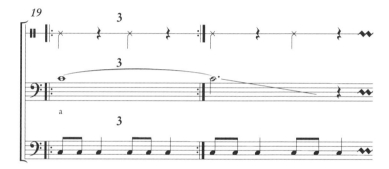

explanations of this song have been given: some suggest that the Tiwi man really was pursued by Wilha, others that he only thought he saw the Dreaming, while others obfuscate the reference to the Dreaming (which is not explicit in the song text) by saying that he was chased by a buffalo.

Barrtjap's song includes not only exhortations to come up to the safety of the hill but also the high-pitched cry *kuu*, associated with the Wilha Dreaming. This cry, which can be heard on Elkin's recordings of a now-discontinued men's ceremony, and was heard on the night that one of the most important Larrakiya ritual leaders died, is one of the most powerfully direct references to a Dreaming in the whole of *wangga*. Does its inclusion in Barrtjap's song suggest that the Wilha Dreaming was really present, or simply that Barrtjap was trying to frighten the man even further by making that cry? As is so often the case with Aboriginal stories, the answer depends on whom you ask, and in what context. There can be little doubt, however, that powerful connections with one of the most important and dangerous local Dreamings reside within this song.

Table 7.6 Text of "Yagarra Delhi Nye-bindja-ng Barra Ngarrka"

Text phrase	Exclamation	Sentence
1	yagarra	delhi nye-bindja-ng barra ngarrka
	Yagarra!	*Wait! Climb up here to me.*
2		ngangganggulhü kanya barram
		Don't be frightened!
3	kuuwa yagarra	nga-bindja-ng werret bangany-nye ngwe
	Kuuwa! Yagarra!	*Quick! I'm singing a song.*
4	yagarra di	
	Yagarra! di	

There is yet another explanation of this text, which rests not on any story that I was given but on an ambiguity inherent in the word *bindja* (which can mean both "climb up" and "sing")—an ambiguity frequently exploited by singers at Belyuen. See, for example, Bobby Lambudju Lane's song "Benmele," which I will consider in chapter 8, or Barrtjap's "Yagarra Tjüt Balk-nga-me Nga-mi," which I will consider next. The translation of the text given in table 7.6 was made with the assistance of the late JS, a man who was present on the day that the incident occurred and who was able to give a number of details, including the identity of the person concerned, and the location of the event. In this version, *bindja* is interpreted in text phrase 1 as "climb up" and in text phrase 3 as "sing." If, on the other hand, *bindja* in text phrase 1 is read as "sing," rather than "climb up," the song is transformed into a classic set of instructions from a song-giving ghost to a songman: "Wait! Sing it to me. Don't be frightened. Quick! I'm singing a song."

One of the factors that pointed me in the direction of this reading is the fact that it is almost impossible to understand JS's version as the utterance of a Wunymalang. This fact alone set the song apart from all other *wangga* in Barrtjap's repertory. Another reason I find the second reading persuasive is because of parallels with "Yagarra Nga-bindja-ng Ngami": in both songs, the ghost both reflects on his own actions and instructs the songman to sing. This interpretation also resonates with Maralung's story about receiving the song "Minmin Light" (chapter 2), and like Maralung's song-giving ghost, Barrtjap's tells the singer, "Don't be frightened."

"Yagarra Tjüt Balk-nga-me Nga-mi" (Rhythmic Mode 4d)

Rhythmic mode 4d (moderate uneven [quintuple] beating in the vicinity of 120 clapstick beats per minute using the quintuple clapstick-beating pattern (♩♪♪♪)) is used in only two songs, "Yagarra Nga-bindja-ng Nga-mi-ngaye" (song 2) and "Yagarra Tjüt Balk-nga-me Nga-mi" (song 16). The former has a text that is typical of Barrtjap's repertory, incorporating not only formulas about singing but also didjeridu mouth-sounds. The latter, however, has a number of unique qualities that are worth exploring. First, it is one of only three songs explicitly attributed to Barrtjap's teacher, Jimmy Bandak. Second, like "Yagarra Delhi Nye-bindja-ng Barra Ngarrka," several interpretations of the song are given. Third, the word *bindja* is used to mean both "climb up" and "sing," thus opening up the song to layers of interpretation that once again underscore its origins in the realms of the dead (see table 7.7).

.I have heard two "mundane" explanations for this song. The first holds that Jimmy Bandak first made it for his "son" Jimmy Havelock, when Havelock was working at Murgenella on the Coburg Peninsula, many hours' drive to the east of Belyuen. According to Barrtjap, Havelock got an infected foot from a cypress pine splinter and had to "climb up" into an airplane and return to Belyuen. A second explanation was that he hurt his foot at Belyuen and had to "climb up"

Table 7.7 Text of "Yagarra Tjüt Balk-nga-me Nga-mi"

Text phrase	Exclamation	Sentence	Vocable
1	yagarra		ni
	Yagarra!		*ni*
2	yagarra	tjüt balk nga-me nga-mi	karra di
	Yagarra!	*My foot is swollen!*	*karra di*
3	yagarra	yine nga-ve me-nung	
	Yagarra!	*What have I come to do?*	
4		nga-p-pindja-ng nga-p-puring djü	
		I'm going to climb up [into an airplane/onto a tractor] and go back.	

onto a tractor in order to be taken to the clinic. The first of these explanations emphasizes traditional trade and ritual links that Belyuen people maintained in the past with people of the Coburg Peninsula, and corresponds, in its emphasis on links outside the immediate vicinity of Belyuen, to explanations that link Barrtjap's songs to his estates near the Daly River mouth (see chapter 1).

The second interpretation localizes the reference and emphasizes the links that Wadjiginy people have with Belyuen, and once again this has parallels with the localized explanations discussed in chapter 1. It is undoubtedly significant that the first time I heard the second explanation was during the final stages of the Kenbi land claim, at a time when Daly people at Belyuen were wishing to establish the right to continue living there. A third layer of meaning turns on the ambiguity of *bindja*. In Batjamalh, phrases 3 and 4 of "Yagarra Tjüt Balk-nga-me Nga-mi" (CD track 19), which I have read as "What have I come to do? I'm going to *climb up* [into an airplane/onto a tractor] and go back," are almost identical to those that in my interpretation of "Yagarra Nga-bindja-ng Nga-mi," I read as the utterances of a song-giving ghost: "What have I come to do? I'm going *to sing* and then go back." As was the case in "Yagarra Delhi Nye-bindja-ng Barra Ngarrka," a song that appears on one level to be about an everyday event can also be read as the utterance of a ghost simply by adopting the alternative reading of *bindja*. Other aspects of the song reinforce this interpretation: in text phrase 1, the ghost sings *ni*, as he did in "Yagarra Nga-bindja-ng Nga-mi," and in reflecting on the reference to a sore foot in text phrase 2, we should remember that one of the actions performed by dancers when representing both Walakandha and Wunymalang is limping.

Table 7.8 Text structure of "Be Bangany-nyaya"

First section (number of syllables)

be bangany-*nyaya* (5)
Be! A song nyaya

nga-bindja-*aya* (4)
I sing aya

bangany bangany-*nyaya* (6)
A song, a song nyaya

nga-bindja-*ya-nyaya* (6)
I sing ya nyaya

nga-bindja (3)
I sing

Core sentence

yine nga-ve me-nung
What have I come to do?

Last section (number of syllables)

be bangany-*nye nye nye* (1 + 5)
Be! A song nye nye nye

bangany-*nye* (3)
A song nye

nga-bindja *nye* (4)
I sing nye

bangany-*nyaya* (4)
A song nyaya

"Be Bangany-nyaya" (Rhythmic Mode 5a)

In song 7, "Be Bangany-nyaya," Barrtjap draws heavily on the formulaic nature of his text to create yet another example of a song in quintuple meter. Performed in rhythmic mode 5a, that is, with fast even beating, all elements of the text—Batjamalh words or untranslatable vocables—are playfully combined to produce a lively and rhythmically varied song.

As can be seen from table 7.8, the sentence that forms the core of the text comprises the same ghostly question that was found in song 5, "Yagarra Nga-bindja-ng Nga-mi," and song 16, "Yagarra Tjüt Balk-nga-me Nga-mi," namely, *yine nga-ve-me-nung* (What have I come to do?). In song 5, it is given the answer "I'm going to sing and then go back," and in song 16, "I'm going to climb up [into an airplane/onto a tractor] and go back" as a primary meaning, with the answer "I'm going to sing and then go back" resonating in the background.

In song 7, the rather more lighthearted song-giving ghost proceeds to answer his own question with a playfully elaborated version of the basic idea "I'm singing a song," in which the key words *bangany* (song) and *nga-bindja* (I sing) are freely combined with untranslated ghost language. In fact, so playful is this text that the question is answered even before it is posed.

The text phrase divisions in the outer sections of each vocal section are created by rhyme, that is, in the same way as subdivisions were created in the first text phrase of "Bangany-nyung Ngaya" (see chapter 4). In the first section, each text phrase except the last is marked by *–aya*, and in the last section the rhyme is *nye*. Each of these text phrases is then set to a two- or three-beat rhythmic cell. These cells, which in musical example 7.4 appear as two- or three-beat measures, or as two- or three-beat subdivisions of a five-beat measure, at first follow each other in an irregular configuration before settling into a regular 5/4 meter (see musical example 7.4; "Be Bangany-nyaya" can be heard on the CD at track 20).

The conventions that determine whether it is a two- or three-beat rhythmic cell that is allocated to a text phrase are fairly, though not totally, consistent. In the first section, each syllable, apart from the initial *be*, takes roughly half a beat

Example 7.4 "Be Bangany-nyaya," vocal section 1, melodic section 1 (Moy68:5, xi)

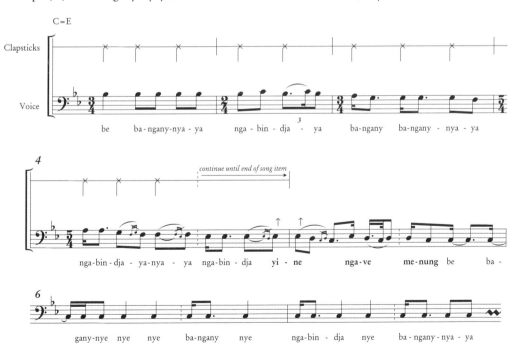

(there is some adjustment because of the swinging of the rhythm): thus the four-syllable text phrase *nga-bindja-ya* (the number of syllables is given in brackets in table 7.8) is set to a two-beat measure, while the six-syllable text phrases *bangany bangany-nyaya* and *nga-bindjaya-nyaya* are set to three beats. To fit text phrases with an odd number of syllables to the two- or three-beat rhythmic cells, some adjustment is required. Hence the first, five-syllable text phrase *be bangany-nyaya* is set to a three-beat cell by prolonging the initial syllable (the vocable *be*, unique to this song), and the three-syllable text phrase *nga-bindja* at the end of the section picks up the first syllable, *yi*, of the core sentence *yine nga-ve menung* to create a two-beat cell. The result is a structure that has measures of the following length in beats: 3 + 2 + 3 + ||:3 + 2:||. The three- and two-beat rhythmic cells enclosed in the double bars comprise a series of 5/4 measures that continue to the end of the vocal section (see musical example 7.4). In the last section, the means by which two- and three-beat rhythmic cells are formed differs slightly from the beginning, but the principles are the same.[5]

As I have observed several times already, any song that is accompanied by even clapstick beating must establish the meter of the song by means other than through the morphology of the clapstick-beating pattern, whether this be through the use of didjeridu patterns or through the rhythmical realization of the text. Regular clapstick beating does not, however, necessarily imply regular meter. We have already seen how, in the Walakandha *wangga* song "Yenmilhi," the text of a song is used to articulate irregular metrical groupings—in that case, groups of three and four clapstick beats. In "Watjen Danggi," on the other hand, text phrases were grouped so as to produce quadruple meter. Further ways of establishing meter in songs with even clapstick beating can found in Barrtjap's repertory. Songs 1 and 15, for example, establish quadruple meter by the repetition of isorhythmic cycles that are four beats in length. Whereas in song 1 each beat is then subdivided into three, thus producing a compound quadruple meter, in song 15 the subdivision is duple, thus producing a simple quadruple meter.

"Dadja Kadja Bangany Nye-ve" (Rhythmic Modes 5b and 5c)

As can be seen from table 7.9, the text of "Dadja Kadja Bangany Nye-ve" comprises a high proportion of vocables (including the didjeridu mouth-sound *didjeremo*) with only one, albeit oft-repeated, meaningful phrase: "You go for a song" (*bangany nye-ve*). Text phrase 1 is entirely cyclic and is set isorhythmically; text phrase 2 comprises a mixture of through-composed and isorhythmically set cyclical text; and text phrase 3 comprises a single vocable, which is sung to a melisma.

As already observed, one of the characteristics of Barrtjap's practice is that, like Maurice Ngulkur, he sometimes performs successive vocal sections of the one song item in different rhythmic modes.[6] There is a group of five songs (songs 8, 9, 12, 13, and 14; see table 7.3) in which, in every performance, the first one or two vocal sections are always sung in rhythmic mode 5b (fast doubled),

Table 7.9 Text of "Dadja Kadja Bangany Nye-ve"

Text Phrase	Text
1	‖:*dadja kadja* bangany nye-ve *Dadja kadja! You go for a song.* *mayeve kadja* bangany nye-ve:‖ *Mayeve kadja! You go for a song.*
2	*yene* bangany nye-ve *Yene! You go for a song.* *yenene didjeremo* ‖:*limaranye*:‖ *yenene didjeremo* ‖:*limaranye*:‖
3	*ii* *ii*

while the next one or two are always sung in rhythmic mode 5c (fast uneven [quadruple]). In all songs in this group, the first melodic section is either largely or totally isorhythmic, and the meter is always compound—that is, with triple subdivisions of the main beats.

Musical example 7.5 shows the second, and part of the third, vocal sections of a performance of "Dadja Kadja Bangany Nye-ve," including the transition from rhythmic mode 5b (here elaborated with interlocking beating) to 5c at the beginning of vocal section 3. This can also be heard on the CD at track 21. In songs like this, in which the rhythmic mode changes between one vocal section and the next, the instrumental section always maintains the mode of the vocal section that immediately preceded it, with the change of rhythmic mode normally occurring at the very end of a instrumental section, that is, immediately before the beginning of the vocal section in the new rhythmic mode.

As a brief aside, I would like to draw attention to one further case where rhythmic mode is changed in the course of a performance, and to do this I will return briefly to "Bangany-nyung Ngaya," the song examined in detail in chapter 4. Here I noted that Barrtjap always performed this song in rhythmic mode 5c, fast uneven (quadruple). In contrast to his father's practice, however, Barrtjap's son Kenny Burrenjuck regularly switches rhythmic mode in the course of this song.[7]

In the example of "Bangany-nyung Ngaya" on CD track 22, we hear him perform the first vocal section in rhythmic mode 5b (fast doubled) and then change to the more usual rhythmic mode 5c (♩♩♪) at the beginning of vocal section 2. In another performance, in which I was in fact his backup singer, Kenny performed the first of a pair of items in rhythmic mode 5b throughout, and the second item of the pair in rhythmic mode 5c. It seems clear that Kenny has evolved his own

Example 7.5 "Dadja Kadja Bangany Nye-ve," vocal sections 2 and 3 (Mar88:5, iii)

distinctive way of performing this, the most popular of the songs in the Barrtjap repertory, but that his innovations rest firmly on broader compositional principles established by his father.

Returning now to "Dadja Kadja Bangany Nye-ve," this is the song for which we have the widest spread of recordings over time. The earliest dates from 1952 and the latest from 1997, although the song continues to be performed today. Musical example 7.6 juxtaposes performances of the opening of a vocal section from each of four recordings (including material also transcribed in musical example 7.5). The first is a recording made by Elkin in 1952 in which the singer is not clearly identified;[8] the second is a recording of Barrtjap that I made in 1988, and the third is a recording of Kenny Burrenjuck that I made in 1997. A fourth version, sung by Laurence Wurrpen and recorded in 1964 by Maddock, will be discussed in chapter 10.

The identity of the singer in the earliest recording is critical, and for this reason I have dedicated quite some effort in trying to clarify the matter. When I played this recording to senior men and women at Belyuen, many of whom were present when Elkin made his recordings in 1952, they were unable to agree on the identity of the singer (see chapter 2). Barrtjap himself was clear on this matter, however, insisting that the singer was Jimmy Bandak, not himself. On the basis of this, and all other evidence, it seems likely that the singer recorded in 1952 was indeed Bandak.

From musical example 7.6, we can see that the degree of difference between the first three recordings is remarkably small, particularly in the isorhythmic first melodic section. The degree of stability in melodic section 1 is perhaps not entirely surprising, since one of the functions of isorhythm is to serve as a mnemonic device. As might be expected, the most conspicuous differences occur in the more melismatic melodic section 2, although even here the degree of variation between the 1952 and 1988 performances is in general no more than might be found between successive performances of melodic sections—particularly melismatic melodic sections—in a single performance.

The evidence from musical example 7.6 suggests that until the end of his life, Barrtjap faithfully preserved a version of this song virtually identical to that which his teacher, Jimmy Bandak, sang in 1952. Moreover, Kenny Burrenjuck closely follows the path laid down by his "grandfather" and father in melodic section 1, although the degree of variability exhibited in his melodic section 2 is consistently greater than in the other performances.

Questions of transmission, and the factors that tend to alter the form of songs, will be taken up in more detail in the course of my discussion of the songs of Bobby Lambudju Lane in the following chapter. Whereas the lines of transmission within the Barrtjap lineage are remarkably direct, with songs being passed down in patrilineal succession from generation to generation, the lines of transmission relating to Lambudju's repertory are more tangled and complex. The fact that Barrtjap's repertory has been passed down within a single family is clearly a major factor in the reliability of its transmission.

Example 7.6 Comparison of four performances of "Dadja Kadja Bangany Nye-ve" from 1952 (Elk52:19B, iv), 1988 (Mar88:5, iii), 1997 (Mar97:7, ix), and 1964 (Mad64:1, xii)

179

chapter eight

Bobby Lambudju
Lane's *Wangga*

In 1993 Bobby Lambudju Lane (1941–1993) was poised to take over from Barrtjap as the leading songman at Belyuen. Until his death in the previous year, Barrtjap had continued to assert his authority as the dominant songman of the community with undiminished vigor. But now, with his passing, the way was open for Lambudju to take on the mantle. Alas, this was not to be. By the end of 1993, Lambudju was himself dead, at the tragically young age of fifty-two. Although a few songs in his repertory are now carried on by younger singers such as Colin Worumbu Ferguson and Roger Yarrowin, the tradition will probably never recover from this blow.

In terms of his education and his personality, Lambudju makes a contrasting figure to Barrtjap. Whereas Barrtjap was an old-fashioned leader—hard, authoritarian, and taciturn—Lambudju was gentle and voluble. Western trained, literate, and for a number of years a teacher at the Belyuen School, Lambudju was a fluent speaker not only of Batjamalh and Emmi but also of English. He had the rare capacity to speak the texts of songs and give their translations the moment he had finished singing and was the only singer with whom I worked who could correct my text transcriptions as I wrote them down.

The character of his songs stands in marked contrast to those of Barrtjap. Whereas Barrtjap's repertory was marked by an economy of lexicon, by adherence to a strict modal practice, and by a vicelike grip on musical form, Lambudju produced texts that were highly varied in terms of both lexicon and structure and even mixed two languages: Batjamalh and Emmi. Lambudju's melodies are diverse and employ a range of different modes; the modal consistency found throughout Barrtjap's repertory is not to be found. The key to this variety is not, however, just education and personality but also the history of his repertory. We have seen already, in chapter 2, that parts of Lambudju's repertory came down to him from a variety of sources, including his two Wadjiginy "fathers," Aguk Malvak and Alalk, as well as his Emmiyangal adoptive father, Mun.gi, and other members of that family. While the line of transmission for Barrtjap's repertory runs straight through a single family and language group, that of Lambudju intertwines at least two families and two language groups in ways that are now difficult to completely disentangle.

Because Lambudju's life was cut short so unexpectedly, and at such a relatively

Table 8.1 Lambudju's repertory

Song number	Title (number of items in this sample)
1	Rak Badjalarr (9)
2	Bandawarra Ngalkin (6)
3	Karra Balhak Malvak (7)
4	Karra-ve Kan-ya Verver Rtedi Ka-ya-nhthi (2)
5	Benmele (4)
6	Winmedje (2)
7	Tjerrendet (1)
8	Tjendabalhatj (8)
9	Bangany Nye-bindja-ng (5)
10	Walingave (3)
11	Djappana (4)
12	Karra Balhak-ve (1)
13	Limarakpa (1)
14	Mubagandi (3)
15	Bende Ribene (5)

young age, his corpus of recordings is not large, although it does have an intriguing historical depth. In all, fifteen songs have been recorded over a forty-five-year period from 1959 to the present. These are set out in table 8.1 together with the number of recorded performances in brackets; details of the recorded sample are given in appendix 4. The first thirteen songs in table 8.1 were recorded by Lambudju at various times in his life, but only eleven of these were still in his repertory in the period I was working with him, between 1986 and 1991. The two he did not record were "Mubagandi," which was composed shortly before his death and given to Roger Yarrowin, who subsequently sang it for me, and "Bende Ribene," which is now sung by Colin Worumbu Ferguson and seems simply to have been overlooked in the performances that Lambudju recorded for me.

The earliest recording, from 1959, was made by Alice Moyle when Lambudju was only in his late teens. "Karra Balhak-ve," the song that he sang on that occasion with Rusty Benmele Moreen, was no longer in Lambudju's repertory by the time I met him in 1986. In 1962, Moyle again recorded Lambudju, now age twenty, singing four songs, "Rak Badjalarr," "Karra Balhak Malvak," "Karra-ve Kan-ya Verver Rtedi Ka-ya-nhthi," and "Limarakpa," the first three of which remained in his repertory until the end of his life. "Rak Badjalarr" will form one of the main focuses of this chapter. It has been recorded in a variety of contexts: in 1961, sung by Rusty Benmele Moreen; in 1962, 1986, and 1991, sung by Lambudju; and in 1997, sung by Colin Worumbu Ferguson. "Rak Badjalarr" provides an ideal focus both for an exploration of the relationship between songs and place and for the study of transmission. Badjalarr, or North Peron Island—the island of the dead that lies to the north of the Daly River mouth—is the place where Lambudju's song-giving ghosts, Mun.gi and Aguk Malvak, reside, as well as the place to which Lambudju's Wunymalang has now gone. Read against the background of an analysis of Lambudju's complete repertory, "Rak Badjalarr" will also provide a vehicle for discussing the most salient features of his musical style.

The key players in the transmission of Lambudju's repertory were discussed in chapter 2, but we would do well to remind ourselves of the details. Some of the songs in Lambudju's repertory were composed by his father's brothers, Alalk and Aguk Malvak. Aguk Malvak appears to have died around 1950, when Lambudju would have been only about nine years old. His father Jack Lambudju therefore asked his brother-in-law, the Emmiyangal songman Mun.gi, to look after the songs until Bobby was old enough to take them on. Mun.gi became not only Lambudju's teacher but also his adoptive father and imparted to him not only the Wadjiginy songs that he was keeping in trust but also his own repertory of Emmiyangal songs. In addition to receiving songs composed by Aguk Malvak and Mun.gi while they were alive, Lambudju also continued to receive songs from them after they died, when they appeared to him in his dreams in Wunymalang form.

Other members of both Lambudju's and Mun.gi's family have also played an important part in this lineage. Mun.gi's son, Rusty Benmele Moreen, joined Lambudju as one of the two leading singers in this tradition, until his own untimely death in the early 1980s. A song about Benmele's death (song 5, "Benmele") forms another major focus in this chapter. In addition, Lambudju's "brother" (father's brother's son) Melan Enda passed songs to his son Brian, who also makes an appearance later in this chapter but was not regarded as a major figure in the song tradition. Mun.gi also encouraged his daughter, Audrey, to sing *wangga* around the campfire in the evening, though because she is a woman, she never performed in ceremony. Audrey Badjawalang Lippo and her sisters, Esther Djerrim Burrenjuck (Barrtjap's widow) and Agnes Alunga Lippo, have played a central role as consultants in the transcription, translation, and elucidation of Lambudju's song texts.

Rak Badjalarr: The Island of the Dead

Badjalarr (*rak* means "patrilineally inherited ancestral country"), the larger and most northern of the two Peron Islands, is the ancestral country of Lambudju, to which he inherited rights through his father. It lies just north of Anson Bay in the vicinity of the Daly River mouth (see figure 1.2). It is regarded as a dangerous place, except to senior people belonging to that country, and to other people who have been properly introduced to it. As already indicated in chapter 1, in recent times Badjalarr has become a generalized land of the dead, a sort of "western paradise," for people at Belyuen, just as the Belyuen water hole, originally a Larrakiya descent Dreaming site, has become a generalized conception site.

Wunymalang ghosts can come from Badjalarr to Belyuen to give songs to songmen, or to menace people who behave inappropriately, or simply to inhabit the country that they knew when alive. Badjalarr is one of a number of sites in the Daly region mentioned in Lambudju's songs. Lambudju's practice of naming places in his songs stands in stark contrast to that of Barrtjap, who, for all his emphasis on the utterances of ghosts, never mentions specific places within the texts of his songs.

Brian Enda, a Wadjiginy man like Lambudju, was descended from one of Lambudju's father's brothers (Tjulatji; see figure 2.2). Because his father, Melan Enda, was in the same generation as Lambudju, Brian called Lambudju "father." Brian Enda described North Peron Island as the place where the ghosts of his grandfathers and fathers live and as a place that should be approached with due ceremony—by the application of sweat and ocher by older relatives, by smoking, and by newcomers paying the same respect to the shades of the deceased as they would to living elders:

> You can't go down Peron now, not even me . . . sacred ground, so sacred you can't even go there. If my auntie wants to go there she can go. She can go to Peron Island but not me, and not even you. Unless they take us there and you know, wipe our sweat, you know, our way. You know, old people, their sweat they got under their arm? Well they got to put it over you [and] ocher [and] white smoke. They got to put it on your arms and your legs and your face, so when you go to that Peron Island, soon as you hit that beach, well something might happen to you now [i.e., then]. It's not dangerous but, you know, old people [ghosts] are there. They're looking at [you] from the bush. You know, like, spirits.
>
> Our [dead] grandfathers, they make you, you know, sit down, sit down and you stand for a little while. Maybe you want water. You're thirsty. All right, next minute . . . next minute you look [i.e., see] water here, or if you're hungry for tucker, anything, wallaby or possum [will appear]. . . . During the night you gotta sleep. You're going to see a lot of [camp] fires here, and all them old people, all my grandfathers and my father, they camp in the saddle here, they watch you. Don't be frightened, you know. Don't be afraid, of these white ones . . . they come out to you. They sing songs.
>
> You know my father Bobby [Lambudju] Lane—you know Bobby Lane? All those new songs [of his] come from that Peron Island. See, when he sleeps, they sing him, you know, sort of a ghost. You know, like all them ghost now, all my fathers, where they sing corroboree. Well Bobby Lane, when he sleeps, he gets that song. They give him a new song, that's the song now, that Wali [song 10, "Walingave"] that [I've just sung for you]. That thing from old man now. He told him a new song.[1]

"Rak Badjalarr": A Song about the Relationship of People to Country

Through their origins with ghosts, all of Lambudju's songs are implicitly associated with North Peron Island, but among these, "Rak Badjalarr" takes pride of place and remains powerfully associated with both Lambudju and North Peron Island today. Close examination of this song reveals much about the complex relationships that people living at Belyuen have both with their ancestral country on the Daly—rights to which are inherited patrilineally—and with the Cox Peninsula, the country on which they now live and to which many people trace their conception. It also reveals much about the cosmologies that sustain these relationships, and about the musical conventions by which they are articulated in performance.

Musical example 8.1 is a transcription of "Rak Badjalarr" as it was performed by Lambudju in 1986. A recording of this performance appears on the CD at track 23.

Example 8.1 "Rak Badjalarr" (Mar86:4, vi)

Table 8.2 The text of "Rak Badjalarr" as performed by Lambudju in 1986

Text phrase	Text
1	‖:rak **ba**dja**larr**-ma**ka** ba**ngany-nyung**:‖ (5x)
	For the sake of a song for my ancestral country, Badjalarr.
2	*ii* win**me**dje ngan-dji-nyene
	I'm eating oysters.

TEXT STRUCTURE AND MEANING

In this performance of "Rak Badjalarr," the text, which is set out at table 8.2, comprises two text phrases, the first of which is cyclical and the second through-composed.[2] As is usually the case, the cyclical text is set isorhythmically, and in this case, the isorhythm is limited at each occurrence to five full repetitions.

In table 8.2, text phrase 1 is translated, somewhat cryptically, as "for the sake of [i.e., in order to give] a song for my ancestral country, Badjalarr." Yet again we observe the elliptical nature of text in *wangga*. In his spoken gloss, Lambudju added the word *nga-bindja-ng* (I am singing) to the end of the phrase in order to give the fuller meaning "I am singing in order to give a song for my ancestral country, Badjalarr."[3]

A variant form of this text phrase occurs in the version of this song sung by Lambudju for Alice Moyle in 1962, namely, *rak badjalarr bangany nye-bindja-ng*, which means "*You* sing a song for your ancestral country Badjalarr." Here we again encounter the dichotomy—first noticed in Maralung's story about "Minmin Light" and noted again in a number of Barrtjap's songs—between self-reflexive statements that focus on the action of the song-giving ghost ("I'm singing . . .") and statements that articulate the ghost's instruction to the songman ("You sing . . ."). Both versions of the initial text phrase of "Rak Badjalarr" survive in recent practice: while Lambudju used the first form in his 1986 performance, in 1997 Colin Worumbu Ferguson used the second.

Text phrase 2 refers to the eating of oysters. Here, once again, the Batjamalh text is somewhat elliptical, omitting the auxiliary verb *nga-mi* (I sit).[4] In his spoken gloss, Lambudju gives the full meaning of the text, *winmedje ngan-dji-nyene nga-mi*. The sung form means "I'm eating oysters," while the spoken form means "I'm *sitting down* and eating oysters." While the most obvious interpretation of text phrases 1 and 2 is that a song-giving ghost is sitting on North Peron Island and eating oysters, Lambudju's account of the creation of this song suggests that more complex meanings are present, and that these primarily concern his dual relationship to the Peron Islands and the Cox Peninsula.

Lambudju told me that at the time he made this song, he had a dream-vision of his "daughter" Audrey Badjawalang Lippo eating oysters at Two Fella Creek, a stream on the north coast of the Cox Peninsula.[5] This account brings into play a rich web of associations. First, Badjalarr is famous for its oysters. Indeed, as

Table 8.3 The text of "Winmedje"

Text phrase	Text
1	Winme**dje** ngan-dji-nye**ne** nga-**mi mm**
	I'm sitting eating oysters.
2	e, a, mm
	e, a, mm

Brian Enda implied, it can be relied on to provide food and drink to those allowed to visit it. It is therefore not surprising that a vision of Audrey eating oysters would make Lambudju think of his ancestral homeland. Second, Audrey herself claimed to have composed another *wangga* about oysters, the text of which is virtually identical to the second text phrase of "Rak Badjalarr" (see table 8.3).[6]

The two text phrases of "Rak Badjalarr" thus unite several forms of relationship that the protagonists had with country. Lambudju and Audrey had a relationship both with country on the Daly (by birthright) and with the country around Belyuen (by dint of living and foraging there). Birthright is indicated in the song by the word *rak*, and foraging is symbolized by the collection of oysters. In addition, both performed ceremony for Belyuen and for Badjalarr—Lambudju as a singer and Audrey as a dancer—and each composed songs that were both for Belyuen and from Badjalarr.

MELODY

The melodies of "Rak Badjalarr" and "Winmedje" are closely related. As can be seen by comparing musical examples 8.1 and 8.2, the melody of "Rak Badjalarr" is based on the five lowest pitches (A–G–E–D–C) of the "Winmedje" melody. The two songs thus share not only text but also melody, both of which unite the two songs in a complex relationships with both North Peron Island and the Cox Peninsula.

While Lambudju was clear that he himself composed "Rak Badjalarr," the ac-

Example 8.2 "Winmedje" (Mar86:4, v, vocal section 1)

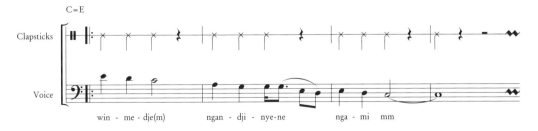

counts of the composition of "Winmedje" are more contested and highlight the fact that, even in the case of songs that were composed within living memory, issues of transmission may be far from simple. According to Lambudju, "Winmedje" was dreamed by Rusty Benmele Moreen, who, in a scenario parallel to that described for the composition of "Rak Badjalarr," dreamed of his sister Audrey collecting oysters at another Cox Peninsula site, Mandorah. According to this account, Benmele then shared this song with Lambudju. But according to Audrey, it was she who composed "Winmedje" and gave it to Lambudju to sing. In yet another version, Lambudju said that he dreamed of Benmele having a vision of Audrey gathering oysters.

Just as different interpretations of songs circulate, so too do different accounts of their composition. Both are heavily dependent on context: on who is being given meaning, and who is giving it. We have already seen this for a number of Barrtjap's songs, and later in this chapter, I will outline how over a number of years, different levels of meaning were revealed to me with regard to the song "Benmele." In assessing the different interpretations, it is not so much a matter of determining which version is "true" as of determining what the speakers are trying to impart to a particular listener at a particular time. In northern Australia, stories are negotiated, and the authority to speak about certain matters derives both from hereditary rights and from whether the speaker "witnessed"—that is, personally experienced—the events being described or not.[7]

Lambudju's version of events highlights a relationship between Audrey Lippo and Benmele by birth (Benmele dreams of his sister foraging) and between himself and Benmele by custom. Benmele, the natural son of Mun.gi, and Lambudju, the young man adopted into Mun.gi's family, frequently sang together in ceremony, so it was only natural for them to share songs. However, as we will see shortly, the two developed their own distinctive versions of "Rak Badjalarr."

Audrey's version of events also emphasizes her relationship to Lambudju via custom (she made the song and gave it to him) and by implication emphasizes the closeness of their family relationship, even though he was an adopted, rather than a natural, member of the family. Indeed, her act of passing a song to Lambudju mirrors her father's passing on of songs to Lambudju: in the former case, the transmission is from the upper to the lower generation; in the latter, from the lower to the upper. Most importantly, Audrey is asserting that although she is a woman, she exercises considerable agency within this *wangga* tradition.

The terms in which Lambudju and Audrey express their relationship to songs—that is, in terms of customary and hereditary rights—are, of course, precisely the terms in which people relate to country.

RHYTHMIC SETTING OF THE TEXT

I have previously established that within the *wangga* tradition, the normal convention for the rhythmicization of texts is for word boundaries to be marked by lengthening. As can be seen from musical example 8.2, this convention is closely followed in "Winmedje." Here meter, rhythmic structure, and the clapstick beating all work to support and clarify the word boundaries of the text: each word occupies a single measure, and the last syllable of each of the three words of the text—*winmedje* (oyster), *ngan-dji-nyene* (I am eating), and *nga-mi* ("am sitting)—is lengthened.[8] Each word coincides, moreover, with one cycle of the clapstick-beating pattern ♩♩♩♪.

In "Rak Badjalarr," however, the relationship between textual and rhythmic structure is not so straightforward. As can be seen from table 8.2, in the setting of the first text phrase, all word boundaries except the one between the words *rak* and *badjalarr* are marked by final-syllable lengthening: *rak **badjalarr**-maka **bangany-nyung***. Instead of marking off *rak*, as one would expect, a prolongation is applied to the first syllable of *badjalarr*, thus creating the impression that the first two words are not *rak* and *badjalarr* but *rakba* and *djalarr*.[9]

In his comments on this song, Lambudju said: "*Rak badjalarr bangany, bangany-nyung nga-bindja-ng*, which means that's the name of the place, *djalarr*. That's where you're going to sing." Why does Lambudju use the word *djalarr* rather than *badjalarr* here? The reason is that Wadjiginy and Kiyuk people cannot say the word *badjalarr*, particularly at night. It is so powerful that its mere utterance might call up Wunymalang from North Peron Island to steal away the *maruy* of the person who uttered it.[10] In the song, the rhythmic setting acts to disguise this powerful name, and Lambudju's use of the word *djalarr* in his explanation of the song text points to, but does not directly explicate, this aspect of the setting. At the same time, the overlapping of different formal divisions in text and song in this way marks the thing that is being obscured as potentially powerful and dangerous. Sitting on the beach at Mandorah one night following a performance of "Rak Badjalarr," I was mildly admonished for saying the word *badjalarr*: "In our language, we don't callim in the night time. We don't call that place . . . No good. Take your *maruy* away."

In "Rak Badjalarr," the setting of the second text phrase of the song, *winmedje ngan-dji-nyene*, also departs from the more conventional setting that the phrase receives in the song "Winmedje." Whereas in "Winmedje," the prolonged syllables always occur at the end of each work, in "Rak Badjalarr," one of the prolongations is transferred to the middle of the word, *winmedje* (oyster). By applying rhythmic distortion to the word "oyster" in the second text phrase, Lambudju highlights oysters as the key to the deeper meaning of this song, namely, the close relationship that people such as Lambudju and Audrey have both with the Cox Peninsula (through customary action) and with Badjalarr (by birth).

TWO OTHER PERFORMANCES OF "RAK BADJALARR"
AND THEIR IMPLICATIONS FOR TRANSMISSION

In addition to the performance of "Rak Badjalarr" already examined, two other performances—one recorded by LaMont West in 1961 and one recorded by me in 1997—are of particular interest with regard to the way matters of transmission are reflected within the fabric of the music.

Table 8.4 The distribution of rhythmic modes in Benmele's 1961 performance of "Rak Badjalarr"

Vocal section	Rhythmic mode
1	1 (melodic section 1) 5b (melodic section 2)
2	5b
3	5b
4	(unique clapstick beating pattern)

LaMont West's recording made at Beswick Creek (Barunga) on November 7, 1961, is of Lambudju's adoptive relation Rusty Benmele Moreen. Benmele's performance comprises four vocal sections—the longest version we have of this song—in which he deploys three different rhythmic modes within a single item, as set out in table 8.4.

As can be heard on CD track 25, the first melodic section of vocal section 1 is sung without clapstick beating, the clapstick beating being withheld until just before the beginning of the second melodic section. Benmele then interposes a short instrumental section between the two melodic sections, in which he takes up rhythmic mode 5b, fast doubled clapstick beating at around mm 250. He continues in this rhythmic mode throughout the second and third vocal sections before moving to a new rhythmic mode—one heard in no other *wangga* performance—in vocal section 4. Here the clapsticks are in the fast tempo band (around 124 beats per minute) in the unique rhythm: ♩♩♩♩♩𝄽. The effect is both powerful and striking.

In contrast to this, all of Lambudju's performances of "Rak Badjalarr" that I witnessed and recorded were performed in the same rhythmic mode (rhythmic mode 5d) throughout, and this practice of only ever using one rhythmic mode for a song is typical of his practice. In view of the fact that Lambudju never switched rhythmic modes within a performance, let alone within a song, it is significant that a change of rhythmic mode, similar to that made by Benmele in the final vocal section of his performance, was also made at the same point in Colin Worumbu Ferguson's 1997 performance of "Rak Badjalarr," which can be heard on CD track 26. In this performance he changes from rhythmic mode 5d, the "standard" fast uneven (triple) mode that Lambudju favors in all his mature performances, to fast even beating. The effect is similar to that of Benmele's performance—it is powerful and striking. In response to my observations about the similarity between his use of rhythmic modes and that of Benmele, Ferguson told me that he learned his version of "Rak Badjalarr" from Benmele rather than from Lambudju, and indicated that his use of rhythmic modes reflects that pattern of transmission.

Ferguson's performance reflects another aspect of Benmele's practice, this time in the realm of melody. In his version of the song, Benmele adds a distinctive melodic flourish similar to Barrtjap's figure z but never encountered in any of Lambudju's performances. In Benmele's 1961 performance, this occurred near

Example 8.3 Four performances of "Rak Badjalarr" (Mar86:4, vi; Moy62:1, i; Wes61, xxvi; Mar97:13, xiii) showing variant endings of vocal sections used by Benmele and Colin Worumbu Ferguson

the end of the first melodic section (boxed in musical example 8.3), and Ferguson's performance retains versions of this phrase in the same position, near the end of his first melodic section as well as earlier in the section (also boxed in musical example 8.3).

Colin Ferguson's 1997 performance of "Rak Badjalarr" was particularly significant because it not only articulated a relationship to Benmele but also laid claim to his being Lambudju's musical heir. While his treatment of rhythmic mode and melody expressed his relationship to Benmele, the fact that this performance called forth Lambudju's ghost in the form of a blue-green light and a cool breeze was a powerful expression of his having succeeded to the position of principal songman for this tradition. This event, drawn to my attention by Ferguson's sister, was witnessed by many of those present and held out to me as evidence of Ferguson's authority in the matter of Lambudju's songs.

Repertories are, however, particularly badly affected when, as was the case with Lambudju (and previously Benmele), a songman dies relatively young. Of the thirteen songs in Lambudju's late repertory, I have heard only four—"Rak Badjalarr," "Benmele," "Tjendabalatj," and "Bende Ribene"—performed by Ferguson. One further song, "Mubagandi," is performed by Roger Yarrowin. While this may not be the full extent of what has survived, it is clear that there has been a massive shrinkage of repertory. This contrasts with the state of Barrtjap's repertory, where more than half of his songs survive in the repertories of his sons. Direct patrilineal succession seems to be a much more reliable way to vouchsafe a tradition. It is particularly significant that Ferguson does not belong to the same language group as Lambudju (Wadjiginy) or Benmele (Emmiyangal). He is a Marri-tjevin man who also sings Walakandha *wangga* songs, and his relationship with Lambudju rests primarily on the fact that he was nursed by Lambudju's mother as a baby, and with Benmele on the fact that they married sisters.

"Benmele," a Song about Sorcery

Several songs other than "Rak Badjalarr" refer to North Peron Island or to other sites in the Daly region and their association with the dead.[11] In "Karra-ve Kanya Verver Rtedi Ka-ya-nhthi," for example, one of the Wunymalang dead sings, "I'm going to North Peron Island forever."[12] Bandawarra Ngalkin, a deep hole in the ocean between Badjalarr and the mouth of the Daly River (see figure 1.2), is another place associated with the dead. It is referred to in two songs, "Bandawarra Ngalkin" and "Karra Balhak Malvak." In the first of these, the coming in of the tide recalls the poetics of the Walakandha *wangga* where it refers to the return of the dead to their totemic source.[13] Elkin, writing of Belyuen in 1949, underscores this parallel when he observes, "The soul is carried on its Dreaming path into the womb to be born, to live in the flesh for a while, and then, when the body dies, to be carried away as the tide goes out, to rest a while, until once again it is reborn" (Harney and Elkin 1949, 146). The second describes the ghost of Lambudju's "father," Aguk Malvak, lying near this site with one leg crossed over the other.[14] At least two other songs mention places in the vicinity of Badjalarr and Bandawarra, namely, "Djappana," a beach on the north bank of the Daly river opposite Bandawarra, and "Walingave," a place that Lambudju claimed was near North Peron Island.[15]

By contrast, only one of Lambudju's songs refers to a Dreaming site on the Cox Peninsula near Belyuen, and that only obliquely. The channel-billed cuckoo, Kurratjkurratj, the traditional harbinger of death that features in Lambudju's song "Benmele" (CD track 27), has a site, a banyan tree, to the south of Milik Beach on the west coast of the Cox Peninsula. The evocation of this site is in the context of a song that Lambudju composed about the channel-billed cuckoo in response to accusations of sorcery at the time of Benmele's death.

One can only imagine the shock that must have befallen Belyuen at the untimely death of Benmele from a heart attack in the early 1980s.[16] Following Benmele's death, Lambudju received a song with the text that is set out in table 8.5, which he first sang for me in 1986.

Text phrase 1 of this song is cyclical and is set isorhythmically. A literal translation of the text is "Benmele! Kurratjkurratj! He sang for him" (see table 8.5). In terms of its grammatical structure, this phrase is ambiguous. There is no indication of which noun is the object and which is the subject. Is Benmele

Table 8.5 The text of "Benmele"

Text phrase		Text		
1	‖:Benmele-maka	kurratjkurratj	ka-bindja	-nung:‖ (4x)
	Benmele!	*Kurratj kurratj!*	*He sang*	*for him.*
2	i, a, n			

singing for Kurratjkurratj? Or is Kurratjkurratj singing for Benmele? As will become clear, this ambiguity, born once again of textual ellipsis, opens the door to multiple interpretations.

Lambudju was unequivocal about how this ambiguity should be resolved when he first explained the song to me in 1986. He first gave me the ambiguous text and then disambiguated it, glossing *kurratjkurratj* as a kookaburra (*Dacelo leachii*).

> *Benmele-maka kurratjkurratj ka-bindja-nung*, means this bloke called Benmele, *kurratjkurratj* means a kookaburra, *ka-bindja-ng ka-mi-nyung*, which means this bird kookaburra has been singing a song to Benmele.

That is, Lambudju said that the song was about a kookaburra giving a song to a songman, and not vice versa. As we have already seen with reference to Maralung and Ngulkur, in the *wangga* tradition it is not unusual for birds to be song giving agents. Barrtjap, however, who was present on this occasion, commented: "That's two words: that's one word," by which he meant, "The meaning that Lambudju is giving you is just one way (one word) of interpreting something that is actually ambiguous (two words)." This ambiguity was later pointed up by Benmele's sisters, who insisted that it was not the bird that sang for Benmele but Benmele who sang for the bird.

The disagreement between Lambudju and Benmele's sisters over the interpretation of this text spurred me on to further inquiry. In this regard, Aboriginal pedagogical method is not unlike that of a Japanese Zen master who puts a logically inconsistent proposition (a koan) to a student in order to force him to dig into his experience. And as a result of gnawing away at this problem, I eventually discovered that this was not so much a song about a bird giving a song to a songman (or a songman giving a song to a bird) as a song about death. I learned that *kurratjkurratj* was not a kookaburra at all but the channel-billed cuckoo (*Scythrops novahollaniae*), the ancestral bird who calls people away to death (Povinelli 1993, 14), and then realized that the song was about Benmele being called away to his death. The translation of *kurratjkurratj* as "kookaburra" is one frequently given to children because the channel-billed cuckoo and its associated site are regarded as particularly dangerous to children.

I next learned that a play was being made on the word *bindja*, which, as noted in the previous chapter, means not only "sing" but also "climb up" or "hang up." "They hung that body in that tree," I was told by one of Benmele's sisters. This is a reference not only to the now-discontinued practice of exposing a dead body on a tree platform but also to "that tree," the banyan tree that is the Dreaming site for the channel-billed cuckoo. Other associations between songs and trees adhere to this song. Wunymalang may be found sitting in trees, and I have been told that the songmen used to climb trees in order to find songs, just as they nowadays might go and sit in a graveyard.

Finally I learned that the song was in fact a rebuttal of an accusation that Benmele had been killed by sorcery. I had heard this accusation made on more than one occasion, so when I learned that in much of northern Australia, the channel-billed cuckoo represents natural death, as opposed to death by sorcery, the pieces fell into place.[17] If the channel-billed cuckoo had indeed called out to Benmele before his death, then clearly he could not have been ensorcelled.

Just as my ongoing discussion of "Rak Badjalarr" opened up multivalent interpretations of the song as an expression of the complex relationships that people at Belyuen have with country, so too did digging into "Benmele" open up a multiplicity of ever-deepening interpretations of the relationship of songs, sorcery, and death.

The Musical Conventions of Lambudju's Repertory

In this final section, I will summarize some of the distinctive features of Lambudju's musical style, focusing particularly on melody and rhythmic mode. As already observed, Lambudju's melodies do not fall within one mode in the way that all but one of Barrtjap's do, and it is clear that this variety of modes reflects his complex lineage. It is nonetheless possible to discern—albeit tentatively—two groups of songs, which have similar modal characteristics and can be associated with a group of composers.

The first group comprises seven songs as set out in table 8.6. Lambudju himself is associated with the composition of all but one of these.

The first three songs—"Tjerrendet," "Tjendabalatj," and "Mubagandi"—two of which are specifically attributed to Lambudju,[18] have a distinctive lydian flavor produced by the presence of F-sharp in the mode. This modal structure is found in no other *wangga* examined in this study. Second, chromatic elements in two of these songs—consecutive semitones in "Tjendabalatj" (G–F-sharp–F–E) and "Mubagandi" (G–F-sharp–F)—produce a melodic association with a further two songs attributed to Lambudju, "Bandawarra Ngalkin" and "Benmele," both of which are highly chromatic. Third, even though they include nei-

Table 8.6 The modal relationship between songs attributed to Lambudju and those close to him

Song	Pitch series	Attribution
Tjerrendet	A–G–F-sharp–D–C	
Tjendabalatj	A–G–F-sharp–F–E–D–C	Lambudju
Mubagandi	A–G–F-sharp–F–C	Lambudju
Bandawarra Ngalkin	chromatic D to C	Lambudju
Benmele	chromatic E to C	Lambudju
Winmedje	E–D–C–A–G–E–D–C	Lambudju/Benmele/ Audrey Lippo
Rak Badjalarr	A–G–E–D–C	Lambudju/Audrey Lippo

Table 8.7 Six modally related songs in Lambudju's repertory

Song	Pitch series	Comments
Karra Balhak Malvak	C–B-flat–A–G–F–E-flat–D–C	Attributed to Aguk Malvak
Walingave	C–B-flat–A–G–F–E-flat–D–C	
Bende Ribene	C–B-flat–G–F–E-flat–C	
Karra Balhak-ve	C–B-flat–A-flat–G–F–E-flat–D–C	Recorded in 1959
Limarakpa	C–B-flat–A-flat–G–F–E-flat–D–C	Recorded in 1962
Karra-ve Kan-ya Verver Rtedi Ka-ya-nhthi	C–B-flat–A-flat–G–F–E–E-flat–D–C	Recorded in 1962

ther the lydian nor the chromatic feel of the other songs in table 8.6, the pentatonic pitch series of "Rak Badjalarr" and "Winmedje" might be derived from a heptatonic lydian series on C by the omission of B and F-sharp. Although this might at first seem far-fetched, we should remember that, as shown in chapter 5, performers in the Walakandha *wangga* tradition manipulated pentatonic forms derived from a single heptatonic series to assert authority in matters of transmission. On this basis, it seems that songs with an actual or implied lydian or chromatic feel are more likely than not to have been composed by Lambudju or singers closely associated with him.

Table 8.7 shows the second set of songs. In this group—which includes modes that are both dorian and aeolian in structure—the modal character is more minor and less chromatic in feel.

Several things suggest that this group might comprise older songs. "Karra Balhak Malvak," the only song that Lambudju identified with a composer from the upper generation, falls within this group, and the three last songs in the group are all ones that Lambudju was recorded singing in the late 1950s or early 1960s, when he was still in his late teens and early twenties. At that age he would have been more likely to have been singing songs composed by his teachers than ones he composed himself.

In the final analysis, however, I can say little more than that the first group of lydian-sounding songs seems to be associated with Lambudju and his contemporaries, while the second group of minor-sounding songs seems to be associated with the upper generation of composers. Further than this I cannot go.

As was the case with Barrtjap's repertory, so the vast majority of Lambudju's repertory comprises measured songs. Of his fifteen songs, only two—"Bandawarra Ngalkin" and "Karra Balhak Malvak"—have unmeasured vocal sections in rhythmic mode 1.[19] His measured songs display a total of no fewer than nine different rhythmic modes over performances of only eleven songs. This

Table 8.8 Rhythmic modes used in the vocal sections of Lambudju's songs

Clapstick beating	Rhythmic mode	Songs	Number of songs
Unmeasured			
Without clapsticks	1	Bandawarra Ngalkin	2
		Karra Balhak Malvak	
Measured			
Slow (mm 64–69)	2	Benmele	1
Slow moderate even (mm 99)	3a	Tjerrendet	1
Slow moderate uneven triple (mm 105–7)	3b	Walingave	1
Moderate uneven quadruple (mm 110–14)	4b	Tjendabalatj	1
Moderate uneven triple (mm 116)	4c	Karra-ve Kan-ya Verver	1
Fast even (mm 121–25)	5a	Djappana	1
Fast uneven quadruple (mm 120–25)	5c	Winmedje	2
		Bangany Nye-bindja-ng	
Fast uneven triple (mm 119–22)	5d	Rak Badjalarr	1
Total			11

means that almost every one of the songs in the sample is performed in a different rhythmic mode. Those used in the sample of recordings between 1986 and 1991 are set out in table 8.8.[20]

Lambudju employs all four tempo bands for his vocal sections, including the slow moderate tempo band that he adopts for the instrumental sections of his unmeasured songs. As can be seen from table 8.8, only two measured songs—"Winmedje" and "Bangany Nye-bindja-ng"—share a rhythmic mode. This large range of rhythmic modes seems to reflect the higher degree of variety found in other aspects of his repertory, such as melody and melodic mode. If *wangga* in general is eclectic, then Lambudju's repertory is the most eclectic of them all.

chapter Nine

The Musical Conventions
of the Daly Region Revisited

This chapter will summarize some of the musical conventions of *wangga* that are shared across the four repertories discussed in the previous chapters. My interest here is not so much in constructing a taxonomy of the characteristics that typify *wangga* as a genre as in locating, and reflecting on, those elements of musical form on which signification primarily rests. The very fact that there are identifiable features that fulfill such a function across all four repertories suggests that there is a web of understandings that is shared across the whole Daly region and activated by the performance of *wangga*.

In the following discussion, I will focus primarily on the elements of *wangga* —in particular, text, melody, and rhythmic mode—that in the previous chapters have been identified as being most central to singers' abilities to enact complex social understandings. The ways in which music does this can be identified only by focusing on specific performative moments at particular points in time. That has been the work of the previous chapters. The time has now come to draw some more general conclusions.

Wangga Texts

The Diversity of Text Structures

One of the aspects of *wangga* that emerges most strongly from this study is the diversity of its text construction. Some text phrases are cyclical, others through-composed, and others a mixture of the two. Such diversity is relatively uncommon in Australian Aboriginal song. In Central Australia, for example, texts are almost exclusively cyclical and are set isorhythmically, while in Arnhem Land there is a strong tendency for public song series of the *manikay-bunggurl* genre to comprise strings of short, through-composed text phrases. This diversity of text structure in *wangga* reflects long-standing ritual, trade, and musical links with these and other areas outside the Daly region.

Texts and Meaning

Within the overall corpus of Australian Aboriginal song, the texts of *wangga* songs are noteworthy for the degree to which they approximate utterances that could be made in everyday speech. As we have repeatedly seen, *wangga* texts serve as sites for the interpenetration of worlds and modes of being, as well as for contestations over matters such as transmission, filiation to land, and history. For the song texts to fulfill this role, the form of the words must be clearly articulated. Several aspects of musical form, such as the rhythmic treatment of texts and the placement of meaningful text within vocal sections, enhance the clear articulation of text and hence its agency in the world.

THE RHYTHMIC TREATMENT OF TEXTS

To enhance the definition of semantic units, and hence the comprehensibility of texts in performance, word and sentence boundaries tend to be marked by lengthening final syllables. While this practice is particularly apparent in Lambudju's repertory, it is also apparent in varying degrees in other repertories. In both Barrtjap's repertory and the Walakandha *wangga*, for example, the longer and more complex the sentence, the more semantic units tend to be marked off in this way.

THE PLACEMENT OF MEANINGFUL TEXT WITHIN VOCAL SECTIONS

Another aspect of musical form that enhances the clear articulation of meaningful text is the tendency for it to occur most frequently in initial text phrases, where the clarity of the upper register of the voice, combined with the volume and articulation associated with the powerful initial breath, gives maximum definition to the text. In Lambudju's repertory, meaningful text occurs almost exclusively in the first melodic section, and a similar tendency is found in the Walakandha and Ma-yawa repertories.

Barrtjap's songs, whose texts tend to be highly formulaic, are somewhat of an exception to this rule. Because his textual formulary is already familiar to his audience, it needs little further definition in performance.

The Multivalency of Meaningful Text

Despite the closeness of many sung utterances to everyday speech, and despite the various musical devices that allow the texts to emerge clearly, texts are rarely totally transparent. Ellipsis and the use of words with double, or even multiple, meanings ensure that texts are always multivalent.

TEXTUAL ELLIPSIS

I have previously discussed text ellipsis in regard to numerous cases. In chapter 1, for example, we saw how ellipsis in Thomas Kungiung's text "This is what the Walakandha have always done" opened up multiple interpretations according to context. When sung by a song-giving Walakandha, it might mean "This [i.e., my singing you a song in a dream] is what the Walakandha have always done."

When sung by a songman in ceremony, it may mean "This [i.e., what I am now singing in ceremony] is what the Walakandha have always done"; and for the dancers, didjeridu player, and the witnessing audience, the text has the meaning "This [i.e., what we are doing now—dancing, playing the didjeridu, witnessing the performance] is what the Walakandha have always done."

The efficacy of Barrtjap's "Bangany-nyung Ngaya," one of the most discussed songs in this study, likewise rests on an ellipsis that opens it to being read either as the utterance of a ghost, "I'm singing for the sake [of giving you] a song," or as the statement of a songman, "I am singing for the sake of [performing] the song."

In such cases, texts serve as sites for the interpenetration of the everyday and the numinous.

WORDS WITH DOUBLE MEANINGS

Multivalency is also achieved by including words that have double meanings within a text. We have seen, for example, how "Yagarra Delhi Nye-bindja-ng Barra Ngarrka," Barrtjap's song about the Cheeky Yam Dreaming, can be interpreted on the one hand as a humorous story about an everyday event—a newcomer sees what he *thinks* is a dangerous Dreaming and runs away—and on the other as a set of instructions from a song-giving ghost to a dreaming songman: "Wait! Sing it to me. Don't be frightened. Quick! I'm singing a song." Here, as in at least two other songs, the dual interpretations rest on the ambiguity of the core element of the verb, *bindja*, which can mean both "sing" and "climb up."

This ambiguity is exploited in another of Barrtjap's songs, "Yagarra Tjüt Balk-nga-me Nga-mi," which can be interpreted either as a story about someone hurting his foot and having to get onto a plane at Murgenella on the Coburg Peninsula, or as an instruction from a song-giving ghost—"What have I come to do? I'm going to sing and then go back." *Bindja* also serves as a site of ambiguity in Lambudju's song about Benmele, which was discussed in detail in the previous chapter. Is this a song about a bird (or possibly a man) singing, or is it about putting a dead body onto a tree platform?

In addition to uniting different ontological realms, the use of words with a double meaning can also open up songs as sites for social contestation and social adjustment. The ambiguity inherent in the word *rak*, which can mean either "patri-country" or "camp," allowed the song "Yagarra Nedja Tjine Rak-pe" to be associated in one historical context with the singer's ancestral country near the Daly River mouth, and in another with a site on the Cox Peninsula. As was shown in chapter 1, these differing interpretations of *rak* were related to the different positions that people were forced to take in the course of the long-running Kenbi Land Claim.

A similar keeping open of options can be detected in another repertory from Belyuen. In Lambudju's "Rak Badjalarr," complex patterns of exegesis relate the song both to his ancestral country on the Daly, on the one hand, and to his country of residence on the Cox Peninsula, on the other.

Stability and Instability of Text

Before leaving texts, I will briefly revisit the question of stability, since this too goes beyond simply formal matters to matters of practice and meaning. In Central Australia, texts tend to be stable from performance to performance, while in Arnhem Land clan song, they are more variable. In three of the repertories studied in the previous chapters—the Walakandha *wangga*, Barrtjap's *wangga*, and Lambudju's *wangga*—the texts tend to remain stable from performance to performance. Only in the fourth, the Ma-yawa *wangga*, do performances of songs regularly vary: text phrases may be added or omitted, the order in which text phrases appear may change, and word order within individual text phrases may be reworked. The presence of such moves is significant in the Ma-yawa *wangga* and reflects the fact that it was rarely, if ever, performed in ceremony. The aesthetics of *wangga*, and in particular the expression of group solidarity in ceremonial performances, demand strong unisonal singing by two or more singers. Textual stability, singing in unison, and the maintenance of an agreed version of song all facilitate this. We have only to observe the complex range of social enactments that emerge from textually (and melodically) unstable performances like Ngulkur's performance of "Walakandha Ngindji" to appreciate the extent to which textual stability and its associated unisonal style enact social solidarity and are hence less risky.

Melody and Mode

In Australian Aboriginal music, the power of melody to signify rests primarily on a widespread convention that associates particular melodic forms with Dreamings, and by extension with the peoples and countries associated with those Dreamings. The precise ways in which this convention is played out differ from place to place, from group to group, and from occasion to occasion. The primary concern in this study is with how this convention informs specific performances of *wangga*. Owing to the rapidly changing circumstances in which *wangga* performers have found themselves, and the needs to adapt their practices in creative ways, however, this matter is far from straightforward.

While something approximating the "classical" relationship between melody, Dreamings, country, and people is to be found in the Ma-yawa *wangga*, the oldest of the repertories considered in this study, this relationship is not articulated with anything like the same degree in other repertories. The progressive alienation, over a period of more than a century, of people in the Belyuen community from their traditional Dreaming sites close to the Daly River has led to significant modification of the "classical" relationship between melodies and Dreamings, as has the new role assumed by the Walakandha *wangga* in the tripartite ceremonial arrangements established in the 1960s at Wadeye. Let us discuss each of these repertories in turn.

The Ma-yawa Wangga

Of the four melodies used in the Ma-yawa *wangga*, two were regularly used to sing songs about Marri-ammu Dreamings or Dreaming sites. Over time they have come to stand both for those Dreaming and sites and for the people associated with them. The only songs in the repertory that were not performed to these two melodies are the two that are not about Dreamings or Dreaming places, namely, "Na-pebel" and "Watjen Danggi"; each of these has its own individual melody.

The Belyuen Repertories: Tommy Barrtjap and Bobby Lambudju Lane

A lack of association between melodies and Dreamings in the Belyuen repertories is not difficult to understand, since the Belyuen people have, for several generations, lived far removed from their patri-estates and their associated Dreaming places on the Daly.

Barrtjap's repertory provides important insights into how the relationships between people, country, and melodies have been modified in the musical practice at Belyuen. As we have seen, Barrtjap's repertory tends to articulate broad relationships between people and broad tracts of country rather than precise relationships between people and specific Dreamings and Dreaming sites. This looser sort of association is reflected musically by a more generalized type of melodic identity. None of Barrtjap's songs share a melody, but all but one song share the same mode. In many ways, this looser relationship—between a vaguer sort of melodic identity and a broader conception of country—functions like ambiguity and ellipsis in text in that it allows people a wider range of interpretative strategies when they think about or explain the way songs relate to country.

In Lambudju's repertory, too, we find a much vaguer relationship between Dreamings and melody than in the Ma-yawa *wangga*, but in this case, the vagueness rests not on modal consistency but on modal complexity. Because Lambudju's repertory derives from so many different sources—from at least two Wadjiginy forebears, as well as from his Emmiyangal mentor, Nym Mun.gi—any relationship between Dreamings and melodies that might have existed in the past is no longer discernible or remembered. As in the case of Barrtjap's repertory, the fact that melody does not clearly signify a relationship to a particular Dreaming or Dreaming site is useful, since it allows interpretative strategies to accommodate the complex and shifting relationship that people at Belyuen have toward their ancestral sites, on the one hand, and their place of residence, on the other.

The Walakandha Wangga

In considering why the sorts of relationships found between the Ma-yawa melodies and Dreamings are not found in the Walakandha *wangga*, we need to consider a different, far more complex, set of factors. The first relates to the role that the Walakandha *wangga* plays within the tripartite ceremonial system, which is almost certainly quite different from the role that the Ma-yawa *wangga* played in the earlier pre-1960s ceremonial practice.

The social groups, or "mobs," associated with songs within that system—with Walakandha *wangga*, *lirrga*, and *dhanba*—are much more complex entities than the relatively small Marri-ammu group associated with the Ma-yawa *wangga*. The Walakandha *wangga* embraces not only the Marri-tjevin—whose mythologies form the basis of the repertory—but also the Marri-ammu and the Matige language groups, members of which regularly participate in the performance of the Walakandha *wangga*. While it is primarily members of the Marri-tjevin group who compose and sing songs, members of all *wangga*-owning language groups work together to produce a performance. The most important manifestation of this is the fact that men and women from all *wangga*-owning groups perform together as dancers. Group solidarity is also expressed in a number of other ways—by members of the mob sitting together during performances and clapping along with the music, by men from any language group providing the didjeridu accompaniment, and even by non-Marri-tjevin men acting as backup singers if absolutely necessary.

Dhanba similarly unites diverse Murrinhpatha clans whose mythologies and countries are different from those celebrated in *dhanba*, just as *lirrga* unites several Marri-ngarr clans. It was the Marri-ngarr whose country lies on or near the Muyil floodplain near Wudipuli who composed *lirrga* about their country and their Dreamings. Other Marri-ngarr-speaking clans whose country and Dreamings lie in other places also identify with this repertory, however, and participate in *lirrga* performances. In none of these "new" repertories is the relationship between the songs and the group who identifies with them as straightforward as it is for the Ma-yawa *wangga* repertory.

The Manipulation of Melody and Text to Reflect Relationships within Wangga-Owning Groups

To see how the complex relationships that exist within and between the groups who identify with the Walakandha *wangga* play out in performance, we need to briefly revisit two examples, Maurice Ngulkur's new *wangga* song, "Walakandha Ngindji," and "Truwu." My aim here is not to replicate the analyses produced in the chapters on the Ma-yawa *wangga* and the Walakandha *wangga* but rather to underscore more general conclusions.

"WALAKANDHA NGINDJI"

By the very act of marrying a Marri-ammu melody with a Marri-tjevin text in the composition of "Walakandha Ngindji," Ngulkur made a powerful statement about the commonality of interests held between the Marri-tjevin and the Marri-ammu. At the same time, however, he mitigated any negative connotations that might derive from the process of subjecting a Marri-tjevin text to the most potent musical symbol of Marri-ammu identity—the melody associated with his key Dreamings and Dreaming places—by significantly modifying the melody itself. The catalyst for this change was, moreover, the need to accommodate a text structure that he had derived from the Walakandha *wangga*.

A balance between Marri-ammu and Marri-tjevin interests is also enacted in other dimensions of the performance. Rhythmic modal settings typical of the Ma-yawa *wangga* and the Walakandha *wangga* sit side by side within the same vocal section, and in setting each of the text phrases of "Walakandha Ngindji," different sets of rhythmic conventions—one Marri-tjevin, the other Marri-ammu—are employed. On the one hand Ngulkur revealed his intimate knowledge of the Walakandha *wangga* repertory—in which he regularly participated as a ceremonial performer—while on the other he created a new Ma-yawa *wangga* song that was clearly related to all the other songs in that repertory. The result is a complex musical enactment of the relationship between the Marri-ammu songman Ngulkur and the primary Marri-tjevin holders of the Walakandha *wangga* tradition present at his performance.

"TRUWU"

Just as the performances of "Walakandha Ngindji" articulated themes of both solidarity and independence between different language groups among the *wangga* owners at Wadeye, so too did the performance of "Truwu." In the latter case, however, these themes were played out *within* the Marri-tjevin group. A theme of group solidarity was implied by the fact that both of the song's pentatonic melodies derive from the dorian modal series, a series associated with core Marri-tjevin interests. At the same time, performers were able to enact competing interests within the Walakandha *wangga* tradition as a whole by emphasizing or erasing differences between the two pentatonic settings of this song—one of which is associated with inland tracts of Marri-tjevin country, and the other with coastal tracts.

Rhythmic Mode and Dance

Here I will summarize the system of rhythmic modes as it is manifested across the four repertories and then briefly compare it first to the rhythmic modal practice in *lirrga*—the other main didjeridu-accompanied repertory at Wadeye —and second with a system of rhythmic modal organization that is more widely distributed in northern Australia. Finally I will explore the context in which rhythmic modes have their greatest significance: dance.

A Summary of Rhythmic Modal Practice across the Four Repertories

We have seen that a considerable number of different rhythmic modes are used in the performance of *wangga* songs, and yet, for all this variety, there is a remarkable degree of consistency in the way these are formed and applied across the four repertories. Although some modes occur in one repertory alone, many are shared, and the principles underpinning all rhythmic modes are consistent.

Rhythmic modes are defined primarily by the intersection of tempo bands and clapstick-beating patterns, though other factors may also be associated with them. These include the metrical relationship between the voice and the clapsticks and the role of the didjeridu. The didjeridu, for example, supports the definition of the unmeasured rhythmic mode (rhythmic mode 1) either by following the vocal rhythms or by remaining metrically independent. In measured rhythmic modes, on the other hand, it plays almost as great a role as the clapsticks in articulating the rhythms associated with the mode. Another feature that adds definition to rhythmic modes is the association of some modes with particular moods: songs in rhythmic mode 1, for example, tend to be imbued with a sense of gravitas, whereas songs in fast rhythmic modes are often described as "happy" (*lerri*). For ease of comparison, however, I have in this book focused primarily on the first two of the foregoing criteria, namely, clapstick-beating patterns and tempo, since it is these that are applied most consistently

Table 9.1 Summary of all rhythmic modes used in vocal sections in the Walakandha, Ma-yawa, Barrtjap, and Lambudju *wangga* repertories

Unmeasured	
Without clapsticks (vocal section only)	*mode 1*
Walakandha *wangga*: 15 of 19 songs	
Ma-yawa *wangga*: 5 of 12 songs (entirely or partly)	
Barrtjap's *wangga*: 2 of 18 songs	
Lambudju's *wangga*: 2 of 11 songs	
Measured	
Slow (mm 55–65/64–69)	
Slow even	*mode 2*
Walakandha *wangga*: 3 of 19 songs (mm 55–65)	
Barrtjap's *wangga*: 3 of 18 songs (mm 58–65)	
Lambudju's *wangga*: 1 of 11 songs (mm 64–69)	
Slow moderate (mm 99–107)	
Slow moderate even	*mode 3a*
Lambudju's *wangga*: 1 of 11 songs (mm 99)	
Slow moderate uneven (triple) (♩♩ ⅜)	*mode 3b*
Lambudju's *wangga*: 1 of 11 songs (mm 105–7)	
Moderate (mm 110–20)	
Moderate even	*mode 4a*
Ma-yawa *wangga*: 1 of 12 songs (mm 117)	

across all four repertories. Table 9.1 shows a complete list of all rhythmic modes used in the vocal sections of the repertories discussed in the previous four chapters, together with the clapstick-beating patterns and tempos that define them.

In all *wangga* repertories considered in this study, there is a primary division between the single "unmeasured" rhythmic mode, rhythmic mode 1, which is performed without clapstick beating, and the other rhythmic modes, all of which are measured and performed with clapsticks. Overall the number of clapstick-beating patterns used in the measured rhythmic modes is quite limited. The most common of these are even beating and uneven quadruple beating (♩♩♩♪). Uneven triple beating (♩♩♪) and uneven quintuple beating (♩♩♪♩♪) are used, but relatively infrequently. Measured rhythmic modes are performed in four tempo bands: slow, slow moderate, moderate, and fast, the last of which includes the interlocking fast doubled pattern described in chapter 4.

The most commonly occurring rhythmic modes are the unmeasured mode (rhythmic mode 1) and three of the four rhythmic modes in the fast tempo band. While rhythmic mode 1 is used in twenty-four songs across all four repertories, there is a significantly higher proportion of songs in rhythmic mode 1 in

Table 9.1 *continued*

Moderate uneven (quadruple) (♩♩♩♪)	*mode 4b*
Lambudju's *wangga*: 1 of 11 songs (mm 110–14)	
Moderate uneven (triple) (♩♩♪)	*mode 4c*
Lambudju's *wangga*: 1 of 11 songs (mm 116)	
Moderate uneven (quintuple) (♩♩♪♩♪)	*mode 4d*
Barrtjap's *wangga*: 2 of 18 songs (mm 117–20)	
Fast (mm 119–25/126–44/133–42/268–88)	
Fast even	*mode 5a*
Walakandha *wangga*: 1 of 19 songs (mm 133–42)	
Barrtjap's *wangga*: 4 of 18 songs (mm 126–44)	
Lambudju's *wangga*: 1 of 11 songs (mm 121–25)	
Fast doubled	*mode 5b*
Barrtjap's *wangga*: 5 of 18 songs (mm 268–88)	
Fast uneven (quadruple) (♩♩♩♪)	*mode 5c*
Ma-yawa *wangga*: 6 of 12 songs (mm 134–46)	
Barrtjap's *wangga*: 7 of 18 songs (mm 126–44)	
Lambudju's *wangga*: 2 of 11 songs (mm 120–25)	
Fast uneven (triple) (♩♩♪)	*mode 5d*
Lambudju's *wangga*: 1 of 11 songs (mm 119–22)	

the repertories at Wadeye, as compared with those at Belyuen, particularly in the Walakandha *wangga*, where fifteen out of the nineteen songs use this mode. This, as we will see in more detail shortly, is related to the fact that the dance style associated with rhythmic mode 1 is dominant at Wadeye, whereas it is rarely danced to at Belyuen.

The predominance of the three most commonly occurring modes in the fast tempo band—rhythmic mode 5a (fast even beating), rhythmic mode 5b (fast doubled beating), and rhythmic mode 5c (fast uneven quadruple [♩♩♩♪] beating)—is also related to dance practice.[1] One or another of the fast rhythmic modes is used in most songs in Barrtjap's repertory, with some songs using more than one, and rhythmic mode 5c is also used in half the songs of the Ma-yawa *wangga*. Rhythmic modes 5a and 5b, moreover, are used for all instrumental sections—the sections in which structured dancing occurs—of the Walakandha *wangga* repertory, a factor that does not emerge in table 9.1, since it deals only with vocal sections.

The slow tempo band, which is characterized by beating at a rate of around mm 55–65 (Lambudju's tempo is a little faster), contains only one rhythmic mode, rhythmic mode 2 (slow even beating). Although this rhythmic mode occurs in all repertories except the Ma-yawa *wangga*, it is used for a total of only seven songs, three of which occur in Barrtjap's repertory and three in the Walakandha *wangga*.

All other rhythmic modes are represented in only one or two songs, and this is probably related to the fact that the dance styles associated with these modes have, by and large, ceased to be performed. The slow moderate tempo band, which employs clapstick beating in the range of mm 99–107, contains two rhythmic modes, rhythmic mode 3a (slow moderate even clapstick beating) and rhythmic mode 3b (slow moderate uneven triple beating [♩♩♪]). These rhythmic modes are used only in Lambudju's repertory, where each is confined to only one song. The moderate tempo band, which has clapstick beating in the range of mm 110–20, is used in all repertories except the Walakandha *wangga* and contains four rhythmic modes, but each of its rhythmic modes is used in only one or two songs. Moderate even beating (rhythmic mode 4a) occurs only in the Ma-yawa *wangga* song "Watjen Danggi"; moderate uneven (quadruple [♩♩♩♪]) beating (rhythmic mode 4b) and moderate uneven (triple [♩♩♪]) beating (rhythmic mode 4c) are found only in Lambudju's repertory and are represented in one song each; and moderate uneven (quintuple [♩♩♪♩♪]) beating (rhythmic mode 4d) occurs in two of Barrtjap's songs (songs 2 and 16). The fourth of the fast rhythmic modes, fast (uneven triple [♩♩♪]) beating (rhythmic mode 5d), is used only in Lambudju's song "Rak Badjalarr."

Rhythmic Modes in Lirrga

A system of rhythmic modes that parallels but does not replicate that found in *wangga* is to be found in *lirrga*, the repertory of songs performed at Wadeye by the Marri-ngarr. In a study of the seventeen *lirrga* composed for performance in the church, Linda Barwick (2002) has identified a system of rhythmic modes formed first by the differentiation of an "unmeasured" rhythmic mode (that is, a mode in which singing is not accompanied by clapstick beating) from a set of measured rhythmic modes.[2]

In the church *lirrga* there are four tempo bands, each of which is identified by indigenous terminology comparable to that used for tempo bands in the *wangga* repertory at Wadeye. Because most of the clapstick beating used in the church *lirrga* is even (uneven [gapped] beating occurs only in the moderate tempo band), Barwick has defined rhythmic mode primarily as an intersection of tempo bands and the meter of texts. Before we can draw more detailed conclusions between the use of rhythmic modes in *lirrga*, a wider range of *lirrga* songs will have to be analyzed. Nonetheless, it is clear that the rhythmic organization of both *wangga* and *lirrga* is underpinned by similar principles.

Rhythmic Mode in Arnhem Land and Beyond

The system of rhythmic modes uncovered in this study rests on principles of rhythmic and metrical organization that are widespread in northern Australia and may have their provenance from beyond its shores. The clear identification of a system of rhythmic modes, based first on a differentiation between measured and unmeasured modes and then, within the measured modes, on an intersection of tempo and clapstick-beating patterns, was first made by Gregory Anderson in his 1992 doctoral dissertation on the Central Arnhem Land *manikay/bunggurl* series Murlarra. A succinct summary of his findings in this regard is published in Anderson 1995. In Arnhem Land styles, unmeasured rhythmic modes are characterized not by an absence of clapstick beating but by a lack of metrical alignment between clapstick beating—which may be either very slow or very fast—and the other elements of the musical texture. Within measured songs, Anderson identifies three tempo bands, which intersect with clapstick-beating patterns, in order to define nine of what he calls "types," and which I would call "rhythmic modes" (Anderson 1995, 14–16).

By far the most detailed account of rhythmic organization in the music of North East Arnhem Land is Peter Toner's analysis of clapstick-beating patterns in Dhalwangu clan *manikay* (Toner 2001, 82–100, 109–19). Here Toner differentiates not one but two unmeasured modes in which a nonmetrical relationship exists between the musical elements: *bulnha*, which involves very slow even beating at a rate of 20–30 beats per minute, and *yindi*, which involves very fast beating at around 240 beats per minute. Within measured songs he differentiates a total of twenty-six beating patterns that are used across a range of tempos. Toner's treatment of tempo does not, however, allow a simple comparison of his findings with mine. Nonetheless, it is clear that, in general terms, a similar system of rhythmic organization is in operation.

There is clearly a large amount of work still to be done on rhythmic mode, particularly in Arnhem Land, and in view of this it may seem premature to raise the question of whether this rather pervasive form of musical organization might be related to systems of rhythmic modes encountered in the music of Sulawesi and other islands of the Indonesian archipelago to the north of Australia. From the early seventeenth century until 1907, traders from Macassar (Ujung Pandang) visited the north coast of Australia on an annual basis to harvest bêche-de-mer (*Holothuria scabra*). It has been shown recently just how profound the legacy of these visits on ceremony and the ceremonial arts has been (see, for example, McIntosh 2000, 144–45; Morphy 1998, 213–16; Toner 2000, 22–41). Fuller description of the distinctive system of rhythmic organization found across northern Australia, coupled with comparison with the musical traditions of Sulawesi, may in the future reveal something startling about northern Australian music, namely, that it represents the southeastern end of a vast continuum of music that bases its rhythmic organization on rhythmic modes and includes Arabic *iqa'at*, Indian *tala*, and the many forms of cyclical rhythm found throughout Indonesia. Is it possible that such studies might eventually reveal continuities in the rhythmic organization of music that sweeps from the Middle East, through India, Southeast Asia, and Indonesia to the northern shores of Australia?

Even if it were possible to show that the rhythmic organization of music in northern Australia derives from Macassan contact, it is unlikely that the influence of Macassan systems of rhythmic organization on *wangga* came from direct contact between Macassans and the peoples of the Daly region. It is more likely to have occurred as a result of the long-standing trade and ceremonial relationships between the Daly region and the regions of Western Arnhem Land where the Macassans regularly came ashore, and where their influence is most deeply felt within the ceremonial arts.

The Relationship of Rhythmic Modes to Dance

The main significance of rhythmic modes stems from their association with dance. Indeed, while some rhythmic modes are named by reference to the action of the clapsticks (for example, the Marri-tjevin *ambi tittil*, "without clapsticks," or the Marri-ngarr *titir kindjerryit*, "clapsticks drag,"), at least one mode is named by reference to the associated dance movement, namely, *tarzi verri* (quick foot).

At Wadeye, where dancing nowadays occurs almost exclusively to songs with vocal sections in rhythmic mode 1 and instrumental sections in either rhythmic mode 5a (fast even) or 5b (fast doubled), all dancing conforms to the same basic pattern. As we saw in chapter 4, this involves unstructured mimetic movement in the unmeasured vocal sections and more structured dancing in the instrumental sections. In a recording made in 1974 (Rei74; see appendix table 1.1), however, we hear a distinctly more complex rhythmic modal practice than that heard today. This suggests that earlier in its history, the Walakandha *wangga* accommodated a wider diversity of dance styles. When questioned, senior performers confirmed that this was indeed the case but dismiss the older dance styles as "old-fashioned." In the *lirrga* tradition, on the other hand, individual

songs continued to be sung in a variety of rhythmic modes with a variety of associated dance styles until at least 1997.

Far from lamenting the loss of an earlier, more complex practice, senior
Marri-tjevin men like Frank Dumoo pragmatically point to the strength of the
unisonal dancing that is made possible by adopting a single style. Just as singing
strongly in unison expresses shared values and agendas, so too does strong
unisonal dancing. To unite the three language groups—Marri-tjevin, Marri-
ammu, and Matige—as well as the diverse interests (such as the different Marri-
tjevin song lineages) within these language groups, the elders appear to have
made a conscious decision to simplify the system of dance. Nonetheless, even as
they point to the virtues of having one dance style, the more senior dancers cannot restrain themselves from occasionally dancing in older styles, such as the
slow stamping associated with rhythmic mode 2—but they do so in solo turns,
usually at the edge of the performance.

At Belyuen the situation is in one sense different, but in another the same.
Whereas at Wadeye most of the dancing occurs to songs whose vocal sections
are unmeasured, at Belyuen most, if not all, dancing occurs to songs whose vocal sections are measured. At Belyuen, songs sung in rhythmic mode 1 seem no
longer to be used to accompany dance (at least not in my experience), and the
songs that are performed for dancing occur primarily in the fast tempo bands.

The similarity between Wadeye and Belyuen is that in both cases a repertory
that included several dance styles has, under the pressure to provide strong
unisonal dancing, been reduced to a repertory that by and large supports a single style of dance. At Belyuen the "boxing up," or unifying, of the diverse language groups is reflected in ceremonial action. Although in the past there were
several song lineages, each based in a separate language group and maintaining
its own repertory, by the mid-1980s, these had effectively contracted to just two,
of which Barrtjap's was the more dominant. Just as the Walakandha *wangga* was
made to serve the interests of diverse language groups, so too at Belyuen, Barrtjap's repertory became the *wangga* to which the whole community performed.

The account given here of musical conventions and their significance is not in-
tended to be exhaustive. A number of important ways in which aspects of music
signify—the association of the didjeridu with conception (see chapter 4), or the
power of voice quality to make permeable the boundaries between the worlds of
the living and the dead (see chapter 5), for example—have not been included in
the summary. My intention is, however, to give a general sense of the musical
and dance conventions of *wangga* and the ways in which they are manipulated
by singers in their home environment in the Daly region.

In the final chapter, I will investigate what happens to these conventions
when songs are taken over by singers who do not belong to Daly region communities and, in many cases, neither speak Daly languages nor fully understand the
wangga style. What happens to the texts and the musical forms of the songs

when they are taken up by singers in the Kimberley and assigned a quite different ceremonial function from that which they have in the Daly region? What happens when new *wangga* songs are created in this environment?

By considering which aspects of the Daly song conventions endure, and which collapse, in the new contexts, and by reflecting on the factors that contribute to these changes, we will gain not only an understanding of the processes by which songs are adapted when they are traded into, or composed within, a wider diaspora, but also further perspectives on the stylistic conventions of this genre in its home environment.

chapter Ten

Wangga beyond the Daly: Performance in the Wider Diaspora

Ceremonial reciprocity is an essential element that binds together the different language groups at Wadeye, which in turn is a microcosm of a wider network of reciprocal relationships between Wadeye and other communities. With the exception of *wangga*, all the song genres performed at Wadeye represent localized forms of genres that belong to other communities or regions. Thus the *lirrga* repertory is a localized form of *gunborrg*, a genre of song associated with communities to the east and northeast, in particular Gunbalanya (Oenpelli), Manigrida, and Barunga. *Dhanba* is a localized form of genres such as *junba* and *balga* from the Kimberley (see chapter 1). The existence of localized forms of these traditions in no way, however, precludes families from Daly communities from engaging singers from Arnhem Land or the Kimberley to perform genres such as *gunborrg* or *bunggurl*. For circumcision ceremonies, singers tend to be drawn from more remote communities, while *burnim-rag* ceremonies tend to draw more on local traditions.

Not only do distant traditions travel to Daly communities, but also local traditions, in particular *wangga* and *lirrga*, travel to communities outside the region. For many decades, *wangga* has been taken from the Daly to Barunga, where it is known as both *wangga* and *walaka*; to communities in the Kimberley, where it is frequently confused with *lirrga*; and to Gunbalanya, where it is known as *djungguriny*.[1] In this chapter, I will first outline the history of *wangga* performance at Barunga, focusing first on performances of Barrtjap's *wangga* by Laurence Wurrpen, a Wadjiginy man resident at Barunga, and second on the localization of *wangga* at Barunga through the compositional activities of Alan Maralung. I will then examine its spread in the Kimberley to the south and southwest of Wadeye, focusing first on performances of items from the Walakandha and Ma-yawa *wangga* repertory in the eastern Kimberley, and then on performances of Walakandha *wangga* songs in the more distant western and northern Kimberley.

Wangga in the Barunga/Beswick Region

A Performance of Barrtjap's Songs at Barunga in the 1960s

The tradition of performing *wangga* at Barunga is a long-standing one, extending back at least to the 1940s.[2] All three *wangga* performances that Elkin recorded at or near Beswick Creek in 1949 and 1952 were from the Daly River area (A. Moyle 1966, 34, 39). The *walaka* [*wangga*] recorded at Tandandjal in 1949 is described as being "owned by the *kungarr* people just north of the Daly River" (Elkin and Jones 1958, 63); the "Brinkin Wongga" recorded at Beswick Creek in 1952 is described as being "of the 'inside' or bush people of the Daly River region" (149); and a second recording made in 1952 at Beswick Creek is described as "A Daly River Wongga," which the songman Lamderod had learned from his maternal relations on the Daly River (151).

In 1964 the anthropologist Kenneth Maddock made two recordings at Barunga of the Wadjiginy singer Laurence Wurrpen, who performed a number of songs from Barrtjap's repertory.[3] Laurence Wurrpen grew up at Belyuen and was a native speaker of Batjamalh, the language of Barrtjap's songs. Wurrpen married into the community of Barunga, some four hundred kilometers to the southeast of Belyuen, and lived there for most of his adult life. Although his precise relationship to the Bandak-Barrtjap-Burrenjuck line is unclear, Wurrpen clearly had the right to sing Barrtjap's repertory and other songs from Belyuen.[4]

Maddock's recordings contain six of the eighteen *wangga* in the repertory recorded by Barrtjap (see appendix table 3.2), of which three ("Dadja Kadja Bangany Nye-ve," "Yagarra Nga-bindja-ng Nga-mi," and "Bangany-nyung Ngaya") were examined in chapters 4 and 7. Maddock's recordings of these songs illustrate three of the things that can happen when *wangga* is removed from its home environment and adopted in a remote community: songs may remain relatively unchanged; the number of text phrases may be significantly reduced while retaining the same melodic structure; and a segment of the original song—one text phrase, for example—may be taken as the basis of what becomes effectively a new song.

"DADJA KADJA BANGANY NYE-VE," "YAGARRA NGA-BINDJA-NG NGA-MI," AND "BANGANY-NYUNG NGAYA" REVISITED

"Dadja Kadja Bangany Nye-ve" is an example of a song that remained relatively unchanged. A transcription of four performances of this song (see musical example 7.6) reveals just how close Wurrpen's 1964 performance was to those of Jimmy Bandak, Barrtjap, and Kenny Burrenjuck. The degree and type of variation between Wurrpen's performance and those of the main Belyuen singers is little different from those that occur *between* the Belyuen singers from 1952 to 1997. The same cannot be said for Wurrpen's performances of the other two songs.

In Wurrpen's version of "Yagarra Nga-bindja-ng Nga-mi," we encounter the second type of effect that transmission outside the home community can have on a song. The number of text phrases is significantly reduced, while the me-

Table 10.1 Melodic section 1 of Barrtjap's version of "Yagarra Nga-bindja-ng Nga-mi"

Barrtjap 1968 (melodic section 1 only)

yagarra nga-bindja-ng nga-mi
Yagarra! I'm singing!

yagarra yine nga-ve me-nung*
Yagarra! What have I come to do?

nga-p-pindja-ng nga-p-puring-djü nüng
I'm going to sing and then go back.

yagarra nye-bindja-ng nya-mu
Yagarra! You sing!

* Text selected by Wurrpen is in boldface.

lodic structure is retained. This sort of change tends to occur particularly in un-measured *wangga* with long and complex texts, of which "Yagarra Nga-bindja-ng Nga-mi" is a prime example. Wurrpen's version, the vocal line of which can be seen in musical example 10.1, comprises two melodic sections that are melod-ically related (albeit in a truncated form) to the two melodic sections of Barr-tjap's performance (see musical example 7.1).

The text sung to each melodic section, however, is based on only the first of the two melodic sections of Barrtjap's performance, and even then, on only two of its four text phrases. Table 10.1 shows the text of melodic section 1 of Barr-tjap's version, in which the text taken up by Wurrpen is highlighted. Table 10.2 shows Wurrpen's version.

Example 10.1 "Yagarra Nga-bindja-ng Nga-mi" as performed by Wurrpen (Mad64:2, xvi)

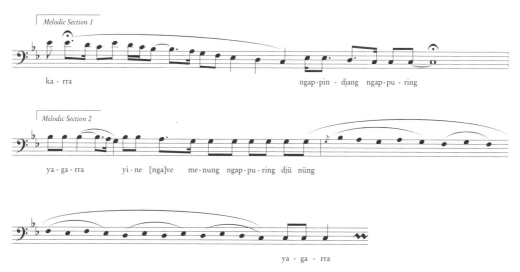

Table 10.2 Wurrpen's version of "Yagarra Nga-bindja-ng Nga-mi"

Wurrpen 1964	
Melodic section 1	karra nga-p-pindja-ng nga-p-puring *I'm going to sing and then go back.*
Melodic section 2	yagarra yine nga-ve me-nung *Yagarra! What have I come to do?*
	nga-p-puring djü nüng yagarra *I will go back. Yagarra!*

Wurrpen's rearranged text, although different from Barrtjap's, nonetheless makes grammatical sense, as one would expect from a native speaker of Batjamalh. Indeed, it might be seen as encapsulating the very core of Barrtjap's text ("What have I come to do? I'm going to sing and then go back"). This suggests that Wurrpen fully understood not just the words but also the cosmological significance of the song—that is, that the song is an utterance of a Wunymalang ghost. As we shall see later, while nonnative speakers in the Kimberley also generate new versions of *wangga* songs from the Daly by selecting fragments of text and rearranging them, their changes tend both to be ungrammatical and to reflect a lack of understanding of the broader cosmological significance of the songs.

In the third and final example, "Bangany-nyung Ngaya," Wurrpen takes up

Example 10.2 "Bangany-nyung Ngaya," as performed by Wurrpen (Mad64:2, xiii, vocal section 2)

only part of the original—melodic section 3—and generates what is effectively a new song. Barrtjap's original form of melodic section 3 from "Bangany-nyung Ngaya" is shown in the lower stave of musical example 10.2. Wurrpen's new version is shown in the upper two staves.

Wurrpen's "new" song has two melodic sections, both of which are clearly based on melodic section 3 of the original. The melodies of the two melodic sections are virtually identical both to each other and to Barrtjap's original, and the text clearly derives from Barrtjap's original. There are, however, significant differences. In melodic section 1, for example, Wurrpen adds new, unintelligible text (shown as [???] in musical example 10.2), and melodic sections 1 and 2 of the original are nowhere to be seen.

We have already seen that at Wadeye, singers sometimes create new songs by taking an existing melody or section of melody and adding new or modified text. This occurs both in the group 2 songs of the Walakandha *wangga* repertory and in certain songs of the Ma-yawa *wangga* repertory.

One reason why I am inclined to regard this as a new song derived from "Bangany-nyung Ngaya," rather than a variant of it, is the fact that later in the same performance, Wurrpen sang "Bangany-nyung Ngaya" in its original form. He clearly could, had he wished, have rendered "Bangany-nyung Ngaya" in its original form. But these matters are rarely simple. When I played a recording of Wurrpen's version to some of the older and more senior men and women at Belyuen, they dismissed it as nothing more than a corrupted version of Barrtjap's best-known song. Some people—most commonly those who did not realize that Wurrpen was in fact Wadjiginy—even went so far as to say, with a degree of anger, that he had "stolen" the song. The changes that Wurrpen made to the text and music clearly fell outside what is acceptable at Belyuen, and this resulted in a good deal of hilarity and derision. As we will see later with reference to performances of Walakandha and Ma-yawa *wangga* at Kununurra, even small departures from the original version of a song by someone living at some distance

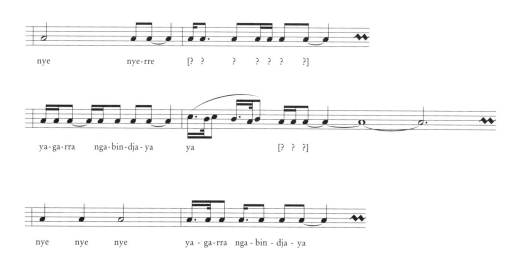

from its home community can result in similarly derisive hilarity or even puzzlement when recordings are played back in the home community.

Alan Maralung's Bunggridj Bunggridj Wangga

Not all *wangga* sung at Barunga in the period from 1960 to 1990 was imported from a Daly community. Another singer active in Barunga in the 1960s, Alan Maralung, was composing unequivocally new songs with the assistance of song-giving spirits. Maralung's detailed account of how he received the song "Minmin Light" from his spirit agents Balanydjirri and Bunggridj Bunggridj was a centerpiece in my consideration of song composition in chapter 2.

In 1961 LaMont West recorded Alan Maralung and noted: "[Maralung] is the actual composer of this song cycle, but alleges that he is inspired and taught in dreams by the ghost of a deceased songman" (West 1974). What exactly did Maralung receive from his song-giving spirits, and in what ways, if any, did this differ from what was given to singers resident in Daly communities?

Maralung's song texts consist entirely of vocables that have no meaning in everyday language. It seems that only singers from the Daly region have the ability to "turn over" texts into human language, and then only if they are descended from the ancestors who first gave the songs.[5] Viewed from the point of view of musical composition, however, Maralung's vocable texts can be seen as providing a wonderful vehicle for the flexible and ever-changing form of his songs. By the time I met him in 1986, Maralung had for many years been too frail to sustain ceremonial performances and was thus freed from any obligation to sing loudly in unison with another singer, or to provide clear musical structures for the dancers. He, like Maurice Ngulkur, was therefore able to explore musical elements more intensively through improvisation. A detailed account of these processes as manifested in performances of the song "Minmin Light" between 1986 and 1988 has already been published (Marett 1992). The following discussion will therefore merely summarize the key points of that analysis in the light of the broader concerns of this book.

Like most songs in Maralung's repertory, "Minmin Light" (CD track 28) is an unmeasured *wangga*, that is, one in which the vocal section does not have a clapstick-beating accompaniment.[6]

On July 14, 1986, Maralung sang the newly composed song "Minmin Light" sixteen times in succession.[7] In hindsight, it is clear that Maralung structured this performance in order to demonstrate his improvisational skills to me. There are clear parallels with Ngulkur's performance of "Walakandha Ngindji" discussed in chapter 6, where in a similar fashion Ngulkur systematically laid out aspects of his musical language for me. Except in a very small number of cases, each of the sixteen items sung by Maralung comprised three vocal sections, and each vocal section consisted of two closely related melodic sections. Melodic sections were made up of four elements, which in my 1992 analysis I labeled "introduction," "main text," "transition," and "closing formula." Of these, the introduction and transition were only sometimes present, and when they were, the form of each was highly variable. The other two elements—"main text" and "closing formula"—occurred in every melodic section, though their precise form also varied from item to item.

Some four weeks later I made another recording of "Minmin Light" and was curious to see whether the song had settled into a more fixed form.[8] If anything, however, the flexible processes evident in the first performance were even more in evidence, and the song had continued to evolve. Maralung had added a short instrumental section, which he inserted into the middle of the main text. Moreover, whereas in the first performance the vocal section almost always comprised two melodic sections, in the later performance he occasionally adopted a one- or three-melodic-section form.

When I heard Maralung sing "Minmin Light" for a third time, on February 29, 1988,[9] the song had developed even further. There was a new optional coda, in effect an additional melodic section. The introduction had now virtually disappeared, and where it did occur, it took on a new form that concluded with a cadence that also effectively produced another melodic section.

While certain aspects of Maralung's practice—for example, the high proportion of vocables—might be seen as typical of *wangga* composed outside the Daly, flexibility of musical form is not, in itself, a feature of diasporic *wangga*. We have already seen elements of this in the Ma-yawa *wangga*, which, although not diasporic, is rarely performed ceremonially.

Wangga in the Kimberley Region

Another area where *wangga* from the Daly region has been adopted is the Kimberley. From my own and others' recordings, it is clear that a very high proportion of what is known as *wangga* in the Kimberley has been imported from Wadeye or Belyuen. However, a high proportion of what they call *wangga* in the Kimberley is not in fact *wangga* but *lirrga*. As in Barunga, new *wangga* songs have been composed in the Kimberley, though it cannot be said to be a major center of *wangga* composition.[10]

In the eastern Kimberley, which lies to the south of Wadeye, there is evidence of a long association with *wangga*—long enough, at least, for themes associated with *wangga* to form part of the local mythology. There is, for example, a site near Police Hole in the Keep River National Park where the ancestral bat, Tjinimin, the central figure in the myth discussed in chapter 3, can be seen standing up in the rock, dancing *wangga* together with one of the dancing birds. A version of the Tjinimin myth, which specifically mentions the didjeridu, is also known at Kununurra, and there is an important Tjinimin site near the Bullo River crossing.

Strong family ties also exist between the Daly region and the eastern Kimberley, and this extends to *wangga* and *lirrga* singers from the Daly: both Charlie Brinken and the *lirrga* singer Jimmy Numbertwo had, or have, family ties in Kununurra. Moreover, performers from Wadeye travel regularly to Kununurra and Timber Creek for ceremony where they perform all the major public genres.

Most of the *wangga* and *lirrga* songs that have been taken up by singers in the eastern Kimberley are acknowledged to come from the Daly, and in many cases the composers of the songs are remembered. The distinction between *wangga* and *lirrga*, moreover, is well understood, although it tends to be eroded by the fact that, in contrast to the practice at Wadeye, the same singers will often perform both genres and will mix *wangga* and *lirrga* songs in the same performance.

The precise dates at which didjeridu-accompanied genres such as *wangga* and *lirrga* entered the northern and western Kimberley are more difficult to ascertain. People living in the northern Kimberley today say that *wangga* arrived there in the 1940s (Sally Treloyn, personal communication, 2002), and this is supported to an extent by the fact that there is no evidence of *wangga* or any other didjeridu-accompanied genre in Andreas Lommel's quite detailed account of ceremony based on fieldwork conducted in the area in 1938 and 1939 (Lommel 1952).

In the western Kimberley, at Mowanjum, and at related communities to the north of Derby, such as Dodnun (near Gibb River; see introduction figure 1), a relatively high proportion of what is truly *wangga* (that is, not *lirrga*) is derived either from the Walakandha *wangga* or from Belyuen *wangga* singers such as Billy Mandji and Jimmy Muluk, both of whom spent significant periods of time in the Kimberley. Although knowledgeable songmen such as Dusty Lejune (who was originally from Wadeye) or Jack Dann may understand that *wangga* and *lirrga* are distinct genres, in this part of the world, both are generally referred to as "*wangga*" and, as in the eastern Kimberley, freely mixed in performance. In the western and northern Kimberley, ritual and family ties to the Daly are significantly less strong than in the eastern Kimberley. Whereas in the east, performances of *wangga* retain enough features of the original songs for their identity to remain clear, in the more remote northern and western areas, songs are often modified beyond the point of recognition. Even though the pronunciation of song texts may become a little distorted in the eastern Kimberley, they remain close enough to the original for them to remain comprehensible to native speakers.

Wangga songs clearly have a different ceremonial role in the Kimberley from that which they have in the Daly region. Even when *wangga* songs from Wadeye are performed at nearby communities such as Timber Creek or Kununurra, the ritual significance and meaning that the songs have within the Daly is not fully replicated. When *wangga* is performed at even more distant communities such as Mowanjum, or at desert communities such as Dagaragu, the significance and even the nature of the songs in their original environment are rarely understood. Stripped of the meanings that adhere to them in their home environments, they take on new significance.

I will now examine four song sessions focusing on a number of specific songs. The first of these was recorded in the eastern Kimberley at Kununurra. The other three were recorded either at Dodnun in the northern Kimberley or at Myall's Bore, near Derby, in the western Kimberley. In most cases these performances comprised a mixture of *wangga* and *lirrga*.

In discussing the Kununurra performance, I will focus on two songs: a Ma-yawa *wangga* song about Jungle Fowl (*Malhimanyirr* in Marri-ammu) that is no longer performed at Wadeye; and a Walakandha *wangga* song about the Marri-tjevin ancestor Wutjeli.

The Performance of Two Songs from Wadeye at Kununurra

On September 2, 1998, I recorded an elicited performance at Kununurra, in which the vocalists were senior singers Philip Pannikin and another singer who wishes to remain anonymous. Jeff Janama played the didjeridu.[11] Many of the songs that were sung were from Wadeye, yet their form differed significantly from that which they had in their home community. As shown in table 10.3, the performance mixed *wangga* items (from both the Walakandha and Ma-yawa *wangga* repertories) with *lirrga* songs, which formed the majority of what was sung.[12]

The performance began with two items of a *wangga* song attributed to "Charlie Port Keats," later identified as Charlie Brinken, the principal composer of the Ma-yawa *wangga* repertory. Marri-ammu people at Wadeye later identified the subject of the song as the Jungle Fowl (Malhimanyirr) Dreaming. This song has been designated "Malhimanyirr no. 2" to distinguish it from "Malhimanyirr no. 1," the song about Jungle Fowl performed by Maurice Ngulkur. The Kununurra singers, however, apparently mistaking it for a Walakandha *wangga* song, identified it as a song about "Full Tide." Six *lirrga* songs belonging to Marri-ngarr singers from Wadeye or Palumpa were then sung (all but one of them twice), and these were followed by a further four *wangga* items: two items of Kungiung's "Wutjeli" and two further items of "Malhimanyirr no. 2." The performance concluded with a single *lirrga* item.

"MALHIMANYIRR NO. 2"

"Malhimanyirr no. 2" seems to have been in the repertory of *wangga* singers at Kununurra for several decades, surviving there long after it was forgotten at Wadeye, and in the meantime undergoing significant change. Over the years, the subject of the song and its origin within the Ma-yawa *wangga* repertory seem,

Table 10.3 **The structure of a song session recorded at Kununurra on September 2, 1998**

Items	Genre: Title
i–ii	Ma-yawa *wangga*: "Malhimanyirr no. 2"
iii–xiii	*Lirrga* items
xiv, xv	Walakandha *wangga*: "Wutjeli"
xvi, xvii	Ma-yawa *wangga*: "Malhimanyirr no. 2"
xviii	*Lirrga* item

Table 10.4 The text of "Malhimanyirr no. 2"

Text phrase	Text
1	aven-[an]dja-wurri aven-[an]dja-wurri *"Where have they gone to?" [they say] to me.* (x 2)
2	kindji-murriny marzi *They call from the edge of the jungle.*
3	ngindji malhimandha [?kagandja?] *One Jungle Fowl is right here now.*
4	yagarra *Yagarra!*

apart from the attribution to Charlie Brinken, to have been forgotten. This is not altogether surprising in view of the fact that the Ma-yawa *wangga* has long since been eclipsed by the Walakandha *wangga* as the dominant repertory at Wadeye. Nowadays at Kununurra the song is believed to be about the tide, one of the central poetic elements of the Walakandha *wangga* repertory. In addition it has picked up a number of musical characteristics that are atypical of the Ma-yawa *wangga* repertory. The text of "Malhimanyirr no. 2" is set out in table 10.4.

Marri-ammu speakers at Wadeye were able, apart from being uncertain about one word (possibly *kagandja*), to pick up and translate the text of "Malhimanyirr no. 2," despite the fact that "Malhimanyirr" was mispronounced as "Malhimandha." Given that they did not know the true subject of the song, it is extraordinary how well the Kununurra singers had preserved this text.

> "Where have they gone to?" [they say] to me. "Where have they gone to?"
> [they say] to me.
> They call from the edge of the jungle. One Jungle Fowl is right here now.
> Yagarra!

The confidence that the Marri-ammu felt in identifying this as a song about Jungle Fowl—despite the mispronunciation of the key word—is not surprising, since in the version current at Wadeye, the Jungle Fowl Dreaming also calls out at the edge of the jungle. Here is part of the text of "Malhimanyirr no. 1":

> Jungle Fowl is forever piling up [earth for her nest] and calling out.
> In the dense jungle she is forever piling up [earth for her nest]
> and calling out.[13]

We do not know for sure why in "Malhimanyirr no. 2" the jungle fowl is calling out, but the expression "Where have they gone to?" resonates strongly with expressions of abandonment in the Walakandha *wangga* repertory, where the ancestors left behind in country that had been depopulated at the time of mis-

Example 10.3 "Malhimanyirr no. 2" (Mar98:4, xvi)

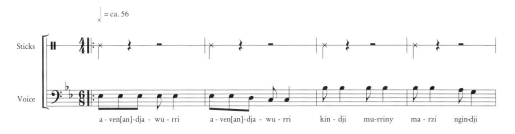

sionization expressed their loneliness in song. The appearance of the word *ya-garra* in the text of "Malhimanyirr no. 2" is also significant, since this word is usually associated with *wangga* from Belyuen and is not found in songs from Wadeye. Here, in the *wangga* songs of Kununurra, we seem to see at work the same magpie approach that I earlier identified as typical of the way *wangga* composers make new songs, but here it is applied to the transformation of an existing *wangga* song by incorporating into it elements from far and wide. Musical considerations confirm this impression.

As shown in musical example 10.3, the vocal sections of "Malhimanyirr no. 2" are performed in rhythmic mode 2 (slow clapstick beating at a rate of mm 56–58). Given the infrequency with which this rhythmic mode is used—it occurs in only seven songs from the four repertories previously surveyed—its use here is striking. But even greater significance lies in the fact that this rhythmic mode is never used today in performances of the Ma-yawa *wangga* repertory. While we can never be absolutely sure that "Malhimanyirr no. 2" was originally sung in one of the rhythmic modes typical of the current Ma-yawa *wangga* repertory, there seems to be a good chance that rhythmic mode 2 has been appropriated to this song from somewhere else since its importation to Kununurra. The Wala-kandha *wangga* repertory might seem an obvious source, since this rhythmic mode is the one used for all but one of the measured songs in that repertory, but without knowing more about which songs have circulated in Kununurra over the past decades, we cannot be sure of this.

One of the most distinctive features of the Ma-yawa *wangga* repertory is the use of a single melody, melody 1, for many of the songs about Dreamings, including "Malhimanyirr no. 1." "Malhimanyirr no. 2," however, does not use melody 1, although it does retain its dorian modal character.

Before leaving this performance, we might consider how Marri-ammu and Marri-tjevin people at Wadeye responded to this performance. It did not produce the same strong reactions of hilarity and anger that Wurrpen's performances of Barrtjap's songs did at Belyuen. Rather, it seemed to trouble people. They were disturbed by the distortion of the key word "Malhimanyirr" into "Malhimandha" and by their inability to decipher the final word of the second text phrase. This is not surprising, given the intimate relationship that exists between language and country. Nor is it particularly surprising that no interest was expressed in restoring this song to the repertory. It is as if the changes that have occurred during the time the song has been in Kununurra have disturbed too many of the elements—both textual and musical—that convey meaning at Wadeye.

"WUTJELI"

"Wutjeli," the other *wangga* song sung in the Kununurra performance, is a group 1 song from the Walakandha *wangga* repertory. As it is performed at Wadeye, it has the same text structure as "Truwu," that is, a pair of through-composed couplets, each of which is sung to an identical melody. Indeed, as can be seen by comparing table 10.5 with table 5.2, the second text phrase of "Wu-tjeli" is almost identical to the first text phrase of "Truwu."

In the performance by Pannikin and an anonymous singer shown in table 10.6, the text-phrase pair of the original is reduced to a single text phrase by conflating the two text phrases of the original. The parts of the original text that are retained are shown in boldface in table 10.5. The following processes have occurred. First, "Wutjeli," the name of the specific Walakandha ancestor, has been replaced by the more general "Walakandha," gleaned perhaps from the second text phrase of the song. The move from the specific to the more general subject reflects, once again, a lesser degree of knowledge about the original significance of the song on the part of the Kununurra singers. Next, the second half of the first text phrase (*kuwa rtidim nidin-ngina*) has been replaced by the second half of the second text phrase (*kuwa-vapa-vinyanga truwu nidin-ngina*). Both these half text phrases begin with *kuwa* (he stands), and it seems likely that *kuwa* has formed the pivot for the conflation, perhaps in the course of misremembering.

This is not unlike what we saw in Wurrpen's performances of "Yagarra Ngabindja-ng Nga-mi," where two phrases of the four-phrase original text were similarly rearranged to create an altered version of the song. While in Wurrpen's case the resultant new text was completely grammatical, at Kununurra it is not. When I played the Kununurra version of "Wutjeli" in Wadeye, it was met with considerable hilarity. In fact, for a while the Kununurra recording of "Wutjeli" was a hit, simply because of its ability to produce near paralytic laughter among the audience.

Turning now to musical structure: musical example 10.4 compares an example of the two melodic sections that make up a full vocal section in Kungiung's performance of "Wutjeli" with the conflated melodic section that makes up a vocal section in Pannikin's performance.

In the Kungiung version, the two text phrases of the couplet are set to the same descending melody, the notes of which belong to the dorian series commonly associated with the Kungiung/Dumoo lineage. The rhythm is free, with final-syllable lengthening conforming to the typical patterns for group 1 songs of the Walakandha *wangga* repertory.

In the Kununurra version, however, the mode is altered, with the E-flat be-

Table 10.5 The text of "Wutjeli" as performed by Thomas Kungiung at Wadeye

Text phrase	Initial vocable	Initial vocative text formula	Core sentence	Concluding vocative text formulas
1	**karra**	wutjeli	**kani-put-puwa** kuwa	rtidim nidin-ngina
	karra	*Wutjeli!*	*He is always standing with one leg crossed over the other.*	*Rtidim! My country!*
2	karra	**walakandha**	purangang devin **kuwa-vapa-vinyanga**	**truwu nidin-ngina walakandha**
	karra	*Walakandha!*	*The lonely sea. It stands up and crashes on them.*	*Truwu! My country! Walakandha!*

Table 10.6 The text of "Wutjeli" as sung by Pannikin and an anonymous singer at Kununurra

Text phrase	Initial vocable	Initial vocative text formula	Core sentence		Concluding vocative text formulas
1	karra	[walakandha]	kani-put-puwa		
			kuwa	-vapa-vinyanga	truwu nidin-ngina (walakandha)

Example 10.4 Kungiung's performance of one vocal section of "Wutjeli" (Eni92, iv) compared with that of Pannikin and an anonymous singer at Kununurra (Mar98:4, xv)

coming natural. Given the close and often very precise relationship that exists between mode, family, and country at Wadeye, this alteration of the melody must again be regarded as significant. It is likely that this alteration occurred unintentionally, but the fact that it persists reflects, once again, a lack of knowledge about the finer points of musical signification at Wadeye.

Apart from the fact that E-flat is replaced by E-natural, however, all the words of the Kununurra text are sung to the same pitches that they were in Kungiung's version. Thus each of the three words that derive from the first text phrase of the Kungiung version (boxed and labeled A in musical example 10.4) is sung to the same pitches (B-flat–A–G) as in the original, while the second half of the text phrase (boxed and labeled B) is—apart from the transformation of E-flat to E-natural—sung to the same basic pitches as the original. Thus, as was the case with Wurrpen's conflation, it is the melody that provides the glue that links the new version with the old.

One final feature of the Kununurra performance should be considered, since it suggests that a new form unique to *wangga* performances of the eastern Kimberley may have evolved. Having produced a single text phrase—let us call it A—

singers generate a new large-scale form made up of two vocal sections, the first of which comprises two occurrences of A, and the second one. This may be represented as follows:

    Vocal section 1 text phrase A (repeated)
    Instrumental section 1
    Vocal section 2 text phrase A
    Final instrumental section

This pattern is followed not only in both performances of "Wutjeli" in the recorded song session but also in all four performances of "Malhimanyirr no. 2."

"Wangga" in the Northern and Western Kimberley

Turning now to the northern and western Kimberley, I will now consider three performances of *wangga*, two recorded in 1997 at Bijili, the ceremony ground near the northern Kimberley community of Dodnun, and the other recorded in 2001 at Myall's Bore near Mowanjum.

Table 10.7 Summary of three performances of "wangga" in the northern and western Kimberley

Bijili (May 3, 1997)[a]	Bijili (May 4, 1997)[b]	Myall's Bore (Feb./Mar. 2001)[c]
	Wangga: 1 song (Barrtjap's "Yagarra Nga-bindja-ng Nga-mi") performed as 2 items	*Wangga*: 12 items
Lirrga: 17 items	*Lirrga*: 15 items	*Lirrga*: 43 items

[a] Recorded by Allan Marett at Bijili on May 3, 1997. AIATSIS: A16952.

[b] Recorded by Allan Marett at Bijili on May 4, 1997. AIATSIS: A16954–55.

[c] Recorded by Sally Treloyn at Myall's Bore on February 22, 2001. AIATSIS: uncataloged.

THE STRUCTURE OF THREE SONG SESSIONS FROM
THE NORTHERN AND WESTERN KIMBERLEY

The first of the performances recorded at Bijili occurred on May 3, 1997, following the main event, a performance of *junba* that had taken place in the late afternoon and evening.[14] The main singer was Jack Dann, and the didjeridu player was Paul Chapman. The performance was extremely relaxed as people unwound from the more serious *junba*. Joking and chatting, people drifted off home to the nearby community of Dodnun. Most of the dancers were boys or young men, and although designated as a performance of *wangga*, all items were in fact *lirrga*, as shown in table 10.7.

The second Bijili performance, which took place on the following night primarily for the purpose of making a recording, included a number of senior *wangga* singers from the region, including Paul Chapman, Scotty Martin, and Jacob Burgu.[15] Jimmy Maline and Morton Moore played the didjeridu. As shown in table 10.7, in this performance, the vast majority of the fifteen items were, once again, *lirrga*, with only one *wangga* song, a version of Barrtjap's "Yagarra Nga-bindja-ng Nga-mi," being performed. The melody in this performance, while somewhat modified, remains recognizably that of Barrtjap—at least to those who know his repertory well—but the text of the original has been entirely lost, transformed into a single vocable, *aa*. Most strikingly, the clapstick-beating pattern used in the instrumental sections is not the original used by Barrtjap but rather the Walakandha *wangga* clapstick-beating pattern. The confusion here of what, in the Daly region, are features of musical form that distinguish repertories is typical of what happens to *wangga*, particularly in the areas of the Kimberley that are most remote from the Daly.

Myall's Bore is a camping area on an old stock route near the famous Prison Boab tree about six kilometers from Derby. In February and March 2001, Sally Treloyn recorded Jack Dann and Jimmy Maline singing fifty-five "*wangga*" items, accompanied by Wallace Midmee on didjeridu. Of these, forty-three were in fact *lirrga* and twelve *wangga*.

Table 10.8 Summary of the Myall's Bore "wangga" performance

Items	Genre: Title	Comments
i–iv	*Lirrga*	
v, vi	*Wangga*: "Walakandha no. 2"	Walakandha *wangga* clapstick-beating pattern
vii–xii	*Lirrga*	
xiii, xiv	*Wangga*: "Yendili no. 3"	*lirrga* clapstick-beating pattern
xv–xviii	*Lirrga*	
xix, xx	*Wangga*: "Walakandha no. 2"	*lirrga* clapstick-beating pattern
xxi–xxvi	*Lirrga*	
xxviii, xxxix	Unknown *wangga*	
xl–xliii	*Lirrga*	
xliv, xlv	*Wangga* (possibly a Billy Mandji song)	
xlvi–l	*Lirrga*	
li, lii	*Wangga*: "Yendili no. 3"	Walakandha *wangga* clapstick-beating pattern
liii–lv	*Lirrga*	

As can be seen from table 10.8, two of the *wangga* songs that were sung at Myall's Bore—"Walakandha no. 2" and "Yendili no. 3"—are from the Walakandha *wangga* repertory. In the following section I will focus primarily on "Walakandha no. 2."

A PERFORMANCE OF "WALAKANDHA NO. 2"
AT MYALL'S BORE (WESTERN KIMBERLEY)

As was the case with the Kununurra performance of "Wutjeli," the Myall's Bore performance of "Walakandha no. 2" conflates the two text phrases of its couplet text and sets them within a single melodic section.

Musical example 10.5 compares the first melodic section of "Walakandha no. 2," as it was performed at Wadeye in 1992 by a group of singers led by Les Kundjil, with a performance of a complete vocal section, sung by Jack Dann, in the Myall's Bore performance.

As is generally the case in performances from the northwest Kimberley, the performance at Myall's Bore distorts the original text a great deal more than did the performances at Kununurra. Only one word, *walakandha*, is even vaguely recognizable, and the text transcription of the Myall's Bore performance is therefore necessarily tentative.

Although the text alone does not permit identification of the song with its Walakandha *wangga* original, aspects of the melody do. In chapter 5 I noted that the modality of "Walakandha no. 2" is distinctive. Whereas most other songs associated with the Kungiung/Dumoo lineage use a dorian modal series, "Walakandha no. 2" uses a major series. The Myall's Bore performance preserves

Example 10.5 The melody of "Walakandha no. 2" as performed at Wadeye in 1992 (Eni92, vi) compared to the melody of the 2001 Myall's Bore performance (Tre01, vi)

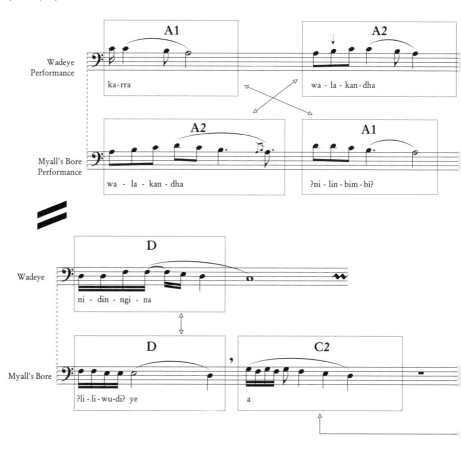

not only this distinctive modality but also a good deal of the original melodic structure.

In musical example 10.5, the melody of each performance has been divided into a number of melodic cells. The first three (A1, A2, and B), which correspond to the section of the melody set to the first three words of the text (*karra wala-kandha ngindji*) in the Wadeye performance, maintain roughly the same shape in the Myall's Bore version. The order of melodic cells A1 and A2, however, is transposed. The two versions then reconverge at melodic cell B, the original text of which, *ngindji*, is distorted beyond recognition in the Myall's Bore version. The Myall's Bore version next transposes the order of two other melodic cells, C1 and C2. The final cell of the Myall's Bore version, melodic cell E, is derived from the end of the *second* vocal section of the Wadeye performance (not shown in musical example 10.5). Despite the alteration in the order of some melodic cells, the original melody is nonetheless identifiable, at least to me. Read against a wider analysis of the sorts of changes that occur as songs move from the Daly

to the western Kimberley, and on the basis of my own broad knowledge of *wangga* within the whole region, I am confident in my identification of this as a version of "Walakandha no. 2." I can say with some certainty, however, that performers at Wadeye would not recognize the Myall's Bore performance as "Walakandha no. 2."

Let us finally consider the clapstick-beating patterns used in the instrumental sections. As can be seen from table 10.8, in the Myall's Bore performance, "Walakandha no. 2" is performed a total of four times in two separate pairs of items. In the first pair (items v and vi), the clapstick-beating pattern is the standard Walakandha *wangga* pattern. In the second pair (items xix and xx), the Walakandha *wangga* clapstick-beating pattern is replaced by a clapstick-beating pattern characteristic of *lirrga*. This represents a significant deviation from the sorts of practices that would be tolerated in the Daly region. Not only do singers in the western Kimberley lump *lirrga* and *wangga* items together and call them both *wangga*, but they allow musical elements from one genre to migrate to the other.

These general observations do not exhaust the ways in which *wangga* from the Daly evolve in Kimberley practice. In some cases, the versions performed in the Kimberley are closer to the "original" than the examples considered above, while in a few cases the deviation has been so great that I am not able to source a song to a repertory, let alone the particular song from which it derives. Nonetheless, the proportion of *wangga* songs that can be linked to originals known to have been composed in the Daly region is sufficiently high to confirm that the Daly region is the major source of the *wangga* performed in the Kimberley.

The Ceremonial Role and Significance of Wangga in the Kimberley

In the Kimberley, locally composed genres such as *junba* most clearly articulate the relationship between people and country. Anthony Redmond, in a recent doctoral dissertation, comments on the potent role that *junba* songs have in this regard. He explains that the transmission of songs along the *wurnan*, a network of exchange routes that links clans and individuals in a system of exchange, is seen as reproducing the action of totemic ancestors in the Dreaming:

> There is a profound analog in contemporary life to ancestral beings making a gift of features of country in the *larlan* [Dreaming]. The transmission of [*junba*] songs into the possession of a group related in the exchange network seems to involve a similar dynamic given that most songs are, above all else, evocations of places. Indeed, it is quite common for an older person offering what they understand to be an exegesis of a song cycle to an outsider to simply list off a series of place names through which the singer "travels" in the course of the performance. . . . While not assuming any sense of ownership of the countries which appear in these transmitted songs, there is no doubt that the new "holders" of songs to whom they have been transmitted feel a deep affection and pride in the places which are sung about. The same term, *duna*, is used for "holding songs" and for "holding country." (Redmond 2001, 348)

The transmission of *wangga* and *lirrga* songs to the Kimberley, and within the Kimberley, is clearly not imbued with the sorts of significance that Redmond notes for the transmission of *junba*. Texts, and their significance within the cosmologies of the Daly, are not generally understood, and in most cases — particularly in the northern and western Kimberley—the texts, including place names, names of ancestors, and other potent lexical items, are distorted beyond recognition. Only the most commonly occurring words in the Walakandha *wangga* repertory—words such as *walakandha* itself—survive in recognizable forms in the northern and western areas, and these, I would argue, are stripped of their power to evoke place or ancestral action. At the level of music, nothing more clearly reveals this lack of understanding of the ways in which melodies, rhythms, and clapstick-beating patterns evoke the countries of Daly than the substitutability of musical markers associated with *wangga* and *lirrga*.

I have witnessed *wangga* only in the context of "winding down" from a more significant performance, in this case a *junba*. I am told that this is in fact the role that *wangga* most commonly performs in the Kimberley, where it also often forms part of the public sections of restricted ceremonies. Deborah Bird Rose writes thus of the role of *wangga* (*Wangka*) in articulating identity within circumcision ceremonies at Yarralin in the eastern Kimberley, Victoria River region.

> The geographical regions based on desert, river, and coast are clearly distinguished through ceremony lines of initiation. *Pantimi* (brought by the Nanganarri women) belongs to the big river country, *Yalaju* to desert country, and *Wangka* to coastal country.[16] Each ceremony demarcates a series of languages which is differentiated from others. Bilinara people, for instance, are responsible for both the pigeon and *Pantimi*. Ngaliwurru people are responsible for both the pigeon and *Wangka*. (1992, 55)

Wangga, then, is clearly associated with identity in the Kimberley, but in ways that do not draw on the original patterns of relationships between song, people, country, and Dreamings indigenous to the Daly region. As is often the case when Aboriginal songs are removed from their home environments, the original patterns of meanings that are inherent in text, music, and dance are weakened and ultimately lost. Having been stripped of their original meanings, songs may then be appropriated to express new identities and to perform new ceremonial roles in new environments. It is only through fully understanding the meaning of the songs in their indigenous contexts, however, that we can fully appreciate these changes.

It is now time to leave the Kimberley and return briefly to the Daly region in order to take our leave of *wangga*, of the people who sing them, and of the country from which they emerge and which they in turn enliven.

Epilogue

It's late October, and I am flying out of Wadeye. Passing below me is a landscape, the outlines of which I knew well enough from maps even before I first came here. But what I see now is a living entity, country that is alive and which throws into life many different phenomena—birds, rain, and fire—as well as the many different orders of being: humans, ancestral spirits, mermaids, ghosts, little people, not to mention language and song. When people call out to it, "My dear country!" the country listens and responds. It feels the presence of its children as they pound the earth with their feet in dance and drop their sweat on the ground. I have learned about this country through the medium of songs.

Looking to the right, I see the Moyle (*muyil*) River snaking through the floodplain—*wuyi-muyil, wuyi-ngina*—as the Marri-ngarr sing: "Muyil country! Our dear country!"

Soon, as the towers of cumulus surrounding us promise, the wet season will be upon us, flooding the land. I remember a song about rain falling on the Muyil floodplain at the beginning of the Wet and the growing abundance of birds:

> What birds are these flocking toward me?
> Green shanks! Green shanks!
> Coming toward me from the big Moyle River.
> The little Moyle has started to fill up with rain.

This song is a *lirrga*, not a *wangga*, but it is one of the songs that can be sung by the *lirrga* mob for *wangga* owners in order to set free their dead and allow them to walk out into their country as Walakandha or Ma-yawa.

For now, though, the country below is still dry, still showing signs of having been burned. For millennia, people have looked after country in this way, and their actions are celebrated in another *lirrga* song.

> Fire!
> The people of the Muyil set fire to Yenmura-Ngurdandar.
> Cold dry season country!
> Burning away from me at Wangnenggi,

> The whole Muyil floodplain will be on fire by now.
> It's burning there, even where I can't see it,
> There at the little Moyle River, far away from me.

Burning country is another of the ways that people make their presence known to the sentient landscape. It is part of what humans are obliged to—to look after country, so that it in turn will nourish them.

Now to the left of the plane I spot Nadirri, the small Marri-tjevin outstation community at the mouth of the Moyle River, where we burned the rags of that young woman back in 1988. I think of her and all the other Walakandha walking around in that country and at night performing their ceremonies at Wudi-dji–rridi. I reflect on the ways that the Walakandha look after the living, on men and women dancing as Walakandha, and on the Walakandha grieving at a human death, but at the same time denying its finality.

> As a matter of inevitability, the tide is always coming in on us.

The country responds: the grasses and trees on the flat top of Yendili Hill stand up like the hair on the back of the neck when someone dies. In response to another death, one of the freshwater springs, an important Dreaming, dried up. And there are the ever-present marks of the tide, which takes away old life and brings in the new.

We pass swiftly on, over the country of the Marri-tjevin's countrymen, the Marri-ammu. I spot Tjindi Creek, and just to the south of it, the cliffs at Karri-ngindji, on top of which the Ma-yawa ancestors eternally dance. Below the cliffs, on the beach, lies the *wudi-pumininy*, the freshwater spring that flows into the salt, just as humans and Ma-yawa interpenetrate in ceremony.

And then on over the country of the Mendheyangal people, over Emmiyan-gal country, and, as we approach the mouth of the mighty Daly River, into Wa-djiginy country. This is the country for which old Tommy Barrtjap sang *wangga* songs full of nostalgia.

> Oh, wherever is my Country?
> Oh, where?
> Oh, where?
> Oh, where?
> Oh, this man here is singing.

To my left I see North Peron Island—Badjalarr—the country of Bobby Lam-budju Lane, and island of the dead for the Belyuen community. Home of Wuny-malang ghosts, and so dangerous that its name cannot be spoken, or sung, at night.

> Rakba Djalarr-maka bangany-nyung

Approaching Darwin across the Cox Peninsula, I look down at Indian Island, at Mica Beach, and at the small community of Belyuen. What a rich place it is. So many wonderful singers over so many years! It was on Indian Island that a man was frightened by the Cheeky Yam Dreaming and a ghost crept up on the Marri-ammu singer Billy Mandji to give him this song:

> The ghost sang: "dagan mele dagaldja dagan mele mele."
> On Duwun [Indian Island] yesterday a ghost crawled
>   and sat down over there, and sang this song to me.

Many years ago at Mica Beach, the ghost of a buffalo gave a song to the great Mendheyangal singer Jimmy Muluk, and this song has traveled everywhere, even to Mowanjum in the western Kimberley and throughout Arnhem Land. The ghost, manifesting as a buffalo, sings:

> "Rimili dje dje dje meme dje
> Rimili dja dja raga mela dje"
> I will dance for you
> On Mica Beach.

There is smoke rising here, too, as people burn this country. It is to this country that these Daly people now belong, and the country feels their presence as they burn it, collect oysters from its rocks, dance, and perform ceremony. Wunymalang inhabit this country too and give their descendants songs.

As we make our final approach to Darwin airport, I reflect on how my view of these places has been transformed through my work with Aboriginal singers. How I have read the country through song. Throughout this flight, as throughout this journey of writing, my head has been full of song. I count myself extremely fortunate.

Recordings of the Walakandha Wangga

Appendix Table 1.1 List of recordings of the Walakandha *wangga*

Recording code	Recording details
1988–2000 sample	
Cro00	Elicited recording made by Mark Crocombe at Wadeye in May 2000. Cassette. Original lodged at Wadeye Aboriginal Languages Centre.
Eni92	Recording of a circumcision ceremony made by Michael Enilane at Wadeye in 1992 (precise date unknown). Original with collector.
Mar88:23–25	Recording of a circumcision ceremony made by Allan Marett at Wadeye on May 17, 1988. Reel to reel. AIATSIS: A16812–14.
Mar88:28–29	Recording of a circumcision ceremony made by Allan Marett at Wadeye on May 18, 1988. Reel to reel. AIATSIS: A16818–19.
Mar88:30	Elicited recording made by Allan Marett at Peppimenarti on June 6, 1988. Reel to reel. AIATSIS: A16820.
Mar88:38–39	Recording of a *burnim-rag* ceremony made by Allan Marett at Nadirri on June 19, 1988. Reel to reel. AIATSIS: A16829.
Mar88:40–43	Recording of a *burnim-rag* ceremony made by Allan Marett at Batchelor on September 11, 1988. Reel to reel. AIATSIS: A16830–33.
Mar88:54	Elicited recording made by Allan Marett at Peppimenarti on November 20, 1988. Reel to reel. AIATSIS: A16930.
Mar98:4	Elicited recording made by Allan Marett at Kununurra on September 2, 1998. Cassette. AIATSIS: A17043–44.
Mar98:11	Recording of a *burnim-rag* ceremony made by Allan Marett at Merrpen on September 27, 1998. DAT. AIATSIS: A17061–62.
Mar98:15	Elicited recording made by Allan Marett at Wadeye on October 15, 1998. DAT. AIATSIS: A17070–72.

Mar99:1	Elicited recording made by Allan Marett at Wadeye on July 6, 1999. DAT. AIATSIS: A17096.
Mar99:2	Recording of a funeral made by Allan Marett at Wadeye on July 9, 1999. DAT. AIATSIS: A17097–98.
Mar99:3	Recording of a funeral made by Allan Marett at Wadeye on July 16, 1999. Cassette. AIATSIS: A16943.
Mar99:4	Elicited recording made by Allan Marett at Wadeye on July 21, 1999. DAT. AIATSIS: A17099–101.
Sim88	Recording of concert given by Martin Warrigal Kungiung and Robert Daly at the Symposium of the International Musicological Society (SIMS) in Melbourne on August 30, 1988. Original in ABC archives.
Walc92	Recording dated 1992 held by Wadeye Aboriginal Languages Centre at DO23. Recordist and precise date unknown. Location of original unknown.

Other recordings

Anon. n.d.	Recordist and date unknown. Given to Allan Marett by a member of the Dumoo family. Location of original unknown.
Rei74	Recording of a circumcision ceremony made by Lesley Reilly (née Rourke) at Wadeye in 1974. Cassette. AIATSIS: uncataloged.
Wal72	Recorded by Michael Walsh at Wadeye in 1972. AIATSIS: A4377.·

Appendix Table 1.2 Location of individual songs in the recorded sample of Walakandha *wangga*

Song	Recordings	Items[a]	Singers[b]
1988–2000 sample			
1. Kubuwemi (11 items)	Mar88:23	i, ii	TK, WD, MWK
	Mar88:30	i, ii	MWK
	Mar88:41	v, vi(a)	TK
	Mar88:42	vii, viii, ix	TK
	Sim88	ix	MWK
	Eni92	i	TK, LK
2. Yendili no. 1 (11 items)	Mar88:23	iii, iv	TK, WD, MWK
	Mar88:24	x(b), xi	TK, WD, MWK
	Mar88:28	i, ii, iii	TK, WD, MWK
	Mar88:30	iii, iv, v	MWK
	Sim88	x	MWK

Song	Recordings	Items[a]	Singers[b]
1988–2000 sample			
3. Yendili no. 2 (30 items)	Mar88:23	vi, vii, viii	TK, WD, MWK
	Mar88:24	vi	TK, WD, MWK
	Mar88:25	i	TK, WD, MWK
	Mar88:28	x, xi, xii	TK, WD, MWK
	Mar88:29	iii, iv(a), iv(b), vii(a), vii(b)	TK, WD, MWK
	Mar88:30	xiii, xiv	MWK
	Mar88:38	iii, iv, v, vi(a), vi(b), vii(a), viii, ix	TK, WD, MWK
	Mar88:39	i	TK, WD, MWK
	Mar88:41	i, ii	TK
	Mar88:42	x, xi	TK
	Sim88	viii(a), viii(b)	MWK
4. Yendili no. 3 (18 items)	Mar98:15	v, vi	LK
	Mar99:1	v, vi, xi	LK
	Mar99:2	ii, iii, vii, viii, xi, xvii	LK
	Mar99:3	ii, iii, iv, xiii, xvi, xxiii, xxiv	LK
5. Yendili no. 4 (4 items)	Eni92	xv, xvi, xvii, xviii	PM, TK
6. Walakandha no. 1 (18 items)	Mar88:23	v, ix, x	TK, WD, MWK
	Mar88:24	ii, viii(a), viii(b), ix, x(a)	TK, WD, MWK
	Mar88:28	iv, v, vi, vii	TK, WD, MWK
	Mar88:29	i, ii	TK, WD, MWK
	Mar88:30	viii, ix	MWK
	Mar88:38	vii(b)	TK, WD, MWK
	Sim88	vii	MWK
7a. Truwu A (16 items)	Mar88:24	v(a), v(b)	TK, WD, MWK
	Mar88:28	viii, ix	TK, WD, MWK
	Mar88:30	vi, vii	MWK
	Mar88:38	i(a), i(b), ii(a), ii(b)	TK, WD, MWK
	Mar88:39	ii	TK, WD, MWK
	Mar88:40	x	TK
	Mar88:41	vi(b)	TK
	Sim88	iii, iv, xi	MWK
7b. Truwu A/B (10 items)	Eni92	viii, ix	TK, LK
	Mar99:1	ix	AP, LK

Song	Recordings	Items[a]	Singers[b]
1988–2000 sample			
	Mar99:3	vi, vii, viii, ix, x	PM, LK
	Mar99:4	iv, v	PM
7c. Truwu B (6 items)	Mar98:15	xi, xii, xiii	LK
	Mar99:2	xiv	LK
	Mar99:3	xiv	LK
	Cro00	ii	LK
8. Nadirri (6 items)	Mar88:29	v(a), v(b), vi	TK, WD, MWK
	Mar88:30	xv, xvi	MWK
	Mar88:43	iii	TK, MWK
9. Yenmilhi (17 items)	Mar88:54	iii, iv, v	MWK
	Sim88	i, xii	MWK
	Eni92	ii, x, xi	TK, LK
	Mar98:15	vii, viii	LK
	Mar99:1	xii	LK
	Mar99:2	xv, xvi	LK
	Mar99:3	xix, xx, xxi	LK
	Mar99:4	ii	LK
10a. Mirrwana A (7 items)	Mar88:30	x, xi, xii	MWK
	Mar88:54	i, ii	MWK
	Sim88	v, vi	MWK
10b. Mirrwana B (5 items)	Mar88:40	xi	TK
	Mar88:42	i, ii	TK
	Walc92	xiii, xiv(a)	TK
11. Wutjeli (9 items)	Eni92	iv, v	TK
	Walc92	vii, viii, ix, xiv(b), xv	TK
	Mar98:4	xiv, xv	PP
12. Walakandha no. 2 (26 items)	Eni92	vi, vii(a), vii(b)	TK, LK
	Walc92	x, xi, xii	LK
	Mar98:15	ix, x	LK
	Mar99:1	vii, viii, x	LK
	Mar99:2	iv, v, vi, ix, x, xii, xiii	LK
	Mar99:3	v, xii, xvii, xxii	LK
	Mar99:4	iii, xvii, xviii	LK
	Cro00	v	LK
13. Walakandha no. 3 (3 items)	Eni92	xix	PM
	Mar99:4	vi, vii	PM

Song	Recordings	Items[a]	Singers[b]
1988–2000 sample			
14. Karra Yeri Ngina (7 items)	Mar98:11	xiii, xiv	PM
	Mar98:15	i	PM
	Mar99:3	xi, xv	PM
	Mar99:4	viii, ix	PM
15. Walakandha no. 4 (3 items)	Mar98:15	ii	PM
	Mar99:4	x, xi	PM
16. Walakandha no. 5 (4 items)	Mar98:15	iii, iv, xix, xx	PM
17. Kinyirr (2 items)	Mar99:4	xx, xxi	PM
18. Lhambumen (3 items)	Mar99:3	xviii	LK
	Mar99:4	xvi	LK
	Cro00	vi	LK
19. Yendili no. 5 (3 items)	Walc92	iv, v, vi	TK
Other recordings			
20. Walakandha no. 6 (3 items)	Rei74	xiii, xiv, xv	SM
21. Wutjeli no. 2 (3 items)	Rei74	xvi, xvii, xviii	SM
22. Niminbandja (2 items)	Rei74	ix, xx	SM
23. Walakandha no. 7 (3 items)	Anon. n.d.	i, ii, iii	TK
24. Walakandha no. 8 (2 items)	Anon. n.d.	iv, v	TK
25. Yendili no. 6 (2 items)	Anon. n.d.	vi, vii	TK
26. Yenmilhi no. 2 (1 item)	Anon. n.d.	viii	TK

[a] The addition of "(a)" and "(b)" signifies items that are run together without a break.
[b] See appendix table 1.3 for key to performers' names.

Appendix Table 1.3 Key to performers in appendix table 1.2

Abbreviation	Singers
AP	Ambrose Piarlum
LK	Les Kundjil
MWK	Martin Warrigal Kungiung
PM	Philip Mullumbuk
PP	Philip Pannikin
SM	Stan Mullumbuk
TK	Thomas Kungiung
WD	Wagon Dumoo

Appendix 2

Recordings of the Ma-yawa *Wangga*

Appendix Table 2.1 List of recordings of the Ma-yawa *wangga*

Recording code	Recording details
Cro00	Elicited recording made by Mark Crocombe at Wadeye in May 2000. Cassette. Original lodged at Wadeye Aboriginal Languages Centre.
Mar98:4	Elicited recording made by Allan Marett at Kununurra on September 2, 1998. Cassette. AIATSIS: A17043–44.
Mar98:14	Elicited recording made by Allan Marett at Wadeye on October 6, 1998. DAT. AIATSIS: A17069.
Mar98:16	Elicited recording made at Peppimenarti on October 7, 1998. DAT. AIATSIS: A17073.
Mar99:1	Elicited recording made at Wadeye on July 6, 1999. DAT. AIATSIS: A17096.

Appendix Table 2.2 Location of individual songs in the recorded sample of Ma-yawa *wangga*

Song	Recordings	Items	Singers*
1. Walakandha Ngindji (3 items)	Mar98:14	i, ii	MN
	Mar98:16	i	MN
2. Wulumen Kimigimi (2 items)	Mar98:14	iii, iv	MN
3. Rtadi-wunbirri (4 items)	Mar98:16	ii, iii, iv, v	MN
4. Menggani (2 items)	Mar98:14	v, vi	MN
5. Tjerri (2 items)	Mar98:14	vii, viii	MN
6. Watjen Danggi (2 items)	Mar98:14	ix, x	MN
7. Malhimanyirr no. 1 (2 items)	Mar98:14	xi, xii	MN
8. Ma-vindivindi (2 items)	Mar98:14	xiii, xiv	MN
9. Karri-ngindji (2 items)	Mar98:14	xv, xvi	MN
10. Thalhi-ngatjpirr (2 items)	Mar98:14	xvii, xviii	MN
11. Na-pebel (3 items)	Mar99:1	i, ii, iii	MN

Song	Recordings	Items	Singers*
12. Wulumen Tulh (4 items)	Cro00	vii, viii, ix, x	MN
13. Malhimanyirr no. 2 (4 items)	Mar98:4	i, ii, xvi, xvii	PP

* See appendix table 2.3 for key to singers' names.

Appendix Table 2.3 Key to performers in appendix table 2.2

Abbreviation	Singers
MN	Maurice Ngulkur
PP	Philip Pannikin

Appendix 3

Recordings of Barrtjap's Wangga

Appendix Table 3.1 List of recordings of Barrtjap's *wangga*

Recording code	Recording details
Elk52:19B	Recorded at Delissaville (Belyuen) by A. P. Elkin on June 9, 1952. "University of Sydney, Arnhem Land Expedition 1952." 16" disk RPX6823. Columbia Gramophone Company (Australia), Sydney. AIATSIS: A4691a.
Elk52:21B	Recorded at Delissaville (Belyuen) by A. P. Elkin on June 9, 1952. "University of Sydney, Arnhem Land Expedition 1952." 16" disk RPX6825. Columbia Gramophone Company (Australia), Sydney. AIATSIS: A4692a.
Mad64:1	Recorded at Beswick Creek (Bamyili/Barunga) by Kenneth Maddock in 1964 (precise date unknown). AIATSIS: A1067b.
Mad64:2	Recorded at Beswick Creek (Bamyili/Barunga) by Kenneth Maddock on November 15, 1964. AIATSIS: A1131.
Mar86:3	Recorded at Belyuen by Allan Marett on June 24, 1986. Reel to reel. AIATSIS: A16734.
Mar88:4–5	Recorded at Belyuen by Allan Marett on March 22, 1988. Reel to reel. AIATSIS: A16792–93.
Mar88:7	Recorded at Mandorah by Allan Marett on April 30, 1988. Cassette. AIATSIS: A16795.
Mar88:40	Recording of a *burnim-rag* ceremony made by Allan Marett at Batchelor on September 11, 1988. Reel to reel. AIATSIS: A16830.
Mar95:3	Recorded at Belyuen by Allan Marett and Linda Barwick on August 27, 1995. DAT. AIATSIS: uncataloged.
Mar97:4	Recorded at Belyuen by Allan Marett on July 31, 1997. DAT. AIATSIS: A16963–64.
Mar97:6–7	Recorded at Wooliana by Allan Marett on August 2, 1997. DAT. AIATSIS: A16971–73.
Mar97:8	Recorded at Belyuen by Allan Marett and Linda Barwick on July 30, 1997. Cassette. AIATSIS: A16960.

Recording code	Recording details
Mar97:9	Recorded at Belyuen by Allan Marett on July 31, 1997. Cassette tape backup of 97:4. AIATSIS: A16981–82.
Mar97:13–14	Recorded at Mandorah by Allan Marett on November 8, 1997. Cassette. AIATSIS: A16974–75 (Mar97:14 is not cataloged).
Moy68:5	Recorded at Delissaville (Belyuen) by Alice Moyle on June 3, 1968. AIATSIS: A1144a

Appendix Table 3.2 Location of individual songs in the recorded sample of Barrtjap's *wangga*

Song	Recordings	Items	Singers*
1. Ya Bangany-nyung Nga-bindja Yagarra (4 items)	Moy68:5	i, ii	TB
	Mar88:4	x, xi	TB, BL
2. Yagarra Nga-bindja-ng Nga-mi-ngaye (10 items)	Moy68:5	iii	TB
	Mar86:3	i	TB, BL
	Mar88:4	viii, ix	TB, BL
	Mad64:1	viii, ix, xxiv, xxv	LW
	Mad64:2	xx, xxi	LW
3. Bangany-nyung Ngaya (30 items)	Moy68:5	iv, v	TB
	Mar86:3	ii	TB, BL
	Mar88:4	iv, v	TB, BL
	Mar88:5	x	TB
	Mar88:7	i, ii	TB
	Mad64:2	xii, xiii	LW
	Mar88:40	i, ii	MB, SM
	Mar95:3	xiv, xv, xvi, xvii, xxvi, xxvii, xxviii	TimB
	Mar97:6	xi, xii, xiv	KB
	Mar97:8	i, ii	KB
	Mar97:9	i, ii, v, ix, x, xviii	KB
4. Kanga Rinyala Nga-ve Bangany-nyung (19 items)	Moy68:5	vi, vii	TB
	Mar88:4	xii, xiii	TB, BL
	Mar88:5	vii, viii, ix	TB
	Mad64:2	xiv, xxxi, xxxii, xxxiii, xxxiv	LW
	Mad64:1	vi, vii	LW
	Mar97:6	iii, vii	KB
	Mar97:8	v	KB
	Mar97:9	iv, xiii	KB
5. Yagarra Nga-bindja-ng Nga-mi (7 items)	Moy68:5	viii, ix	TB
	Mad64:2	xvi, xvii, xviii, xix, xxii	LW

Song	Recordings	Items	Singers*
6. Yagarra Bangany Nye-ngwe (1 item)	Moy68:5	x	TB
7. Be Bangany-nyaya (1 item)	Moy68:5	xi	TB
8. Nyere-nyere Lima Kaldja (7 items)	Mar88:4	i, ii	TB, BL
	Mar88:5	iv	TB
	Mar88:7	viii	TB
	Mar97:6	iv	KB
	Mar97:8	iii	KB
	Mar97:9	xii	KB
9. Nyere-nye Bangany-nyaye (11 items)	Mar88:4	iii	TB, BL
	Mar88:5	xii	TB
	Mar88:7	iv, vi	TB
	Mar95:3	v, vi, vii	TimB
	Mar97:8	iv, xiv	KB
	Mar97:9	vi, xiv	KB
10. Karra Ngadja-maka Nga-bindja-ng Nga-mi (6 items)	Mar88:4	vi, vii	TB, BL
	Mar88:5	v	TB
	Mar88:7	v	TB
	Mar97:6	x, xv	KB
11. Yerrerre Ka-bindja-maka Ka-mi (6 items)	Mar86:3	iii	TB, BL
	Mar88:4	xiv	TB, BL
	Mar88:5	i, xi	TB
	Mar88:7	iii	TB
	Mar97:7	viii	KB
12. Yagarra Ye-yenenaye (9 items)	Mar88:5	ii	TB
	Elk52:19B	xiii	JB
	Elk52:21B	xiii	JB
	Mar95:3	xxx, xxxi, xxxii, xxxiii, xxxvii, xxxviii	TimB
13. Dadja Kadja Bangany Nye-ve (14 items)	Mar88:5	iii	TB
	Elk52:19B	iv, v, vi	JB
	Elk52:21B	iii, iv	JB
	Mad64:1	xii	LW
	Mad64:2	xv	LW
	Mar97:7	ix	KB
	Mar97:8	vi, vii	KB
	Mar97:9	vii, xvi, xix	KB
14. Yagarra Nedja Tjine Rak-pe (1 item)	Mar88:5	vi	TB

Song	Recordings	Items	Singers*
15. Ya Rembe-ngaya Lima-ngaya	Mar88:5	xiii, xiv	TB
(5 items)	Mar95:3	iv, xiii	TimB
	Mar97:6	xiii	KB
16. Yagarra Tjüt Balk-nga-me Nga-mi	Mar86:3	iv	TB, BL
(6 items)	Mad64:1	x, xvi, xvii	LW
	Mad64:2	vi, vii	LW
17. Karra Tjine Rak-pe	Mar86:3	vi	TB, BL
(1 item)			
18. Yagarra Delhi Nye-bindja-ng Barra Ngarrka	Mar86:3	v	TB, BL
(2 items)	Mar97:14	v	KB
19. Nga'ngatbat-ba Mangalimpa	Mar97:7	x	KB
(4 items)	Mar97:8	xv	KB
	Mar97:9	iii, xi	KB
20. Ngaya Lima Bangany-nyaya	Mar97:6	viii	KB
(3 items)	Mar97:7	vii	KB
	Mar97:8	xiii	KB
21. Nyala Nga-ve Bangany	Mad64:1	xx, xxi, xxii	LW
(5 items)	Mar97:9	viii, xv	KB
22. Anadada Bangany-nyaya	Mar95:3	iii, viii, ix, x, xi, xviii, xix, xx, xxi, xxii, xxiii, xxiv	TimB
(14 items)	Mar97:9	xvii	KB
	Mar97:6	ii	KB
23. Karra Bangany-nyaya Nga-p-pindja	Mar95:3	i, ii, xii, xxv, xxix, xxxiv, xxxv, xxxvi	TimB
(8 items)			

* See appendix table 3.3 for key to singers' names. Shaded recordings are by singers other than TB.

Appendix Table 3.3 Key to performers in appendix table 3.2

Abbreviation	Singers
BL	Bobby Lambudju Lane
JB	Jimmy Bandak
KB	Kenny Burrenjuck
LW	Laurence Wurrpen
MB	Major Banggan
SM	Simon Moreen
TB	Tommy Barrtjap
TimB	Timothy Burrenjuck

Appendix 4

Recordings of Lambudju's Wangga

Appendix Table 4.1 List of recordings of Lambudju's *wangga*

Recording code	Recording details
Eni92	Recording of a circumcision ceremony made by Michael Enilane at Wadeye in 1992 (precise date unknown). Original with collector.
Har79	Recorded by Adrienne Haritos at Kalaluk on May 19, 1979. Original with collector.
Mar86:4	Recorded at Belyuen by Allan Marett on June 24, 1986. Reel to reel. AIATSIS: A16736.
Mar91:3	Recorded at Belyuen by Allan Marett on November 13, 1991. Reel to reel. AIATSIS: A16937.
Mar91:4–5	Recorded at Belyuen by Allan Marett on November 15, 1991. Reel to reel. AIATSIS: A16938–39.
Mar97:5	Recorded by Allan Marett and Linda Barwick at Belyuen on August 1, 1997. DAT. AIATSIS: A18966–67.
Mar97:10	Cassette backup of 97:5 recorded at the same time. AIATSIS: A16965
Mar97:13	Recorded at Mandorah by Allan Marett on November 8, 1997. Cassette. A16974–75.
Moy59	Recorded by Alice Moyle in 1959 (precise date unknown). AIATSIS: A1243.
Moy62:1	Recorded by Alice Moyle at Bagot on May 21, 1962. AIATSIS: A1370.
Wes61	Recorded at Beswick Creek (Barunga) by LaMont West on October 27 and November 7, 1961. AIATSIS: A399.

Appendix Table 4.2 Location of individual songs in the recorded sample of Lambudju's *wangga*

Song	Recordings	Items	Singer*
1. Rak Badjalarr (9 items)	Mar86:4	vi	BL
	Mar91:4	x, xi	BL
	Moy62:1	i	BL
	Wes61	xiv, xvi	LW
	Wes61	xxv, xxvi	LW, RBM
	Mar97:13	xiii	CWF
2. Bandawarra Ngalkin (6 items)	Mar86:4	ii, iii, vii	BL
	Mar91:3	iii, viii	BL
	Mar91:4	i	BL
3. Karra Balhak Malvak (7 items)	Mar86:4	viii	BL
	Mar91:4	xii, xiii	BL
	Mar91:5	i, ii, iii	BL
	Moy62:1	ii	BL
4. Karra-ve Kan-ya Verver Rtedi Ka-ya-nhthi (2 items)	Mar86:4	i	BL
	Moy62:1	iv	BL
5. Benmele (4 items)	Mar86:4	ix	BL
	Mar91:4	ix	BL
	Mar97:13	xiv, xv	CWF
6. Winmedje (2 items)	Mar86:4	v	BL
	Mar91:4	viii	BL
7. Tjerrendet (1 item)	Mar86:4	iv	BL
8. Tjendabalhatj (8 items)	Mar86:4	x	BL
	Mar91:3	i, ii, v, vi, vii	BL
	Eni92	xxiv, xxv	CWF
9. Bangany Nye-bindja-ng (5 items)	Mar91:3	iv	BL
	Mar91:4	ii, iii, iv, vii	BL
10. Walingave (3 items)	Mar91:4	v, vi	BL
	Har79	iv	BE
11. Djappana (4 items)	Mar91:5	iv, v, vi, vii	BL
12. Karra Balhak-ve (1 items)	Moy59	i	BL, RBM
13. Limarakpa (1 item)	Moy62:1	iii	BL, DR
14. Mubagandi (3 items)	Mar97:5/Mar97:10	i, ii, iii	RY

Song	Recordings	Items	Singer*
15. Bende Ribene (5 items)	Eni92	xii, xiii, xiv	CWF, LK
	Mar97:13	xi, xii	CWF

* See appendix table 4.3 for key to singers' names. Shaded recordings are by singers other than BL.

Appendix Table 4.3 Key to performers in appendix table 4.2

Abbreviation	Singers
BL	Bobby Lambudju Lane
BE	Brian Enda
CWF	Colin Worumbu Ferguson
DR	Douglas Rankin
LK	Les Kundjil
LW	Laurence Wurrpen
RBM	Rusty Benmele Moreen
RY	Roger Yarrowin

Notes

Preface, p. xv–xvii

1. Statement on Indigenous Music and Performance issued by the Garma Symposium on Indigenous Performance Research, convened at Gunyangara, Gove Peninsula, August 10–12, 2002, by Mandawuy Yunupingu, Marcia Langton, and Allan Marett. The full statement may be read at www.garma.telstra.com/statement. music02.htm.

Introduction, pp. 1–14

1. "Karra walakandha kimigimi-wurri kavulh-a-gu" ("Walakandha no. 8," Walakandha *wangga* song 24; see appendix table 1.2). Appendix 1 lists all known songs of the four repertories that form the focus of this study together with details of all known recordings of these songs. For explanation of orthographic conventions, see "A Note on Orthography."

2. "Bangany nye-bindja-ng nya-mu-ngarrka ya-mara / bangany nye-bindja-ng nya-mu-ngarrka ya-mara / ya-mara nye-dja-ng-nganggung bangany-e ya-mara" ("Bangany Nye-bindja-ng," Bobby Lambudju Lane's *wangga* song 9; see appendix table 4.2).

3. The headings "The Gunborg and Gunbalanya" (32–37), "The Djarada" (53–62), "The Walaka" (62–63), "The Djedbangari" (82–97), and "Wongga" (*wangga*) (149–52) all refer to musical genres. Others are the names of specific repertories: "The Ngorungapu" (46–52), "The Djerag" (82), "The Mulara of Central Arnhem Land," and "Kamalangga" (144–47) are all names of clan song (*manikay-bunggurl*) repertories; "The Nyindi-yindi: A Wadjigan Corroboree" (152–53) refers to Barrtjap's *wangga* repertory (see chapter 7 of this volume). Others headings name ceremonial complexes such as "The Ngurlmag or Uwara" (162–70), and "The Kunapipi" (170–76).

4. The following is an incomplete list of such work conducted in northern Australia: Anderson (1992, 1995), Clunies Ross and Wild (1984), Knopoff (1992), Stubington (1978), and Toner (2001) have investigated *manikay-bunggurl* in east and central Arnhem Land; Mackinlay (1998) has described several genres of women's music from the gulf country; Keogh (1989, 1990, 1995) wrote extensively on the musical conventions of the *nurlu* genre from the western Kimberley region; Treloyn (2000) has written on the *junba* of the northern Kimberley; Barwick (2002) has recently written on *lirrga*; a number of preliminary studies have been published on

the musical conventions of *wangga* music and dance (Marett 1992, 1998, 2001; Marett and Page 1995).

5. Jones nonetheless attempts this type of analysis when he investigates the musical characteristics of "sacred and secret music" as opposed to "secular music" or speculates on the role of vocal strength in comforting secluded initiands (Elkin and Jones 1958, 341–43).

6. The titles of these works are *The Rise of Music in the Ancient World, East and West* (Sachs 1943); *Music in Primitive Culture* (Nettl 1956).

7. Elkin's recordings also inspired and were part of a wave of interest in Aboriginal music and dance. Some of Elkin's recordings were incorporated into the sound track of the landmark Australian film *Jedda* (1955). Directed by Charles Chauvel, *Jedda* was the first Australian film to use Indigenous actors in leading roles and was the first Australian film to be shown at the Cannes Film Festival. The Australian composer Peter Sculthorpe also drew on the Elkin recordings in composing his 1977 work *Port Essington*.

8. For a more comprehensive assessment of Ellis's contribution, see Barwick and Marett 1995.

9. Richard Moyle, for example, has implied that Ellis's analysis is overly complex and does not reflect indigenous perceptions of the music (Moyle 1997, 185). In North East Arnhem Land, the Yolngu people have evolved a more highly developed analytical language, perhaps under the influence of Islamic thought, in the course of centuries of interaction with Macassan traders from Sulawesi. Knopoff, for example, documents the use of the word *yutunggurr* (thigh) for a song verse, the word *dhambu* (head) for melody, and words for the four commonly used clapstick patterns: *bulnha* (slow), *ngarrunga* (walking), *yindi* (big, important), and *barka* (arm) (1992, 141, 144, 148).

10. For a succinct account of the development of the idea of absolute music and musical autonomy, see McClary 1993, 326–28.

11. In "On Grounding Chopin," for example, Subotnik argues, through close analysis of passages from a number of Chopin's works, that a shift of focus from harmonic structure to the "dense, leisurely, undulating, and iridescent quality of the so-called musical 'Surface'" marks "a shift in Western thought away from metaphysical beliefs, and even away from complete confidence in the innate rationality of structure, or hence ultimately, I would say, from confidence in the universal rationality of science" (1987, 123). In the conclusion to her paper, she suggests, but does not pursue, ways of further grounding her analysis in social reality: "To obtain a more integrated view of Chopin's stylistic relationships to his culture, one would want to establish, I would argue, some dialectal sort of movement between Chopin's music and various other selected structures in his society" (130).

12. Recent scholarship on Western music does not, of course, rest entirely on traditions of what Cook calls "hermeneutic criticism" and Martin calls "rhetorical analysis" (Cook 1998, 78; Martin 2002, 144). Martin observes that to challenge many of the assumed positions of musicology, McClary adopts models that are little different from those that Martin himself espouses: "For Susan McClary, it is precisely the distinctive features of African-American music—its orientation to performances 'as the means whereby the community enacts consolidation' rather than the production of 'works,' and its burgeoning influence in the twentieth century—that calls into question many of the traditional procedures and assumptions of musicology" (Martin 2002, 140).

13. Ford records with regard to Batjamalh, for example, "The number of Wad-jiginy fluent in Batjamalh is small. I have located twenty speakers aged from 20 to 82" (1997, 3). Ford estimates that there are probably no more than five fluent speakers of Marri-ammu. The number of fluent speakers of Marri-tjevin is greater but is probably no more than about twenty.

14. The forms of names used in this study are those preferred by the people themselves. The senior Marri-ammu singer, for example, asked me to name him as Maurice Ngulkur (Ngulkurr), so that his father's name, Ngulkur, and hence his patriline, was recorded. The orthography adopted is in general that used by people today for official purposes. These forms of the names, which reflect the linguistic limitations of the government officials and missionaries who first wrote them down, are often at variance with the orthographic conventions adopted by linguists to transcribe their languages.

15. In 1988, in a paper presented to the ICTM Symposium on Music and Dance in the Pacific, convened by Alice Moyle in Townsville, I said, with regard to my work with *wangga* singer Alan Maralung, "I believe that there is a relationship between what he reveals to me and his assessment of my ability to communicate accurately about it, and I believe that he trusts me to present my understanding in modes appropriate to my traditions of knowledge." This was subsequently published in Marett 1992, 195.

16. "Yine nga-ve menung / nga-p-pindja-ng nga-puring djü nüng / nye-bindja-ng nya-mu" ("Yagarra Nga-bindja-ng Nga-mi," Barrtjap's repertory song 5; see appendix table 3.2).

1. *Repertories, Histories, and Orders of Being, pp. 15–38*

1. This story was recorded in 1996 by Mark Crocombe and is reproduced on a CD accompanying Wadeye Aboriginal Languages Centre 2003. It was translated from the original Marri-ammu by Lysbeth Ford and edited by me. Passages in square brackets are not in the original text but were supplied in the course of translation to explain ellipses in Edward Nemarluk's version of the story.

2. I use the term "language group" rather than "tribe," which was the term adopted by Falkenberg to describe these social units. He notes that "the tribal name denotes the language" and that "the population inside a tribal territory has, on the whole, a common culture" (1962, 11, 17). The term "tribe" is still, however, in wide use today in the English of Aboriginal people at Wadeye.

3. The ancestral dead appear as named Dreamings elsewhere in northern Australia. Ganbulapula, for example, is an ancestral *mokuy* (ghost) who resides at Gulkala (the site of the annual Garma Festival run by the Yothu Yindi Foundation), and Murayana is another "same but different" manifestation of the *mokuy* who resides at a *renggitj* estate at Gapuwiyak (Corn 2002, 135).

4. There is no single word in English for a freshwater spring that flows into the salt water below the high-water mark. I have therefore retained the Marri-ammu word *wudi-pumininy* throughout. Where appropriate the *wudi-pumininy* at Karri-ngindji will be referred to as the Karri-ngindji *wudi-pumininy* to distinguish it from other *wudi-pumininy* found along the coast.

5. In other paintings, Ma-yawa may be represented as more human than Tulh (who is something of a special case). The frontispiece (also by Charlie Brinken) shows the Ma-yawa doing what they are renowned for, namely, performing ceremony.

6. The painting is suffused with imagery that reflects the themes of danger, liminality, and creativity. Danger is symbolized by the snake, the Hairy Cheeky Yam itself, the tree to Tulh's right that bears a dangerous inedible fruit, as well as a number of totemic species that cannot be eaten. Liminality is symbolized by the pairs of ducks and turtles (see further in the text), and creativity (which is both dangerous and liminal) is symbolized by the juxtaposing and linking of the Ma-yawa, the song subject (Hairy Cheeky Yam), and the songman. In the process of creation, the song passes through two dangerous media, namely, the Hairy Cheeky Yam and the snake, and it is the song that creates liminality between the worlds of the dead (as represented by the Ma-yawa) and the living (as represented by the songman).

7. These two ducks also figure in a Murrinhpatha myth discussed in chapter 3, where they represent *wangga* dancers invited to a ceremony by the ancestral Bat, Tjinimin.

8. "Wulumen Tulh," sung by Maurice Ngulkur with Columbanas Wanir (didjeridu), CD track 1 (Cro00, viii); CD track 2 (Cro00, vii). All song titles are given in their original languages rather than in translation; "Wulumen" is Aboriginal English for "Old Man." The codes used to identify the recordings are explained in the appendixes. "Cro00, viii," for example, is a recording made by Crocombe in the year 2000; "viii" refers to the item number.

9. Fuller definitions of technical terms such as "vocal section," "instrumental section," "text phrase," "melodic section," and "melodic subsection" are given in chapter 4.

10. This division was first noted by Jones: "The songs are of two distinct rhythmic types. The first type has a regular movement in all parts in simple quadruple or triple time. The second type is free and declamatory, with the voice rhapsodizing without any rhythmic restriction and didjeridoo droning in irregular groups of two. In the latter type, the vocal sections are separated by instrumental interludes in strict tempo, with simple syncopation by the didjeridoo" (Elkin and Jones 1958, 212–13).

11. Even though songs of this type include measured beating in their instrumental sections ("interludes in strict tempo," to use Jones's phrase), the term "unmeasured" has been adopted because within indigenous terminology, it is the unmeasured quality of the vocal sections that most clearly defines this style. The Marri-tjevin term used to describe this style of performance, for example, is *ambi tittil* (without clapsticks).

12. In musical examples 1.1 and 1.2, the transcription focuses on the sung melody; the didjeridu part is not notated.

13. Irrespective of its actual pitch, the didjeridu drone—which provides the tonic of most songs—is in all musical examples transcribed as C, and all other pitches are adjusted to conform to this. This facilitates comparison between performances sung to didjeridus of different pitch. The actual pitch of the didjeridu is given at the beginning of each musical example.

14. Because this was the first item in his performance, the first vocal section was rather atypical, and so I will focus on the second vocal section, where the performance is more settled and more representative of his practice. In listening to track 2 of the CD, the reader should take care to remember that it is vocal section 2, not vocal section 1, that is transcribed in musical example 1.2 and table 1.2.

15. There are a number of permanently populated outstations at Nadirri and Perrederr in Marri-tjevin country; at Kuy and Yederr (Matige); Wudipuli, and

Nama (Marri-ngarr); Merrpen (Ngan'giwumerri); and Wudikapilderr (Marri-thiyel). Other outstations (for example, Rtadi-wunbirri in Marri-ammu country) are not permanently occupied but are visited regularly by their traditional owners.

16. For further information on the history of these settlements, see Povinelli 1993; Pye 1973; Stanley 1985; Stanner 1989; and later in this chapter.

17. I am relying here on the accounts of senior men such as Frank Dumoo, Laurence Kolumboort, and John Nummar, who were adults at the time the new repertories began. Precise dates are difficult to ascertain. The present owners of the *dhanba* repertory date the compositions of its first songs to the late 1950s, which is also the period given by the Marri-ngarr for the beginning of *lirrga*. Frank Dumoo has told me that the Walakandha *wangga* began a little after the other two. Although the details are now lost in the mists of time, it is clear that the process of composing the three new repertories began in the late 1950s and continued into the 1960s.

18. We know that *balga* was performed at the Port Keats mission in the 1950s immediately before the composition of the first *dhanba* songs. Stanner recorded two *balga* serics at Wadeye in 1957. One was from Turkey Creek, and the other is said to have come from Kununurra via Legune cattle station. See Stanner's tape 10 from 1957, which is held at the Australian Institute of Aboriginal and Torres Strait Islander Studies (AIATSIS) at catalog number A8200.

19. The only time I ever heard a song from Stan Mullumbuk's repertory was when Ambrose Piarlum performed one for me in 1999 as a historical curiosity.

20. Strehlow maintained that "Dreaming" was a mistranslation. Nonetheless the word has now gained such wide currency in both Aboriginal and non-Aboriginal usage that it is difficult to avoid it. We must always bear in mind, however, that "Dreaming" refers to "self-creating" or "self-actualizing" beings, rather than to "dreaming" in the sense of the visions we have while sleeping, although the two domains are related. *Wangga* songs are both dreamed (in the sense that they are taught to singers during sleep visions) and of the Dreaming (in the sense that the beings who teach the songs are in many cases self-actualizing).

21. "Wulumen vindivindi kavulh-a-gu / wulumen vindivindi kavulh-a-gu / nidin-gu rtadi wunbirri-wunbirri kisji" ("Rtadi-wunbirri," Ma-yawa *wangga* song 3; see appendix table 2.2).

22. "Menggani kimigimi kavulh-a-gu" ("Menggani," Ma-yawa *wangga* song 4; see appendix table 2.2).

23. For other discussions of the sentient nature of country in Aboriginal cosmologies, see Myers 1986; Povinelli 1993; and Rose 1996.

24. "Ngadja windjeni ngumunit-nginyanga-ndjen / wudi yendili kil-dim-nginyanga-ndjen" ("Yendili no. 5," Walakandha *wangga* song 19; see appendix table 1.2).

25. "Mana walakandha nadirri karri-tik-nyinanga-ya / aa mana karri-tik-nyinanga-ya" ("Nadirri," Walakandha *wangga* song 8; see appendix table 1.2).

26. See Marett 2002 for an account of how the senior Marri-tjevin lawman Frank Dumoo led me to an understanding of this existential journey and the metaphors used to express it in song.

27. See chapter 5, table 5.6.

28. "Karra mana meri kani-djet kuwa kagandja kisji / meri-gu mana kagandja kisji/mana ma-yawa wudi-pumininy-pumininy" ("Karri-ngindji," Ma-yawa *wangga* song 9; see appendix table 2.2).

29. In her survey of Aboriginal conception beliefs, Francesca Merlan enumerates three "ideal types" of Australian societies with regard to the relationship of conception. In the first of these, a child is usually believed to have come from totemic wells in the father's country. In the second, "conception totemism is itself a primary mode of affiliation to land and totem," and in the third either conception totemism or descent totemism can, according to circumstance, provide the basis of filiation to particular land (1986, 483–84). The situation at Wadeye, where conception Dreamings in the form of child spirits emerge from descent Dreaming sites (and where songs also come from descent Dreamings), falls firmly within the first category. The belief systems at Belyuen fall mainly into the second category.

30. Povinelli has written of the Belyuen water hole as follows: "As the Northern Territory government began forcibly interning them onto the Delissaville settlement, Larigiya, Wagaitj [Wadjiginy and Kiyuk] and Beringgen [Emmiyangal and Mendheyangal] Aborigines' actions were increasingly restricted to the confines of the community, and their children were increasingly 'caught' by *maroi* from the water hole. Although a score of Belyuen residents have *maroi* from sites around the Cox Peninsula, older Belyuen men and women state that the local Aboriginal children now 'come from Belyuen' itself" (Povinelli 1993, 165).

31. Elkin, in terms that largely concur with the account by Falkenberg (1962), describes the system on the Daly as follows: "A person's cult-totem, 'dreaming' (or *dorlk*), is the 'dreaming' of the locality in which his (or her) conception totem or *maroi* . . . is 'found' by the father. This usually occurs in the father's part of the tribal territory and so the child's 'dreaming' will be the same as the father's unless there be more than one 'dreaming' in the latter's clan country, which is sometimes the case. The child's 'dreaming' might then be different from his father's, though would still belong to the father's country" (Elkin 1950, 68). He then goes on to describe the changes that had occurred at Belyuen. "But now that so much time is spent out of their own clan countries, either at Delissaville or in Darwin, the local aspect of the descent operates much less, and a pure patrilineal principle is being recognized. As one informant put the matter with reference to three of his children: 'Got no other *dorlk* and *maroi* (cult and conception totems) for these, because sit down here' (that is at Delissaville)" (ibid.).

32. "Yagarra nedja tjine rak-pe / yagarra rama rama kama" ("Yagarra Nedja Tjine Rak-be," Barrtjap's *wangga* song 14; see appendix table 3.2). *Yagarra* is an exclamation expressing strong emotion. It is often translated into English as "Oh no!"

33. Given the multiplicity of interpretations that a song text can attract, and allowing for the possibility of a degree of misunderstanding, one wonders whether Elkin was referring to this song when he wrote: "In 1946 I was present at a Delissaville [Belyuen] corroboree. The songman sang of his deceased wife; her spirit was reported in the song as saying that she was now finished (with the surroundings of the camp) and was going away" (Elkin and Jones 1958, 153).

34. The report of the Aboriginal land commissioner, the Hon. Justice Peter Gray, into the Kenbi (Cox Peninsula) Land Claim no. 37 was dated December 20, 2000. It recommended that some six hundred square kilometers of the Cox Peninsula to the west of Darwin be granted to, and for the benefit of, six traditional Aboriginal owners and some sixteen hundred Aboriginal people having traditional affiliation to the land. A report on *wangga* songs was submitted in evidence to the land commissioner on behalf of Daly people's claims to residency rights on the Cox Peninsula (Marett, Barwick, and Ford 1998).

35. Elkin writes about *ngirrwat* at Belyuen as if it were primarily a system of name exchange and without any explicit indication of the fact that in most Daly languages it is cognate with *durlk* (Dreaming) in Batjamalh. He does, however, use the expression "one dreaming" to describe the relationship established through name exchange and states, "There is in every totemic *ngirrwat* the one 'dreaming' or totem line" (1950, 76, 81). Evidence that the term *ngirrwat* was used in the past by speakers at Belyuen to refer to Dreamings is provided by Ewers, who—drawing on observations made in the late 1940s—writes with reference to the Rainbow Serpent Dreaming in the Belyuen water hole (Ingrapooroo): "To the Wargaitj [Wadjiginy], Ingrapooroo is the Pool of the Rainbow, a dreaming or *Ngerewat*" (1964, 65).

36. Povinelli notes that the Kiyuk and Wadjiginy groups have *durlk* sites in their traditional country on the Daly that are linked by tracks to related sites on the Cox Peninsula (1993, 161).

37. The extent to which Wunymalang (or *ngutj*, as they are known in other Daly languages spoken at Belyuen) are identified with the *maruy* aspect of being is shown by the fact that people use both terms almost interchangeably to refer to the dead.

38. Redmond writes of yet another land of the dead, Dulugun, an island of the dead off the west coast of the Kimberley where composers of *junba* travel to receive songs (Redmond 2001, 120).

39. In the past, the traditional owners of the Cox Peninsula, the Larrakiya people, also adopted *wangga* to celebrate Dreamings and Dreaming sites local to the Cox Peninsula. There is at least one surviving example from the archival record that reflects the Larrakiya association with *wangga*, namely, the song that the last of the Larrakiya songmen, George King, recorded for Peter Hemery at Belyuen in 1942 (recorded May 15, 1942, by Peter Hemery, ABC war correspondent, disc NAT3, ABC archives number 72/10/543 [with commentary], 72/10/544 [without commentary], AIATSIS archive number A2915). In this didjeridu-accompanied song, which is clearly of the *wangga* type, George King sings of a Larrakiya Dreaming, the Wudut or Frog Dreaming, whose site lies on the western side of the Cox Peninsula. The only other *wangga* associated with a local Belyuen Dreaming is Mosek's song about the Belyuen water hole, recorded in 1948 by Colin Simpson. Simpson documented this as a song that Mosek said "was given by Belyuen, the manifestation of the Rainbow Serpent that resides in the Belyuen water-hole." Mosek Manpurr was a renowned Kiyuk dancer and native doctor (*dawarrabürak*) who died in the early 1950s.

2. *Dreaming Songs, pp. 39–54*

1. "Minmin Light" is an Aboriginal English word for a spirit light or will-o'-the-wisp. The Aboriginal langauge terms used by Maralung were *namarroto* (Ngalkbon/Rembarrnga) and *namol* (Jawoyn). A recording of Maralung's songs, including "Minmin Light," is available on Maralung 1993. A recording of the song "Minmin Light" is also included on track 28 of the CD accompanying this book.

2. This account was recorded by me at Barunga on July 13, 1986 (cassette, AIATSIS A16759). The version of the story published here streamlines the narrative for ease of comprehension, omitting redundant or confusing material, and slightly rearranging the order of some statements.

3. Maralung has a quite different relationship to Balanydjirri from that which

songmen in the Daly region have with their song-giving ancestors, whether these be Dreamings such as Walakandha and Ma-yawa, or Wunymalang ghosts. In the Daly region, the song-giving ancestors are always of the same patriline as the songman, whereas in Maralung's case the ancestor is of the opposite patri-moiety.

4. LaMont West, who worked in Barunga in the early 1960s and recorded Maralung at that time, mentioned only ghosts in relation to song composition: "[Maralung] alleges that he is inspired and taught in dreams by the ghost of a deceased song-man. . . . The pattern of dreaming and ownership is typical of Central Arnhem Land, Alan's homeland. But the dance and music are patterned upon the Wongga [*wangga*] type corroborees prevalent further west" (West 1984).

5. For a more detailed account of the role that birds play in the composition of songs in the Kimberley, see Marett 2000.

6. Namarroto is also one of the song subjects of the Murlarra clan song (*manikay-bunggurl*) series that I also recorded at Barunga during the period I was working with Maralung. Anderson describes Namarroto as follows: "This is a malevolent spirit being who may appear as a yellow or green falling star, and who impregnates people with a baby that proceeds to eat them from the inside" (1992, 73).

7. "Yenmilhi," Walakandha *wangga* song 9; see appendix table 1.2. A recording of this song may be heard on the accompanying CD at track 11. The Marri-tjevin text and a musical transcription of the song are given in chapter 5, in table 5.9 and musical example 5.7 respectively.

8. "Karra yeri-ngina / karri yitjip wandhi nginanga kani tenggi-diyerri / karra yeri-meri-yigin-ga djindja-wurri / ka-ngi-nginyanga yenmungirini na-pumut / pumut kurzi" ("Karra Yeri-ngina," Walakandha *wangga* song 14; see appendix table 1.2).

9. I do not normally include *karra* in my translations of texts into English. The fact that it marks an utterance as being "of the dead" gives it rhetorical strength and emotion. If pushed, people will translate it as "poor bugger" or some such expression.

10. "Karra yene yene yene yene / karra walakandha kiminy-ga kavulh." Ambrose Piarlum performed this for me in 1999 (Mar99:4, items xiv, xv), but only as a historical curiosity. It was not in the ceremonial repertory during the period I conducted research and is not therefore included in appendix 1.

11. Stanner recorded Malakunda in September 1954. The tape, which Stanner numbered 4B, is cataloged at AIATSIS at A8196A. Malakunda was also recorded by Lesley Reilly in 1974 (a digital transfer of Reilly tape 1 is lodged at the Wadeye Language Centre at D034; the original is lodged at AIATSIS and is as yet uncataloged).

12. Lambudju used the term "Wunymalang" interchangeably with *maruy* (conception Dreaming) to refer to ghosts. In the following discussion, however, I will use the term "Wunymalang" for ghost and reserve *maruy* for conception Dreaming.

13. "Yagarra Nga-bindja-ng Nga-mi," Barrtjap's *wangga* song 5; see appendix table 3.2. The text of this song is given at table 7.4 in chapter 7, where it is discussed in some detail. A recording of the song may be found on the accompanying CD at track 16.

14. "Bangany nye-bindja-ng nya-mu-ngarrka ya-mara / bangany nye-bindja-ng nya-mu-ngarrka ya-mara / ya-mara nye-dja-ng-nganggung bangany-e ya-mara" ("Bangany Nye-bindja-ng," Lambudju's *wangga* song 9; see appendix table 4.2).

15. A recording of the performance may be found at Maralung 1993, track 1, "New Song."

16. Kundjil, the surname of Les Kundjil, one of the two principal Walakandha *wangga* singers at Wadeye in the late 1990s, derives from a mishearing of his father's name, Ngurndul.

17. For references to Berida and Munggumurri, see "Walakandha no. 4," Walakandha *wangga* song 15, the text of which is given in table 5.6. For a reference to Munggum, see "Truwu," Walakandha *wangga* song 7, the text of which is given in table 5.2. "Wutjeli," Walakandha *wangga* song 11, is discussed in chapter 10.

18. Aguk Malvak is named as one of the two main songmen at Delissaville in 1947; the other was Barrtjap's "father" Jimmy Bandak (Ewers 1964, 25). "Old Argok" is reported to have used fish traps on "the Cullen beach" (probably Kahlin Beach, the site of the Darwin Native Compound from about 1913 to 1940).

19. Lambudju was famous for mixing Batjamalh and Emmi in his everyday speech, and at least one song, "Karra Ve Kan-ya verver Rtedi Ka-ya-nhthi," Lambudju song 4, has a macaronic text. Some songs, such as "Karra Balhak Malvak," Lambudju song 3, which refers directly to Lambudju's "father," Aguk Malvak, can be identified as songs transmitted from the upper generation of Wadjiginy singers (see chapter 8). See also Marett, Barwick, and Ford 2001.

3. Ceremony, pp. 55–77

1. See Merlan 1998 for a more detailed examination of the significance of accounts of the death of the Rainbow Serpent in northern Australia.

2. Immediately as you enter the Kanamkek Yile Ngala Museum, you see before you a painting of Tjinimin by Simon Ngunbe, the original of which is said to have been presented to Sir Paul Hasluck, governor-general of Australia from 1969 to 1974. To the right is a series of paintings depicting the principal episodes of the myth, and to the left are various visual representations of the Rainbow Serpent, including an image, originally reproduced from rock engravings at Purmi by Stanner (1989, 98), of Kunmanggurr with a spear entering his side. The Christian resonances of the Tjinimin myth, so obvious in this painting, have been commented on variously by Stanner (1989), Swain (1993), and Rose (1998). A nearby photograph shows the parallel rock grooves at Kimul that are the embodiments of Tjinimin's spear and Kunmanggurr's didjeridu.

3. As Stanner pointed out, there is no univocal version of the myth. Different narrators may, and do, start at somewhat different points, omit or include details, vary the emphasis, describe events differently, and attribute them to different causes and persons (1989, 84). Stanner made the recording from which he translated this version of the story in September 1954; the recording is cataloged at 8195B in the sound archives of the Australian Institute of Aboriginal and Torres Strait Islander Studies.

4. *Anhinga melanogaster*, better known in English as a darter.

5. *Grus rubicundus*.

6. *Ardeotis australis*, better known in English as the Australian bustard.

7. *Xenarhynchus asiaticus*.

8. *Anas castanea*, the chestnut teal (*mudjigin* in Marri-tjevin and Marri-ammu).

9. *Tadorna radjah*, the burdekin duck or radjah shelduck (*tindirrgam* in Marri-tjevin, Marri-ammu and Marri-ngarr).

10. Stanner observes that in the middle of this largely opaque text, the word *mutjingga*, "Old Woman," stands out. The Old Woman is the central figure in the cult that replaced that of the Rainbow Serpent (1989, 92).

11. Falkenberg (1962) notes many instances of an association between the death of totemic ancestors and the creation of Dreaming sites.

12. Although today they sing *lirrga*, the present repertory dates only from the late 1950s. Before this, the Marri-ngarr were associated with *wangga*. Although we have no way of knowing what song subjects were performed in the now-extinct Marri-ngarr *wangga* corpus, it may be significant that the darter (*wamandhi* in Marri-ngarr) is now the subject of a number of songs in the *lirrga* repertory.

13. *Dinggirri* (*dingari, tingarri*) is a mythical complex and associated song series that is widely spread in the central and western desert (R. Moyle 1979, 26–27, 104–5; Berndt and Berndt 1964, 266–67; Petri and Petri-Odermann 1988, 267). In general the complex is secret and restricted to initiated men only. The Berndts record that the country of the Djamindjung, the language group to the immediate south of the Murrinhpatha, is the northernmost extent of the complex, where it functioned as one of the preliminary rites leading up to circumcision. The predominance of this style in the 1930s and 1940s reflects an overall pattern of strong influence on Murrinhpatha culture from the south during this period (see also Falkenberg 1962 and Stanner 1989).

14. In addition to the Muyil *lirrga*, the Marri-ngarr composed a body of songs with Christian themes for use in the church (see Barwick 2002, 2005).

15. A fourth repertory of four songs called *wurlthirri* was composed by Thimararr and is associated with Nangu country to the south of Wadeye. While it too is performed by Murrinhpatha singers, sometimes together with *dhanba* and sometimes in place of it, it predates the creation of *dhanba* by several decades. *Wurlthirri* is unique among the Murrinhpatha genres because it uses didjeridu to accompany the singing. So far as I know, *wultherri* is the only didjeridu-accompanied genre of Aboriginal music that is sung by women. A fifth repertory, *malkarrin*, is now primarily associated with Christian revelation and is not performed in traditional ceremonial contexts.

16. What people mean by "sweat" varies according to local ontologies, and for this reason, I will delay more detailed discussion of this term until later in the chapter.

17. Stanner records the use of the word "clear" to describe the effect of completing a circumcision ceremony. He glosses the Murrinhpatha word *tarangga*, of which "clear" was the given English translation, as "limpid and translucent" water, or "a place . . . free of obstructions" or "a situation in which grievances have been adjusted satisfactorily" (1989, 116). Elkin records a similar use of the word "clean" with regard to the effects of a *kapuk* ceremony (Elkin and Jones 1958, 153).

18. "Karra mana wudi purangang kisji" ("Karri-ngindji," Ma-yawa *wangga* song 9; see appendix table 2.2).

19. It is precisely these principles that also allow the Dreamings and country celebrated in songs of one of the clans or language groups within a *wangga, lirrga,* or *dhanba* company, to stand for the country and Dreamings of others in the company.

20. "Karra walakandha" ("Walakandha no. 1," Walakandha *wangga* song 6; see appendix table 1.2).

21. "Mana walakandha nadirri karri-tik-nyinanga-ya" ("Nadirri," Walakandha *wangga* song 8; see appendix table 1.2).

22. The text of this song is given in table 5.2.

23. The text of this song is given in table 4.2.

24. Because Marri-ngarr no longer perform *wangga*, it has not been possible to elicit the Marri-ngarr word for song-giving ancestors who are the equivalent of the Marri-tjevin Walakandha and the Marri-ammu Ma-yawa.

25. "Karra-ve ka-nya verver rtedi ka-ya-nhthi / karra-ve kak-ung-bende bad-jalarr" ("Karra-ve Kan-ya Verver Rtedi Ka-ya-nhthi," Lambudju's *wangga* song 4; see appendix table 4.2).

26. "Nye-me-nung/nye-bindja-ng nya-mu ngangung-djü."

27. Simpson records that immediately before the act of circumcision, an initiand is "sung dead" by the songman (1951, 169). Elkin states, in reference to the removal of a young man for initiation: "A ritual death has taken place" (Elkin and Jones 1958, 157).

28. "Wandhi wandhi kimi kayirra watjen-danggi / mana kani-tjippi-ya kayirra watjen-danggi / yilhiyiliyen-gu" (Ma-yawa wangga song 6; see appendix table 2.2).

29. Stanner records the following: "The traditional circumcision ceremonies ceased at Port Keats about the middle 1940s. The local missionary, alarmed at a sup-posed risk to life or well-being from loss of blood and septicemia, persuaded the elders to let him perform the operation on several boys. Soon afterwards, a hospital was established at the mission. It then became customary to have infant males cir-cumcised by a trained sister. The traditional institution lapsed. The elders put up no great resistance and the youths, one need scarcely add, were in favor of the change. . . . The flow of candidates for initiation dried up when all infant males were circumcised at the mission hospital and, as they came to a right age, were withheld from the other rites. The number of visitors fell off when, because of their interference with the work of the mission, they were made to feel unwelcome, and because the shrunken ceremonies were a disappointment. But in my judgement, it would have been possible to revive the entire ritual complex as late as the early 1950s since there were still alive a sufficient number of older men possessing both the secrets and the interest" (1989, 108, 148–49).

30. I attended and recorded the 1988 ceremony on both audio- and videotape and have listened to audio recordings and viewed photographs of the 1992, 1996, and 1997 ceremonies.

31. For a more detailed account of this phase of the ceremony, see Stanner 1989, 113.

32. Elk52:21B (see appendix table 3.1). See also Elkin and Jones 1958, 149–50.

33. Elkin mentions a number of aspects of the circumcision ceremony that I have not witnessed at Wadeye or heard described for Belyuen. These included a taboo called *warabatj* whereby a boy and the guardian who conducted him through the ceremony cannot speak or associate for about a year; after circumcision "a young man is taken by his father to visit his *dorlk* [Dreaming] centre and is told the myth connected with it" (Elkin adds, "Perhaps too, he will dream a song about it"); "after initiation, the new man must be introduced by his guardian, *nanga*, to these places and objects which are dotted over the tribal territory and just off shore"; and "after a circumcision wound is healed, he is taken out of his camp by his guardian and made to throw two spears in the direction of his Dreamings" (1950, 74, 76, 77, 80).

34. According to Rose (1995, 26), two of the four main traveling Dreamings in the Belyuen area are associated with freshwater and two with salt water. The two freshwater Dreamings are Kenbi (Didjeridu, which is symbolically associated with men) and Ngarrmang (Baler Shell, which is symbolically associated with women). Their travels are similar in that they travel underground to link the major fresh-

water sources of Belyuen with other freshwater sources in the area. The other two main traveling Dreamings are associated with salt water. Kenbi Kenbi, the Old Man Crocodile, and Wilha, the female Cheeky Yam, both travel in the salt water. As I have already noted, freshwater/saltwater oppositions occur in the mythology of the Marri-ammu and are common throughout the coastal communities of northern Australia.

35. After World War II, during which many Aboriginal people had been interned in camps at Mataranka, Tandandjal was selected as the site of a government settlement. The settlement was moved not long after to Beswick Creek, which is known today as Barunga.

4. *Conventions of Song and Dance, pp. 79–110*

1. For a more detailed discussion of what is meant by "same melody," see R. Moyle 1979 and Ellis 1984.

2. This performance is listed in appendix table 3.2 as "Moy68:5, v." A recording of this item was previously released on the LP disc *Aboriginal Music from Australia*, Unesco Collection, Philips 6586034. A preliminary analysis of the song was presented in 1988 at the ICTM symposium entitled "Music and Dance of Aboriginal Australia and the South Pacific: The Effects of Documentation on the Living Tradition" and was published later as Marett 1992. The analysis presented in the present context benefits from a much deeper familiarity with Barrtjap's repertory and the *wangga* repertory in general.

3. Much of the linguistic analysis in this section was carried out by Lysbeth Ford and is based on a forthcoming paper in which we put forward a more comprehensive technical description of the use of Batjamalh in *wangga* (Marett and Ford, n.d.).

4. Lysbeth Ford has provided the following explanation of these signs: + means a free morpheme, originally another word; = means a bound morpheme that can exist only as part of a word, for example in English, "black+bird" as opposed to "small=ish." The general practice in this book is that unless there is some reason to distinguish free from bound morphemes, morphemes that are components of a single word will be linked by hyphens, as in musical example 4.1.

5. Ford and I have constructed the glosses in table 4.1 in consultation with senior Batjamalh speakers, all of whom have a deep knowledge of song.

6. Only sentient beings qualify as core arguments. To the Aborigines of the Daly region, humans, spirits, all living creatures, and the land itself are sentient, and all may be marked on the verb as core arguments.

7. Although nowadays children at Belyuen are obliged to attend school and learn to read, people of Barrtjap's generation were rarely literate.

8. Nonmetrical relationships between the voice and didjeridu also occur in Arnhem Land clan song, for example in the *ngarkana* style of performance used in the Murlarra song series described by Anderson (1995), the "formal" style of performance of Djambidj songs described by Clunies Ross and Wild (1982), and the *bulna* and *yindi* styles of North East Arnhem Land described by Toner (2001). Although in these cases stick beating is also part of the style, it is, like the voice and the didjeridu, unaligned to any metrical pulse.

9. In ordinary speech, *ye ngina* is two words, meaning "I walk to my children." On the basis of what we have been told by speakers, however, in this and other contexts, *ngina* indicates emotional intensification or longing. Aboriginal people will

express this emotional quality by translating expressions such as *nidin=ngina* into English as "Poor fellow, my country." The intonation pattern used in speech supports the view that *ye=ngina* is one word. The emphasis on *ye* rather than *ngina* confirms that *ngina* is an enclitic, where the clitic adds emotion to the host.

10. "Aa ninimbandja kuninggi meri ngindji nginanga-wurri kunya" ("Ninimbandja," Walakandha *wangga* song 22; see appendix table 1.2).

11. The analysis presented in this section and the following section is based on material previously presented in Marett and Page 1995. I am indebted to JoAnne Page for her assistance in creating this analysis.

12. If, as is sometimes the case, there is no second clapstick player, the main clapstick player will simply maintain the short-long pattern throughout A^1. In some cases the second clapstick player delays his entrance for a few beats, and in this case the effect is the same, namely, a series of short-long beats that precede the more complex interlocking form.

13. The most frequent exception to this convention occurs when an individual dancer does not participate in the dancing in the first sequence of phrases. When a dancer makes a late entry to the dance ground in this way, he will often join in at the second sequence with a W phrase before the usual sequence of RHSE.

14. For the purposes of this analysis, the beats notated as ♪♪ in pattern B are counted as one beat when determining the rhythmic mode of instrumental sections. Within any one performance occasion, the beating tends to stay within a range of about ten clapstick beats per minute. Some performances might be faster than the norm, and some slower, and this is often affected by factors such as the vigor of the dancers or the general excitement level generated by the performance. Martin Warrigal Kungiung consistently performs rhythmic mode 5a more slowly, generally in the range of 117–22 clapstick beats per minute, although in one performance the lower end of his range slips to 109 beats per minute. His performances cannot, in this regard, be regarded as typical of the Walakandha *wangga* tradition.

15. For the purposes of this analysis, the interlocking beats interposed by the second singer are disregarded (since they are not always present), and the lopsided nature of the beating is accommodated by averaging the beating rate within each pair of beats.

16. The 1988 Barunga Festival was an occasion of immense significance for the relationship between Aboriginal and non-Aboriginal people in Australia. On this occasion, the prime minister, Bob Hawke, promised a formal treaty to Aboriginal people, a promise that was never delivered. Three years later the popular music band Yothu Yindi released their song "Treaty" on the album *Tribal Voice* (Mushroom D30602), and this has subsequently become the anthem of the Aboriginal struggle for land rights and political recognition.

17. I have incorporated the rhythm in which the pattern is sung into the reconstruction of the performance represented in musical example 4.3.

18. In his transcription of the song, Stanner adds a word, *purima* (wife), that is not in fact in the original recording.

5. The Walakandha Wangga, *pp. 111–33*

1. Thirty-two items of "Truwu" (including Truwu A, Truwu B, and Truwu A/B: A and B signify different forms of the melody) were performed in the period

1988–2000. The next most frequently performed were "Yendili no. 2" (thirty items) and "Walakandha no. 2" (twenty-six items).

2. Titles of songs are, wherever possible, those used by performers themselves. The title "Truwu," for example, was used by Frank Dumoo when, as ceremonial leader, he called out to the singers to take up this song. In cases where I have not heard a piece named in this way, I have given it a title according to its central theme. In some cases the same title is given to different songs, and in these cases numbers are added to distinguish between them. There are, for example, eight songs about Walakandha, numbered from "Walakandha no. 1" to "Walakandha no. 8." Similarly there are six songs focused on Yendili Hill, numbered from "Yendili no. 1" to "Yendili no. 6." Not all of these are listed in table 5.1, but all can be seen in appendix table 1.2.

3. I made most of the recordings discussed in this chapter between 1988 and 1999, supplementing them with a small number of recordings made by others in 1988, 1992, and 2000. This body of recordings is set out in the upper section of appendix table 1.1 under the heading "1988–2000 sample." Three other recordings, which do not fall within this period and are not included in the present analysis, but which are referred to from time to time, are set out in the lower section of appendix table 1.1 under the heading "Other recordings." Songs by Ambrose Piarlum have not been included in the sample. The location of individual items within the recordings is set out in appendix table 1.2.

4. Munggum, together with Kungiung and Mullumbuk, was one of three brothers to whom a number of Marri-tjevin singers active over the course of this study traced their ancestry (see figure 2.1).

5. See table 5.2 for the Marri-tjevin text.

6. In four of the six group 1A songs ("Truwu," "Wutjeli," "Walakandha Ngindji," and "Walakandha no. 3"), both text phrases of the couplet are sung to the same melody, while in the other two ("Kinyirr" and "Walakandha no. 5"), different melodies are used for each of the two text phrases of the couplet.

7. The terms "dorian" and "major" are used here solely to describe the form of the pitch series and carry none of the wider meanings associated with the former term in classical Greek or European church modes, or with the latter within the Western harmonic system.

8. In this table, I have assigned each of the melodies a proper name. Where a melody is associated with one, and only one, song, the name of the melody is the same as that of the song. In cases where several songs are sung to the same melody, the melody is named after the song that first used that melody (where this is known) or after the song that most frequently uses that melody.

9. The other is "Mirrwana." Thomas Kungiung and Martin Warrigal Kungiung sing slightly different forms of the text to different but related melodies that I have called Mirrwana A and Mirrwana B. These will not be discussed here.

10. While it is hardly possible on the basis of this example alone to conclude that such complexity is a feature of rhythmic mode 2, it is worth noting that some vocal sections sung in rhythmic mode 2 in Thomas Kungiung's performance on Anon. n.d. reveal a similar level of complexity.

11. The performance by Martin Warrigal Kungiung that appears on track 11 of the CD is somewhat atypical of the Walakandha *wangga* tradition in that, as is usual when he performed alone, Warrigal performs at a slower-than-normal tempo. In this performance, his clapstick beating is at a rate of 117–19 beats per

minute, that is, at a tempo that would normally be considered moderate and would make the rhythmic mode 4a. Because Warrigal's tempos are consistently a notch lower when he sings solo—irrespective of what song he is singing—I regard his performance here as being in rhythmic mode 5a.

6. The Ma-yawa Wangga, pp. 135–52

1. Ngulkur confirmed that the first twelve songs listed in table 6.1 made up his complete repertory. The titles used here reflect the nomenclature by which Ngulkur referred to the songs.

2. To distinguish the two versions, I will refer to the Ma-yawa *wangga* version as "Walakandha Ngindji" and the Marri-tjevin version as "Walakandha no. 2."

3. *Kanda ma-walakandha ngirri munggit-pini-ni.*

4. There is a slight divergence from this pattern at the beginning of text phrase 2, where *ngata devin* (a solitary house) is not a vocative text formula but simply the subject of the sentence that follows.

5. Syllables in boldface in tables 6.3, 6.4, 6.6, 6.7, and 6.8 indicate syllables that are lengthened.

6. Textual variation occurs not only between item i and item ii but also between the first and second vocal sections of item i: in the second text phrase of the second vocal section of item i, the morpheme *nanga* (for him) was omitted, and two new vocative text formulas, *mana* and *walakandha*, were added. (In table 6.3, the omitted material has been placed in parentheses, and the added material in square brackets.)

7. I am grateful to Linda Barwick for this observation.

8. While in his performance of "Walakandha Ngindji" Ngulkur mixed rhythmic modes at the level of the vocal section, in the performance of "Wulumen Tulh" examined in chapter 1, the contrast of rhythmic modal settings was made at a higher level of structure. In that case, it was whole items, rather than individual vocal sections, that were either in rhythmic mode 5c or in rhythmic mode 1.

9. Although I do not want to engage in analysis of this level of complexity, it is worth noting that similar principles apply in the unmeasured vocal section (vocal section 2), where the length of the rhythmic cells is variable (between five and fourteen beats rather than six beats or multiples thereof).

10. The reason for this is that the group 2B songs are in rhythmic mode 2, a slow simple duple meter, rather than in the fast compound duple meter used in "Walakandha Ngindji."

11. As in the Walakandha *wangga*, a contrast may be drawn between the melodies (melodies 1 and 2) that use a dorian series and those that use a major series (melodies 3 and 4). The significance of this distinction is nowadays no longer understood.

12. By way of contrast, Ngulkur sang two songs, "Na-pebel" (a sandbar in the shape of a dilly bag near the mouth of Tjindi Creek) and "Watjen Danggi" (Dingo), that are explicitly not about Dreamings or Dreaming places. Each has its own individual melody, and significantly this melody is quite different from those used for songs about Dreamings. The text of "Na-pebel" makes it quite explicit that this place, while both dangerous and important, is not a Dreaming site. By referring to Na-pebel as *thawurr-nidin* (*thawurr* marks *nidin*, "country," as inanimate), Ngulkur differentiates this site from animate, life-giving Dreaming sites. "Watjen

Danggi" is the only song in the repertory that was composed without ancestral assistance. According to Ngulkur, Charlie Brinken made up the song after he had seen a dingo walking along the beach at Yilhiyilhiyen.

7. Barrtjap's Wangga, pp. 153–79

1. Barrtjap (or Berrtjap) and his descendants have taken on the family name "Burrenjuck." Moyle uses the spelling "Barandjak" in her notes. I use "Burrenjuck" when referring to other members of the family and reserve "Barrtjap" to refer to Tommy.

2. In table 7.1 and throughout this chapter, I have in most cases adopted all or part of the first line of each song as a working title. This practice reflects the means by which Barrtjap, Kenny Burrenjuck, and I referred to songs when discussing them, namely, by singing the first text phrase. In a small number of cases (songs 10 and 16), the second phrase, rather than the first, is picked up to identify the song. A summary of all recordings of the Barrtjap repertory is given in appendix table 3.1.

3. While the rhythmic modes summarized in table 9.1 represent those most commonly used in *wangga*, this list is not exhaustive. In rare and inevitably striking cases, a rhythmic mode may appear that does not fall within this pattern (see, for example, the discussion of Rusty Benmele Moreen's performance of "Rak Badjalarr" in chapter 8).

4. In Arnhem Land unmeasured performances are similarly weighty. According to A. P. Borsboom, the most important songs are the unmeasured ones performed with elaborate dancing (1978, 91–92). Greg Anderson refers to this category of dancing by its Rembarrnga name *ngarkana* (bone) and describes the music as follows: "The main distinguishing characteristics of the [*ngarkana*] songs are that there is no regular metrical pulse in any of the sound component's parts, and therefore no regular metrical relationship between the sound components" (1992, 350).

5. While the setting of the three-syllable text phrase *bangany-nye* to a two-beat cell by prolonging the last syllable, and the setting of the four-syllable text phrase *bangany-nyaya* to a two-beat rhythmic cell, follow the conventions already established, the other two phrases are set less conventionally. The initial syllable of the first text phrase, *be bangany-nye nye nye*, is incorporated into the measure that takes the core sentence, leaving the remaining five syllables to be set to a three-beat rhythmic cell. In the setting of the remaining text phrase, *nga-bindja nye*, a desire to echo the rhythm of the preceding measure seems to override the normal conventions, so that in this case a four-syllable text phrase is set to a three-beat, rather than a two-beat, rhythmic cell.

6. As was also the case with the Ma-yawa *wangga*, not only vocal sections but also complete song items can be sung in different rhythmic modes. For example, song 1 is performed both in rhythmic mode 5a and in rhythmic mode 5b.

7. The other conspicuous difference is that Kenny Burrenjuck performs at a faster tempo than his father. Barrtjap's performances range between 134 and 136 clapstick beats per minute; Kenny's are around 144 beats per minute.

8. This recording can be heard on the commercially available CD *Arnhem Land: Authentic Australian Aboriginal Songs and Dances (The A. P. Elkin Collection)*, Larrikin CD LRH 288, where it appears as item i of track 2.

1. Har79; see appendix table 4.1.

2. Although Lambudju regularly included a lower-octave phrase as an integral part of his song, I do not count the text of the lower-octave phrase as a separate text phrase.

3. The use of the expression *bangany-nyung* in this song recalls its use in Barrtjap's song, "Bangany-nyung Ngaya," which includes the text phrase *banganynyung nga-bindja* (I am singing in order to give you a song).

4. In translating into English, one needs to translate only the aspectual information conveyed by the auxiliary verb, but it cannot be omitted in spoken Batjamalh.

5. Audrey's father, the Emmiyangal songman Nym Mun.gi, was in the same generation as Lambudju. She therefore called Lambudju "Dad" (uncle in the European way) and Lambudju called her "daughter" (niece in the European way). Despite this generational difference, Lambudju was close in age to Audrey and her siblings (including Rusty Benmele Moreen), with whom he grew up.

6. In this case, the literal meaning of the auxiliary *nga-mi* is included in the translation of text, following Lambudju's own gloss, "that means I'm sitting eating oysters."

7. Sansom describes in detail some of the ways in which "collective representations" of events are arrived at (Sansom 1980, 79).

8. Both *winmedje* and *nga-mi* are elided with a concluding hum, which for the purposes of analysis is regarded as an extension of the final syllable.

9. Lysbeth Ford has observed that when sung, *rakba* is indistinguishable from *rak-pe*, which means "eternal country" in Batjamalh.

10. At the launch of the CD *Rak Badjalarr: Wangga Songs from Peron Island by Bobby Lane*, the late Kiyuk elder JS expressed concern that "Badjalarr" was contained in the title of the CD and warned a young female Aboriginal journalist not to say the word. (The title of the CD had previously been approved by other elders at Belyuen.) It might seem strange that Lambudju utters *badjalarr* in its undisguised form at the beginning of his explanation and then disguises it later, were it not for the fact that he often used such apparent inconsistencies as a way of drawing attention to important points, as we will see in the discussion of "Benmele" later in the chapter.

11. Recordings of all the songs mentioned in this paragraph may be heard on Marett, Barwick, and Ford 2001.

12. "Karra-ve kan-ya verver rtedi ka-ya-nhthi / karra-ve kak-ung-bende badjalarr / ribene ribene" (A cool breeze is forever blowing on my back / [I'm] going to North Peron Island forever. / [ghost language]) ("Karra-ve Kan-ya Verver Rtedi Ka-ya-nhthi," song 4; see appendix table 4.2). The first text phrase of this song is in Emmi, and the second in Batjamalh. The orthography adopted for Emmi in this short phrase follows that given for Marri-tjevin and Marri-ammu. While the presence of Emmi in the text suggests that it might originally have been composed by Mun.gi or given to Lambudju by his ghost, the fact that Lambudju was famous for mixing the two languages, even in everyday speech, urges caution in jumping to such a conclusion.

13. "Bandawarra ngalgin ka-djen-mene / nya-muy-ang nye-dja-ng-nganggung / bandawarra ngalgin ka-djen-mene / ngalaviyitj nya-mu-nganggung" (The tide is coming in at Bandawarra. / The women are dancing for us. / The tide is coming in

at Bandawarra. / Sit and clap hands for us) ("Bandawarra Ngalkin," song 2; see appendix table 4.2). The order of these text phrases may be changed in different performances of the song.

14. "Karra balhak malvak karrang-maka ngan-rdut-mene-ng / ka-bara bandawarra ngalgin-bende nguk ka-maridje-ng ka-yeve / karra balhak werret-bende müng ya-mara nya-buring munguyil-malang / ngawardina ngawardina-djenenung-bende" (Brother Malvak! He has gone and left me behind. / He is now lying with one knee bent over the other at Bandawarra Ngalkin. / Quick now, brother! Go and catch him up! Paddle like mad! / Use a floating log now" ("Karra Balhak Malvak," song 3; see appendix table 4.2). Like Walakandha and Ma-yawa, Wunymalang lie with one knee bent over the other—the position is known as "number four leg" in Aboriginal English—when they are in the process of giving songs. The references to paddling are expressive of the belief that the spirits of the dead paddle to Badjalarr on the outgoing tide.

15. According to Lambudju, "This song is about a place called Wali, Walingave. It's near Peron Island there somewhere." Brian Enda, however, gave a different explanation: "Wally, that's the name of the Toyota at Port Keats [Wadeye] when I was working up there. They call that Toyota 'Wally.' He [Lambudju] had an accident, somewhere near Daly River. You know the crossing. My father Bobby Lane [asked] what time they're going to fix it. My father said [sings] *wali muvu maka*—'what time you going to move again?' My old man made that song you see, that's the one we're singing now" (Har79; see appendix table 4.1).

16. Although the exact date of his death is not known, Benmele was still alive in 1979 when he was photographed performing for a circumcision ceremony at Belyuen.

17. In Arnhem Land, for example, it is believed that "a person should announce his or her death in advance, and absolve all living relations and members of other clans from any responsibility of involvement in it. This is what the *guwak* [channel-billed cuckoo] does" (Morphy 1991, 269).

18. Although not specifically attributed to Lambudju, the third song, "Tjerrendet," is so similar in construction to "Tjendabalatj" that it seems likely that both were composed by him.

19. As in other repertories, Lambudju uses even clapstick beating in nonfinal instrumental sections and doubled beating in the final instrumental sections of these unmeasured songs. The tempo of these—slow moderate tempo, in the range of 110–14 clapstick beats per minute—is, however, slower than that used in the Walakandha *wangga* and Ma-yawa *wangga* repertories.

20. As noted elsewhere, there is evidence that aspects of rhythmic mode, in particular the range of tempo bands, shift over time. For this reason, I have excluded both the earlier recordings and the recordings made since Lambudju's death.

9. *The Musical Conventions of the Daly Region Revisited, 197–210*

1. Because the recorded sample contains so many examples of songs in this tempo, the tempo range is somewhat artificially inflated. To make sense of it, we must first consider the practice of individual singers. Lambudju's fast tempo, for example, is significantly slower than that of most other singers, with his fast beating falling in the range of mm 119–25, and his fast doubled beating (which occurs only in instrumental sections) roughly twice that. Martin Warrigal Kungiung, while fol-

lowing the normal practice when singing with other songmen in the Walakandha *wangga* tradition, regularly performed more slowly when he performed alone. In all other cases, however, the range of the fast tempo band in the Walakandha *wangga* is mm 126–44, although in fact most performances fall within a range of 134–44 beats per minute. The factor that most commonly influences the precise tempo used in a performance is context. In general, the tempo of danced ceremonial performances, in which there is a high degree of excitement, tends to be slightly faster than in more casual performances. Except in Lambudju's repertory, the fast doubled tempo is in the range of 268–88 beats per minute—that is, almost exactly twice the most commonly encountered rates of fast beating.

2. The church *lirrga* is a subset of the *lirrga* repertory, which in total numbers more than one hundred songs.

10. Wangga *beyond the Daly, 211–31*

1. Alice Moyle recorded *djungguriny* at Gunbalanya in the 1960s, examples of which are included on *Songs from the Northern Territory*, disc 1B, track 1 (track 7, disc 1 of the 1991 CD reissue), and discussed in the accompanying handbook (A. Moyle 1967, 7). Moyle states in the handbook that the singer Lofty Nabadayal "learnt this song from Wagaitj men at Delissaville [Belyuen]," but in her Ph.D. dissertation, she states, "The singer Lofty Nabadayal, learnt the song at Beswick where some . . . Delissaville boys were living at the time" (A. Moyle 1974, 163). The similarity of these items to Maddock's recordings of Laurence Wurrpen and Rusty Moreen made at Barunga (Beswick) in 1964 suggests that the latter explanation is the correct one. Although the term *djungguriny* is still used today at Gunbalanya, I have conducted insufficient fieldwork there to be able to speak authoritatively about its role today.

2. Until 1965, Barunga was known as Beswick Creek, and from 1965 to 1984 as Bamyili.

3. Mad64:1 and Mad64:2; see appendix table 3.1.

4. This is indicated by the fact that in Maddock's recordings he was accompanied by Rusty Benmele Moreen, one of the leading singers from Belyuen at the time.

5. *Wangga* texts obtained by Elkin and Alice Moyle outside the Daly region were mostly untranslatable, even when they are known to have originated from within the Daly region. This is probably because the singers did not know the original languages, as is the case today when songs from Wadeye are disseminated to the western Kimberley with similar losses of meaning. In the case of the *wangga* sung by Dick Palduna, a Maielli man with no known links to the Daly region, who was recorded by Elkin at Barunga, only minimal documentation of the texts was obtained. This consisted mainly of syllables such as *a:la:la: a:la:da*, which are almost certainly meaningless vocables (Elkin and Jones 1958, 149). By contrast, in the other two cases of *wangga* from the Daly that Elkin recorded at or near Barunga, he was assisted in transcribing texts by Lamderod, a Jowayn singer with maternal relations on the Daly and perhaps some knowledge of the languages of the song. In these cases (Elkin and Jones 1958, 62, 151), Elkin was able to get translations for at least parts of the texts. Similarly, Alice Moyle states that song words and translations could not be obtained for the *djungguriny*—which had almost certainly came to Gunbalanya from Belyuen via Barunga—that she recorded at Gunbalanya (1967, 7).

6. Recorded by Allan Marett at Barunga on November 24, 1988. AIATSIS: A16933.

7. AIATSIS: A16760/17013.

8. Recorded by Allan Marett at Barunga on August 8, 1986. AIATSIS: A17029–30.

9. AIATSIS: 16790.

10. Philip Pannikin composed a number of *wangga* songs, which he said were in Murrinhpatha. Because Pannikin died shortly after I recorded these songs in 1998, I was not able to work with him on them. When I subsequently played them to people at Wadeye, they confirmed that they contained Murrinhpatha words, but said that the texts were scrambled and largely unintelligible.

11. This recording is listed as Mar98:4 in appendix tables 1.1 and 2.1. At the time, Pannikin had only recently taken over from Binggal as principal *wangga* songman at Kununurra. Both Binggal and Pannikin were recorded by Alice Moyle in the 1960s.

12. The choice of songs may have been influenced by the fact that immediately before the performance, we had been discussing *lirrga*. On the other hand, the high proportion of *lirrga* items reflects a general pattern encountered in other performances that I have recorded in the Kimberley. The following day, Pannikin performed for me again (recorded on Mar98:5, AIATSIS: 17047). He began with a bracket of *wangga* songs, some of which he had composed himself, and followed them with a bracket of *dhanba* songs also composed by him.

13. "Malhimanyirr karri-mi-gagap ka-vulh / mungerini kapil karri-gap ka-vulh" ("Malhimanyirr no. 1," Ma-yawa wangga song 7; see appendix table 2.2).

14. Like *wangga* and *lirrga*, *junba* are received from the spirits of the dead in dream. The morphology of the songs is, however, radically different, conforming more to a desert style than to the didjeridu-accompanied genres of the Daly region and Arnhem Land. They are accompanied by clapsticks but not didjeridu, and the texts are cyclical and set isorhythmically, usually to a single melody. *Junba* may be heard on Barwick 2003.

15. Scotty Nyalgodi Martin is known primarily as a composer and singer of his own Jadmi *junba* series. The late Jacob Burgu also owned and sang a separate *junba* series. Paul Chapman is famous as a *junba* dancer.

16. Rose (1992, 145) refers to "strings" of songs or "*Wangka* lines." While it is possible that she may have heard people refer to *wangga* in these terms, it is important to bear in mind that unlike most of the series sung in the Kimberley and Victoria River region, *wangga* songs are not organized in "song lines" whereby songs tend to follow a prescribed order and describe the journey of an ancestor through country.

Anderson, Gregory D. 1992. "Murlarra: A Clan Song Series from Arnhem Land." Ph.D. diss., University of Sydney.

———. 1995. "Striking a Balance: Limited Variability in Performances of a Clan Song Series from Arnhem Land." In *The Essence of Singing and the Substance of Song: Recent Responses to the Aboriginal Performing Arts and Other Essays in Honour of Catherine Ellis*, ed. Linda Barwick, Allan Marett, and Guy Tunstill, 13–25. Oceania Monograph no. 46. Sydney: University of Sydney.

Barwick, Linda. 1990. "Central Australian Women's Music: Knowing through Analysis versus Knowing through Performance." *Yearbook for Traditional Music* 22:60–79.

———. 1995. "Unison and 'Disagreement' in a Mixed Men's and Women's Performance (Ellis Collection, Oodnadatta, 1966)." In *The Essence of Singing and the Substance of Song: Recent Responses to the Aboriginal Performing Arts and Other Essays in Honour of Catherine Ellis*, ed. Linda Barwick, Allan Marett, and Guy Tunstill, 95–105. Oceania Monograph no. 46. Sydney: University of Sydney.

———. 2002. "Tempo and Rhythmic Mode in Marri Ngarr Lirrga Songs." *Australasian Music Research*, 67–83.

———. 2003. *Jadmi Junba: Public Dance Songs by Nyalgodi Scotty Martin, Northern Kimberleys*. Recordings by L. M. Barwick, commentary compiled by L. M. Barwick and S. Treloyn in association with Nyalgodi Scotty Martin and the Ngarinyin Aboriginal Corporation (Derby, Western Australia). Sydney: Undercover Music RRR135, 2003, ISBN 9780646424613.

———. 2005. "Marri Ngarr Lirrga Songs: A Musicological Analysis of Song Pairs in Performance." *Musicology Australia* 28 (in press).

Barwick, Linda, and Allan Marett. 1995. Introduction to *The Essence of Singing and the Substance of Song: Recent Responses to the Aboriginal Performing Arts and Other Essays in Honour of Catherine Ellis*, ed. Linda Barwick, Allan Marett, and Guy Tunstill, 1–10. Oceania Monograph no. 46. Sydney: University of Sydney.

Basedow, H. 1906. "Anthropological Notes on the West Coastal Tribes of the Northern Territory of South Australia." *Transcripts of the Royal Society of South Australia* 31:1–62.

Becker, Howard. 1989. "Ethnomusicology and Sociology: A Letter to Charles Seeger." *Ethnomusicology* 33 (2): 275–85.

Berndt, R., and C. Berndt. 1964. *The World of the First Australians*. Sydney: Ure Smith.

Blacking, John. 1995. "Deep and Surface Structures in Venda Music." In *Music, Cul-*

ture and Experience: Selected Papers of John Blacking, ed. Reginald Byron, 54–72. Chicago: University of Chicago Press. Originally published in *Yearbook of the International Folk Music Council* 3 (1972): 91–108.

Blum, Stephen. 1992. "Analysis of Musical Style." In *Ethnomusicology: An Introduction*, ed. Helen Myers, 165–218. New Grove Handbooks to Music. London: Macmillan.

Borsboom, A. P. 1978. *Maradjiri: A Modern Ritual Complex in Arnhem Land, North Australia*. Nijmegen: Katholieke Universiteit.

Christie, H. W. 1906. "Down upon the Daly." *Adelaide Weekly News*, May 5.

Clifford, James. 1988. *The Predicament of Culture: Twentieth-Century Ethnography, Literature and Art*. Cambridge: Harvard University Press.

Clunies Ross, Margaret. 1978. "The Structure of Arnhem Land Song Poetry." *Oceania* 49 (2): 128–56.

Clunies Ross, Margaret, Tamsin Donaldson, and Stephen Wild. 1987. *Songs of Aboriginal Australia*. Oceania Monograph no. 32. Sydney: Oceania Publications.

Clunies Ross, Margaret, and Lester Hiatt. 1978. "Sand Sculptures at a Gidjingali Burial Rite." In *Form in Indigenous Art: Schematisation in the Art of Aboriginal Australia and Prehistoric Europe*, ed. Peter Ucko. Canberra: Australian Institute of Aboriginal Studies.

Clunies Ross, Margaret, and Johnny Mundrugmundrug. 1988. *Goyulan the Morning Star: An Aboriginal Clan Song Series from North Central Arnhem Land*. Canberra: Australian Institute of Aboriginal Studies. Book and cassette.

Clunies Ross, Margaret, and Stephen Wild. 1982. *Djambidj: An Aboriginal Song Series from Northern Australia*. Canberra: Australian Institute of Aboriginal Studies. Book and cassette.

———. 1984. "Formal Performance: The Relations of Music, Text and Dance in Arnhem Land Clan Songs." *Ethnomusicology* 28:209–35.

Cook, Nicholas. 1998. *Music: A Very Short Introduction*. New York: Oxford University Press.

———. 2002. "We Are All Ethnomusicologists Now." Paper read at the International Congress of the Musicological Society of Japan, Shizuoka, November 2002.

Corn, Aaron. 2002. "Dreamtime Wisdom, Modern-Time Vision: Tradition and Innovation in the Popular Band Movement of Arnhem Land." Ph.D. diss., University of Melbourne.

Dean, Beth, and Victor Carell. 1956. *Dust for the Dancers*. Sydney: Ure Smith.

Dixon, R. M. W. 1984. "Dyirbal Song Types." In *Problems and Solutions: Occasional Essays in Musicology Presented to Alice M. Moyle*, ed. J. C. Kassler and J. Stubington, 206–27. Sydney: Hale and Iremonger.

———. 2002. *Australian Languages: Their Nature and Development*. New York: Cambridge University Press.

Dixon, R. M. W., and Grace Koch. 1996. *Dyirbal Song Poetry: The Oral Literature of an Australian Rainforest People*. St. Lucia: Queensland University Press.

Donaldson, Tamsin. 1984. "Kids That Got Lost: Variations in the Words of Ngiyampaa Songs." In *Problems and Solutions: Occasional Essays in Musicology Presented to Alice M. Moyle*, ed. J. C. Kassler and J. Stubington, 228–53. Sydney: Hale and Iremonger.

———. 1987. "Making a Song (and Dance) in South-Eastern Australia." In *Songs of Aboriginal Australia*, ed. M. Clunies Ross, T. Donaldson, and S. Wild, 14–42. Oceania Monograph 32. Sydney: Oceania Publications.

Dussart, Françoise. 2000. *The Politics of Ritual in an Aboriginal Settlement: Kinship, Gender, and the Currency of Knowledge.* Washington, D.C.: Smithsonian Institution Press.

Elkin, A. P. 1950. "Ngirawat, or The Sharing of Names in the Wagaitj Tribe, Northern Australia." In *Beitrage zur Gesellungs- und Völkerwissenschaft,* ed. I. Tönnies, 67–81. Berlin: Gebrüder Mann.

Elkin, A. P., and Trevor A. Jones. 1958. *Arnhem Land Music.* Oceania Monograph no. 9. Sydney: Australasian Medical Publishing Company.

Ellis, Catherine J. 1980. "Aboriginal Music and Dance in Southern Australia." In *New Grove Dictionary of Music and Musicians,* ed. Stanley Sadie, 722–28. London: Macmillan.

———. 1984. "Time Consciousness of Aboriginal Performers." In *Problems and Solutions: Occasional Essays in Musicology presented to Alice M. Moyle,* ed. J. C. Kassler and J. Stubington, 155–70. Sydney: Hale and Iremonger.

Ellis, Catherine, Linda Barwick, and Megan Morais. 1990. "Overlapping Time Structures in a Central Australian Women's Ceremony." In *Language and History: Essays in Honour of Luise A. Hercus,* ed. P. Austin, R. M. W. Dixon, T. Dutton, and I. M. White, 101–36. Canberra: Australian National University (Pacific Linguistics).

Ellis, Catherine J., A. M. Ellis, M. Tur, and A. McCardell. 1978. "Classification of Sound in Pitjintjatjara-Speaking Areas." In *Australian Aboriginal Concepts,* ed. L. R. Hiatt, 68–80. Canberra: Australian Institute of Aboriginal Studies and Humanities Press.

Ewers, John K. 1964. "Aboriginal Ballet." In *Walkabout in Australia,* ed. A. T. Bolton. Sydney: Ure Smith.

Falkenberg, Johannes. 1962. *Kin and Totem: Group Relations of Australian Aborigines in the Port Keats District.* Oslo: Oslo University Press.

Feld, Steven. 1987. "Dialogic Editing: Interpreting How Kaluli Read Sound and Sentiment." *Cultural Anthropology* 2 (2): 190–210.

Ford, Lysbeth. 1990. "The Phonology and Morphology of Bachamal (Wogait)." M.A. thesis, Australian National University.

———. 1997. *Batjamalh: Dictionary and Texts.* Fyshwick, Australian Capital Territory: Panther Publishing and Printing.

———. 2005. "Marri Ngarr Songs: A Linguistic Analysis." *Musicology Australia* 28 (in press).

Geertz, Clifford. 1983. *Local Knowledge: Further Essays in Interpretive Anthropology.* New York: Fontana Press.

Gummow, Margaret. 1992. "Aboriginal Songs from the Bundjalung and Gidabal Areas of South-Eastern Australia." Ph.D. diss., University of Sydney.

Harney, W. E., and A. P. Elkin. 1949. *Songs of the Songmen.* Melbourne: F. W. Cheshire.

Herndon, Marcia. 1974. "Analysis: The Herding of Sacred Cows." *Ethnomusicology* 18 (2): 219–62.

Hiatt, Lester. 1965. *Kinship and Conflict: A Study of an Aboriginal Community in Northern Arnhem Land.* Canberra: Australian National University.

———. 1989. "On Aboriginal Religion: An Introduction." Introduction to *On Aboriginal Religion,* by W. E. H. Stanner, xix–xxxix. Oceania Monograph 11. Sydney: Oceania Publications.

Jones, Trevor. 1956. "Arnhem Land Music Part II: A Musical Survey." *Oceania* 26 (4): 252–339.

Keen, Ian. 1994. *Knowledge and Secrecy in an Aboriginal Religion*. Oxford Studies in Cultural Anthropology. Melbourne: Oxford University Press.

Keogh, Raymond. 1989. "*Nurlu* Songs from the West Kimberley: An Introduction." *Australian Aboriginal Studies*, no. 1:2–11.

———. 1990. "Nurlu Songs of the West Kimberleys." Ph.D. diss., University of Sydney.

———. 1995. "Process Models for the Analysis of *Nurlu* Songs from the Western Kimberleys." In *The Essence of Singing and the Substance of Song: Recent Responses to the Aboriginal Performing Arts and Other Essays in Honour of Catherine Ellis*, ed. Linda Barwick, Allan Marett, and Guy Tunstill, 39–51. Oceania Monograph no. 46. Sydney: University of Sydney.

Knopoff, Steven. 1992. "*Yuta manikay*: Juxtaposition of Ancestral and Contemporary Elements in the Performance of Yolngu Clan Songs." *Yearbook of the International Council for Traditional Music* 24:138–53.

Leppert, Richard, and Susan McClary. 1987. *Music and Society: The Politics of Composition, Performance and Reception*. Cambridge: Cambridge University Press.

Lommel, Andreas. 1997. *The Unambal: A Tribe in Northwest Australia*. Trans. Ian Campbell. Carnarvon Gorge, Queensland: Takarakka Nowan Kas Publications. Originally published in 1952.

Mackinlay, Elizabeth. 1998. "For Our Mother's Song We Sing: Yanyuwa Women Performers and Composers of A-nguyulnguyul." Ph.D. diss., University of Adelaide.

Marett, Allan. 1992. "Variability and Stability in *Wangga* Songs of Northwest Australia." In *Music and Dance in Aboriginal Australia and the South Pacific: The Effects of Documentation on the Living Tradition*, ed. Alice M. Moyle, 194–213. Oceania Monograph no. 41. Sydney: Oceania Publications.

———. 1993. *Bunggridj Bunggridj: Wangga Songs by Alan Maralung, Northern Australia*. Sung by Alan Maralung, accompanied by Peter Manaberu (didjeridu). Recorded by Allan Marett. Commentary by Allan Marett and Linda Barwick. Traditional Music of the World 4. Smithsonian/Folkways SF 40430. Compact disc.

———. 1994. "*Wangga*: Socially Powerful Songs." *The World of Music* 36 (1): 67–81.

———. 1998. "Northern Australia." In *Encyclopedia of World Music: Oceania*, ed. Adrienne Kaeppler and J. Wainwright Love, 418–27. New York: Garland.

———. 2000. "Ghostly Voices: Some Observations on Song-Creation, Ceremony and Being in NW Australia." *Oceania* 71 (1): 18–29.

———. 2001. "Australia, Aboriginal Music, Northern Australia." In *New Grove Dictionary of Music and Musicians*, 2nd ed., ed. Stanley Sadie, vol. 2, 193–202. New York: Macmillan.

———. 2002. " 'The Tide Has Gone on Him': *Wangga* Songs, Walakandha Dances and the Eternal Ebb and Flow of Existence." *Cultural Survival* 26 (2): 22–25.

Marett, Allan, and Linda Barwick. 2003. "Endangered Songs and Endangered Languages." In *Maintaining the Links: Language, Identity and the Land; Proceedings of the Seventh FEL Conference, Broom, 22–24 September 2003*, ed. Joe Blyth and R. McKenna Brown. Federation for Endangered Languages.

Marett, Allan, Linda Barwick, and Lysbeth Ford. 1998. *Ethnomusicology of the Belyuen Community on the Cox Peninsula*. Unpublished report commissioned by Northern Land Council, Darwin.

———. 2001. *Rak Badjalarr: Wangga Songs by Bobby Lane, Northern Australia*.

Booklet accompanying compact disc recorded by Allan Marett and Linda Barwick. Canberra: Aboriginal Studies Press.

Marett, Allan, and Lysbeth Ford. n.d. "Bobby Lane's *Wangga:* A Musicological and
Linguistic Analysis of Australian Aboriginal Song Texts." Typescript.

Marett, Allan, and JoAnne Page. 1995. "Interrelationships between Music and
Dance in a *Wangga* from Northwest Australia." In *The Essence of Singing
and the Substance of Song: Recent Responses to the Aboriginal Performing
Arts and Other Essays in Honour of Catherine Ellis,* ed. Linda Barwick, Allan
Marett, and Guy Tunstill, 27–38. Oceania Monograph no. 46. Sydney: Univer-
sity of Sydney.

Martin, Peter. 2002. "Over the Rainbow? On the Quest for 'The Social' in Musical
Analysis." *Journal of the Royal Musical Association* 127:130–46.

McClary, Susan. 1987. "The Blasphemy of Talking Politics during Bach Year." In
Music and Society: The Politics of Composition, Performance and Reception, ed.
Richard Leppert and Susan McClary, 13–62. Cambridge: Cambridge University
Press.

———. 1993. "Narrative Agendas in 'Absolute' Music: Identity and Difference in
Brahms's Third Symphony." In *Musicology and Difference: Gender and Sexuality
in Music Scholarship,* ed. Ruth A. Solie, 326–44. Berkeley and Los Angeles: University of California Press.

———. 2000. *Conventional Wisdom: The Content of Musical Form.* Berkeley and
Los Angeles: University of California Press.

McIntosh, Ian. 2000. "Sacred Memory and Living Tradition: Aboriginal Art of the
Macassan Period in North-Eastern Arnhem Land." In *The Oxford Companion to
Aboriginal Art and Culture,* ed. Sylvia Kleinert and Margot Neale, 144–55. Mel-
bourne: Oxford University Press.

McKenzie, Kim. 1980. *Waiting for Harry.* Canberra: Australian Institute of Aboriginal Studies. Film and video.

Meggitt, Mervyn J. 1955. "Djanba among the Walbiri." *Australia Anthropos*
50:375–403.

Merlan, Francesca. 1986. "Australian Aboriginal Conception Beliefs Revisited." *Man*
21:474–93.

———. 1987. "Catfish and Alligator: Totemic Songs of the Western Roper River,
Northern Territory." In *Songs of Aboriginal Australia,* ed. M. Clunies Ross,
T. Donaldson, and S. Wild, 142–67. Oceania Monograph no. 32. Sydney: Oceania
Publications.

———. 1998. *Caging the Rainbow: Places, Politics and Aborigines in a North Australian Town.* Honolulu: University of Hawai'i Press.

Morphy, Howard. 1984. *Journey to the Crocodile's Nest: An Accompanying Monograph to the Film "Madarrpa Funeral at Gurka'wuy."* Canberra: Australian Institute of Aboriginal Studies.

———. 1991. *Ancestral Connections: Art and an Aboriginal System of Knowledge.*
Chicago: University of Chicago Press.

———. 1998. *Aboriginal Art.* London: Phaidon Press.

Moyle, Alice. 1966. *A Handlist of Field Collections of Recorded Music in Australia and
Torres Strait.* Occasional Papers in Aboriginal Studies no. 6, Ethnomusicology
Series no. 1. Canberra: Australian Institute of Aboriginal Studies.

———. 1967. *Songs of the Northern Territory.* Canberra: Australian Institute of

Aboriginal Studies (rev. ed., 1974). Companion booklet for five 12-inch LP discs (catalog no. M-110/5). These recordings were reissued as CDs with reduced documentation in 1991.

———. 1974. "North Australian Music: A Taxonomic Approach to the Study of Aboriginal Song Performances." Ph.D. diss., Monash University.

Moyle, Richard. 1979. *Songs of the Pintupi: Musical Life in a Central Australian Society.* Canberra: Australian Institute of Aboriginal Studies.

———. 1986. *Alyawarra Music: Songs and Society in a Central Australian Community; With the Help of Slippery Morton, Alyawarra Interpreter.* Canberra: Australian Institute of Aboriginal Studies.

———. 1997. *Balgo: The Musical Life of a Desert Community.* Nedlands: Callaway International Resource Centre for Music Education (CIRCME), University of Western Australia.

Munn, Nancy. 1973. *Walbiri Iconography: Graphic Representation and Cultural Symbolism in a Central Australian Society.* Ithaca: Cornell University Press.

Myers, Fred. 1986. *Pintupi Country, Pintupi Self: Sentiment, Place and Politics among Western Desert Aborigines.* Canberra: Australian Institute of Aboriginal Studies.

Nettl, Bruno. 1956. *Music in Primitive Culture.* Cambridge: Harvard University Press.

Petri, H., and G. Petri-Odermann. 1998. "Stability and Change: Present-Day Historical Aspects among Australian Aborigines." In *Australian Aboriginal Anthropology: Modern Studies in the Social Anthropology of the Australian Aborigines,* ed. R. Berndt, 248–76. Nedlands: UWA Press.

Povinelli, Elizabeth A. 1993. *Labor's Lot: The Power, History and Culture of Aboriginal Action.* Chicago: Chicago University Press.

Pye, J. 1973. *The Port Keats Story.* Darwin: Coleman.

Qureshi, Regula. 1987. "Musical Sound and Contextual Input: A Performance Model for Musical Analysis." *Ethnomusicology* 31:56–86.

Redmond, Anthony. 2001. "Rulug wayirri: Moving Kin and Country in the Northern Kimberley." Ph.D. diss., University of Sydney.

Rice, Timothy. 1994. *May It Fill Your Soul: Experiencing Bulgarian Music.* Chicago: Chicago University Press.

Rose, Deborah Bird. 1992. *Dingo Makes Us Human: Life and Land in an Australian Aboriginal Culture.* Cambridge and Melbourne: Cambridge University Press.

———. 1995. *Kenbi (Cox Peninsula) Land Claim: Anthropologist's Report on Behalf of the Tommy Lyons Group.* Darwin: Northern Land Council.

———. 1996. *Nourishing Terrains: Australian Aboriginal Views of Landscape and Wilderness.* Canberra: Australian Heritage Commission.

———. 1998. "Signs of Life on a Barbarous Frontier: Intercultural Encounters in North Australia." *Humanities Research* 2:17–36.

Sachs, Kurt. 1943. *The Rise of Music in the Ancient World, East and West.* New York: Norton.

Sansom, B. 1980. *The Camp at Wallaby Cross.* Canberra: Australian Institute of Aboriginal and Torres Strait Islander Studies.

Seeger, Anthony. 1987. *Why Suya Sing: A Musical Anthropology of an Amazonian People.* Cambridge Studies in Ethnomusicology. Cambridge: Cambridge University Press.

Simpson, Colin. 1951. *Adam in Ochre: Inside Aboriginal Australia.* Sydney and London: Angus and Robertson.

Stanley, Owen. 1985. *The Mission and Peppimenarti: An Economic Study of Two Daly River Aboriginal Communities*. ANU North Australia Research Unit Monograph. Darwin: Australian National University.

Stanner, W. E. H. 1989. *On Aboriginal Religion*. Oceania Monograph no. 36. Sydney: Oceania Publications. Originally published in 1963.

Strehlow, T. G. H. 1971. *Songs of Central Australia*. Sydney: Angus and Robertson.

Stubington, Jill. 1978. "Yolngu Manikay: Performances of Australian Aboriginal Clan Songs." Ph.D. diss., Monash University.

Stubington, Jill, and Peter Danbar-Hall. 1994. "Yothu Yindi's 'Treaty': *Ganma* in Music." *Popular Music* 13 (3): 243–60.

Subotnik, Rose R. 1976. "Adorno's Diagnosis of Beethoven's Late Style." *Journal of the American Musicological Society* 29:242–75.

———. 1987. "On Grounding Chopin." In *Music and Society: The Politics of Composition, Performance and Reception*, ed. Richard Leppert and Susan McClary, 105–31. Cambridge: Cambridge University Press.

Swain, Tony. 1993. *A Place for Strangers: Towards a History of Australian Aboriginal Being*. Cambridge: Cambridge University Press.

Tamisari, Franca. 2000. "Knowing the Country, Holding the Law, Yolngu Dance Performance in North-East Arnhem Land." In *The Oxford Companion to Aboriginal Arts and Culture*, ed. S. Kleinert and M. Neale. Melbourne: Oxford University Press.

Toner, Peter G. 2000. "Ideology, Influence and Innovation: The Impact of Macassan Contact on Yolngu Music." *Perfect Beat* 5 (1): 22–41.

———. 2001. "Where the Echoes Have Gone: A Yolngu Musical Anthropology." Ph.D. diss., Australian National University.

Treitler, Leo. 1975. " 'Centonate' Chant: *Übles Flickwerk* or *E pluribus unus*." *Journal of the American Musicological Society* 28 (1): 1–24.

Treloyn, Sally. 2000. "An Investigation of Scotty Martin's Jadmi Junba—a Song Series from the Kimberley Region of Northwest Australia." Paper delivered at the 23rd National Conference of the Musicological Society of Australia, Sydney.

Tryon, D. T. 1974. *Daly Family Languages, Australia*. Canberra: Australian National University (Pacific Linguistics).

von Sturmer, John. 1987. "Aboriginal Singing and Notions of Power." In *Songs of Aboriginal Australia*, ed. M. Clunies Ross, T. Donaldson, and S. Wild, 63–76. Oceania Monograph 32. Sydney: Oceania Publications.

Wadeye Aboriginal Languages Centre. 2003. *Mi-Tjiwilirr i Wulumen Tulh: Hairy Cheeky Yam and Old Man Tulh*. Batchelor, Northern Territory: Batchelor Press.

West, Lamont. 1974. *Notes, Dubbings and Vocabularies relating to Research in Arnhem Land, Cape York and Torres Strait, 1960–1965*. Dubbings of West's 1961–62 field recordings of Aboriginal music in northeastern Australia, prepared by P. Hamilton for Trevor Jones. AIATSIS: MS 2456/1, item 1.

Widdess, Richard. 1999. "Spatial Concepts and Musical Structure in a Nepalese Stick-Dance." http://www.santacecilia.it/italiano/archivio/cthnomusicology/esem99/musicspace/papers/widdess/widdess.htm.

Wild, Stephen. 1986. *Rom: An Aboriginal Ritual of Diplomacy*. Canberra: Australian Institute of Aboriginal Studies.

Index

Page numbers in italics refer to illustrations, tables, and musical examples; page numbers in boldface refer to principal treatment of a subject in the text.

Kungiung, Charles, 47, 137
Kungiung, Martin Warrigal, 47, 52, 114–15, 118, *238–40*
Kungiung, Ned Narjic, 47
Kungiung (Kanggiang), Thomas, 13, 25, 31, 47, *48*, 49, 52, 62, *73*, 113–15, 117–21, 132–33, 150, 198, 219, 223–25, *238–41*
Kungiung family and lineage, 46–47, 52, 117, 120, 223, 227
Kunhbinhi, 24, 47, 58, **63–64**
Kunmanggurr. *See* Rainbow Serpent Dreaming
Kununurra, 2, 135, 215, 217, **218–25**, 227
Kuy, *16*, 24, 61, 71

Lambudju, Jack, 50, 183
Lambudju's *wangga*, 6, 13, **181–96**, 234, *245–47, 248–50*
    country, 5, 37, 55, 67, 234
    instrumental sections, 93, 190, 196
    lineage, 25, 48–51, 53, 67
    melodic sections, 185, 190
    melody, 116, **187–88**, 190, 194, 201
    modality, 181, 194–95, 201
    musical conventions of repertory, 181, **194–95**
    repertory, 6, 181–83
    rhythmic modes, 158, 161, 186, 188–89, 190–92, 194–96, 204–6
    song dreaming, 43–45, 182–84, 186–88, 192–94
    text, 5, 170, 181, 183, 186, 192–93, 198–200
    transmission, 177, 181–82, 188, **189–91**, 195, 201
Lane, Bobby Lambudju, 5, 13, 25, 37, 55, 67, 93, 116, 234. *See also* Lambudju's *wangga*
Larrakiya people, 26, 33, 49, 58, 167, 169, 183, 207
learning songs. *See* transmission of *wangga*
Lejune, Dusty, 218
Leppert, Richard, 10
Lhambumen (place), *16*
"Lhambumen" (song), 112, 117–18, 120, 122, 126–27, 146, *241*
"Limarapka" (song), 182, 195, *249*
liminality, **5**, 17, 62
lineages, 80
    Belyuen, 25, 49–52, 177, 181, 191
    Wadeye, 38, 42, 46, 48–49, 52–53, 117–21, 124, 126, 136
    See also transmission of *wangga*
Lippo, Agnes Alunga, 68, 183

Lippo, Audrey Badjawalang, 50, 183, 186–89, 194
Lippo, Michael, 50
lirrga genre, 4, 24, 58–59, 68, 70, 74, 202, 233
    outside Daly region, 211, 217–19, 226–27, 229–30
    rhythmic modes, 203, **206–7**, 209
living and dead
    relationship between, **3–4**, 40
    song composition and ceremony, 14, 17, **31–32**, 38, 53, 62–66, 68–69, 109, 113, 128, 155, 209
Lommel, Andreas, 218
Luckan, Pius, 59
Lyons, Tommy Imabulk, 49

Macassar (Ujung Padang), 208
Maddock, Kenneth, 154, 177, 212
malh. See ritual cries
Malhimanyirr (Jungle Fowl Dreaming), 28, 136, 219
"Malhimanyirr no. 1" (song), 136, 144, 147–48, 219–20, 222, *242*
"Malhimanyirr no. 2" (song), 135–36, **219–22**, 225, *243*
Maline, Jimmy, 226
Malvak, Aguk, 44, 50, 181, 183, 192, 195
Manaberu, Peter, 40, *41*
Mandji, Billy, 25, 47–48, 51–52, 67, 218, 227, 235
Mandorah, 80, 188–89
manikay-bungurl genre, 26–27, 152, 197, 207
Maningrida, 2, 73, 211
Manpurr, Mosek, 50
Maralung, Alan, 13, 38, 45, 94, 193, 211, 216–17
    "Minmin Light," **39–42**, 43–44, 170, 186, 216–17
marri. See ritual cries
marriage, 49, 66, 76, 191, 212
Marri-ammu language group (people), 2, 33, 222, 234
    country, 5
    dance, 107, 209
    lineages, 43, 45–46, 49
    mythology, 15–18, 37, 57–59, 64
    orders of being, 26, **27–31**
    wangga (*see* Ma-yawa *wangga*)
Marri-dan language group (people), 24
Marri-ngarr language group (people), 24, 58–59, 66, 117, 125, 202, 207–8, 219, 233
Marri-thiyel language group (people), 24, 58, 60

Milik Beach, 35, 37, 192
Minmin Light Dreaming, 40–41
"Minmin Light" (song), **39–42**, 43–44, 170, 186, 216–17
"Mirrwana" (song), 112, 118, 122, *240*
modality, 80, 88
    Barrtjap's *wangga*, 50
    Kimberley *wangga*, 222–24, 227–28
    Lambudju's *wangga*, 181, 194–95, 201
    Ma-yawa *wangga*, 148
    Walakandha *wangga*, 111, 116, 117–21, 124, 126, 158, 195
moods, 87, 162, 204
Moreen, Rusty Benmele, 50–51, 182–83, 188, 190–94, 199, *249*. *See also* "Benmele" (song)
Moreen, Simon, 51, *245*
Morphy, Howard, 152
mortuary ceremonies. *See burnim-rag* ceremonies
Mowanjum, 2, 26, 218, 225, 235
Moyle, Alice, 7, 81, 86, 153, 160, 162, 166, 182, 186
Moyle, Richard, 9, 79
Moyle, Tommy Karui, 24, *99*, 100
Moyle River, 2, *16*, 23, 46, 233–34
"Mubagandi" (song), 182, 191, 194, *249*
Mullumbuk, Philip, *19*, 42, 45, 47, *48*, 49, 52–53, 112, 117–18, 125–26, 137, 150, *239–41*
    "Truwu," 118, 120–21
    "Walakandha no. 4," 30, 111, 118, **122–24**, 131
Mullumbuk, Roy, 47
Mullumbuk, Stan, 25, 42, 46, 49, 52, 117, 132–33, *241*
Mullumbuk family, 46–49, 117, 120–21, 123, 126
multigin (saltwater turtle), 17
multivalency. *See* text of *wangga*
Muluk, Jimmy, 25, 47, 49, 51–52, 67, 80, 218, 235
Mumbil, Anne, 50
Munggum, 42, 47, 65, 112–14, 121, 139
Munggumurri, 42, 47, 118, 122–23
Mun.gi, Nym, 50–51, 67, 181–83, 188, 201
Munn, Nancy, 152
Murgenella, 170, 199
Murlarra song series, 207
Murrinhpatha language group (people), 24–28, 43
    ceremonies, 63–64, 66, 69
    myths, 41, 53, 55–57, 60, 202

orders of being, 26
    See also Diminin clan
musical analysis, 6–12, 79
    social analysis and, **9–11**
musical features of *wangga*, **18–23**
musical structure, 7–10, 13, 79–81, 217, 223–24, 226. *See also* instrumental introductions; instrumental sections; melodic sections; melody; song conventions; vocal sections
musicology, 6–7, 9–12, 152
Muyil floodplain, 59, 202, 233–34
Myall's Bore, 218, 225–26, **227–30**
mythology, 7, 110, 202, 217
    Old Man Tulh, **15–18**
    Rainbow Serpent, 53, **55–57**, 60, 79

Nadirri, *16*, 30, 46, 48, 61–66, 68, 70, 74, 79, 95, 101, 104–6, 112, 138, 234. *See also* Kubuwemi (place)
"Nadirri" (song), 74, 112, 117–18, 122, *240*
Na-pebel (place), 136
"Na-pebel" (song), 136–37, 148, 210, *242*
Na-pumut, 42, 62
Narjic family, 59
Nemarluk, Edward, 15, 17, 18, *99*, 100
Nemarluk family, 46
nganang (persons), 26
"Nga'ngatbat-ba Mangalimpa" (song), 154, *247*
Ngan'gityemerri language group (people), 24, 58, 60
Ngan'giwumerri language group (people), 24
ngarrith-ngarrith. *See* baby spirits
"Ngaya Lima Bangany-nyaya" (song), 154, *247*
Ngenawurda family, 49
ngepan. *See* conception Dreaming
ngirrwat. *See* Dreamings
ngugumingki. *See* Dreaming sites
Ngukurr (place), 71
Ngulkur, Maurice Tjakurl, *18*, *48*, *73*, *242–43*
    ceremony, 62, 70, 93–94
    country and Dreamings, 27–29, 32
    lineage, 46, 49
    performances, 19, 93–94, 126–27, 133, **135–52**, 161, 174, 200, 202–3, 216, 219
    song creation, 193
    "Wulumen Tulh," 18, 19, 21, 31
Ngura-nyini (Penis Dreaming), 75
Ngurndul family. *See* Kundjil family
nguwatj. *See* ghosts

song texts. *See* text of *wangga*

sorcery, 37, **193–94**

southern Daly region, 12, *16*, 27, 35, 43–44, 51, 53–54, 61–63, 66–67, 71, 75

South Peron Island (Barakbana), 35

spelling, xxi–xxiii

spirit children. *See* baby spirits

Stanner, W. E. H., 27, 54, 55–58, 60, 62, 69–73, 76, 108–9

stories. *See* mythology

Strehlow, T. G. H., 27

Subotnik, Rose, 10, 11

Swain, Tony, 28, 37

sweat (*maruy, meri-men.ngu*), 51, 61–62, 67, 75, 184, 233

Tandandjal, 76, 212

Tchinburur, Clement, 59

teaching songs. *See* transmission of *wangga*

tempo
    Barrtjap's *wangga*, 92, **159–61**, 167, 174 75
    instrumental introductions, 81, **86–87**
    Lambudju's *wangga*, 190, 196
    Ma-yawa *wangga*, 21, 141, 144, 151
    rhythmic modes and, 13, 52, 204–9
    Walakandha *wangga*, 106, 129, 131–32

terminating patterns. *See* codas and terminating patterns

text of *wangga*, 3, 7, 9, 53, 87, **88–92**, 94, 96, 98–100, 203
    Barrtjap's *wangga*, 153, 155–57, 163–64, 167, 169–74, 199–200, 212–15
    burnim-rag ceremonies, **60–69**
    Kimberley *wangga*, 218, 220, 222–24, 226–28, 230–31
    Lambudju's *wangga*, 5, 170, 181, 183, 186, 192–93, 198–200
    manipulation to reflect relationships, **202–3**
    Maralung's *wangga*, 41, 43, 216
    Ma-yawa *wangga*, 18–21, 23, 28, 30–31, 67, 127–29, 136–37, **138–50**, 151–52, 155–56, 198–200
    meaning and, **197–98**
    multivalency and ambiguity, 35, 170–71, 192–93, **198–200**, 201
    placement in vocal sections, **198**
    prolongation (*see* prolongation, repetition, and truncation of text)
    repetition (*see* prolongation, repetition, and truncation of text)
    rhythmic treatment (*see* rhythmic treatment of text)

song creation, 38, 43, 45

stability and instability, 41–42, 152, **200**

truncation (*see* prolongation, repetition, and truncation of text)

Walakandha *wangga*, 29, 111, 113–14, 152, 155–56, 192, 200

See also ghost language; text structure

text structure
    Barrtjap's *wangga*, 35, 50, 81, **88–92**, **155–57**, 163, 172
    diversity, **197**
    Kimberley *wangga*, 222
    Lambudju's "Rak Badjalarr," **186–87**
    Maminmangga's song, 108–9
    Ma-yawa *wangga*, 138–41
    Walakandha *wangga*, 111–14, 116, 120, **122–31**, 138–39

Thalhi-ngatjpirr (Fish Dreaming site), 136, 144, 147

"Thalhi-ngatjpirr" (song), 136, 147–48, *242*

Thangguralh company, 46, 49

tide metaphor
    Barrtjap's *wangga*, 167
    Kimberley *wangga*, 219–20
    Lambudju's *wangga*, 192
    Walakandha *wangga*, 2, 4–5, 30, 55, 62, 65, 74, 123, 192, 234

Timber Creek, 2, 26, 217–18

Tiwi Islands, 167, 169

"Tjendabalhatj" (song), 182, 191, 194, 196, *249*

"Tjerrendet" (song), 182, 194, 196, *249*

Tjerri (Sea Breeze Dreaming), 27–29, 31, 136

"Tjerri" (song), 27, 136, 144, 147–48, *242*

Tjindi, 71, 234

Tjinimin (Bat), 55–58, 60, 71, 76, 79, 108–9, 217

tjiwilirr. See hairy cheeky yam

Tjulatji, 50, 184

Tomlinson, Gary, 10

Toner, Peter, 207

trade songs, 76–77, 171, 197, 210, 230

tradition. *See* transmission of *wangga*

transcription, 6–7, 9–12

transmission of *wangga*, 38, 198
    Belyuen, 25, 43–45, **49–52**
    Belyuen: Barrtjap's *wangga*, **49–51**, 153–54, 162, 170, 177, 181, 183
    Belyuen: Lambudju's *wangga*, 177, 181–82, 188, **189–91**, 195, 201
    performances beyond Daly region, 6, 12, 23, 26, 38, 41, 154, 197, 209–10, **211–31**

Allan Marett is professor of musicology at the University of Sydney and was formerly professor of music at the University of Hong Kong. A recognized authority on Aboriginal music and culture, he is currently working with Indigenous and non-Indigenous scholars and intellectuals to establish a National Recording Project for Indigenous Music and Dance in Australia. He has also published widely on Japanese music and Sino-Japanese music history, having received his Ph.D. in this field from Cambridge University. Professor Marett is a former president of the Musicological Society of Australia, a member of the editorial board of its annual journal *Musicology Australia*, and chair of the Australian National Committee of the International Council for Traditional Music.

The *Wangga* of North Australia: CD Track List

The codes used to identify the recordings are explained in the appendixes. "Cro00, viii," for example, is a recording made by Crocombe in the year 2000; "viii" refers to the item number.

Track 1 "Wulumen Tulh" (Ma-yawa *wangga*), sung by Maurice Ngulkur with Columbanus Wanir (didjeridu) (Cro00, viii) (1:14)

Track 2 "Wulumen Tulh" (Ma-yawa *wangga*), sung by Maurice Ngulkur with Columbanus Wanir (didjeridu) (Cro00, vii) (1:24)

Track 3 "Bangany-nyung Ngaya" (Barrtjap's *wangga*), sung by Tommy Barrtjap with Djagabunbun (Jackie Woody) (didjeridu) (Moy68:5, v) (1:40)

Track 4 "Yendili no. 2" (Walakandha *wangga*), sung by Thomas Kungiung, Wagon Dumoo, and Martin Warrigal Kungiung, with John Dumoo (didjeridu) (Mar88:38, v) (2:25)

Track 5 "Truwu" (Walakandha *wangga*), sung to the Truwu A melody by Thomas Kungiung, Wagon Dumoo, and Martin Warrigal Kungiung (Mar88:39, ii) (2:36)

Track 6 "Truwu" (Walakandha *wangga*), sung to the Truwu B melody by Les Kundjil (Mar98:15, xii) (1:32)

Track 7 "Truwu" (Walakandha *wangga*), sung to the Truwu A/B melody by Thomas Kungiung and Les Kundjil (Eni92, viii) (1:29)

Track 8 "Truwu" (Walakandha *wangga*), sung to Truwu A/B melody by Philip Mullumbuk (Mar99:4, iv) (1:49)

Track 9 "Walakandha no. 4" (Walakandha *wangga*), sung by Philip Mullumbuk (Mar99:4, xi) (1:43)

Track 10 "Kubuwemi" (Walakandha *wangga*), sung by Thomas Kungiung, Wagon Dumoo, and Martin Warrigal Kungiung (Mar88:42, viii) (1:06)

Track 11 "Yenmilhi" (Walakandha *wangga*), sung by Martin Warrigal Kungiung (singer) with Robert Daly (didjeridu) (Mar88:54, iii) (1:11)

Track 12 "Walakandha no. 2" (Walakandha *wangga*), sung by Thomas Kungiung, Les Kundjil, and Philip Mullumbuk (Eni92, vi) (2:08)

Track 13 "Walakandha Ngindji" (Ma-yawa *wangga*), sung by Maurice Ngulkur with Benedict Tchinburur (didjeridu) (Mar98:14, i) (0:49)

Track 14 "Wulumen Kimigimi" (Ma-yawa *wangga*), sung by Maurice Ngulkur with Benedict Tchinburur (didjeridu) (Mar98:14, iv) (1:09)

Track 15 "Watjen Danggi" (Ma-yawa *wangga*), sung by Maurice Ngulkur with Benedict Tchinburur (didjeridu) (Mar98:14, x) (0:55)

Track 16 "Yagarra Nga-bindja-ng Nga-mi" (Barrtjap's *wangga*), sung by Tommy Barrtjap with Djagabunbun (Jackie Woody) (didjeridu) (Moy68:5, ix) (2:07)

Track 17 "Kanga Rinyala Nga-ve Bangany-nyung" (Barrtjap's *wangga*), sung by Tommy Barrtjap with Djagabunbun (Jackie Woody) (didjeridu) (Moy68:5, vii) (1:47)

Track 18 "Yagarra Delhi Nye-bindja-ng Barra Ngarrka" (Barrtjap's *wangga*), sung by Tommy Barrtjap with Eric Martin (didjeridu) (Mar86:3, v) (1:36)

Track 19 "Yagarra Tjüt Balk-nga-me Nga-mi" (Barrtjap's *wangga*), sung by Tommy Barrtjap with Nicky Jorrock (didjeridu) (Mar86:3, iv) (1:38)

Track 20 "Be Bangany-nyaya" (Barrtjap's *wangga*), sung by Tommy Barrtjap with Djagabunbun (Jackie Woody) (didjeridu) (Moy68:5, xi) (1:26)

Track 21 "Dadja Kadja Bangany Nye-ve" (Barrtjap's *wangga*), sung by Tommy Barrtjap with Nicky Jorrock (didjeridu) (Mar88:5, iii) (1:39)

Track 22 "Bangany-nyung Ngaya" (Barrtjap's *wangga*), sung by Kenny Burrenjuck with Peter Chainsaw (didjeridu) (Mar97:4, v) (2:45)

Track 23 "Rak Badjalarr" (Lambudju's *wangga*), sung by Bobby Lambudju Lane and Tommy Barrtjap with Nicky Jorrock (didjeridu) (Mar86:4, vi) (1:41)

Track 24 "Winmedje" (Lambudju's *wangga*), sung by Bobby Lambudju Lane with Nicky Jorrock (didjeridu) (Mar86:4, v) (1:18)

Track 25 "Rak Badjalarr" (Lambudju's *wangga*), sung by Rusty Benmele Moreen and Laurence Wurrpen with Billy Brap (didjeridu) (Wes61, xvi) (2:42)

Track 26 "Rak Badjalarr" (Lambudju's *wangga*), sung by Colin Worumbu Ferguson with Nicky Jorrock (didjeridu) (Mar97:13, xiii) (2:07)

Track 27 "Benmele" (Lambudju's *wangga*), sung by Bobby Lambudju Lane and Tommy Barrtjap with Nicky Jorrock (didjeridu) (Mar86:4, ix) (2:02)

Track 28 "Minmin Light" (Maralung's Bunggridj Bunggridj *wangga*), sung by Alan Maralung with Peter Manaberu (didjeridu) (AIATSIS: A16933, i) (1:41)